The Complete Book of

Sewing and Fabrics for the Home

CAVENDISH HOUSE

Edited by Lindsay Vernon

Published by Marshall Cavendish Publications Limited
58 Old Compton Street
London, W1V 5PA

© Marshall Cavendish Limited 1972 – 83

This volume first published 1973

Printed in Hong Kong

ISBN 0 85685 028 4

This volume is not to be sold in the U.S.A., Canada
or the Philippines.

Designers:
Gwen Edwards, Cheryl Fry, Margaret Hamilton, Marjory Hastie Smith, Ike Rosen, Lindsay Vernon.
Illustrator:
Margaret McNally.
Manufacturers and stockists
Fabrics and carpets:
Borg Textiles, Du Pont, T. Forsell & Sons, Gomshall Tanneries, George H. Herman,
International Wool Secretariat, John Lewis, Lister & Co., Moygashel, Parker Knoll Textiles,
Sandersons, Sundour Fabrics, Villa-tex.
Furniture and accessories:
Armitage Shanks, Cane Contracts, Casa Pupo, Craftsmen Potters Shop, Heals, John Lewis,
Winchmore Whitewood Furniture.
Equipment:
Arrowtip Ltd., Dylon International, Grant Baxell of Putney, Gripperrods, Rexel International,
Rufflette, Whiteleys of Queensway.

About this book . . .

Why spend a fortune buying soft furnishings when you can learn how to make them yourself? The methods described here are those used by the professionals. All *you* have to do is follow the step-by-step instructions, the diagrams, colour photographs, and you will be able to sew elegant drapes and bedspreads, loose covers and make unusual lampshades and cushions.

Soft furnishings from curtains to floor coverings make a house into a home, adding both to its comfort and decoration. They need not be expensive, but like most things they are a lot cheaper if you make them yourself. And soft furnishings can be tackled by anyone who can use a tape measure and a sewing machine. Nor is soft furnishing all plain sewing. From the chapters on rug-making, embroidered table linen and crochet you can make those extra touches which add so much to a home.

Try out the techniques of upholstery, dyeing and patchwork; discover the age-old art of batik; see how to use fabric as a wall covering and on furniture; employ leather and fur as decorative aids; transform rags and offcuts into beautiful rugs.

The shops are full of lovely fabrics, innumerable wallpaper designs and colourful paints. The problem is knowing where to begin and what to choose. It is not enough to be able to *make* soft furnishings — they must look right in their setting. Start by understanding colour, pattern and texture, how they affect you and how you can use them to make the most of your home and possessions. See how you can create the mood of a room and how simple tricks can camouflage its proportions.

Whether your preference is for the ultra modern or traditional, you will certainly find just the ideas to appeal to your taste here. No matter what you make, or adapt to your individual needs, you can be sure that you are creating a more beautiful and luxurious home.

Contents

Choosing colour for effect

Most colours in your life are probably passed by without even a casual glance. They are so familiar to you and everyone else that they are taken for granted. So, when you get down to redecorating, you are faced with a new world: harmonious colours, complementary colours, clashing colours, favourite colours . . . so the question is, 'where to begin?'

But, as with all problems, once you know some facts, then half the battle is over. Facts like whether colours are 'warm' or 'cold'; how they affect each other; which go together without 'fighting'. And also facts about your own house flat or bungalow, since no colour scheme is 'right' or 'wrong' in itself.

What is colour?

The so-called 'white light' we see as daylight is made up of all the colours of the rainbow; it is the mixture of light waves of different wavelengths that creates a white look. The 'wheel' of colour, or spectrum, is made up of red, orange, yellow, green, blue, indigo and violet. The in-between colours with fancy names, so often found on paint manufacturers' colour charts, are made by combining colours, pure and impure. They can be *shades,* colours with black added, or *tints*; colours with white added. You can go on mixing colours indefinitely, but eventually the resulting hues or tints will be too 'close' to be distinguished.

Colour, and the perception of colour, is a complicated matter. For example, what we see as a red cushion is an object which has absorbed all the other colours in the spectrum, and is reflecting just red.

A white wall looks white because it reflects all colours, absorbing none, whereas black absorbs all colours, reflecting none. Black is the total absence of any light or colour.

The brightest, purest colours—red, yellow and blue—are known as 'primary' colours because they are unmixed with any others. Generally, pure colours are strong and vibrant—they seem to shout for attention. Hence, of course, their use for road signs, fire appliances, and other things which must be identified quickly.

The 'non-colour' colours

Black, white and grey, although strictly non-colours, are considered in decorating as colours in their own right. Used together, these three can do a lot for a room, without necessarily having a dull, restrained effect. They also give good functional value when used alone, and in some cases can be quite dramatic.

White, often rightly used to frame doors or windows, separates colours excellently, showing up even pastel tints to good advantage. As well as being fresh looking, it is naturally harmonious. It partners most other colours without a 'fight', and flatters them positively by reflecting its neighbouring colours. A white area surrounded by a dark area will appear to swell in dimension.

Black, although traditionally associated with anything sinister, and with death and mourning in particular, need not be depressing. Small touches of black are usually enough to provide 'drama' for an otherwise weak setting. Ebonized furniture or a couple of black cushions can bring out, by contrast, the richness of other colours. Black-painted woodwork, however, usually ranges from unsuccessful to disastrous in a colour scheme. It can make a room a weird shape, and certainly will not flatter anything in it.

Grey can be used effectively as a background for more brilliant colours, providing a welcome rest for the eye. It can be mixed with other colours to soften them, or used on large areas against which something 'stronger'—an orange sofa, for example—is set.

Black, white and grey have been used together, with splashes of primary colours, by professionals for many successful interiors.

How colour affects you

Yellow is the brightest primary colour, nearest to sunlight and most luminous. Consequently it has a cheering effect, even in winter—but as with all primary colours, if too much is used in a small area it will soon tire the eye.

Red is the most aggressive and demanding colour in the whole spectrum. Used widely for danger signals, it has an immediacy which seems to force itself on you. It is also sexually suggestive, vital (the colour of blood, the essence of life) and advancing. This exhibitionist colour can have an unsettling effect, even challenging, like a 'red rag to a bull'. Mixed with orange and cunningly lit, it can provide an intense warmth for a cold room—a 'Christmassy' feeling.

Orange is also stimulating, but psychological tests have shown that if it is used extensively in a room, the occupants will fast feel 'driven out' by its sheer forcefulness.

Green, the colour of nature, is well known for its restful effect on the eye. In many ways it is the exact opposite of red, in that it is so un-stimulating as to be positively sedative.

Purple, on the other hand, stimulates the brain. Its associations with grandness, royalty and ceremonials can make people shy of using

Above. A landscape in the bathroom—walls and ceiling camouflaged as a background for dreaming while relaxing in the bath.

it in their homes but, provided it is used in large rooms, it can add a richness and dignity to its surroundings. Used in smaller areas, such as halls, purple can be overpowering.

Brown is restful and, if used in harmony with another 'warm' colour, can make for a cosy setting. Brown on its own, or teamed unimaginatively with pallid cream, can be depressing—as that 1930s craze for 'brown everywhere', a survival from dull Victorian decorating, showed. Brown enjoyed a great revival in the early 1970s, but think carefully before you splash it everywhere; as with

clothing fashions, revivals can go too far.

Blue, as your skin demonstrates in bitterly cold weather, is generally a cold, slightly uncomfortable colour. It has the effect of retreating and, like green, is sedative. Moreover, it is traditionally associated with the chill of holiness. The Virgin Mary's robes, in traditional painting, were almost always blue, and the blue robes of the saints induced feelings of respectful distance, and even melancholia.

Highlighting and camouflaging

Most homes have at least a few good features which can be accentuated by skilful decorating. And almost every home has potential strong points which can be brought out by colour-emphasis.

A cramped-looking room facing the sun can be helped by painting at least one wall in a cool blue or green. This area will seem to 'back away', giving the impression of spaciousness. But beware of using cold colours in a room on the shaded side of the house—you would be just adding to the 'iceberg' effect. It is far better to use pastel tones of a warmer colour. The white in the pastel shades will give the desired illusion of space, while the warm colour will retain its warmth and help correct the room's coldness.

Long, narrow rooms can be given a wider look by painting the shorter walls in warm, advancing colours—tints of yellow, red or orange. Small, boxlike rooms can be made to appear longer by reversing this idea.

Similarly, oppressively low ceilings can be 'raised' by painting them with soft, receding colours, and high ceilings 'brought down' by giving them a bold, advancing colour.

If you are wallpapering, using stripes is a useful aid to correcting badly-proportioned rooms. Women know that vertical stripes will make them seem taller and slimmer; horizontal stripes will have the opposite effect. The same applies to rooms. Vertical stripes add height to a squat room by carrying the eye upwards, unconsciously beyond the limits of the wall. This may over-correct, though, by making your ceiling seem 'miles away'; in this case, painting the ceiling in a shade of a warmer colour could lower it to the right height. The purer this colour, the lower it will seem. Horizontal stripes add length to a short wall by leading the eye out sideways and 'stretching' the actual distance.

In a room not receiving much light, pure colours can create a sunnier feeling. If you have seen the jewel-like intensity of the golds, scarlets, and indigos which are still to be found in high, dark medieval churches, you will realize that these striking colours would look absurdly garish in a naturally well-lit room. But to darker interiors, they add a touch of richness.

Large picture windows should be framed with a warm colour; in winter, a blue window frame would give the impression of framing the glass with ice.

Angular and aggressive shapes in rooms are more noticeable—and usually considered more of an eyesore—than soft rounded shapes, nooks and crannies. You may decide against ripping out an offending chimney breast, and simply want to 'lose' it by camouflage. In this case, use dark receding colours or gentle patterned wallpaper, while emphasizing the adjoining recess with light pastel shades, or a pure, vibrant colour as a focus for the eye. If you do want to emphasize a chimney breast or some other projection, then reverse the process just described.

As armies have discovered, the best way to be inconspicuous is to dress in the colour of the background they will be patrolling (shades of green in jungles, soft khaki in deserts). If you have a room with many doors which break up the walls into small, ugly areas, camouflage is the best answer for them, too. Paint the doors, frames and all, precisely the same shade as the surrounding walls. If you have papered the walls, then pick out the most retreating, unnoticeable tone from the pattern and paint your doors in it. Radiators or projecting pipes can be camouflaged in a similar way by painting them exactly the same colour as the walls behind.

Equal *tones* will camouflage, even where the *colours* are different. Tones of the same 'weight' will neutralize bad features in a room, whereas a blatant contrast in tone (or intensity) will highlight. Remember that any colour mixed with grey can be used in camouflaging because of its muting, receding effect. Seldom used doors—to store or cellar, say—can be hidden by painting them a deep grey. Alternatively, a shade of your main colour, but deeper and greyer, will help fade them away.

Under-stair cupboards or panelling should, as a general rule, be made to disappear. Darkish colours will help disguise panelling which is

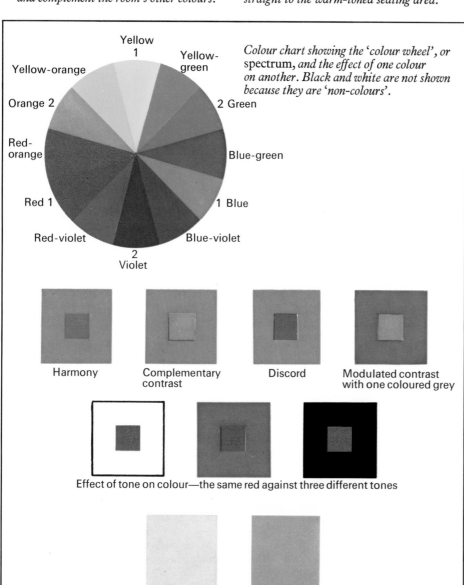

Above left. How one strong colour can create a striking 'wall' from different-sized doors, —and complement the room's other colours.

Above right. The neutral cream and white of the low roof beams and walls take the eye straight to the warm-toned seating area.

Colour chart showing the 'colour wheel', or spectrum, *and the effect of one colour on another. Black and white are not shown because they are 'non-colours'.*

Yellow 1

Yellow-green

2 Green

Blue-green

1 Blue

Blue-violet

2 Violet

Red-violet

Red 1

Red-orange

Orange 2

Yellow-orange

Harmony

Complementary contrast

Discord

Modulated contrast with one coloured grey

Effect of tone on colour—the same red against three different tones

Cool colour recedes   Warm colour advances

HEIDEDE CARSTENSEN/STUDIO HUELSTA

COLOUR PATTERN AND TEXTURE BY WILLIAM GRAHAM/ARTIST LIZ BENNETT

broken up by small doors, or boards which are not well finished. Similarly, the margins beside a stair carpet are best painted in a 'retreating' tone chosen from the colours in the carpet.

Where your skirting board is deep (perhaps 15in.) and in one or two sections or bands, use a neutral colour (grey, light tan, soft beige) on the lower section. This makes the floor space look wider. Then add a crisp, light colour to trim up the upper section, giving a sharp framing line to the wall.

If you have picture rails which you dislike but do not want to remove, you can still make your ceiling interesting by painting the picture rails the same colour as the walls and using a high-lighting colour—the best is always white—on the cornice to frame the walls and ceiling.

Where panel mouldings on ceilings, walls or framing to niches are in good repair, and you want to draw attention to them, apply the highlighting rule. Where they are battered or ugly, apply the camouflaging rule.

So, to summarize the general rule: Use bright, vivid colours to pick out any surface that you like and that projects forward into the room, and use deeper hues on surfaces you want to hide or which are recessed. This magnifies the natural light-and-shade effect of both daylight and artificial light. The projections catch the light, and recesses are naturally in shadow anyway.

The balance of colour

The secret of a professional-looking colour scheme is the skilful use of a *few* colours, or simply many shades of the same colour. The inexperienced person tends to introduce too many colours—giving himself more problems than he can cope with.

To create a harmonious look, there should be a delicate balance among the colours you use. Only a professional designer with precise colour knowledge can deal successfully with discords of the boldest, clashing colours. Large areas of pure colour, such as deep blue walls with a scarlet carpet, can have a very irritating effect. One pure colour should be allowed to be the focus—and if it is a pure colour it *will* stand out, even if used on small areas.

Colours affect each other

Never try to visualize the impact of a single colour on any particular room. Try to see it in your mind's eye alongside the other colours you

MICHAEL BOYS

will be using. Better still, try to get swatches of appropriately coloured card or material; hold them up against walls, furniture and each other. This will help you to gauge how they are going to 'live' together.

If the same colour is used in several places, it will appear to be different in hue, because of variations in the amount of light bouncing off it, and its nearness to other colours. For example, a bright yellow cushion will not look the same yellow on a grey settee as on a tan one. Yellowish-green can make some shades of blue look purple when used close beside them. A very dark mulberry can make a tint of the same colour—such as light mauve—look white. An area painted yellow (the most luminous colour) seems larger than one painted orange (slightly less luminous), and an orange area bigger than one painted red.

A pale grey-green may flatter a room—until you decide to add a *bright* green feature such as curtains, cushions, or an ornament. The grey-green will then 'die', looking very washed-out by contrast.

If you are thinking of an ultra-colourful room, consider how visitors might react. Op-art pictures and decor can have a dizzying effect on people unused to optical illusions. Vibrant colours can be similarly disturbing. But if the *entrance* to a living room is painted in colours complementary to those in the room, it prepares the eye to receive the total colour scheme. This gradual build-up (in some cases perhaps a warning) is known as creating a 'colour climax'.

If you use patterned wallpaper *and* patterned carpet, the room will certainly look smaller. Pattern tends to make even large rooms look 'busy' and cluttered, calling for less furniture in plain designs and colours. As an extreme example, think of the claustrophobic Victorian parlour—a 'jungle' of fussy accessories, surrounded inevitably with heavy, plush-looking wallpaper. Too many bright colours, plus crammed-in furniture, can make a similar impression even in a modern setting.

As with all other aspects of home design, your personal taste will dictate the colours in your home. Rooms that can be categorized as 'trendy' or 'go-ahead' will usually contain some primary colours, stimulating and young in effect. Formal, quiet rooms need a dignified and limited palette. Whatever style you choose, do all you can to ensure in advance that it will please you. After all, you will have to live with it.

PAUL REDMAN

Above. *A whole room decorated overall in muted cream shows how subtle colour can make for an interesting setting.*

Below. *Taking a strong line with a whole wall. The blue and yellow lines framing the wall are echoed in the settee and cushions.*

Colour
for living rooms
and bedrooms

Living rooms are primarily family rooms —a homely place to watch television, entertain visitors, and simply relax. As with all other colour scheming, decorating living rooms depends very much on personal taste—and on personality. The danger is in trying to force your particular taste on other members of the family. Many families span a fairly wide age group, with widely differing tastes in colour so that some sort of compromise may be needed if everyone is to feel at home. So try to make colour planning a family decision.

There are other considerations. If you do a good deal of entertaining, and go out a lot in turn, you can afford to be a little bolder in your choice of colours than if you spend most of your time at home and want something more restful. But generally, as living rooms are semi-public in function, you should aim for something more acceptable, to friends and family, than the decor you would choose for a strictly personal room.

If you aim for a restful decor, you might choose soft sage greens, beige, oatmeal—some of the discreet colours. You can buy attractive shades of most colours now. For a more exciting scheme, you might choose whatever are the current fashion colours, and stimulating tints such as white, orange and cerise, or purple, blue and green.

Below. A warm bedroom setting, using only shades of orange and oatmeal to effect.

Where to start

Unless you are moving into an unfurnished house, you will probably want to base your colour scheme on some existing feature, if only because it costs less to redecorate a room than to refurnish it. In this case, you should take into account the textures and tones of carpets, a woodblock floor, curtains, light oak furniture—whatever is going to be a permanent feature in the room. This gives you an immediate advantage—as in a crossword puzzle, the first clue solved helps with the next.

Having established the 'base', of unalterable colour, you can build on it in one or two ways. One way, if one colour is predominant, is to build on that colour with a 'tone on tone' scheme. Starting from a blue carpet, for example, you can use other blues—a paler one on walls, a greyer one on woodwork, a greener one for upholstery. Neutral white on the ceiling and on

woodwork trim helps to set off the blues, while accessories in red, orange or black can add dramatic sparkle.

Alternatively, the fixed colour can be part of a complementary scheme. Starting with the same blue, for example, you can make it the contrasting element to soft yellows, corn colour and white, with perhaps both blue and one of the other colours in a patterned curtain fabric.

If a woodblock or planked floor is going to be your starting point, you will already have a large area of rich colour. This can be the trigger for a series of 'natural' colours and materials—hessian for walls in a warm colour; broad striped curtains in browns, greys and off-white; off-white paintwork; Danish rugs in dark brown and off-white.

Which way do you face?

An important consideration is the aspect of the room. Notoriously, a north-facing room has the coldest aspect—although artists prefer north light, because it is the least changeable. South- and west-facing rooms have warm light, and plenty of it.

But all rooms need corrective action to balance out their overall 'temperature.' Adding warm colours—reds, oranges and yellows—helps to overcome the cool north light. Rooms with a south or west aspect, on the other hand, benefit from cool blues, blue-greens and greys, especially where the light is bright and strong.

Colour and artificial light

Artificial lighting does not normally create a colour problem in living rooms and bedrooms, although all artificial light changes the appearance of most colours to some extent. This effect is known as 'metamerism'. Fluorescent lighting can make some colours look 'washed out', while the tungsten filament bulbs most used in homes give a warmer cast to most colours. Normal eyes easily adapt to such slight changes but, when choosing colours, it is a good idea to view them in both daylight and artificial light.

Colour and fashion

Fashion, in colour as in clothing, is a fickle thing. You may decide against 'trendy' colours for that reason.

Keeping up with fashion means almost constant redecoration, since colour fads, wall-covering designs and ideas for using materials change rapidly. The 1960s and early 1970s, for example, saw an upsurge of interest in purples. Then browns, in many shades from beige to peat, became the rage—only to be threatened immediately by an onslaught from sharp lettuce green and deep strong pinks! And while on the one hand there was increased interest in plain textures and natural colours, on the other there was a Victorian revival.

All this shows that fashion for its own sake is only for outgoing people with either great colour tolerance or ample time and money.

Keeping up with progress is quite another matter. Paint and wallcovering manufacturers constantly come up with new colours and textures, and materials of greater durability. It is worthwhile keeping abreast of these developments. Old materials and methods tend to look outdated to the discerning eye.

Colour in small houses

Small houses, flats and bungalows often need the illusion of greater space. This can be achieved by using 'receding' colours (see page 9), and by creating continuity or colour. For instance, you could put down exactly the same floor covering in all the main rooms. When all the doors are open, a large expanse of floor will seem to open up, flowing from room to room. Muted or neutral colours are best for this, because you can arrange several colour schemes round them—a different one in each room.

Colour for children's bedrooms

Whereas the living room is a semi-public room where visitors are entertained, a bedroom is private territory. This is the room which should be allowed to express the occupant's personality, with no need to 'keep up' with anybody, or to follow any particular fashion at all.

Nurseries, quite rightly, are often painted in pastel shades, or with delicately coloured fairy-tale wallpaper. Very young babies need a restful surrounding, with perhaps just one wall papered with nursery-rhyme or fairy-tale characters, preferably facing them.

As they grow into toddlers, they crave visual stimulation and begin to show a marked interest in the 'loudest' of primary colours. This is when the delicate nursery colours can give way to reds, yellows, oranges, electric blues; children have a built-in tolerance for vibrant colours which adults seem to lack. (On a practical note: remember that toddlers are apt to chew and suck on the corners of furniture, so be careful to use lead-free paints *throughout* their rooms.)

The period between starting school and the early teens often sees a fad for collecting things—almost *any* things. Try not to force more sophisticated patterns on the children's rooms, thinking they will appreciate your tact in implying they are so grown-up. A new coat of paint, or a change of plain colours, will keep rooms smart, but their own accumulations of belongings provide pattern enough.

Teenagers, students and young adults should have a major say in the decoration of their rooms, if not the ultimate responsibility. At this stage, too, their own belongings and bright posters will make a room of thrusting colour and shapes. Usually the bedroom is treated as a private sitting room, with friends visiting—it is, in effect, a bedsitting room. Psychedelic colours and posters are likely to be much in evidence. Whether parents like them is beside the point: colour is a personal thing, and should therefore be tolerated.

Colour for double bedrooms

Double bedrooms are almost inevitably dominated by feminine tastes. Once this meant profusions of flounces and frills, delicate pinks and masses of rosebud pattern. Now there is so much to choose from in both colours and textures that there is little restriction left. A more imaginative palette can make for an acceptably asexual, but still intimate, colour scheme.

Shades of the cool section of the spectrum, such as blues, mauves and aquas, can mingle

Top left. *This inviting room combines the colour of sunshine with the natural materials of rush matting and wicker seats. The dominant colour is picked out in the curtains and echoed by the wallprint.*
Below. *Superbly dramatic bedroom setting achieved with a limited palette. Black and white dominate, unashamedly picking out the strong lines of the furnishings and outlining the shape of the room. Grey is used well to deepen one wall, adding a new dimension.*
Below bottom. *This striking living room employs the blue/green motif to perfection. Usually too sedative, green is enlivened here by splashes of electric blue and bold white furnishings which compel attention. The carpet reflects the green of the leaves.*

"ANNABELLE", ZURICH

effectively to create a cool, sophisticated look, especially if some greenery is provided as a foil.

Pinks still have their place—but these days tend to be allied with salmon, orangey-reds and some pure red to emphasize the warm tones.

All-white bedrooms are always popular, but really succeed only if 'dressed up' with another colour. If the dressing table is the focal point, then its clutter of bottles and jars may provide an adequate splash of colour, as will flowers and perhaps a picture or two.

If you decide on a black and white scheme, then you could paint the walls, ceiling and paintwork white, and use a black rug or bedspread to add drama, and a wall-hanging or two (such as black and white Beardsley prints) to add formal line and dignity. If you have a black wrought-iron balcony, then white alone could give your bedroom a Spanish look. In colder climates, this could be warmed up with bright cushions, vivid ikons, or flowers: in colour scheming, *all* possessions and accessories should be taken into account, since everything contributes to the overall impression. Their shapes liven up the colours too.

Strong greys, deep browns, and restrained colours generally can make a room look 'business-like' and over-masculine. However, if the room is also to be used as a study, this arrangement may provide the necessary compromise between the tidy 'study' look and a restful bedroom scheme. If brown is your central colour, then pretty brown floral fabrics in cushions or curtains could offset any severity. If a deep grey is chosen, then a lighter, brighter colour is an essential to liven it up. A buttercup yellow or bright orange in paintwork trim or fabric accessories, would make all the difference.

Guest rooms

Because guest rooms are primarily 'surprise' rooms, then all types of people with widely differing colour tastes will be staying there, if only for short periods. If this always seems a problem when you come to decorate, you could either play safe by using a black-white-grey or brown scheme, or take the bit between your teeth and decorate the room in *your* favourite colours. As a middle course, you can use several shades of one colour, such as green, which will look smart, be restful, and not cause shocked comments or headaches. If you think an all-green room is monotonous, add floral or striped curtains in yellows or orange trimmings. If you start with one colour, you are less likely to make the room look 'fussy', especially as guest rooms tend to be smallish.

HEIDEDE CARSTENSEN/STUDIO HUELSTA

Opposite, top left. *A bedroom children would love. The whole room throbs with brilliant primary colours—blue, yellow and bold red. The Mickey Mouse poster echoes the gay mood and the eye is drawn to the floor, where children love to play. Bedtime might even be fun in a room like this!*
Opposite, below. *Bedroom for an older child or for a teenager uses bright, but more subtle, colours than for youngsters. The yellow and orange duvet motif is taken up throughout the room, including accessories such as the giant clock and Beatle posters.*

CINDY CASSIDY/PHOTO PAUL RADKAI

HEIDEDE CARSTENSEN/STUDIO DIE WOHNFORM

Above right. *A muted, 'mood' effect for a feminine, single bedroom. The warmth of the pinkey-mauve is subtly brought out by the period lamp, and the whole atmosphere carefully sustained through accessories.*

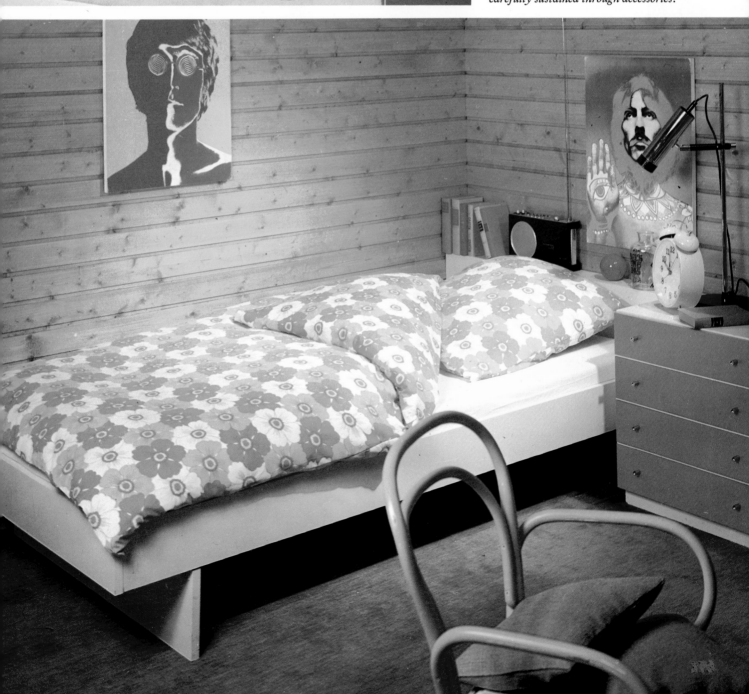

How to use pattern and texture

Most people choose their furnishings on colours first and pattern second. Texture is considered last of all—or, more often, it is chosen unconsciously because it is part of the basic material and cannot be divorced from either pattern or colour.

Pattern and texture play an essential part in most interior decorative schemes and, while it is possible to keep successfully to plain, flat colours, pattern and texture should be intro-duced to give contrast and extra visual interest. By their composition, they also help create the 'mood' of the room, by making it restful or stimulating, traditional or 'trendy', formal or casual.

About pattern

Pattern is not just a linear design printed on wallpaper or fabric—it is also formed by the juxtaposition of one material with another, or by building up independent objects. The joints of tiling, bricks and timber boards, the shapes of furniture and of books on shelves, all make some sort of pattern which must be taken into con-sideration.

Pattern usually looks best against a plain background because, while plain areas can be mixed, too much or conflicting pattern is distracting and tiring and one strong pattern will kill another if placed next to it. Equally a bold pattern, which looks fine in relatively small areas—in curtains or for a bedspread—can be overwhelming in a wall or floor covering.

However, there are occasions when strong pattern and texture can actually complement each other if one is used as a focal point and the other is the background.

In rooms which have few built-in focal points, a well-designed repeat pattern on the walls—structural or introduced—gives intermediate interest to link the focal points with the plain areas. In a room with several strong architectural features, an introduced repeat pattern will be broken up and appear muddled. Here texture should be used to give the room contrast.

STUDIO HUELSTA/HEIDEDE CARSTENSEN

Pattern and colour

Many of the principles governing the use of colour affect pattern too. Just as colours can alter the illusion of space, so can pattern. Strong patterns advance, giving a feeling of intimacy and comfort to a large room, particularly if the colours are dark. Small-scale patterns retreat, giving an impression of solid colour and bareness when seen from a distance. Yet in a small area, a strong pattern used in quantity would be over-dominant and even claustrophobic, and a small pattern would give a welcome illusion of space.

Like colour, pattern can also be used to camouflage. The trick of painting the end walls of a narrow room in a strong colour to make the room seem wider works equally well with a strong pattern, and not necessarily in strong colours. The idea, popular in the 1950s, of papering one or two walls or the ceiling of a square room in a contrasting paper from the other walls was not just a fashion—it was a technique used to lessen the 'boxed in' feeling. Pattern can be used to disguise ugly doors or

JANET & FRANK BEYDA

projections, if they are papered to match their surroundings. By using a co-ordinated fabric and wallpaper, the proportions of a window can be improved.

Because one's eye tends to follow straight lines, horizontal lines make a room look long and low. Vertical lines increase the feeling of height (see page 9) but they can also make a very large room appear smaller by preventing the eye from moving sideways along the wall. A disadvantage of using a geometric wall-covering, such as a striped one, is that it can show up such flaws as unevenness or the corners not being exactly plumb. So, even if you would like the effect stripes give, it would be wiser to have a textured non-patterned paper in a poorly finished room.

About texture

Houses built in Britain since the second world war have not only a simpler shape, but a different texture, from older houses. They have less decoration and are more functional. This leads to a need for added embellishment but, if it is to be in keeping with the plain structure, the decoration must be 'rough' or functional in texture rather than pretty or fancy. Natural stone, natural wood, natural wool—textures apparently untreated or unpolished—all follow this theme. Where pattern is kept to a minimum, texture for its own sake assumes greater importance.

Texture is both visual and sensual; it can be smooth or rough, shiny or matt, soft or hard, cold or welcoming, formal or informal. Every surface has both colour and texture, and colour is affected by texture. On a flat surface, some colours can appear dull, although on a textured surface they can seem alive and interesting. Smooth surfaces reflect light and can appear lighter than something supposedly the same colour on a rough surface which, because it absorbs light, gives a darker tone. Thus a maroon velvet would seem darker than maroon satin, even though both had been dyed with the same pigment.

A dark, highly polished surface reflects the colour and shape of its surroundings and can

BRIAN MORRIS

DOUGLASS BAGLIN

Left. Strong pattern and texture normally 'kill' each other when mixed, but when one is the focal point and the other is the background, they can be complementary.
Top. Small areas of pattern become co-ordinated when repeated on different pieces of furniture throughout the room.
Second from top. Different patterns for walls and bedspread team well together when the same colours are used.
Bottom. A classic fireplace stands out against rose-coloured walls which are reflected in the mahogany. The darkness is relieved by the white carpet.

become almost a mirror of the room. It can even, in some circumstances (black ceramic tiles, for instance), help improve the room's proportions if used on one wall to give a suggestion of greater space through reflection.

A dark matt surface absorbs light and gives a rich, comfortable feeling, best seen by artificial light. A light matt surface, on the other hand, both reflects and diffuses light and is the most popular texture for wallcovering because it enhances both natural and artificial light.

Texture can also alter the character of a pattern. A pattern printed on a silky surface can have elegance and an air of formality, whereas on a rough background the same pattern can be casual and almost masculine. Plate glass, stainless steel, marble, silks, satins, velvets and polished rosewood are other examples of 'formal' textures. Casual or even 'rustic' ones are cork, brick, earthenware tiles, pine or oak furniture, felt, slub linens and fibreglass, 'rough' fabrics like hessian or tweed, shaggy and cord carpets. Vinyl and leather, which might seem sophisticated textures, in fact team better with the more casual ones.

While the textures in each group can combine well with each other, some can also be combined with the other group. But they should always be appropriate to the surface they cover and there should be a definite contrast between them—such as smooth plaster with coarse brick, ceramic tiles with towelling, grasscloth with silk, polished furniture with a shaggy carpet. Glaring contrasts, such as satin cushions on a tweedy sofa, are better avoided.

A room in which the textures are even and of the same type, although of a different colour and substance, can be boring and sometimes oppressive or cold (the all-ceramic bathroom, for instance). Yet one with too many varied and indiscriminately chosen textures (a living room with brocade curtains, flock wallpaper, velvet upholstery, silk ruched lampshades and satin cushions for instance) can be as confusing as too many different patterns or colours.

Starting off

Pattern and texture can be introduced into a room by the carpet, upholstery, wallcovering, curtains, pictures and other accessories like lamps and cushions. Professional designers usually recommend beginning with the floor, arguing that this is probably the most expensive —and, therefore, should be the most long-lasting—single item. This is fine if you are a designer, have a limitless budget, or are starting from scratch. Many people, however, are limited by something, be it budget or choice. Their starting point may have to be a three-piece suite, which meets their needs in shape but

perhaps not entirely in its covering. And, although it is not ideal, it seems more practical to keep it and build up from it, rather than going to the expense of having it re-covered. This can even apply if you are starting from scratch—you find just what you want and even though the manufacturers' upholstery range is wide, it is still easier to find a carpet to go with that, than the other way round.

It is nearly always simplest to leave curtains and wallcovering until last. The range available is enormous, and although wallpapers are designed to be seen flat and curtain fabrics draped, manufacturers are increasingly designing them to co-ordinate, if not match, so the task of choosing can be simplified.

Regardless of the motif or design of the pattern you choose—which is largely a matter of taste—its colours should always go with the rest of the room. It need not match exactly, but

BERNARD HAMILTON

it should tone. It can also be a very useful way of marrying two apparently unco-ordinated colours by combining both in the design.

Applied pattern and texture

Following the principle that one strong pattern or texture can kill another, you will be safer if you keep them to one, or possibly two, major items, and tone down everything else in the room. But this does not mean that having a patterned carpet limits you to completely plain, flat things without even textural interest. An invariably successful combination is an Axminster carpet (which is always patterned) with velvet upholstery or curtains in one of the carpet colours. A plain Wilton, with its velvet-like pile, would be overdoing the velvet theme, and a very shaggy carpet would kill its softness.

The Wilton, on the other hand, would be fine with nearly any other fabric, particularly if patterned. The shaggy, because of its 'outdoor' nature, fits better with rougher fabrics. To combine well with more silky ones, it would need to be in a much smaller area, like a fireside rug.

Similarly, pictures—especially oil paintings— should be hung on plain walls, but they can still have texture. Some wallcoverings, such as neutral-coloured hessian or felt, actually enhance pictures.

Delicate furniture and mouldings are also 'killed' by strident pattern or rough texture. For example, a fine Louis XIV chair would be spoiled by upholstery in a large abstract fabric in black and white. Or the mouldings of an Adam fireplace would be overpowered by a really bright or geometric wallpaper. Designs of the more traditional kind on the other hand—Regency stripes or brocades with a silky finish, for example—can be exactly right. Conversely, massive furniture overpowers the delicacy of a small floral pattern. Unless you want a large sofa to dominate the room, the cover fabric should be a plain one with the curtains or floor 'bearing the brunt' of pattern.

Smaller, modern chairs or sofas with simple lines can take strongly patterned covers, but it is easy to overdo it by having too many pieces in a confined space. It would be far better to have, for example, the sofa covered in a pattern to match the curtains, with the chairs in a plain

RICHARD EINZIG

Left. *Horizontal stripes make a wall seem longer and offset the geometric pictures. The black tiles make the room appear even larger by becoming its mirror and the leather chairs echo this effect, but soften it, while still keeping the 'mood' of the room.*
Above. *Natural architectural features, such as stone and wood beams, should be seen against plain backgrounds; any pattern introduced into the room should be in the furnishings, rather than the walls where pattern would be too broken up.*

fabric picking out the main colour of the pattern and the carpet in a toning shade.

Used in small amounts, the same pattern can be used to co-ordinate different areas of a room —curtains to match a bedspread or the upholstery of an occasional chair, the panels of a door, cushions or lampshades. And in small amounts, two unobtrusive non-matching patterns can be used in one room, particularly if one of the patterns is almost more of a texture, such as brocade curtains with a Persian carpet.

Planning your rooms

Furnishing a room well is not just a matter of buying pieces of furniture that look well together, and putting them in the room in a neat arrangement. To be successful, a room must be planned as a complete unit.

When you are planning or re-planning a room, you should consider how you and your family are going to use it. This applies to living rooms as well as kitchens. The type of points to pay attention to are: Is there a clear passage from one door to another? Is there room for several people to watch the television in comfort, and is the screen placed so that there are no annoying reflections in it from lamps or windows? If you have your neighbours in to tea, can you get from your seat to the kitchen without treading on their feet?

It may be a help to draw a rough plan of the room, and sketch on to it the main areas serving different purposes in the room, and the routes that people can take when they walk through it. This should give you some idea of the amount of furniture you need in it, and where it should be put.

In nearly any room, it is desirable to create an impression of simplicity. The cluttered, messy look of a Victorian room may seem picturesque, but it is hard to live in—and to clean. The Victorians, after all, had servants to do their boring domestic chores. And even so, during the great period of English house and furniture design in the eighteenth century, when Thomas Chippendale and Robert Adam were working, interiors were simple to the point of starkness. You could do worse than follow their example.

Part of the secret of a simple interior is just not to over-furnish it. Put in only the furniture you need to feel comfortable, and ruthlessly throw out anything else, even if it is an interesting piece in itself.

The other part of the secret is to preserve the continuity of line in a room, so that the eye can travel around it without continually jumping about. In practice this means, for example, table-tops that are the same height as each other; bedside units that match the height of either bed or bedhead; occasional tables where tops align with the seats of neighbouring arm-chairs; wall units that match either the door height or the ceiling height, and so on—there are dozens of examples. Thus a line created by the top or edge of a piece of furniture is continued or echoed by another line along something else.

For the same reasons, do not hang pictures blindly in the middle of walls. Hang them where they line-up with, or balance, something else. Groups of small pictures look good hung together in a formal arrangement—for example six pictures arranged in two rows of three. Try to hang all the pictures in a room with their tops at the same height (depending on the size of the pictures, this might also align with the door frame, or the top of a dresser), since the top of a frame is more noticeable than the bottom. However, a picture containing a perspective view should hang where the perspective looks right. As an easy example, a soaring bird should be placed where you will look up at it.

Creating the right mood in a room is also important. An impression of warmth and comfort, or cool elegance, is created mainly by the use of colour (see page 12) but the shape of your furniture can also have an effect.

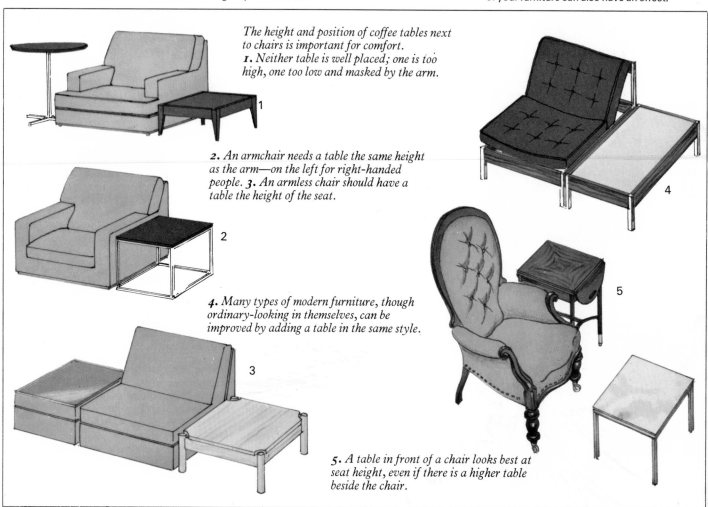

The height and position of coffee tables next to chairs is important for comfort.
1. Neither table is well placed; one is too high, one too low and masked by the arm.

2. An armchair needs a table the same height as the arm—on the left for right-handed people. *3.* An armless chair should have a table the height of the seat.

4. Many types of modern furniture, though ordinary-looking in themselves, can be improved by adding a table in the same style.

5. A table in front of a chair looks best at seat height, even if there is a higher table beside the chair.

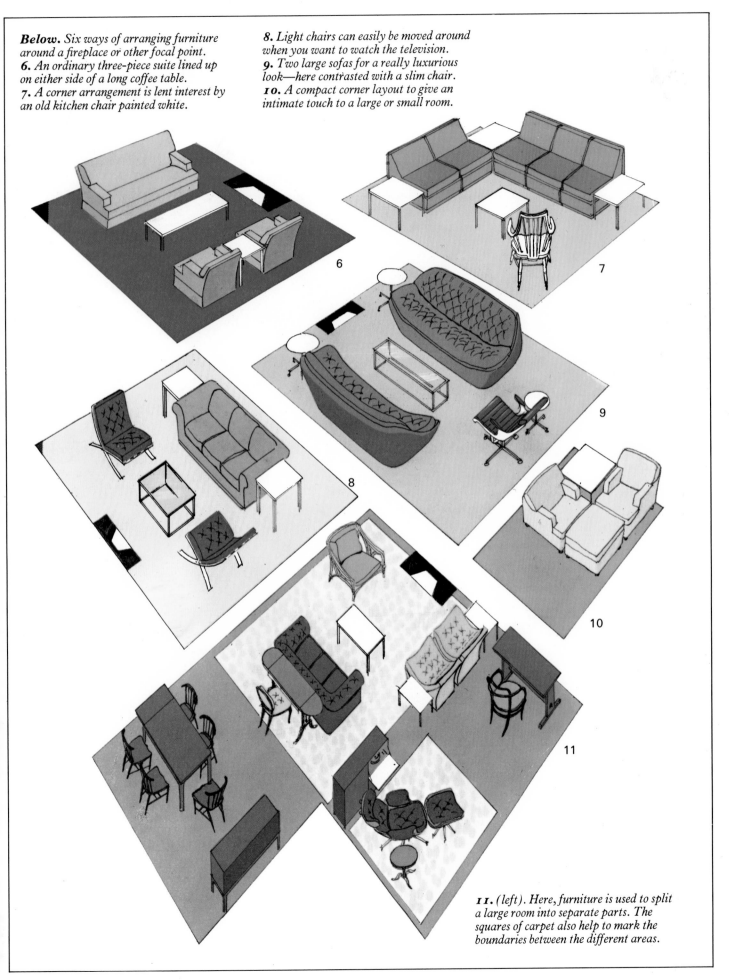

Below. *Six ways of arranging furniture around a fireplace or other focal point.*
6. *An ordinary three-piece suite lined up on either side of a long coffee table.*
7. *A corner arrangement is lent interest by an old kitchen chair painted white.*

8. *Light chairs can easily be moved around when you want to watch the television.*
9. *Two large sofas for a really luxurious look—here contrasted with a slim chair.*
10. *A compact corner layout to give an intimate touch to a large or small room.*

11. *(left). Here, furniture is used to split a large room into separate parts. The squares of carpet also help to mark the boundaries between the different areas.*

Below. *In most rooms, a single tall, narrow window in a wide wall has a mean, pinched look.* **12.** *The curtains on this narrow window do not extend beyond the outer edge of the frame, so that its bad proportions are apparent.* **13.** *The height of the window can be turned to advantage by extending the curtains out to the side to rectify its proportions.* **14.** *The curtains can be carried right across the wall to give a wide, modern effect.*

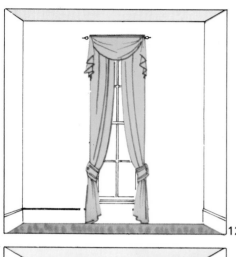

12

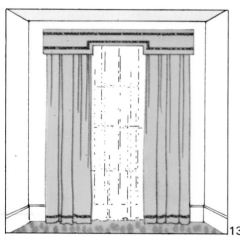

13

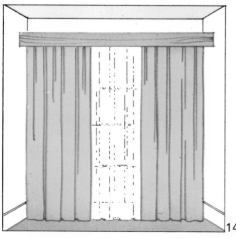

14

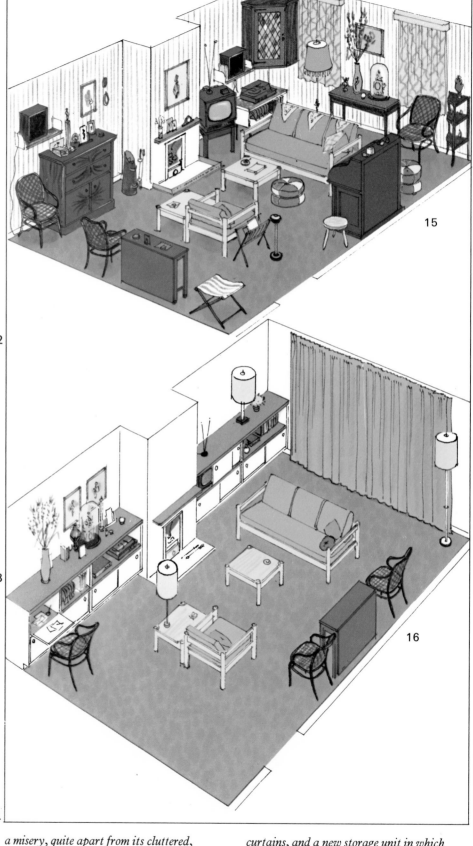

15

16

Above, right. *One of the main troubles with most rooms is that they have too much furniture in them. They can nearly always be improved by a drastic clean-out.* **15.** *This room may be cosy, but it is so over-furnished that living in it would be* a misery, quite apart from its cluttered, messy appearance. Note that most of the seating would never be sat on, because it is in impractical places. **16.** *The same room after throwing out all unnecessary items. Nothing has been added except new lamps and* curtains, and a new storage unit in which all the items that cluttered up the room have been put. Note the TV behind a sliding door. The stereo record player has been built in as well. The room has now become spacious and easy to live in.

For example, a living room should look reasonably cosy. If it is furnished entirely with starkly simple modern furniture, it may seem barren and uncomfortable, no matter how elegant it looks. A few old-fashioned easy chairs might easily improve it; or you can be really generous with the 'soft touches' like curtains and cushions.

Mixing styles in this way is not necessarily something to avoid. Obviously, flowery chintz and Scandinavian chairs look terrible together. But a subtle mixture, planned with taste and care, can often look far more successful than one style on its own.

A mixture of old and new furniture needs some visual link between the two if it is to succeed. This can be done in any of several ways. If the wood is the same colour it is often enough. Surfaces of the same height, or even just an impression that the two pieces have been planned on the same scale, can often link old and new successfully. It does not necessarily matter if one piece is plain and the other very ornate, as long as the proportions make sense. There is no set of rules that can be given here: the success or failure of the mixture will depend on your own judgement.

Once you have chosen all your furniture and fittings and arranged them to your satisfaction, do not spoil the effect with poor lighting. Harsh light can ruin the look of an otherwise comfortable living room or bedroom; weak light impairs the efficiency of an otherwise functional kitchen.

One final point: do not overdo your designing. If you are too careful and thorough, you may easily create a room that looks so perfect that you cannot bear to use it. Even a newspaper left on a chair will look out of place, and you will tiptoe around the room straightening the ornaments. What you should aim for is to strike a balance between a jumbled mess and an over-perfect room like a film set. It is not easy, but the effort is worth it: an evening or two's hard thinking may well produce a better result than many pounds' worth of the wrong furnishings.

Above, right. One of the most important matters in room design is balance. **17.** In this living-room, the cool, uncluttered look is mostly achieved in this way. The curtains are echoed by the coloured panel around the picture; the sofa by the two low stools; the bookcase by the table and chair. But the room is not over-symmetrical.

18. The furniture in this bedroom has been slowly collected over the years, without a thought for the final appearance. The room is a jumble of wardrobes, chests and chairs, all different and most of them in the way. Visually, it is a mess. **19.** The same room completely remodelled. The new built-in wardrobes hold a lot of clothes without breaking up the room. The bed is given the prominence it deserves as the room's main feature. There is more seating space than before, but it is far less obtrusive.

20 & 21. Two examples of old furniture successfully blended with new: a Thonet rocking chair and a Victorian bentwood chair in modern settings.

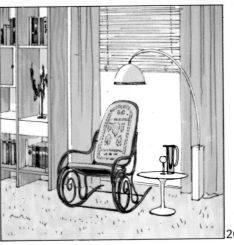

Long, low rooms, as in *32* (right), can
have an oppressive air. This is best
overcome by using furnishings with a strong
vertical stress, and also by splitting it
up with room-dividers or shelving (*31*).

33 shows furniture of a quality out of
most people's reach, but there is the same
strong vertical element. Tall bookcases,
floor-length curtains and even lampshades
all help correct the room's bad proportions.

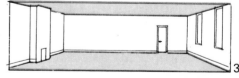

Left. *Six ways of altering the apparent shape of rooms to improve their proportions.* **22.** *Concentrating colour on the low part of the wall will hold the onlooker's eye down and make the room look wider.* **23.** *To make a room look higher, use vertical stripes on the wall and a matching floor covering to draw the eye up to the white ceiling.* **24.** *Warm colours, such as reds and oranges, make walls look nearer. Cool colours, such as blues and greens, make them look farther away. A room painted as shown here will look wider and shallower than it really is.* **25.** *The opposite effect, making the room look deeper and narrower.* **26.** *Another way of making a room look wider is to lay flooring with a linear pattern so that the lines run across the room. The ceiling is in a colour that tones with the floor, concentrating the eye on the white side and rear walls and adding to the width.* **27.** *The opposite effect: this room is made to look narrow and deep by boarding running from front to back.*

Right. *Similar techniques can be used for increasing or decreasing the apparent area of floors.* **28.** *This floor is made to look smaller by putting a bright-coloured carpet in the middle of its dark surface. The eye concentrates on the carpet and ignores the rest of the floor.* **29.** *A fitted carpet makes a floor look wider, and the effect can be increased by painting the skirting board in a matching colour. Continuing the colour up the walls, as in example 22, would make the floor seem even wider.* **30.** *The widest effect of all is created by laying tiles on the diagonal. This creates three sets of lines, two of which run from corner to corner—the longest way across the room.*

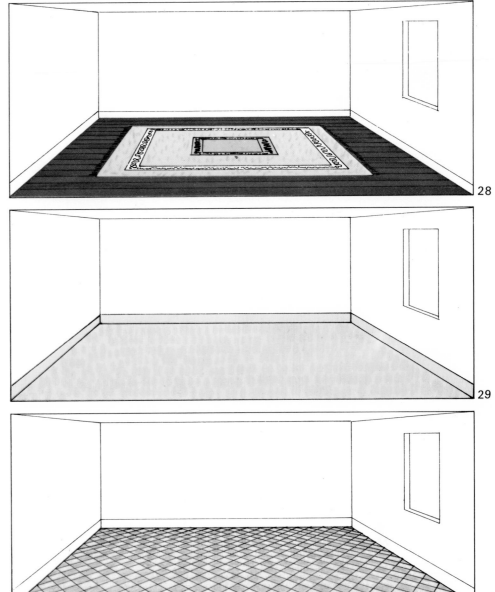

28

29

30

34

Left and below. *Pictures should not be arranged in a meaningless jumble.* **34.** *A typical arrangement, which does nothing for the pictures or for the room.* **35.** *A more satisfactory arrangement, with the bottoms of a row of pictures aligned with the top of the furniture. An alternative would be to line up their tops with a door or window frame at one side.*

36. *This is a more formal arrangement, with the pictures grouped in a rectangle. The right-hand side of the group is aligned vertically with the edge of the sideboard, and the whole layout is balanced by the vase on the left.* **37.** *One or more pictures can be grouped on a coloured backing painted on the wall and framed by a wooden moulding pinned direct to the plaster.*

35

36

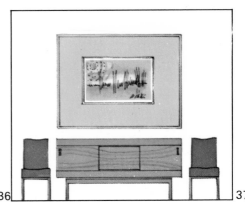

37

Top left. Where the surround of a window is decorative, the curtains should be simple and a pelmet is not needed.

Top right. Grand treatment of a bay window makes a frame for the garden.

Above left. Where the window is small, less light will be lost if the curtain track is taken round on to the side wall.

Above right. A lace curtain adds an elegant touch to French doors, and is heavy enough to screen the room from sun and flies when needed.

Choosing curtains for your windows

Curtains have two main functions—first, to screen windows at night, giving privacy to lighted rooms and shutting out the darkness; and second, to form part of the room's decoration, by softening the hard outline of the windows during the day and by becoming an expanse of wallcovering at night when they are closed.

To decide on the style of curtaining, have a good look at your windows in relation to the room and its other furnishings. Curtains can enhance or disguise the shape of windows and, if the window is out of proportion to the rest of the room, you can alter its apparent shape or size by adjusting the position of the curtain track. If daylight is restricted, the maximum amount of glass should remain uncovered when the curtains are drawn back. For this reason it is usually better to hang curtains outside reveals, but if you do have to hang them inside, take the track right round to the sides of the reveals so that no light is lost.

Next, decide on the length of the curtains—sill length (or no more than 2in. below), or floor length (in fact $\frac{1}{2}$in. above to prevent the hems from wearing and soiling). Anything

This page, top. Blinds are used to give privacy, and sheer curtains soften the outline of the windows and cover the wall gap between them.
Left. With café curtains, the lower tier can be drawn to give privacy without blocking out all the light.
Below left. Sheer curtains tied back are pretty and help hide an ugly outlook.
Below. Tall sash windows in a large room look splendid with draped-swag pelmets with tails and tied-back curtains, provided the furniture is in keeping.
Opposite page, top. Where main curtains are not needed, nets can give privacy and deflect glaring light, while 'sham' side curtains relieve the outline of the window and add decoration.
Centre, left. A contrasting border and trimming give interest to plain curtains where a pattern is not wanted.
Centre, right. The lower tier of these café curtains is made floor-level to give importance to a small window.
Bottom. A 'sham' curtain breaks up the broad expanse of window and helps define the dining area from the living area. This effect is increased by hanging the curtain from the ceiling, rather than from the top of the window.

between these looks unbalanced. If you are unsure about it, look at the height of the window in proportion to the room, and decide whether you need a pelmet or a modern track which needs no pelmet. In all cases the curtains must be full enough—at least one and a half times the width of the window—so they are well draped when closed.

Sash windows

Double-hung sash windows—common in Britain in Georgian, Victorian and Edwardian houses—tend to be narrow and tall, often in rooms with high ceilings, so they look splendid with heavy, floor-length curtains. To make the windows appear wider, the curtain track should extend 6-9in. either side of the window so that the curtains can be pulled right back.

To minimize the height, have a pelmet—this is one of the few places where the traditional, elaborate swags and tails can look really good if the furniture is in keeping. The depth of the pelmet should be one sixth the length of the curtains. If there is no need to minimize the height, give interest at the top of the window with a decorative rod. Short sash windows should be treated as for casement windows.

For sash windows with a rounded top, place the curtain and pelmet track immediately above the highest part. Have a pelmet with a straight upper edge and a lower edge which follows the curved line of the window.

Casement windows

Casement windows can be of all sizes, with two, three or more sashes, but they are usually not very high, nor in high-ceilinged rooms. Full-length curtains can give them importance in a living room. Often they have to be ruled out, however, because of the siting of a radiator. Or, because many casement windows with two or three sashes are only about half the height of the walls, full-length curtains look odd when drawn back—and furniture cannot be pushed against the wall under the window, which is a snag in a small room.

If you have a pelmet, make it a simple shape and shallow—allow $1\frac{1}{2}$in. depth to every foot of curtain length. Anything more elaborate or deeper than this will make the ceiling appear low. If the window is small and there is bare wall above it, position the pelmet and curtain track 2-3in. above the window so that the pelmet does not detract from the light. The pelmet will usually look best if it is made from the curtain fabric, but a plain fabric should be used if the curtain fabric has a large pattern. Avoid trimmings and fringes if your other furnishings are modern and simple. Gathered valances, which are less formal, should always match the curtains.

If you have a modern curtain track—such as a Swish type—which needs no pelmet, make a feature of the heading by using one of the gathering tapes which makes deep pencil pleats. Unless the ceiling is very high, position this sort of track for full-length curtains at ceiling height, even if the window is a few inches below, to prevent the wall from looking 'cut up'.

Picture and pivot windows

This rule also applies to large picture windows which need bold, but simple, treatment. The curtains should be full and heavy, so they drape well, and should have a decorative heading rather than a pelmet. As these decorative gathering tapes are more expensive than the standard sort, however, economize on these and not on the amount of fabric, because skimpy curtains will look far worse than a plain heading.

For pivot windows, the curtain track should be long enough so that the curtain can be pulled completely out of the way when the window is opened—the fuller the curtains, the more the track should extend past the window.

Where picture or pivot windows take up almost the entire wall and you can spare the space either side, have a track the full length of the wall, so that when the curtains are closed the wall is completely covered, and during the day they hang in the corners of the room.

Group treatment

Where windows are set close together on one wall or on either side of a French door, treat them as a group with one pair of curtains and not individually, which gives a bitty effect. A pelmet can give the necessary link between them, and when the curtains are closed the effect will be of one large window. If the windows are too far apart for this and it would look unbalanced when the curtains are drawn back, curtain each window separately but on a combined track, so that during the day the wall space between the windows is covered. Alternatively, have three curtains, each of the same width, and wide enough to cover the windows singly. One of the curtains remains stationary and covers the wall space between the windows; the other two hang at the other sides of the windows and are drawn to meet the stationary one.

Bay windows are often unattractively treated, with each part of the window having its own curtain made from one width of fabric, which looks skimpy and detracts from the daylight because it is not drawn completely to the sides. Instead, it is better to fit a curved track with a cording set, and have one full pair of curtains for the whole window. A pelmet or gathered valance will relieve any bareness at the top. Never, whether it be for reasons of economy or warmth, hang curtains across the face so that they cut off the bay when closed, thus robbing the room of its attractive feature and the added space which a bay gives.

Problem windows

Fabric curtains in kitchens and bathrooms can often be impractical, particularly if the windows are above the sink or hand basin. A roller blind can be the answer here and even when it is pulled up out of the way, it softens the outline of the window to some extent. Blinds are also better than curtains for glass doors, or for dormer windows where it is not possible to take the track round to the side walls (a roman blind will be 'softer' than a roller).

Choosing the fabric

Unless you are offered a large bale of fabric at a knock-down price, it is boring to have the same curtain fabric in every room because with so many different fabrics available, curtains can be a good and relatively inexpensive way of

ALBERTO PERUZZO EDITORE

HEIDEDE CARSTENSEN/STUDIO DIE WOHNFORM

AUSTRALIAN HOME JOURNAL

DU PONT FABRICS

experimenting with colour, texture and design. And with some cheaper fabrics, if you make a mistake, you need not live with it too long. Although they should not be considered as part of the exterior adornment, curtains do give a house a 'lived-in' look, and if you are worried about the fabric clashing with the exterior colour scheme, or feel that by having a different colour and pattern at every window the overall effect from outside will be unco-ordinated, line all the curtains with a neutral colour.

In any case, lining improves the hang of all curtains and can also intensify the colour of the fabric when seen against the light. It protects them from soiling and fading on the window side, makes them shadow-proof and helps to keep out draughts, particularly if the curtains are also interlined. (However, for frequent laundering, unlined curtains are more practical.)

Often a good combination is to have summer curtains in a lightweight fabric, possibly unlined, which you can discard when they are worn or move to the spare bedroom when you are tired of them, and have lined and interlined winter curtains in a more expensive, heavy fabric, which will wear longer because they are in use for only half of each year. If you never draw curtains in the summer, a further economy is to have sham curtains which are full enough not to look skimpy when drawn back, but which are not wide enough to close fully across the window.

The fabric—colour, pattern and texture—should complement, rather than dominate, the rest of the room. In a room where all the other coverings are plain, curtains can add all the pattern and colour necessary to prevent it from being drab; where there is already enough pattern, they can act as a foil for it. A small room can appear larger if the curtains are in the same colour as the surrounding walls; an ugly, or awkwardly placed window can be improved if the curtain fabric 'matches' the wallpaper.

When using a patterned fabric, it should look good draped, because for much of the time the curtains are drawn back and it should look good by artificial light, which is when you will mostly be seeing them closed. With any pattern you will achieve the best result by allowing a minimum of four, and a maximum of seven, repeats per curtain length.

While plain fabrics usually look better than bold patterns on narrow sash windows, they can look dull on very large windows. For these, choose a fabric with a textured weave or add a decorative border to a plain fabric. These borders can be positioned horizontally or vertically, or both, and look best between 4-6in. in from the edge. However, they can also be used as an emergency measure to add length or width to curtains which have shrunk or which were made for a smaller window. In cases like this, the border will not look so noticeably added on if it is quite deep, and added to both the heading and the hem.

Glass curtains

These are hung between the main curtains and the glass to give privacy to an overlooked window, in which case they may cover the lower part only, or to screen an ugly view, in which case they should also be decorative. Fine net curtains should be in white if you want to see through them or to deflect a glaring light, but for screening with some of the heavier mesh fabrics, the colour should be chosen to suit the room. Hang heavy or full-length nets from standard track with runners but, for easy removal for laundering, light or short curtains can be hung from a wire slotted through a casing at the top and hooked to each side of the window frame. A similar casing and wire, instead of a hem, at the foot of the curtains will prevent the curtains from flapping when the window is open. If you cover only part of the window, choose a logical point—such as a glazing bar—to place the curtain wire.

Below. *Where net curtains cover part of the window only, choose a logical position, such as the middle rail, for the wire.*

If you want privacy and protection from the sun, don't clutter the window by having main curtains, glass curtains and sunblinds—instead, hang sheer curtains in a heavy-mesh sun-filter fabric which are permanently drawn but will screen the windows and let in enough light; and have a separate lining hung on a different track which can be drawn as needed.

Where you want privacy and the room is very light, café curtains—curtains hung in two tiers, the lower of which is permanently drawn—might be the answer. The upper tier covers a little over half the depth of the window, and overlaps the lower tier by an inch or two.

Café curtains can also be used to make a small, high window look larger. The upper tier is made the length of the window, or even to reach the floor. The lower tier covers the wall below the window.

ANTHONY VERLAG/PHOTO NILSON

make it possible to find one which will blend with them.

The main alternative to net curtains is a slatted blind, but these are expensive, tedious to clean and cut out a lot of light. And unless they are in a neutral colour, they do not allow for a radical change in colour schemes.

There are three main types of net curtains.

Sheer fabrics: The most popular type of net curtain is made from a sheer fabric. This is hung right against the window and, although it does not detract from the amount of daylight entering the room, it gives privacy from outside while allowing those inside to see out. It is usually used with main curtains in ordinary fabric which are drawn at night.

Sheer net curtain fabric is mostly white, although some pale colours are available, and has a plain, close weave with a variety of textures, decorative borders and hems. The fabric used to be cotton, but these days it is usually a man-made fibre such as Terylene because this can be made in a really fine weave which is strong and resistant to sunlight. This attracts the dirt more quickly than cotton, but it is easily washed and drip dries quickly.

Sheer net fabric is not a difficult fabric to sew provided fine pins and machine needles are used to prevent snagging, and the machine is set with a slightly loose tension to prevent puckering. If you are using a man-made fabric, use a polyester thread, such as Trylko or Drima, because this will 'behave' in the same way as the fabric. Even if you normally don't bother to tack, it is always advisable to tack all folds and seams because the fabric tends to slip while it is being machine stitched.

If you have difficulty with feeding the fabric through the machine, or if it still slips in spite of being tacked, it is often worth putting strips of tissue paper under the fabric as it is being fed into the machine. This can be torn away afterwards.

Another important point about making sheer curtains is that all the hems—side, bottom and top—must be made double (with equal first and second turnings), so that you will not get an ugly raw edge showing through on to the right side of the curtain.

Semi-sheer fabrics: The other main type of net curtaining is made from a semi-sheer open-weave fabric. This cuts off more light than sheer nets, but is more suitable for screening an unattractive outlook. It is made in a variety of weaves and colours, mostly from acrylic fibres which have a warmer 'feel' than Terylene net. Cotton, linen and blends of fibres are also used.

Like sheer nets, semi-sheers are usually left drawn across the window during the day, and main curtains are drawn across at night. Alternatively, because they are heavy enough to hang outside the window reveal, it is possible to make linings which can be pulled across between them and the window for night-time screening.

Curtains made from very open-weave fabrics can be tricky to sew because it is important to plan the size of all the turnings so that the spaces in the weave fall on top of each other and the

Net curtains – light with privacy

Net curtains—the traditional method of screening windows—are back in fashion. With the modern preference for large windows, they are an ideal way of giving privacy and disguising an unpleasing outlook where necessary.

They are inexpensive and simple to make, modern fabrics make them easy to wash, and they soften the light entering the room rather than reducing it. Whether your other furnishings are modern and traditional, the new fabrics and designs being produced by the manufacturers stitching can be worked on a solid section of the weave.

Vision nets: These are similar to sheer nets, but have an open weave like semi-sheers, so the special techniques needed in sewing both types of fabric have to be used.

Hanging net curtains

Where net curtains are to cover the whole window, they can be made with a standard or deep curtain tape, and hung with hooks from a track which has an inner 'lane' specially for nets, but because they usually hang against the window, with the main curtains outside the reveal, it may not be possible to have a combined track. Where you do have to have separate tracks, choose one for the nets which is neat and unobtrusive and can be fixed to the ceiling of the reveal, such as Swish Furniglyde.

With sheer nets which will be kept permanently drawn across the window, you can use a rod or an expanding wire which is fixed to the window frame at either side. Wire should not be used for semi-sheer curtains because the fabric is too heavy and would make it sag in the middle.

A curtain tape can be used with this type of fixing, and the hooks are clipped on to the wire itself. More often, the wire or rod is slotted into a casing at the top of the curtain and the gathers are arranged evenly by pulling the curtain along it. This method is also best if you are covering only the lower part of the window. Always choose a logical place, such as a glazing bar, for fixing the rod.

Headings for net curtains

The most common heading for sheer nets is a casing (see above), but if you are using curtain tape, buy one of the kinds made specially for net curtains. These have an open weave which blends well with the curtain fabric, and are made in a synthetic fibre—usually nylon or Terylene—and so are easily washable and drip dry. They are available in three main widths—$2\frac{3}{4}$in. for tall pencil pleats (such as Rufflette's Tervoil 60), and 1in. or $\frac{5}{8}$in. for ruched gathers.

The deep tape is more expensive than the others, but if the main curtains have been made with a pencil-pleated heading, using it on the nets too gives a co-ordinated effect.

On semi-sheer fabrics, try to use a curtain tape which is the same colour as the fabric so that it will not show through unattractively on to the right side of the curtains. Alternatively, if you are using a deep heading tape which is available in white only, on a very open-weave fabric, you could insert a strip of plain fabric in a matching colour between the curtain and the tape. The strip must be in a similar fibre to the curtains, so that it will react in the same way when the curtains are washed—in most cases a cotton/polyester dress fabric can be used.

Calculating the amount of fabric

The method for measuring and making semi-sheer curtains is very similar to unlined curtains of regular fabric (see page 35), but for sheer curtains there are several very important differences.

With most unlined curtains which are gathered with a conventional narrow curtain tape, between $1\frac{1}{2}$ times or double the required width of fabric is used to give fullness. This can appear skimpy on very fine net curtains, so double or even three times the required width should be used.

Achieving the right amount of fullness leads to another difference between regular and net fabrics. Most furnishing fabrics are 48in. wide, so for any window where the curtain track is longer than 4ft you would have to join on more fabric to the main width in each curtain. The line of the seam would be hidden by the folds of fabric and the turnings out of sight on the back of the curtain.

With net, however, the turnings would show through unattractively on to the right side and, because it is difficult to neaten the raw edges by the conventional method, you would have to join on the fabric by the selvedges. This can lead to the seam puckering if the selvedges are more tightly woven than the rest of the fabric.

Fortunately, most net curtain fabrics are made in a variety of widths up to 165in., so on many windows the problem of joining will not be encountered. You should work out the minimum width you need, and buy the required length in the standard width which is next above it. There is no need to trim off the excess width because the extra fullness can easily be incorporated.

If you cannot buy the fabric you want in the right width, it is usually better to make up separate curtains with a full width of fabric in each. When these are hung, the edges will be hidden by the folds and the effect will be of one complete curtain.

Alternatively, with sheer fabrics you can solve the problem by buying what are known as 'short nets', which are sold in a variety of standard lengths. Conventional fabrics are sold in set widths and you buy the length you require (sheer curtains of this type are known as 'long nets'). With short nets there is often a ready-made casing heading and a frilled or decorative hem, and you buy the required width in the standard length which is nearest above your own.

In measuring the length for long nets, if you are making a casing you may have to adapt the amount allowed at the top so that the turnings do not show through. Measure the basic length of the curtains from the suspension point of the rod to the window sill, and add on the 6in. for a double bottom hem in the normal way. Decide on the depth of the casing, making it large enough for the rod or wire to be inserted easily, and add on twice this depth to the length.

If you also want a heading, which protrudes above the rod in a frill and looks very attractive on half nets, decide on the depth of this—usually between $\frac{1}{2}$in. and $\frac{3}{4}$in. because anything greater will fall back—and add on three times this amount to the length. This allows for the turnings to be double.

When you make the curtains, you add together the depth of the heading and casing and turn over this amount for the first and second turnings: Machine stitch along the lower fold and again at a distance equal to the depth of the heading from the top. The rod is inserted into the casing formed by the two rows of stitching.

If you are using cotton net, allow an extra 12in. length per curtain in case of shrinkage. It is also a good idea to wash the fabric before you cut it out.

Finishing 'short nets'

If the curtains are the right length, before you make the side hems you should unpick the heading for about 3in.-4in. on each side. This frees the fabric so that hems can be made to the top edge and the heading turned down on top of them. If you do not do this, but simply turn down the side hems, you would not be able to insert the rod because you have stitched over the opening.

Trim the side raw edges exactly level with the grain of the fabric, if necessary, and then turn them on to the wrong side for $\frac{1}{2}$in. Fold over a second turning of $\frac{1}{2}$in. to make a double hem, tack and machine stitch. Press the hems lightly and then restitch the heading.

If the curtains are too long, unpick the casing across the entire width and press the fabric carefully. Measure the exact length you want the curtain to be from the bottom of the hem up, add on twice the depth of the casing and trim off the excess. Turn the top edge down on to the wrong side of the curtain for the depth of the casing and tack. Fold over a second turning of the same depth, tack and machine stitch. Press lightly.

Crossover drapes

These are a more decorative style of net curtain, and are ideal where it is more important to distract attention from the outlook than to provide privacy. They are also good in a room like the kitchen, where you might not have main curtains, and for frosted glass windows.

Using a fabric tape, measure from the top left-hand corner of the window in a loose curve to the right-hand side at the point you want to tie the curtains back, and then to the window sill.

RUFFLETTE

SYNDICATION INTERNATIONAL

HEIDEDE CARSTENSEN/STUDIO DIE WOHNFORM

Above left. Where it is important to disguise an unpleasing outlook, festoon curtains are ideal for a traditional setting. If you have main curtains with them, these should be as simple as possible.

Above centre. Crossover drapes are another form of decorative net curtain and are more suitable for an informal, 'country' setting.

Above right. *In a room where you may not want main curtains, semi-sheer nets give an attractive touch of colour. These have been made as café curtains as on page 37.*

Decide on the depth of casing you need and add on twice this amount to the top, plus 2in. for a 1in. double hem at the foot. This is the maximum length, which you should double to calculate the amount of fabric needed for the pair of curtains. For the width, measure the length of the curtain track or rod. Buy the width of fabric which is nearest to double this length.

Cut both curtains to the maximum length. Next, work out the minimum length of each curtain by measuring from the curtain track or rod to the window sill. Add on the same allowances as for the maximum length.

Start by cutting the left-hand curtain first. Lay out the fabric flat and mark on the left-hand edge the minimum length, measuring from the top down. Draw a line from this point to the bottom right-hand corner and cut along it. Cut the right-hand curtain in a similar way, but marking the minimum length on the right-hand edge and cutting from this point to the left-hand corner.

Make 1in. double hems along the lower slanting edge and along the side edges. To finish the top, place one curtain over the other, with the short sides on the outside and their 'right' sides facing downwards. Pin and tack them together and then make a 1in. double hem along the top edge for the casing, treating the two curtains as one piece of fabric.

Insert the rod or wire into the casing and hang the curtains in position. Cut the offcuts of net into long strips and make narrow hems along the edges. Use these to tie back the curtains.

If you would like the cross-overs to have a flounce on the inner vertical edge, it is possible to use 'short nets' sideways. Work out the length and width as above, and buy the standard length which is nearest above the required width, in a width equal to the required length. Cut the fabric so that the flounced edge in both curtains is the maximum length and the casing edge is the minimum length. In many cases, you will be able to use the casing as the side hem.

Festoon curtains

These are ideal for a more formal setting on a large staircase windows or frosted glass windows. Basically they are curtains which are about three times as long as the window and gathered to the right size by vertical tapes stitched at intervals across the curtain. One curtain is used at each window, rather than the usual pair.

Use a fine Terylene net in a plain weave and allow about three times the required height and one-and-a-half times the required width. Decide on the number of festoon gathers you want, placing one at each side of the curtain and then at 8in.-10in. intervals across the width (the tapes will be closer together when on the window). If you have to join the fabric to make the full width, plan the gathers so that one will fall on the join. To calculate the amount of gathering tape required, multiply the length of the ungathered curtain by the number of gathers. Terylene curtain tape in the $\frac{5}{8}$in. width is ideal for the purpose.

Make a $\frac{1}{2}$in. double hem along the bottom edge of the curtain and machine stitch with Terylene thread. Fold over 1in. at each side of the curtain and tack down along the fold and along the raw edge. Press lightly.

Mark the position of the festoons down the length of the curtain, making sure that you keep the lines true to the grain of the fabric. Cut the tape into pieces the same length as the curtain, plus 2in. Pull out the cords for about 2in. from one end, and then fold under the tape at each end for $\frac{1}{2}$in. Pin the tape to the 'wrong' side of the curtain with the ends where the cord has been pulled out at the top and so that the side tapes come $\frac{1}{8}$in. from the outside folds and just cover the raw edges of the turning. Place the remaining pieces centrally over the marks. Tack and machine stitch in position, including the short ends of the tape.

Pull up the cords evenly to make the curtain the right length, adjusting them if necessary so that the loops of fabric fall in regular sweeps. Stitch at intervals to hold in position. To finish the top of the curtain, anchor the gathering cords by making a couple of back stitches with it, and cut off the excess. Then make a $\frac{1}{2}$in. double hem for the casing.

If you want to be able to pull the curtain up, stitch on curtain rings and finish it as for a roman blind (see page 49).

A fringe or gathered flounce can be stitched along the bottom edge as a final touch.

33

Above. *Where the net curtains cover a large area, a deep hem will make them hang better.*

Below left. *As well as giving privacy, net curtains can screen an ugly view.*

Below right. *If the side curtains are floor length, make the nets that length too.*

ELIZABETH WHITING

Above. Full net curtains can be a feature of a room where side curtains are unnecessary.

Unlined curtains

The Victorians called them lace curtains. Now they are known as 'sheers', 'nets', 'inner', or 'glass' curtains. Their purpose is still the same, however – to screen an overlooked window. Unlined side curtains are made by the same method.

Calculating the amount of fabric

There is a formula for calculating the fabric needed for net and unlined curtains, and this should be worked out accurately and then adjusted to make best use of the width of the fabric. If the window is set in a reveal (recess), with the curtain track outside it, always take the measurements from the track as this will probable extend 3–6in. either side of the reveal and 2–3in. above it (Fig. **1**).

Man-made fibres have revolutionized the field of net curtains. They do not shrink or pull out of shape and some, such as Terylene, are extremely resistant to deterioration from light. Use a nylon curtain tape and Terylene sewing thread for the best results.

Measuring the width

For a pair of unlined curtains, gathered with a standard pocketed curtain tape, the width of each curtain should be between $1\frac{1}{2}$–2 times half the length of the track so that the curtain looks nicely full when gathered to fit its half of the track. To this, add 2in. for each side hem, and about 6in. for the overlap if required. Then compare the total with the width of the fabric being used.

For a window 3ft wide, for example, the curtain track might extend 3in. either side of the reveal and be in two 2ft halves, so that the curtains can overlap for 6in. in the centre. As each curtain should be at least 3ft wide before being gathered, plus 4in. for the side hems, you would need pieces of fabric 40in. wide. However, if you buy 48in. or 54in. wide fabric, there is no need to cut off the excess, as the additional amount will be absorbed into the gathering and the curtains will be improved by the additional fullness.

For windows over 4ft 6in. wide you will need to join the fabric to get the right width. It is easiest and most practical to base your calculation in full widths and half widths – use the chart in Fig. **2** to decide how many you need for your window. If the fabric is particularly lightweight, add a half-width to the amount given.

The principle for measuring for net curtains is the same, but as some fabrics are made in widths up to 108in., calculating the amount is easier.

Measuring the length

Use a steel tape or long rule to measure from the track to either the window sill or floor (see Fig. 1). To this, add 6in. for a double hem at the foot (12in. for net, floor-length curtains) and $2\frac{1}{2}$in. for the heading. The total, multiplied by the number of widths calculated above, will give the length of fabric required for a pair of curtains. If the fabric has a large pattern, you will have to buy extra for matching it at the seams on each curtain, and also so that it falls at the same level on both curtains. As a simple guide, you should allow an extra pattern on each width. For example, if each curtain is made from 2 widths, you should allow 4 extra pattern repeats on the total.

If the fabric is not guaranteed non-shrink, allow an extra inch per yard, and wash the fabric before cutting out.

Cutting and joining the widths

Lay the fabric on a really large flat surface for cutting out – you must be able to see a complete curtain length at once. Use the floor if you haven't a table long or wide enough. Make the top edge absolutely straight by drawing a thread at right-angles to the selvedge, and then cut along the line. Measure the curtain length from this point, draw another thread and cut along it. Cut the next lengths in the same way, matching the pattern if necessary (Fig. 3). For a half width, fold one of the pieces in half lengthwise and cut down the fold.

Use a ½in. plain seam to join the pieces for each curtain, placing the 'right' sides of the fabric together, selvedge to selvedge. If using half widths, place them to the outside of each curtain. Machine stitch the pieces together, using a loose tension and a long stitch. Press the seams open and clip into the selvedges if they are tight.

Matching the pattern

To join two pieces of fabric so that the pattern matches exactly needs a slightly different technique from that usually used for a plain seam. Begin by finding the same point in the pattern on both pieces of fabric. With 'right' sides facing, pin the pieces together at this point, with the pin at *right-angles* to the edge (normally the pins are placed on the seam line parallel to the edge).

Continue pinning the pieces together at 1–3-in. intervals, still placing the pins at right-angles to the edge. At about 12in. intervals turn the pieces to the 'right' side to check that the pattern still matches. If it has started to 'slip', take out the pins and repin the pieces, making sure you are not stretching one of them.

Tack the pieces together along the seam line in the normal way, but leaving the pins in position (if your tacking stitches are usually large, make them a bit smaller for this). Still leaving the pins in, machine stitch, following the tack-ing line. Remove the tacking and the pins, and press the seam open.

Making the side hems

Use 1in. double hems at the sides on unlined curtains as these are heavier than single hems, and will prevent the sides from curling back. To make a double hem, fold over the edge 1in. to the wrong side of the fabric, and then fold this over another inch, so the raw edge is completely enclosed. Pin and tack the hem down and then machine stitch (if the fabric has a nap – like velvet – hand stitch it using a strong thread, as machine stitching might spoil the surface). Press the hem and remove the tacking.

Attaching the gathering tape

Turn over the raw edge at the top of the curtains 1½in. and tack down. Cut a length of curtain tape the width of each curtain, plus 2in. for turnings. Pull out about 1½in. of the cords from their slots at both ends of the tape. Knot the cords at one end, but keep the other end free for gathering. Place the tape on the curtain so that it covers the raw edge centrally and the top edge of the tape is not more than 1in. from the top of the curtain. (Fig. 4) Tack it along the top edge. Turn the ends of the tape under at both ends so that the knot is enclosed at one end, but the cords are free at the other (Fig. 5). Tack down the tape along the bottom edge.

Machine stitch, outside the cords, along both edges of the tape (stitch in the same direction to prevent any drag which would show on the finished curtain). Stitch down the ends. Remove all the tacking, and then press.

Gathering the curtains

Pull the fabric along the cords until it is all at the knotted end. Pull out again to the right width, distributing the gathers evenly (Fig. 6) and knot the cords to secure the width. Catch the knot to the tape with a few stitches to prevent it from hanging down, but do not cut off the surplus cord. When the curtains need washing or cleaning, the gathers can be released by unpicking the stitches and undoing the knot.

Insert curtain hooks into the pockets at each end of the curtains, and at 3in. intervals between. (Fig 7). Hang the curtains for a few days before taking up the bottom hems, as some fabrics may stretch during this time.

Making the hem

When you are ready to do the hems, mark the line for the length at each side of the curtain while it is still hanging. Full-length curtains should finish 1in. above the floor to allow them to hang properly and prevent them dragging and wearing through constant chafing. Sill-length curtains should either just clear the sill, or be about 1in. below the sill so the curtains hang outside it.

Take down the curtains and mark the hem line completely. Turn it up and tack loosely along the bottom fold. Turn in the raw edges, half the depth of the hem allowance, and make double hems. Tack them down and machine or hand stitch. Remove the tacking and press the hems and then the complete finished curtains.

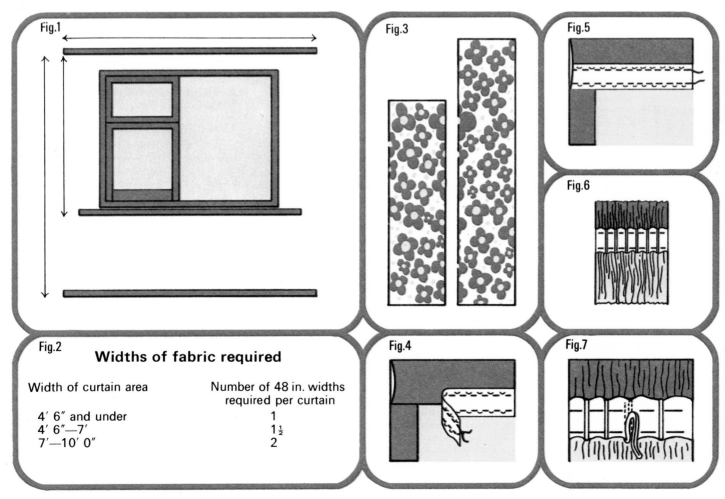

Fig.1

Fig.3

Fig.5

Fig.6

Fig.2

Widths of fabric required

Width of curtain area	Number of 48 in. widths required per curtain
4' 6" and under	1
4' 6"—7'	1½
7'—10' 0"	2

Fig.4

Fig.7

Café curtains

Most people solve the problem of combining large windows and privacy by hanging net curtains. If you feel that this is like putting your house into purdah, café curtains can be a decorative and unusual alternative.

Café curtains are really short curtains, hung from a rod which is placed halfway down the window. They are usually kept permanently drawn closed, thus giving privacy or hiding an unattractive outlook without blocking too much light. They are frequently used with other curtains which are hung from the normal place above the window and are just long enough to overlap the lower tier.

The lower tier can be made in two separate curtains in the normal way if the window is wide, or for a small window it can be one single curtain. The upper tier is usually best made in two parts so they will look balanced when drawn back.

In order to let the maximum amount of daylight filter through, café curtains are best made in cotton and left unlined. On the other hand, if enough daylight comes through the top half of the window and the backs of the curtains are

Below. *Café curtains can be made in the same way as ordinary curtains, but they look more attractive with a scalloped heading and hung from a pole with rings.*

RUTH RUTTER

easily seen from outside, lining will improve their appearance.

Choosing the heading

The simplest type of heading for café curtains where there is a lower tier only is plain casing, through which a dowel rod or length of expanded wire can be inserted for hanging them in the same way as for net curtains. It is not very easy to draw the curtains with this type of heading, so it is suitable only where they will be kept closed.

Alternatively—and this is more attractive but more complicated in the initial calculations and cutting out—the heading can be scalloped. By this method the curtains can be hung from a decorative curtain rod by rings which are stitched to the top of the straps between the scallops, or these straps can be made to loop round the rod. As an extra decoration on curtains to be hung with hooks, the straps can be pinch pleated. Where the straps are used to suspend the curtains, the scallops could be pinch pleated.

Plain heading

First decide where the rod or wire should be placed—usually about halfway down the window and preferably in line with a glazing bar. Fix the rod or wire in position and then measure its length between the fixing points. Double this measurement for the total width of the curtain, to give enough fullness, adding about 2in. if you are making two separate curtains.

For the length, measure from the level of the wire to the window sill and add 1in. (or the circumference of the rod plus $\frac{1}{2}$in.) allowance at the top. Add a minimum of 4in. at the foot for the hem if the curtains are to be sill length, or 6in. if they are to finish just below the sill.

To calculate the amount of fabric needed, divide the width of the fabric into the total width of the curtain, taking it to the nearest half or whole width above, and multiply this figure by the total length. Add on extra if you have to match the pattern when joining pieces to make up the full width.

Cut out the fabric, joining the pieces to make up the full width if necessary with a $\frac{1}{2}$in. plain seam. Turn over 1in. at each side of the curtain on to the wrong side and press down. Turn over another 1in. thus making a double hem, and tack and stitch down. Press.

Turn over the allowance at the top of the curtain and press down. Turn under the edge of the allowance again for $\frac{1}{2}$in. and tack and stitch down. Press.

Below. Where windows which overlook the street come down to floor level, you may want temporary screening, say at meal times. Café curtains do not block too much light when closed, and are cheaper than slatted blinds.

Insert the rod or wire through the hem at the top of the curtain, arranging the gathers evenly along its length, and try the curtain in position. Leave it for a couple of days in case the fabric stretches and then mark the exact position of the lower edge of the hem line with pins while it is still hanging.

Take down the curtain, mark the hem completely and make a double hem. Tack and stitch down. Press the finished curtain completely and re-hang it.

As a variation to the plain hem casing, you could make a casing with a frill above it. Add an extra 2in. to the allowance at the top of the curtain and turn over 1in. of this with the main allowance. Stitch the hem as before and make a second line of stitching 1in. below the top fold. Insert the rod or wire in the casing between the hem stitching and the second row. By gathering the curtain up to fit the rod, the fabric above it will form a frill (Fig.1).

Scalloped heading

First decide on the height of the curtain rod, as above. If you are having an upper tier, decide on the position of this too. Fix both rods in position and measure the distance between the brackets on each side of the window. Add on a half of this measurement, plus 4in. for turnings, for the total width of a curtain with a plain heading, or double it for a pleated heading. If you are making the top tier in two halves, add

on an extra 4in.

For the length of the top tier, first measure from the upper curtain rod to the lower curtain rod. Next, decide on the depth of the scallops—usually between 3in and 4in.—and add this measurement plus 2in. for turnings to the top of the curtain. If you are using straps to hang the curtains, add on an amount equal to the circumference of the rod plus about 1in for ease. So that the top tier will be long enough to cover the scallops of the lower tier when closed, add the depth of the scallops plus 4in. for the hem to the bottom of the curtain.

For the length of the lower tier, measure from the lower curtain rod to the sill, or just below, and add the depth of the scallops plus 2in. for turnings to the top of the curtain, and 4in. for the hem allowance to the bottom.

To calculate the amount of fabric needed, divide the width of the fabric into the total width of the curtain and multiply this figure by the total length.

Making a pattern

The safest way of ensuring that all the scallops and straps are the same width and a good shape is to make a paper pattern. (Fig.2). Use a piece of paper the exact width of the curtain excluding the seam allowances, and about 6in. wider than twice the depth of the scallops.

Start by marking a line (A-B) across the width of the paper about 2in. from the top edge.

Draw another line (C-D) the depth of the scallop below this.

To determine the exact number of scallops and to show whether any adjustments are necessary, decide on an approximate width for both the scallop and the strap and add them together. Divide this figure into the width of the paper. Use the remaining figure to make another strap, so that there is a strap at each end of the curtain, and 'lose' any excess in the width of the scallops or possibly by adding it to the seam allowances at the sides of the curtain.

For example, if you are using fabric at its full width of 48in., making the curtain 44in. wide when the hems are taken, with 4in. wide scallops and $1\frac{1}{4}$in. wide straps, you would start off by having eight scallops and straps. The extra strap would come out of the remaining 2in. still leaving $\frac{3}{4}$in. to lose. The simplest way of doing this would be to make each side hem $\frac{3}{8}$in. wider, so the finished curtain would then be $43\frac{1}{4}$in. wide.

Make any necessary adjustment to the width of the paper, then draw a line down the paper (E-F) half the width of the strap from the left edge. Draw another line (G-H) the same

Below. *If you want to cover the lower part of the window during the day, and the whole window at night, make two-tier café curtains. The upper tier should overlap the lower one by 2in.-3in. for complete screening.*

distance away from this and then a third line (I-J) half the width of the scallop from the second line. Add together half the width of a scallop and strap, and continue marking lines equal to this figure across the paper. At the right-hand edge this should leave an amount equal to half a scallop and a whole strap.

Mark a point (X) on the line I-J half the width of a scallop from the line C-D. Mark a similar point (Y) on the line G-H. Then, using X as the centre, draw an arc to join J and Y. This gives the curve for the scallop.

Keeping all the marked lines uppermost, fold under the paper along the line I-J, then continue folding the paper concertina-wise along the remaining marked lines to the right of I-J. A section, equal in width to half the strap, will extend beyond the folds at each end of the paper (Fig.3).

Cut through all the folds of paper along the top line (A-B), then cut out the scallop (along G-Y-J). When the paper is opened out, the pattern for the complete scalloped edge will be formed.

Making up the curtain

Turn over half the amount allowed for the hems on to the wrong side on each side of the curtain and press down. Turn over the same amount again and make a double hem. Press.

Turn over the amount allowed at the top of the curtain on to the 'right' side and press down.

If the fabric is flimsy, cut a piece of iron-on interfacing to fit the width of the curtain and slightly deeper than the scallops. Iron it on to the heading allowance so that its edge comes level with the fold.

Pin on the paper pattern so that the top edge of the straps is level with the fold of fabric. Tack round the edge of the pattern through all the thicknesses of fabric, keeping your stitches as close to the edge of the paper as possible. Unpin the pattern and machine stitch along the tacked lines (Figs.5 and 6).

Cut out the scallops to within $\frac{1}{4}$in. of the stitching. Clip the remaining seam allowance round the curves of the scallops and at the top corners of the straps, then turn the heading 'right' side out. Poke out the corners of the straps carefully, then tack along the seam line so that none of the facing shows on the 'right' side of the curtain. Press. Turn under the raw edge at the bottom of the facing for $\frac{1}{2}$in. and slip stitch it to the curtain, making sure that no stitches show on the 'right' side.

If you are making the straps into pinch pleats,

form these by hand or stitch on tape, following the method given on page 57.

Sew brass or plastic curtain rings to the top of the straps on the 'wrong' side, using strong thread. Stitch fairly loosely, as if sewing on a heavy coat button, to allow the ring to twist round when it is fitted on the rod.

If you are using the straps to hang the curtains, turn over the amount allowed for fitting it round the pole and stitch firmly in position.

Hang the curtains and turn up the hems as above.

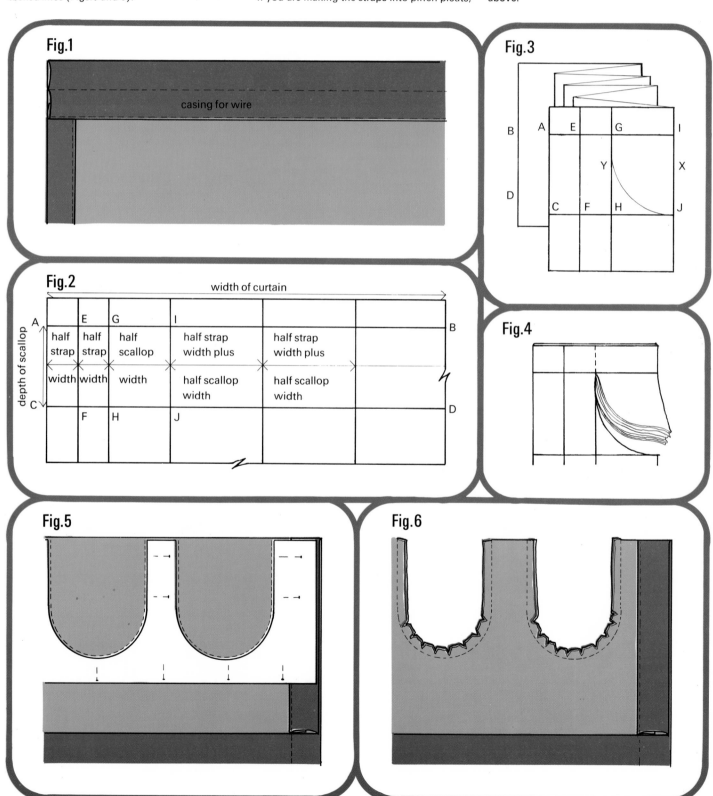

Fig.1   casing for wire

Fig.2

width of curtain

depth of scallop

	E	G	I	
half strap	half strap	half scallop	half strap width plus	half strap width plus
width	width	width	half scallop width	half scallop width
	F	H	J	

Fig.3

Fig.4

Fig.5

Fig.6

Two methods to make lined curtains

Lining improves the look of all curtains, making them seem fuller and better draped. It protects them from fading and soiling on the window side—particularly if the curtains are a pale colour (as above, where the dark border on the edges most handled also helps). In addition, lining intensifies the curtains' colour when seen against daylight, makes them shadowproof and keeps out draughts, especially if they are also interlined.

41

Buy a neutral-coloured sateen, specially made for curtain lining, in the same width as the curtain fabric and in a comparable quality—if your fabric is an expensive one, don't buy the cheapest quality lining, since it will wear out long before the curtains and you will have the bore and expense of remaking them with a new lining. A good alternative to plain sateen is the type which is metal insulated (the wrong side is silver-grey) as this is completely draught-proof.

For the interlining, use a fabric known as 'bump' which is made in a 48in. width. It is woven like chenille, with a heavy weft thread and a fine cotton warp, and looks like a thick, fleecy flannelette sheeting.

There are two methods of making lined curtains. One is known as the 'bag' or 'sack' method and should be used only for short curtains made from single widths of fabric. The other method involves more work—and a great deal of hand stitching—as the lining is 'locked' to the curtains at intervals across the width, but it is worth doing as it prevents it from dropping or flapping in the wind when the windows are open.

Making the curtains

Measure the window and calculate the amount of fabric needed for both curtains and lining as for unlined curtains (see page 35) but allow only 4in. for the hem. Cut out the fabric for the curtains and join it if necessary. Cut and join the lining, making it 3in. shorter and 4in. narrower than the curtains. Mark the centre points down the length of the curtain and lining with tacking stitches.

Making the lining
'Bag' method

With the 'wrong' side of the lining fabric uppermost, turn up the bottom edge $\frac{1}{2}$in., then turn up 1in. and make a machine-stitched hem. Lay out the curtain fabric 'right' side up and make a tuck of about 4in. down the middle (to make curtain the same width as the lining). Place the lining 'right' side down on the curtain

Left. *A curtain lining can be decorative as well as functional. These were made by the 'bag' method but with the lining and curtain pieces cut to the same length. The bottom was seamed at the same time as the side seams to make a neat hem.*

Fig.1. *With a 'bag' lining, the lining top is placed 1½in. below the curtain top.*
Fig.2. *When the pieces are stitched, the lining is positioned so there is a 2in. border of curtain on each side.*
Fig.3. *When the top edge of the curtain is tacked down, the gathering tape can be stitched on.*
Fig.4. *To mitre the corner for the hem the corner is folded in and the excess fabric cut off ¼in. from the fold.*
Fig.5. *The hem is turned up and tucked under the lining, which is then caught down.*
Fig.6. *The side hems are stitched down with large herringbone stitches.*
Fig.7. *Locking stitch is similar to a large blanket stitch.*

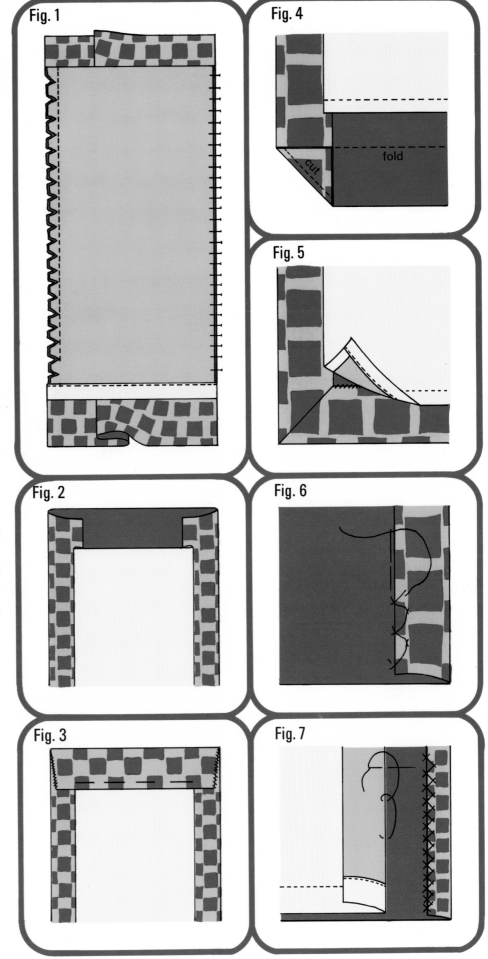

Fig. 1

Fig. 2

Fig. 3

Fig. 4

Fig. 5

Fig. 6

Fig. 7

so that the lining top is $1\frac{1}{2}$in. below the curtain top. Pin the sides together, tack and machine stitch $\frac{1}{2}$in. from the edges and 2in. from the foot of the lining. Clip the turnings and then press the seams on to the lining.

Turn the curtain 'right' side out and match the centre points together. Lay the curtain out flat and position the lining so that it is centred on the curtain and there is a 2in. border of curtain. showing on each side of the lining. Press. Turn down the top edge of the curtain $1\frac{1}{2}$in. on to the lining and tack through all thicknesses. Attach the gathering tape and draw up the threads.

Hang the curtains for a few days and then mark and turn up the hem (leaving the lining free), and mitre the corners by folding under the excess fabric (rather like folding the ends of a parcel).

'Locked' method

Make $2\frac{1}{2}$in. turnings on to the wrong side at each edge of the curtain, tack and herringbone-stitch down. Lay the curtain 'right' side down on a large flat surface and smooth completely flat. Make a 1in. hem on the lining and then position it face down, so that its top edge is $1\frac{1}{2}$in. below the top of the curtain and the centre points are matching at the top and bottom. Pin the lining to the curtain down the centre line, then turn back one half of the lining (Fig.7) and 'lock' it to the curtain.

Starting 9in. from the bottom, and working from left to right up the curtain, pick up two threads of the curtain and lining with the needle, place the sewing thread round it as in Fig.7, pull the needle through and draw up the thread (rather like blanket stitch). Continue working up the curtain in this way, making the stitches 2-3in. apart. Do not pick up more threads than this or the stitches will show on the right side of the curtain, and do not draw the thread too tight or the stitches will pucker. Repeat this locking process at approximately 18in. intervals across the width of the curtains and at the seams. Press the lining completely and then tack it to the curtains about 5in. from each edge.

Turn under the sides of the lining for $\frac{1}{2}$in. and pin them to the curtain, placing the pins at right angles to the fold. Slip stitch the lining to the curtain and then press. Make the heading and hems as above.

Making the interlining

Cut the interlining to the same size as the curtains, joining it with a lapped seam where necessary because this is much flatter than a plain seam. To make a lapped seam, have both pieces of fabric right side up and lay one edge $\frac{1}{2}$in. over the other. Backstitch down the centre of the overlap (do not machine stitch this fabric as it tends to stretch).

Lay the curtain face down on a large flat surface and smooth it flat. Place the interlining on it, with the edges meeting. Turn over the edges $2\frac{1}{2}$in. on both sides, tack and herringbone stitch down. Place on the lining, lock it to the curtain and interlining, and then finish the curtains as above.

Right. *An inset border (above) should be stitched on before the lining, but an edging (below) can be attached afterwards.*

Roller blinds

A roller blind is one of the simplest and most effective window treatments where curtains are inappropriate. With an inexpensive kit, and fabric you buy yourself, you can make up and install a blind within a couple of hours.

Measuring the window

Roller blind kits can be bought with rollers of two widths, and in lengths from 36in. to 7ft. To decide which size to buy, measure the width and height of the inside reveal of the window. If there is no reveal, or the blind is to hang outside it, measure the width and height of the window and add 3in. to the width and 4–6in. to the height, so that the blind will hang straight because it is supported all the way round.

If there is not a kit the same size as the width of the window, buy the next size up and cut it down to fit (see below). In any case, if your window is more than 7ft. high, buy a kit with a roller at least 4ft. long, and cut it down if necessary, as the roller must be heavy enough ($1\frac{1}{2}$in. diameter as opposed to the 1in. of rollers up to 4ft long) to take the weight of the fabric.

In each roller blind kit you should be supplied with: the wooden roller, at one end of which is the spring device (this must *never* be oiled); a round metal cap and lipped nail, which fit into, or over, the other end of the roller; two metal wall brackets, one slotted and one with a round hole; a wooden slat, for the bottom of the blind; a plastic cord holder; a plastic (or wooden) acorn, with a cap; a length of cord; several tiny screws and tacks. (You have to supply your own screws for fixing the brackets to the wall—and rawlplugs, if necessary.)

Choosing the fabric

Pvc coated fabrics are ideal for roller blinds, because they need little or no sewing, and can be sponged down to clean while still in position. Alternatively, use a thin, but closely-woven fabric—such as linen, canvas or a glazed chintz—as this will not crease or go out of shape when rolled up.

Buy a length of fabric equal in length to the window's height (or outside measurement, as calculated above), plus 6in. if you are using pvc, or 12in. for other fabrics, to allow for possible shrinkage when washed. If your window is wider than the standard fabric widths, buy a double quantity and join it following the method for the panelled table-cloth (see page 143).

Fitting the roller

Begin by screwing the roller brackets to the window frame, or to the adjacent walls, or to the ceiling. If the brackets are face or wall fixed, the top should be 1in. from the ceiling, to give enough clearance for the roller and fabric. Allow more if the fabric is a thick one, or if the roller is of the larger width. The bracket with the slot must go on the left and the one with the round hole on the right; the flanges should face inwards. Leave the right-hand side of the roller bare and insert the spring end of it into the left-hand bracket to fit the roller in position. If it is too long, mark a cutting line on the right-hand side so that it will fit the width. Allow for

Below. *A roller blind is ideal for a kitchen door because during the day—when the door is mostly in use—the blind can be rolled up safely out of the way.*

TUBBY

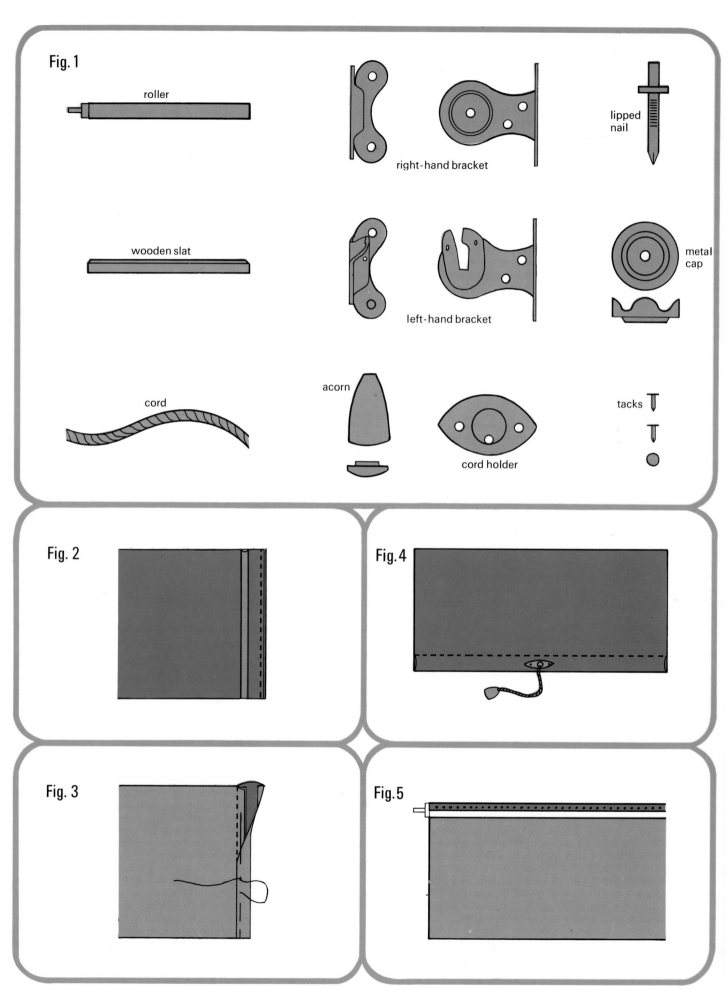

Fig. 1

roller

right-hand bracket

lipped nail

wooden slat

left-hand bracket

metal cap

cord

acorn

cord holder

tacks

Fig. 2

Fig. 4

Fig. 3

Fig. 5

Above. Larder windows are usually best left unadorned but, if they have a sunny aspect, a roller blind in spongeable pvc will keep the room cool but still let light in.

Above right. A blind in a colourful furnishing fabric can brighten up a dull half-glazed front door and give privacy at night. Here, a fringe has been hand stitched to the lower casing.

Below. Instead of the wooden slat supplied with the kit, a decorative rod can be used at the foot of a roller blind. To make the casing for this blind, the bottom was finished with a narrow hem, and 4in. square strips of fabric with hemmed sides were doubled over and stitched to the hem on the wrong side of the blind. A pelmet, finished in the same way, hides the rollers and fittings at the top of the window.

the thickness of the metal cap, plus $\frac{1}{8}$in. for 'play'.

Remove the roller from the window and, if necessary, saw it down to fit. Sawing a straight line—necessary to keep any wobble out of your finished blind—through a circular section of wood is not easy, since there is no ready way of making a cutting line and you must cut 'by eye'. If you have no bench hook, put two chopping boards or lengths of scrap timber, endways on, on a kitchen worktop. Rest the roller on the boards, and push it against two temporary nails, one driven into each board. This will keep the roller steady, lift it high enough that you can sight accurately along the length of the saw while you cut, and provide some support so that the wood does not splinter away as you near the bottom of the cut. Next, sand the rough edge. Fit the metal cap over the end and hammer in the nail so that the lip is flush with the cap. Put the roller back in the brackets, to check that it fits.

Making the blind

The sides of the fabric may be turned over to make a hem, or they may be bound—which with ordinary fabrics looks more attractive when the blind is pulled up and the 'wrong' side shows at the top.

To make hems, cut the fabric to fit the wood part of the roller, plus 2in. If using ordinary fabric, turn $\frac{3}{4}$in. hems (enclosing the raw edges by turning them under $\frac{1}{8}$in. first) and machine stitch them in the normal way. If using pvc, turn over a 1in. fold (don't fold over the raw edge first) and stick the hems down with a latex-based adhesive such as Copydex.

To bind the sides, cut the fabric to fit exactly the wood part of the roller. For ordinary fabric,

use bias binding. To stitch it on, unfold one of the pressed edges and place it to the edge of the 'wrong' side of the fabric. Tack it to the fabric along the crease line and machine stitch (Fig. 2). Press the binding over to the 'right' side of the fabric so that an equal amount of binding shows on both sides. Tack the binding down on to the 'right' side along the fold, and machine stitch (Fig. 3). Press the fabric and use a spray-on starch to give it body if necessary.

Pvc can be bound at the edges by using a broad adhesive tape, stuck on so that an equal amount of binding shows on both the 'right' and the 'wrong' sides.

Making the lower casing

For either type of fabric, turn up a 1in. hem at the bottom and machine stitch it, leaving the ends open (use a long stitch for pvc). Alternatively, pvc can be stuck with adhesive tape. Cut the wooden slat to the right length and insert into the hem. Now stitch up the ends of the hem so that the slat is completely enclosed.

Knot the cord at one end and thread the other end through the acorn from its widest end. Put the acorn's cap into this end. Thread the cord through the centre hole of the cord holder from the domed side and knot it on the other side. With the tiny screws supplied, screw the cord holder to the centre of the slat on the 'wrong' side of the blind, so that the knot of the cord is now enclosed and the cord hangs down with the acorn at the bottom (Fig. 4).

Attaching the blind to the roller

If you are using a pvc fabric, it can go on to the roller with the top edge unfolded. If you are using an ordinary fabric, turn back about $\frac{1}{2}$in., 'right' side to 'right' side, along the top and press flat.

Next, lay the blind flat on your work bench with the 'right' side of the fabric uppermost. Place the roller, with the spring on the left, on to the top edge of the blind and tack the blind to the roller, using the $\frac{1}{4}$in. tacks, and following the line marked on the roller (Fig. 5).

Roll up the blind, place it in the brackets and pull it down to test the tension of the spring. If, when you pull the cord again, the blind does not roll up smartly, the tension needs tightening. Pull the blind down again, remove it from the brackets and roll it up evenly by hand. Replace it in the brackets and test it again, repeating the procedure if necessary.

Roman blinds

Roman blinds are ideal for those places where curtains would take up too much room at the sides of the windows. They are also more economical than curtains because they use half the amount of fabric, and are more attractive and unusual than roller blinds.

Roman blinds differ from roller blinds in that when they are pulled up they form soft folds at the top of the window, rather than a roll. Unlike rollers, no mechanical spring device is used. Instead, rows of rings are stitched to vertical tapes on the back of the curtain and long cords are tied to the bottom ring of each row. These are threaded upwards through the rings to a row of screw eyes on a wooden batten, to which the blind is also attached, at the top. The cords are led through the screw eyes to one side of the blind and, as they are pulled, each one tightens and draws the blind up. The rows of rings ensure that each fold forms evenly.

The cords are then secured around cleat hooks at the side of the window.

Calculating the amount of fabric

Most furnishing fabrics can be used for Roman blinds, provided they drape well and do not crease excessively. If your window is much wider than the fabric, two smaller blinds often look better and are easier to handle than one very wide one. In all cases the blind should be lined.

To calculate the amount of fabric, measure the height and width of your window. If you are fixing it inside the reveal, make it 1in. narrower than the window, because the blind will swing from side to side slightly when it is pulled up. If you are fixing it outside the reveal, make it

*Opposite page. In this room, long full curtains would get in the way of the built-in furniture, but Roman blinds are ideal. **Below.** Blinds can 'show off' an unusual geometric pattern effectively, where the folds of curtains would hide it.*

3in. wider to ensure full coverage. To these measurements, add 1¼in. to each side, 2in. at the top and 1in. at the foot for hems. The lining fabric should be cut 1½in. narrower than the blind fabric.

Other materials

Tape, ½in. wide. Allow four pieces of tape, each equal to the length of the unmade blind, for every 48in. width of fabric used.

Brass rings, ½in. diameter. Allow enough to be spaced at 6-8in. intervals along each tape.

Nylon cord. Allow twice the amount of the tape, plus extra for leading it across the top of blind (see 'threading the cords', below).

Wooden batten, 2in. x 1in. x the width of the blind, if you have no wide wooden architrave around the window to which the blind can be fixed. The blind is fixed to the batten, which can be screwed inside or outside the reveal. Alternatively, if the blind is being fixed outside the reveal, a *wooden decorative curtain pole* may be used. This should be at least 4in. wider than the blind and is hung on brackets which are fixed to the wall at either side of the blind. Ball ends can be fitted to the end of the pole to finish it attractively.

Stretcher batten or dowel, ½in. thick for smaller blinds or 1in. thick for larger ones x the width of the blind. This is inserted into a pocket at the foot of the blind and helps to stabilize it.

Tacks or *gimp pins,* to fix the blind in position.

Screw eyes, the same number as pieces of tape.

Screws to fix batten, if used, and wall plugs if necessary.

Cleat hooks, to secure the cords when the blind is pulled up, and screws to fix these.

Making the blind

Cut the fabric, including the hem allowances; cut the lining 1½in. narrower. Mark the centres at the top and bottom of each piece of fabric and then, with 'right' sides facing, stitch the pieces together down the sides, taking ½in. turnings. About 6-8in. from the foot of the blind, break off the stitching for ½-1in. (the width of the stretcher batten or dowel) at exactly the same point on both sides, and then continue stitching to the end (Fig.1).

Press the seam allowance on to the lining. Match the centre points of the fabric and lining together at top and bottom, and smooth out the fabric towards the sides until it is completely flat and there is a ¾in. border of blind fabric showing on either side of the lining. Stitch the pieces together along the bottom, taking a 1in. turning. Turn the pieces 'right' side out and press again, making sure that no lining fabric shows on the 'right' side along the bottom hem. Leave open the top edge until last.

To complete the pocket for the stretcher batten, machine stitch twice across the blind, through both thicknesses, joining up the points where the stitching was broken in the side hems (Fig.2).

Next, pin and tack on the tapes. Position the side tapes so that they cover the seam line of the hems, with the remaining tapes spaced at equal distances of 8-12in. across the blind. Machine stitch the tapes to the blind, starting 1in. below the top edge and stitching along both edges of

BILL MACLAUGHLIN

Above. A decorative curtain pole can be used instead of a plain batten for Roman blinds, and is just as easy to fix in place.
Below. Where curtains would hide an attractive window frame, a Roman blind sets it off and is more graceful than a roller blind.

JOHN BETHELL

the tape and through all thicknesses. Break the stitching each time to leave the pocket open for the stretcher batten (Fig.2).

Mark the position on the tapes for the hooks, starting just above the stretcher batten, and leaving an equal space of 6-8in. between them. It is essential to measure accurately here, so that each row of rings is exactly horizontal across the blind—otherwise the folds will be uneven when the blind is pulled up. Stitch on the rings securely, making sure your stitches do not show on the 'right' side of the blind.

Hanging the blind

If the blind is to hang inside the window reveal, the batten may be top fixed (to the ceiling) or face fixed (to the wall) if there is room above the window. In either case, the screw holes should be drilled from the 2in. side of the batten (Fig.3).

Cut the batten to size, paint it to match the wall or window frame, and drill the necessary screw holes. Test the blind for length, allow ½in. for fixing, and turn in the hems at the top of both the blind fabric and lining so that they face each other. Stitch them together along the top edge. Tack the blind to the batten on the side which will be facing the ceiling. Attach the screw eyes behind the blind along the front edge of the bottom of the batten, placing each one in line with a row of rings. Do not fix the batten in position yet (Fig.4).

If you are using a decorative pole instead of a batten, turn the blind fabric with the lining on to the lining to make a hem which will form a deep enough pocket for the pole. Stitch the hem firmly and insert the pole. Push the points of the screw eyes through the fabric at the back of the blind and screw them into the pole (Fig.6).

If you are attaching the blind to the window architrave, turn in the hems as for the batten method, and thread the cords, as below, but without the screw eyes at this stage. Make sure you leave enough cord on each length.

Threading the cords

First decide on which side of the blind you want to have the cleats, and start threading at the opposite corner. Unroll a length of cord but do not cut it off yet. Tie the end securely to the bottom ring, and thread it upwards through all the rings on that tape and then through the row of screw eyes at the top. Let the cord hang loosely down the other side of the blind, and cut it off at the foot. Repeat this for all the rows of rings and, when the threading is completed, pull them up and arrange the folds evenly. Press or weight them down, and leave for 24 hours so that the folds will form permanently.

Then fix the batten in position and insert the stretcher batten in the pocket at the foot. Let the blind down, check that the cords are taut but not pulling, and knot them together at the bottom (Fig.5). Fix the cleat hooks behind the blind at one side, and wind the cord round it in a figure of eight.

If you are fixing the blind to the architrave, tack it along the top and fix the screw eyes to the window frame behind the blind, as above. Thread the cords through the screw eyes and down the side, test the tension and knot as before.

Fig.1

stitching broken   stitching broken

Fig.2

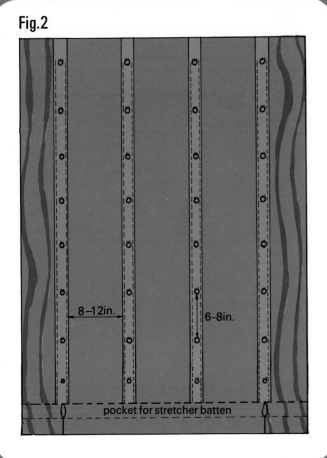

8–12in.   6-8in.

pocket for stretcher batten

Fig.3

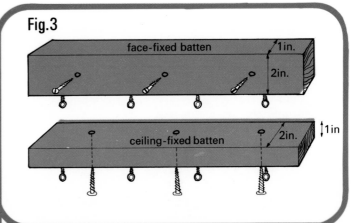

face-fixed batten   1in.   2in.

ceiling-fixed batten   2in.   1in

Fig.4

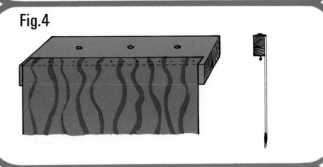

Fig.5

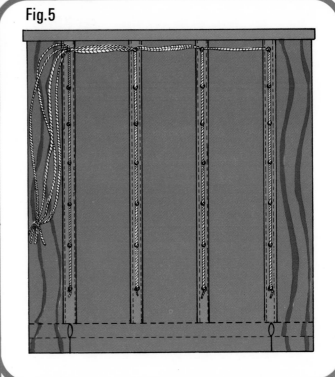

Fig.6

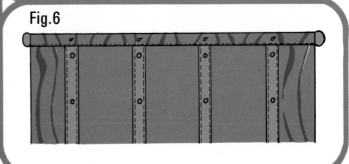

Choosing
curtain tracks

Curtain tracks these days are made for use with or without pelmets and with conventional or deep headings. Some tracks can be bent to fit round curves; some are made in plastic or nylon, others are made from metal or wood. Some have a perfectly plain 'front', others have a decorative finish.

When you choose a track, you should first consider the type in relation to the shape of the window, then to the room, its other furnishings and the style and weight of the curtains. It is always worth actually selecting the track in a store which has a large number of different types displayed so you can compare them and examine the fittings (you can always buy it locally, if that is more convenient). Many shops also show tracks complete with curtains so you can judge them for smooth running and noise.

Choosing for the window

If your windows are straight, with a few inches of wall above, almost all types of track are suitable. You simply have to decide on the best style (see below). With bay and some dormer windows, however, the choice is more limited.

Where the bay is either square or angled, it may be possible to fit a separate track to each section. This means that on the most common style of bay, which is made up from three sections, you would need a minimum of four curtains—a pair for the centre section and one for each side. This works quite well, although it can be a little inconvenient and also reduces the amount of daylight allowed into the room when the curtains are open.

The alternative—and the only style possible on a circular bay—is to use a track which can be bent to the right shape. There are some tracks which you buy in the straight piece and bend it yourself, such as Harrison Drape or Swish Nylonglyde. Or for heavy curtains you can have the track custom-made.

On some dormer windows, if you fit a straight track, the curtains may block out too much light when they are open. Here it may be a good idea, if the walls at each side of the window are deep enough, to buy a track 6in. longer than the width of the window and bend it 3in. at each end round into the room. Then the curtains can be pulled right round to hang against the wall at each side.

It is usually best to hang curtains outside a window reveal, but often this is not practical—in a bathroom or kitchen, for example. So that the curtains do not have to rub against the window (which they might with a track fixed to the wall above it), it may be better to use an unobtrusive neat track which can be fixed to the ceiling of the reveal (soffit), such as Swish Furniglyde.

Choosing for the room

In choosing the style of curtains, one of the

NIGEL MESSETT

main decisions is whether or not to have a pelmet (see pages 26-29). If you have decided against one, you are then plunged into the next decision: the style of curtain track.

The standard type of metal track which was the only sort available for many years, is considered by many people to be too ugly for use without a pelmet. The 'works' of the runners are visible from the front, and on most windows two sections of track are needed so that the curtains can overlap in the middle when they are drawn. Other disadvantages are that it collects dust and is noisy in use, although application of a little silicone wax helps this.

The nylon equivalent of this type is much quieter and easier to clean, and is often used for curtains with a plain heading where there is no pelmet. Its other advantages are that it is cheap and is easily bent to fit bays.

For a more streamlined effect, a plain strip, where the mechanics of the runner are hidden behind, is very popular. There are several different makes, all very similar. Some versions, however, such as Swish de Luxe or Rufflette Trimtrack, look best with curtains which have deep headings, because plain headings tend to drop or fall back.

With this type of track, only one length is needed on straight runs because there is a special fitting which can be used on one of the curtains so that it will overlap the other when closed.

The overlap fitting is about 2-3in. long and slots on to the track in the same way as the runners. It normally has two or three holes into which the hooks at the end of the curtain can be fitted, and it moves along the track with the curtain. Because the arm is curved to come out about $\frac{1}{2}$in. from the track, the edge of the other curtain can fit in behind it when the curtains are closed. When the curtains are open, the arm is not noticeable at all, but the curtain to which it is attached does not pull back quite as far as the other one.

Another point about this fitting, which might be a drawback in some cases, is that the curtain it is attached to has to be about 4in. wider than the other one after the gathers are pulled up. If possible, you should allow for this in the initial cutting out of the curtains. Where doing this would upset the balance of the fabric's pattern, it might be better to make both curtains the same size before gathering, and to settle for the overlapping one's being slightly less tightly pleated.

If you want the effect of the plain band, but also want to fit it round a bay, an aluminium track, such as Harrison Drape, may be a better choice. This track can be bent to a curve (not a sharp angle) with a 5in. radius without affecting its performance or breaking it. It has a combined glide hook which is clipped on to the track from the front. The prong of the hook can be inserted into the pockets of the gathering tape, thus holding a plain heading upright. For a deep heading, separate hooks can be used and hung from the ring at the base of the glide.

Most plain tracks are designed so that they are concealed by the curtains when closed, but if you have one of the decorative types you can sew on deep heading tape so that the pockets come at the top in order to reveal the track when the curtains are closed.

At the opposite end of the scale for straight runs, there are the decorative curtain poles. Curtain poles were the original way of hanging curtains with rings which were attached to the curtain and slid along the pole. They did not run very smoothly or quietly, and because the rings were sewn to the curtains these had to be removed each time the curtains were cleaned, and then sewn on again.

Nowadays this method has been modified to give the same effect, but the curtains run more smoothly because the rings, which encircle the pole, have much smaller rings at their base into which the curtain hooks can be slotted. In other versions no large rings are used, but small ones glide along a groove at the base of the pole. With most poles it is possible to fit an overlap arm and a cording set.

The poles are made in different finishes— brass, aluminium or wood painted in different colours—so you can choose the best one for your room. They also have a variety of end pieces which can be screwed into place.

All these poles look best with curtains with a deep heading—pinch pleats especially—and they also need a fairly 'grand' setting. They are more expensive than most other kinds of curtain track, but some have the advantage of being expandable, so if you move house you can normally adjust the pole to fit another window.

Choosing for the curtains

If you are having a pelmet or valance, the best sort of track to use is the standard metal kind, or its slightly less strong nylon equivalent. It is the least expensive type of track to buy, it is easy to fit, can be bent easily, and all the mechanics are hidden by the pelmet.

If you are having a gathered valance, you can combine it with a valance rail. The curtain track is fixed in the usual way and the valance rail is clipped on to it by a nylon bracket so that it stands away from the track to allow easy movement in closing the curtains.

If you also want net curtains with this type of track, it is possible to use a bracket which holds both tracks about 1-2in. apart. Alternatively, for straight runs, you can buy a special top-fixed combined track which has two channels.

If you are not using a pelmet but have curtains with a plain gathered heading, the best sort of track to use is one with a combination glide hook (see above), because this prevents the heading from falling back, and when the curtains are closed the track is completely covered.

Most kinds of track can be used with a deep heading, providing there is enough clearance above the track—a minimum of $\frac{1}{4}$in.—to allow the curtain to move along freely. With decorative curtain poles, however, this is not a problem because they are designed to allow the pole to be visible when the curtains are closed.

Whichever sort of track is used, it is essential to check that it will be strong enough for the weight of the curtains. With most fabrics there is no need to worry, as long as the track has been fixed securely. But on full length, lined and interlined velvet curtains, for example, a lightweight plastic or aluminium track is not strong enough and you should use a heavy duty metal track.

Measuring for the track

In order to allow as much light as possible to come into the room when the curtains are open, it is usually better to hang curtains outside a window reveal, rather than immediately next to the window. Unless you want to use the curtains to camouflage the shape of the window (see pages 26-29), the track should be long enough to extend about 6in. on each side of the reveal so that the curtains can be pulled right back. On extra wide windows, or when the curtains are very bulky, you may want to make the track even longer.

If you are limited in space, and are using a decorative pole, remember that the end pieces may add about 2-3in. on each end but without actually increasing the length of usable track. With some other tracks, adding a cording set may make a difference to the length of track you buy, because the fittings can add a couple of inches at each side.

Most tracks are sold in set lengths, increasing at 6in. or 1ft intervals. You simply buy the length nearest your own, and cut it to the right size if necessary. Some other types are expandable and simply need adjusting to size.

Before you buy the track, decide on whether you are going to fix it to the ceiling or to the wall above the window. Fixing to the wall is more satisfactory in most cases, but where there is no room above the window or where the curtains are to come within a reveal, it may be preferable to fix it to the ceiling. Some tracks are supplied with brackets which can be used either way, but with others you may have to buy a special bracket.

Fitting a cording set may seem like an extravagance, but in fact they are well worth the money. Most tracks work better with one, and there is less strain put on them. They also save the edges of the curtains from soiling and wearing out through constant handling.

Some more expensive tracks are supplied already fitted with a cording set. With others you buy a kit, complete with cord, pulleys and weights, and fit it to the track yourself.

Fixing the track

Most tracks are supplied with instructions and all the necessary brackets and screws for fixing it into position. If you are securing the track to a wall, it is essential that the holes for the screws are correctly and adequately plugged, and for heavy curtains it is more than likely that the screws supplied by the manufacturer will not be long enough.

One of the simplest methods of fixing the brackets for a straight run is to screw them to a wooden batten (2in. x 1in.), which can then be screwed to the wall. In this way, you can ensure that all the brackets are level, which is never easy if you are drilling several holes into the wall, and you can use the edge of the batten to mark the fixing line.

Using a batten is also a neat way of bringing the track away from the wall enough to allow the curtains to clear the window sill. Alternatively, you can use special extension brackets which are made to go with most tracks.

If you are bending the track for a bay window, be careful to make smooth curves, not angles, or the curtains will not run smoothly.

Types of curtain track

Figs.1-3. *Swish De Luxe—a plain, off-white, plastic band, where all the fittings are hidden behind—is the sort of track which suits most modern houses. It can be painted or even 'wallpapered' to blend with decorations, and can be bent round curves although then a cording set cannot be fitted. It looks best with curtains which have a deep heading because when closed, the track is completely concealed.*

Figs.4-6. *If you like pelmets, a modern nylon version of the standard, old-fashioned metal track is made by most manufacturers. With Swish Nylonglyde the valance rail is clipped on to the main fixing brackets, and the valance is clipped, with standard hooks, on to this. Nylon track is easier to fit than metal because it can be cut with a knife and bent by hand.*

Fig.7. *With decorative tracks, the runners are designed so that the track still shows when the curtains are closed. An unusual kind of decorative track is Rufflette Royal (shown on page 52). Behind the wooden fascia is a metal heavy duty track, which can be used alone.*

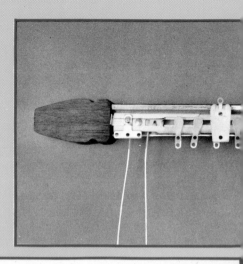

1

2

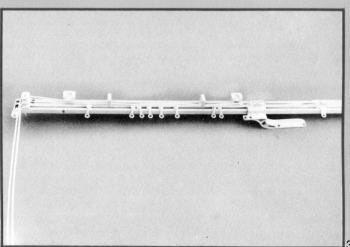

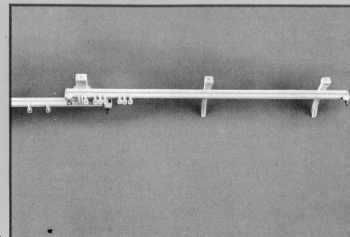

3

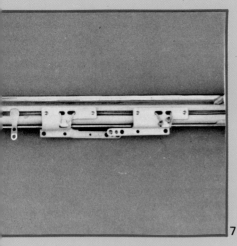

Figs.8-10. *Where you have curtains with a standard gathered heading, the sort of track which has clip-on combination gliders and hooks is specially designed to hold the heading upright. This sort of track can also be used with deep headings, in which case standard or pleater hooks can be slotted into the rings at the base of the gliders. Swish and Harrison Drape both make versions, and Antiference Decorail, shown here, has the added modification of special channels which hold the cording set.*

Figs.11-13. *The most common decorative track is a modern version of the traditional brass pole. Variations of this type are made by nearly all the manufacturers and, although* expensive, some are expandable, so you don't lose if you move house. One different version which blends well with an 'oak beam' setting is Kirsch Atavio, shown here. All decorative tracks look best with curtains which have a deep heading. If you want the top to overlap the track slightly, the pleating tape should be stitched on with the hook pockets on the lower edge. For the top of the curtain to clear the track completely, the tape should be stitched on the other way up. For pinch-pleated headings formed by hooks, you should buy hooks which have special long necks. Because the curtains hang below the pole and within the end pieces, decorative poles are not suitable for use inside a reveal where you would not get full window coverage.

7

8

11

9

12

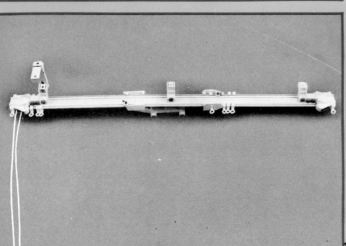

10

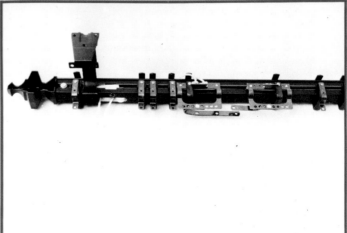

13

This page. Pinch pleats, whether hand stitched or made with commercial tape, make the most attractive heading with a curtain pole.

Deep
curtain headings

Decorative curtain poles and tracks that need no pelmet look best with curtains which have more than plain, simply functional headings.

At one time, curtains with 'fancy' deep headings—pencil, pinch and box pleats—were the prerogative of the rich. They were expensive because they had to be made professionally—their construction and the working out of the pleating formulae were too tricky for many home sewers—and it was not worth making them from cheap fabric because of the amount of hand stitching involved.

Nowadays it is as easy to make a deep heading as a standard gathered one by using one of the special tapes available. Most of these tapes have a set formula for working out the amount of fabric required in each curtain, and are attached to the curtain in a similar way to standard tape. The tapes stiffen the heading and take care of the pleating process. They are expensive—at least twice the cost of standard

Above. By hand stitching pinch pleats, a softer effect can be achieved.

gathering tape—and some of them need special hooks which are more expensive than ordinary hooks. In terms of the time and trouble they save, particularly for pencil pleats which are laborious to handstitch, they are well worth it and give excellent results.

Professional soft furnishers, however, still swear by the old, hand stitched methods. They allow greater flexibility in the use of the fabric because the pattern can be 'studied' and the pleats formed to complement it, and because the heading is not spoiled by machine stitching showing on the 'right' side of the fabric. If you enjoy hand sewing, and have the time to spare and a mathematical mind, it is worth making the headings this way.

Stiffening the headings

All deep headings must be stiffened in order to make them stand up well, particularly after the curtains have been cleaned and their natural stiffness, from the fabric's dressing, disappears.

Commercial tapes are made from a material which also stiffens the headings, and will withstand cleaning, although some should be used with deep hooks to give them extra body. With hand stitched headings, the fabric should be stiffened before the pleats are formed. For stiffening, use a heavy-weight dressmaker's bonded type (such as Vilene 237), or tailor's canvas. Even if you are not fully interlining the curtains with bump, it is worth underlining just the heading (as well as stiffening it), because this will give a rich, full look. The interlining

should be tacked in position on the 'wrong' side of the curtains before the stiffening.

Cut the stiffening to the same width as the curtains, less the allowance for the side hems, and to the total depth allowed for the heading. Tack it in place along both edges—there is no need to stitch it down more permanently because the stitching of the pleats will be enough to hold it.

Measuring the window

Always take measurements from the curtain track. Full length curtains should end 1in. above the floor to prevent them from soiling and chafing; sill length ones should either just clear the sill or finish 1in. below. Allow at least 4in. for the bottom hem and 1½in. for each side hem. Decide how much of the curtain heading will come above the curtain track, and add twice this amount to the length. (Half the amount allowed will be the turning.)

The amount required for the width of the curtains and heading depends on the style (see below). Generally, very deep headings—more than 4in.—look top heavy on short curtains, and are better kept for full-length ones.

Details on measuring and joining widths for curtains are given on pages 35-36. For lining them and making hems see pages 41-44. Allow enough lining fabric to make each piece equal in length to the curtains.

Pencil pleats

Gathering tape (such as Rufflette's Regis)

Make the width of each curtain equal to 2¼—2½ times the length of half the curtain track, and allow 8in. for the heading and hem.

Turn over the raw edge at the top ⅝in. on to the 'wrong' side and tack in position. Cut a length of tape equal to the width of the curtain, plus 2in., and from one end of the tape pull out

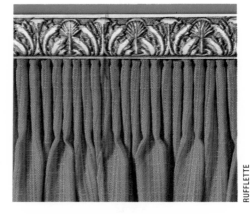

Above. To expose the decorative track, the tape is stitched with the pockets at the top.

about 1½in. of cord and knot it. Pull out the same amount from the other end of the tape, but leave it free.

Place the top of the tape flush with the top of the curtain, with the pockets of the tape facing outermost and running along the *bottom* edge of the tape if there is a clearance of at least 2⅛in. above the gliders on the track, or with the pockets running along the *top* edge if there is less than 2⅛in. Turn under the raw edges of the tape at both ends, enclosing the knotted

end of the cord but leaving the other end free, and tack the tape to the curtains along both edges. Stitch along both edges of the tape, outside the cords.

To pleat the curtains, pull the fabric along the cords until the fabric is all at the knotted end. Pull out again to the right width, distributing the gathers, and knot the cords to secure it. Catch the cord to the tape, but do not cut off the excess amount, as this allows the curtains to be pulled flat for cleaning.

Hand pleating

Allow the same width of fabric (or even more) as if using a commercial pleating tape, with additional amount for the heading. Make up the basic curtains, stiffen the heading and turn over the raw edge for the amount allowed on to the 'wrong' side. Tack in position.

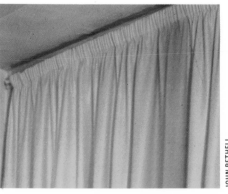

Above. For hand stitched pencil pleats to look good, the curtains must be really full.

Using strong sewing thread or doubled regular thread, make a row of gathering stitches for the lower edge of the heading, making the stitches about ⅝in. long on the 'wrong' side of the fabric and about ⅛in. long on the 'right' side. It is sometimes wise to work another row ½in. below the top of the curtain, placing the stitches and spaces to correspond with the first row. To prevent the thread from breaking when it is pulled up, work in sections across the width of the curtain, securing the thread at the beginning of each section. To prevent any gap in the pleats between sections, double up the stitches at each junction (see Fig.1).

To form the pleats, draw up the threads and gather the curtain to the right width, distributing the pleats evenly. Secure all threads.

Cut a length of 1in. plain, or pocketed curtain tape equal to the width of the pleated curtain, plus 2in., and place it centrally over the raw edge. Turn under the edges of the tape for 1in. at both ends and tack the tape in position. Oversew the tape securely to the curtain along the top edge, making sure the stitches do not show on the 'right' side of the curtain. Stitch the lower edge of the tape from the 'right' side of the curtain, using tiny back stitches placed on the underside of each pleat (Figs.2 and 3).

If you did not make the second row of gathering, 'lock' the pleats along the top edge of the curtain to hold them firmly in position (use the stitch given on page 43 to do this). If you used plain tape, sew on brass curtain hooks at both ends and at 3in. intervals across the curtain (Fig.4).

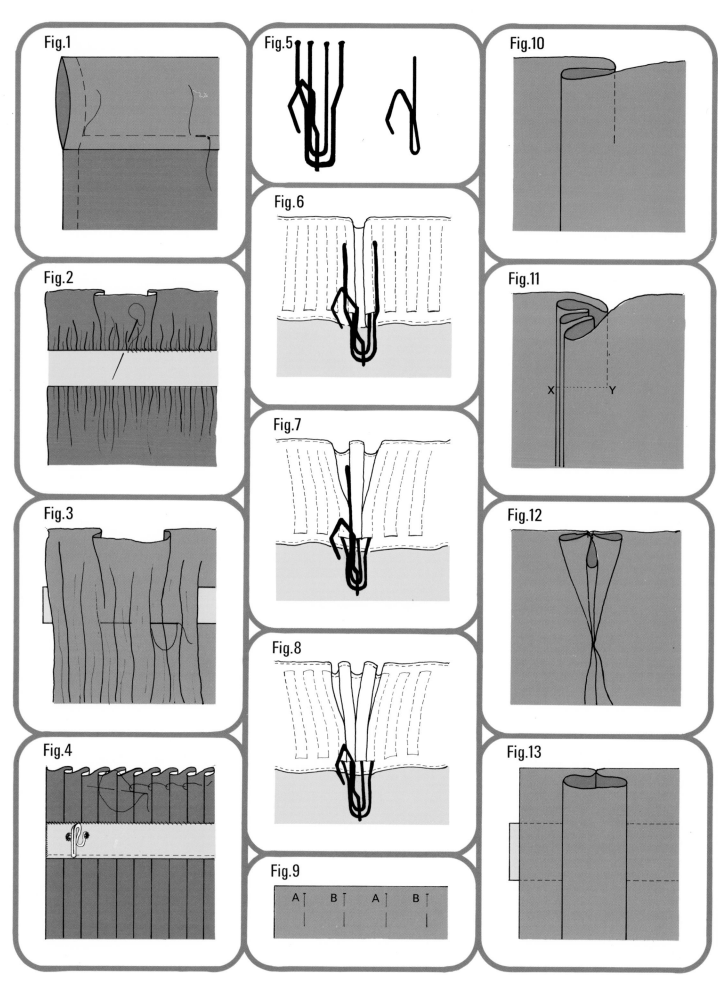

Fig.1

Fig.2

Fig.3

Fig.4

Fig.5

Fig.6

Fig.7

Fig.8

Fig.9

A   B   A   B

Fig.10

Fig.11

X   Y

Fig.12

Fig.13

Pinch pleats

Gathering tapes

There are two main types of commercial tape for making pinch pleats. One type (such as Silent Gliss and Rufflette's Auto Pleat) works like other tapes and the pleats are formed in groups of three when the cord is pulled up.

Allow double fullness in each curtain and attach the tape as for pencil pleats. Place the tape on the curtain so that a space (where the cords are not exposed) falls at each side.

Above. *With gathering tape, the cords can be adjusted to vary the 'tightness' of the pleats.*

The other type (such as Rufflette's Deep Pleat) does not have gathering cords, because its pleats are formed by the insertion of 4-pronged pleater hooks. The amount of fabric needed depends on the pleating arrangement— single, double or treble pleats—and how many hooks you use (see chart below). This is worked out before the tape is attached to the curtain. The width of each finished curtain should equal half the length of the track, including overlap. Allow 8in. for the heading and hem.

Hooks. Use the short-stemmed pleater hooks for tracks which are face fixed to the wall, or long-stemmed hooks if the track is ceiling fixed. Use single-pronged hooks at each end of the curtain (Fig.5).

Single pleats. Insert the two centre prongs of the pleater hook into the two alternate pockets on the tape. Miss three pockets at each end of the curtain and between pleats (Fig.6).

Double pleats. Insert three prongs of the hooks into three alternate pockets on the tape. Miss three pockets at each end of the curtain and between pleats (Fig.7).

Treble pleats. Insert each of the four prongs into four alternate pockets on the tape. Miss three pockets at each end of the curtain and between pleats (Fig.8).

Before you sew the tape to the curtain prepare it in your chosen pleating arrangement and check against your track, rearranging the pleats if necessary to obtain the best effect. Mark the pockets used before removing the hooks.

Turn over the raw edge at the top of the curtain ⅝in. to the 'wrong' side and tack down. Place the tape flush with the top of the curtain, and with the openings of the pockets at the lower edge of the tape. Tack and machine stitch the tape to the curtain, taking the stitching outside the pocket openings. Insert the pleater hooks into the marked pockets.

Hand pleating

Make the width of each curtain equal to 2½ times the length of half the curtain track, and allow the extra for the heading. The total depth of the heading should be determined by the size of the window—on short curtains a very deep heading would be top-heavy. The amount you allow for each pleat can be between 4—6in., and should be increased in proportion to the depth of the heading and the width of the curtains. If you allow more than 6in. for each pleat, use more fabric in each curtain—up to three times the length of half the curtain track.

Make up the curtains, stiffen the heading and turn over the amount allowed for. Turn in the lining fabric the same amount and slip stitch them together along the top edge.

Measure the width of the curtain exactly and subtract the width of the finished curtain from this. Divide the amount allowed for each pleat into the remainder to calculate the number of pleats. If it does not divide exactly, adjust the size of the pleats to suit the difference.

To calculate the size of each space, add one to the number of pleats (because there should be a space at each side of the curtain) and divide this figure into the width of the finished curtain. If it does not divide exactly, divide the remainder and add it to the spaces at each end.

For example, if you want each curtain to be 4ft wide, you should allow 2½ widths of 48in. wide fabric per curtain. When joined with ½in. seams, and with 1½in. hems taken at each side, the unpleated curtains would be 115in. wide with 67in. allowed for the pleats. This, divided by the 4½in. allowed per pleat, gives 15 pleats. There will be 16 spaces, giving approximately 3in. in each.

out with metric measurements.)

Above. *With a hand-made heading, the only stitching that shows on the back is that attaching the hooks. No stitching at all should show on the 'right' side.*

Above. *Single pleats can be made by using standard curtain tape with small double-pronged hooks. The prongs are inserted into two alternate pockets, with two or three pockets left in between the hooks.*

To form the pleats, first mark all the divisions with tailor's chalk or tacking (Fig.9). Make a simple pleat on the 'right' side of the curtains by joining the divisions marking the position of the first pleat (Fig.10). Leave a space and join the next pair. Work across the curtain until all the pleats have been joined, and machine stitch them to the depth of the heading. Then divide the pleats into three equal smaller pleats.

Starting at the outer folds at the foot of the pleats (point x, Fig.11), stab stitch (tiny back stitch) through the pleats to meet the line of machine stitching (point Y, Fig.11). Catch the tops of the pleats to the curtain at the top with neat oversewing (Fig.12). Sew on brass hooks at each pleat, placing them about halfway down the pleats.

Box pleats can be formed as for pinch pleats up to the stage of the machine stitched fold. The fabric is then folded back so that an equal amount falls either side of the stitched line (Fig.13). Stay tack all the pleats down, and then attach the curtain tape so that is secures the back of the pleat enough to hold it in position, but, without any stitches showing on the face of the curtain. Press firmly, then remove the stay tacking. Attach the hooks to the centre of each pleat.

'Dressing' the curtains

When the curtains are finished, hang and 'dress' them, so they will drape well, Pull the curtains to the sides of the window and, starting at the top and working down the curtains in sections of about one foot, push the pleats into their natural folds with your fingers and tie round the curtains with cotton tape. Leave the curtains tied like this for a few days.

Pleating chart	Triple pleats		Double pleats		Single pleats	
	width	hooks	width	hooks	width	hooks
48in. width material pleats down to	22½in.	5	24in.	7	26in.	9
54in. width fabric pleats down to	22¾in.	6	26in.	8	29in.	10
72in. width fabric pleats down to	32in.	8	38in.	10	39in.	14
These measurements allow 1½in. for each side hem.						

Pelmets

In spite of the popularity of curtain tracks which are designed to be used without pelmets, there are many rooms where a pelmet can add to the decoration. They can make a large window seem less bare and, by varying their width or depth, they can alter the apparent size of a window.

The difference between a valance and a pelmet is that a valance is like a very short curtain and is hung from runners on a track. A pelmet is usually a stiffened piece of fabric which is attached flat to a pelmet board above the curtain track. A pelmet board is like a narrow shelf, about ¾-1in. thick, 3-4in. deep and 2in. longer on each side than the track. The pelmet is attached to it with pins, and wraps round the sides to the wall to conceal the track.

Choosing the style

With full-length curtains, the pelmet or valance should be one-sixth the length of the curtains. With short curtains, allow 1½in. to every foot of curtain length.

Unless you actually want to make the window appear lower, the bottom of the pelmet or valance should come about 1in. below the top of the window. However, if you are having a shaped pelmet, the bottom edge may have to come lower than this to avoid revealing the curtain track or wall in the curves.

If the furnishings in the room are modern with simple lines, keep the pelmet simple too, with a plain trimming being the only decoration. Keep more fancy shapes and fringe trimmings for large rooms and tall windows or where the furniture is more in keeping. (Fig.1 gives ideas for different shapes.)

Making a valance

The method for making a valance is very similar to that for making lined curtains by the 'bag' method shown on pages 43-44. The heading should either be simply gathered or pinch pleated by using a curtain tape.

For a *plain gathered* valance, allow enough face fabric to make a strip equal to twice the length of the valance track, plus 3in. for turnings and 1in. extra per seam if you have to join the fabric. Use plain ½in. seams for joining it, matching the pattern carefully. The width of the strip should be 2in. more than the depth of the valance. Cut a strip of lining fabric to the same width and 2in. shorter.

Left. A valance is less formal than a pelmet and is ideal for a kitchen or bedroom. This one has a pinch-pleated heading.

Mark the centre point on both long edges of the face fabric and lining. With 'right' sides together, stitch the lining to the face fabric along both short edges, taking ½in. turnings. Press the turnings on to the lining. Match the centre points of the face fabric to the lining, then pin and stitch them together along the lower edge only, taking a ½in. turning. This will make a 1in. border of face fabric on each short edge. Take the stitching up to the outer folds.

Snip away the turning at the lower corners and turn the valance right side out, poking out the corners with a pencil to give a good shape. Press the lower edge carefully so that no lining shows on the right side of the valance (it often helps to tack it first).

Treating the face fabric and lining as one piece, turn down the top edge 1½in. to the back of the valance and tack down. Cut a length of gathering tape to the same length as the valance, plus 2in. for turnings. Pull out about 1½in. of the cords at each end of the tape, knot them together at one end but leave the other end free for gathering.

Place the tape on the back of the valance so that it covers the raw edge centrally and its top edge is 1in. below the top of the valance. Tack along the top and bottom edges and turn under the ends, enclosing the knotted cord on one side but leaving the cord free at the other. Machine stitch outside the cords along both edges of tape.

To gather the valance, pull the fabric along the cords to the knotted end and then pull out again to the right width, distributing the gathers evenly. Knot the cords to secure them and

catch the knot to the tape with a few stitches, but do not cut off the surplus cord. When the valance needs cleaning, the gathers can be released by undoing the knot. Insert the hooks into the pockets of the tape at 4in. intervals.

For a *pinch-pleated* valance, use a tape which gathers the pleats by cords, rather than one which needs special hooks. Both Silent Gliss and Rufflette's Auto Pleat are suitable.

Make up the valance in the same way as for a plain gathered one (above), but cut the fabric only 1in. wider than the depth of the valance. Turn over the top edge ½in. and tack down. Place the tape so that its top edge is level with the top of the valance.

Making a pelmet

Measure the length of the pelmet board, including the returns at both ends. If you are making a shaped pelmet, cut out a piece of paper to the same length x the total depth wanted. Fold the paper in half and sketch out the design on one side only so the finished pelmet will be symmetrical. If you have no compasses for drawing curves, use a plate.

Cut out the paper through both thicknesses, open it out and try it against the window for the effect, modifying it if necessary. It is usually a good idea to make two or three paper patterns in different shapes and compare them.

Stiffening the pelmet

Use special pelmet buckram or the heaviest grade of Vilene. Buckram is a coarsely woven canvas, impregnated with glue which stiffens it. It gives a much sharper edge than Vilene, and is easier to work with for this reason, but it is not washable or cleanable.

Cut out the stiffening to the same size and shape as the paper pattern. If you have to join it to get the right length, do it before cutting out by laying one edge flat over the other and machine stitching down both sides.

Cut out the face fabric to the same shape and

Below. A simple pelmet can link widely spaced curtains in a way which a plain track would not, and it looks just as right in a modern room.

HEIDEDE CARSTENSEN/BAYER

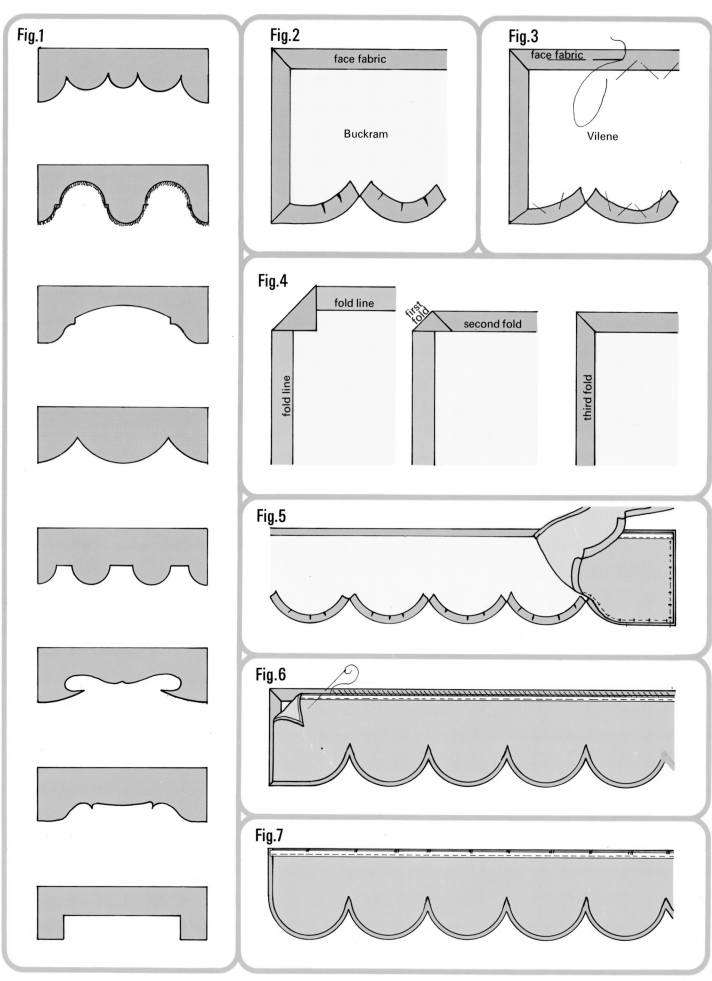

Fig.1

Fig.2

face fabric

Buckram

Fig.3

face fabric

Vilene

Fig.4

fold line

fold line

first fold

second fold

third fold

Fig.5

Fig.6

Fig.7

Above. A different way of finishing a shaped pelmet is to bind the edges with contrasting fabric, rather than a bought trimming.

1in. larger all round. If you have to join it, place the main piece in the middle and, matching the pattern carefully, join pieces at each side to make up the right length.

If the curtains are interlined, or if the face fabric is lightweight or has a coarse weave through which the buckram would show, cover one side of the buckram with bump. (Bump is specially sold for curtain interlining, and is like flannelette.) This also acts as a safeguard in case the colour comes out of the buckram. Since Vilene stiffening is white and does not have a weave you probably need not interline it, although you may want to back the fabric with a matching lining if you do not want the white to show through.

To attach the bump to the buckram, cut it out to the same size and shape. Lay the buckram flat on the ironing board and dampen it with a wet cloth. Place the bump on top and press down with a fairly hot iron, being careful not to press in any creases. Allow to cool. This wetting and ironing releases some of the glue in the buckram and sticks it to the bump.

Lay out the face fabric with the right side down and place the buckram centrally on top, with the bump sandwiched between the two. Turn the edges of the fabric over to the buckram and press down with your fingers, keeping the fold of the fabric following the edge of the buckram exactly. Snip the fabric where necessary round the shaping, and mitre any square corners (Figs.2 and 4). Dampen the edges of the buckram and press the fabric down on to it.

If you are using Vilene, tack on the backing (if any), lay out the face fabric with wrong side up and place the Vilene centrally on it, with the backing lining between the two. Press over the turnings as above, and herringbone stitch them down (Fig.3). Press carefully.

Trimming the pelmet

If you are using a fringe or braid, attach this next. For a fringe, pin it along the bottom edge of the pelmet so that the lower edge of the braid heading, from which the fringe hangs, lies level with the bottom of the pelmet. If you have to make any mitres to fit the braid to the shape of the pelmet, make them all to face away from the centre.

Attach the fringe with doubled thread, stab stitching it along the top edge through all the layers. Stab stitch is really a form of back stitch, but all the stitches on the 'right' side should be so small that they are hidden in the braid. The stitches on the 'wrong' side are made larger to compensate. There is no need to stitch the fringe along the bottom edge.

With an inset trimming, mark its line on the pelmet first, using tailor's chalk. Place on the trimming, keeping the edge level with the mark and mitring where necessary. Attach along both edges with stab stitching.

Lining the pelmet

Cut out the lining fabric to the same shape as the paper pattern and ½in. larger all round. Turn under ¾in. turnings, snipping and mitring where necessary, and press down. Cut a piece of 1in. wide tape to the same length as the pelmet and pin it to the right side of the lining with the top edge ½in. below the top of the lining. Turn under the short ends and machine stitch along the bottom edge of the tape only.

Place the lining centrally on to the back of the pelmet and pin it to the turnings only (ie. so that the pins do not go through to the front of the pelmet). Slip stitch the lining to the turnings all round (Fig.6).

Along the top edge of the tape, catch it down to the pelmet with two or three oversewing stitches, placed at 3½-4in. intervals to form pockets. If possible, take the stitches through the layers to catch in the stiffening and interlining, but not the face fabric (Fig.7).

To attach the pelmet to the board, place a drawing pin in each pocket of tape and press into the board.

Below. Basing the shape of the pelmet round the design of the pattern is a simple idea which can look most effective.

Sewing
for the bedroom

In a bedroom which makes no attempt or pretence at being anything else, the focal point is inevitably the bed. In the average-sized British bedroom, a double bed usually takes up most of the space so it needs some sort of special treatment to complement its status.

The most basic and obvious treatment is a bedspread. Simply making the bed can turn a rather untidy room into something much neater, and even with a Continental quilt or brightly coloured bedclothes, a bedspread gives the finishing touch. In cases of emergency, it can also disguise an unmade bed !

The simplest kind of bedspread is the throwover. These can be very cheap to buy—especially the sort made in striped Indian cotton—but they can also be just as cheap to make. Any one who can use a tape measure and stitch a plain seam can make one (see pages 68-69), and, in a fabric to match or blend in with the curtains and other furnishings, a home-made bedspread can give the whole room a co-ordinated effect you probably could not achieve with a shop-bought one.

It you don't take off your bedspread at night, try to use a fabric which has body and has been treated to drip dry and resist creases. A crumpled bedspread looks terrible and, because of its size and weight, it is a bore to iron.

You can make a throwover bedspread extra warm by lining and interlining it and then stitching the layers together by quilting. Use a washable interlining which is fairly lightweight —use flannelette or the thinnest grade of Terylene wadding—or you will find you are making a full-scale quilt rather than a bedspread. A quilted throwover bedspread is made in a very similar way to a plain one, the main difference being that the edges are finished with a seam rather than a plain hem, so you need allow only $\frac{1}{2}$in. all round for turnings.

After making up the panels for the bedspread, pin and tack on the interlining to the wrong side of the top cover so that all the edges are level. Make up the lining to the same size as the top cover. (If you are joining pieces for the lining fabric, although it looks better if you have two seams, it doesn't really matter if you have a central seam because it will not show.)

With the 'right' side of the lining facing the 'right' side of the top cover, stitch the layers together $\frac{1}{2}$in. from the outer edge, leaving an

Below. *A canopy suspended over the bed, and in fabric to match the bedspread, is a simple idea which looks most effective.*

HEIDEDE CARSTENSEN/STUDIO HUELSTA

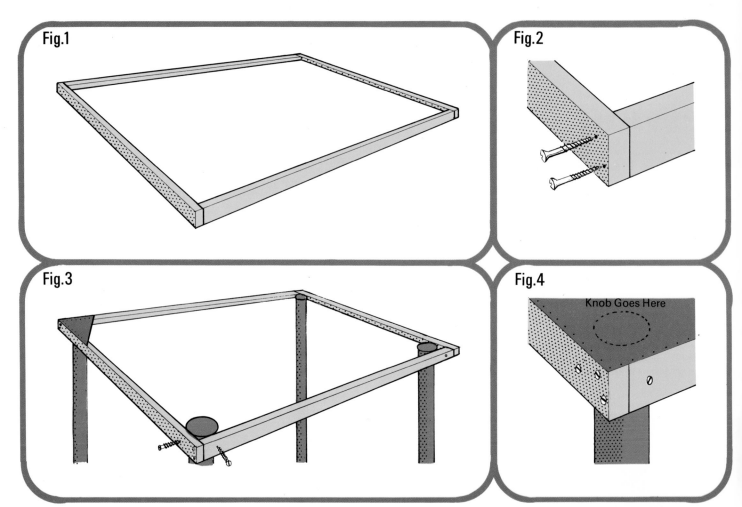

Fig.1

Fig.2

Fig.3

Fig.4

Knob Goes Here

opening of about 18in. on one side. Press the seams, turn the bedspread right side out, and stitch up the opening. Instructions on quilting stitching are given on pages 90-92.

If you make a crochet bedspread, it usually looks best if you put a plain cover underneath it. This should be separate, rather than attached like a lining, because it will hang better. It can be made very cheaply from a crease resistant cotton/polyester mixture dress fabric, and it will show off the crochet more effectively if it is in a different colour.

Throwover bedspreads are usually made large enough to cover the bed and reach down to floor level on each side because this looks neatest, even on a smart divan. However, on some modern divans which have a wooden frame with the mattress inset, this is not really necessary and the bedspread can be made to tuck in which is more economical of fabric. Additional interest can be given to the base by sticking on panels of the same fabric.

Fitted bedspreads with gathered or pleated flounces are more expensive to buy and, although they do need a little more sewing skill, it is, as a general rule, worth making your own (see pages 70-74). Unless you remove all of the pillows from the bed when you make it, it is advisable to include some allowance to prevent the bedspread from being raised at the head of the bed because of the height of the pillows.

This can be done by attaching a pillow 'scarf' or throwover flap. The bedspread is put on to the bed without the pillows. These are then put in position and the throwover flap is folded back

over them and tucked underneath. Unless the fabric is reversible and does not have a one-way pattern, the flap should be made of a separate piece of fabric which is stitched 'back to front' and upside down. The 'right' side of the flap should be facing the 'wrong' side of the bedspread and the top of a one-way pattern towards the seam, so that it is the correct way up when in position and the seam allowance is hidden inside. The flap can be lined for a really neat effect.

Alternatively, you can make wedge-shaped gussets to allow for the pillow rise. When calculating for the platform section of the bedspread, include an allowance of about 4in. at the top for a 3in. overhang and 1in. hem. Cut out two gussets, basing the lengths of the two straight sides on the height and width of the pillow plus $\frac{1}{2}$in. all round for turnings. On the side of the gussets which is equal to the height of the pillows (the shorter side), turn under the $\frac{1}{2}$in. allowance and make a narrow hem.

Then, with right sides together, pin the curved edge of the gusset to the platform so that the hemmed edge of the gusset comes 4in. from the top edge of the platform. Stitch the seam, taking $\frac{1}{2}$in. turnings and clipping the seam allowance of the platform where necessary to fit it smoothly.

With 'right' sides together, pin and stitch the flounce to the platform and gusset (which now forms one continuous edge). The top short edge of the flounce should be level with the edge of the gusset.

Figs.1 & 2. The frame for a four-poster bed is glued and screwed together. The screws should be staggered to stop the wood splitting.
Fig.3. To keep the frame in square, a triangle of hardboard should be nailed at each corner. The posts are screwed into the corners of the frame.
Fig.4. A decorative knob can be placed over the hardboard and screwed into the posts.
Opposite page, left. The days when the curtains of a four-poster bed were needed for warmth and privacy are long past, but they still look very decorative today.
Opposite right. A curtain hung on a pole makes an attractive alternative to a bedhead. This bedspread has wedge-shaped gussets to allow for the pillow rise.

Dressing up with a headboard

While footboards have become unnecessary with a modern divan bed, headboards are still needed because they prevent the pillows from slipping off and protect the wallcovering behind from becoming marked. A padded bedhead is obviously more comfortable than a wooden or metal one for sitting up in bed, and it is not difficult to make (see pages 78-82). It usually looks best covered in the same fabric as the bedspread.

If you do not want a bedhead which is actually attached to the bed, you can achieve a similar effect simply by attaching a panel of fabric to the wall. This can be stuck on with adhesive but, to remove for cleaning, it could be pinned on to a wooden frame or panel which is permanently

fixed to the wall.

Alternatively, for a purely decorative effect, you could fix a curtain pole to the wall about 3ft above the bed and hang floor length curtains. Or you could hang a boxed cushion from a curtain pole. The cushion could be suspended from 2in. wide strips of fabric which are inserted into the seams when the box strip is attached to the main panels of the cushion.

Making a canopy

The idea of attaching a panel of fabric at the head of the bed can be extended into a bed canopy. To make this you need a piece of fabric 1 in. wider than the bed and about twice as long, depending on the height of the ceiling, plus the same amount of lining fabric if you want to back the canopy. To suspend the canopy you need two pieces of 1 in. dowel x the width of the bed and two pieces 3in. longer; four pieces of thick cord about 3ft long or the distance you want the canopy to be from the ceiling plus a few inches for fixing; four hooks for fixing the cord to the ceiling; wall plugs and screws.

Start by drilling two holes in one of the short dowels about 3in. from each end. Mark the position of these holes on the wall above the bed at the exact height you want the canopy to be, and drill and plug the holes in the wall to correspond.

Next, mark the position for the hooks on the ceiling, lining them up above each side of the bed about halfway down and at the foot. Drill the holes and plug them. Use spring toggles if you are unable to drill into a joist (i.e., solid timber in the ceiling).

Insert a length of cord into each hook and pull through the end for about 2in. Secure the loop by binding the end to the main length firmly. Make a loop at the other end in the same way, checking that each length is exactly the same and that, when the hooks are screwed in place, the bottom of the loops will be level with the holes on the wall. Screw the hooks to the ceiling and hang the two longer dowels across the bed through the loops of cord.

To decide the exact length of the canopy fabric, try it in position, working from the foot of

the bed towards the wall, adjusting the loops of fabric as necessary. Hold it in position against the wall at the height of the drilled holes and let it fall to the floor at the head of the bed. Trim off any excess at the foot.

Make a narrow hem on three sides of the fabric, and a 1½in. hem on the edge which will come at the foot of the bed. Or, if you are lining the canopy, stitch the lining and fabric together on the side edges and top, with 'right' sides facing and taking ½in. turnings. Turn right side out and press. Finish the fourth side with a 1½in. hem.

Hang the canopy over the dowel rods as before, with the 'right' side facing down. Insert the undrilled short dowel rod into the hem at the foot of the canopy and insert the drilled dowel into the part of the fabric which meets the wall, and wrap it round the rod tightly. The rod should be above the canopy. Screw the rod to the wall, putting the screws through the fabric on each side of the rod. Attach the fabric to the wall behind the bed.

Curtains for the four-poster

Many people think that a four-poster bed is too cumbersome to have in the average-sized bedroom, but modern four-posters are actually no larger than a standard bed, nor are they too high to fit most rooms. They are usually supplied fitted with tracks for curtains. The curtains should be made with an attractive lining because it will be 'on show' and the easiest way of doing this is to use the 'bag' method.

Measure from the track to the floor and cut out the fabric to the same length, plus 1in. at the top for turnings. There is no need to add turnings to the bottom since the curtain should finish ½in. above the floor to prevent chafing. Cut the lining fabric to exactly the same size as the curtains.

With 'right' sides facing, stitch the lining and fabric together at the sides and bottom, taking ½in. turnings. Turn the curtains 'right' side out and press the seams carefully so that no lining shows on the 'right' side and vice versa. Then, treating the lining and curtain fabric as one piece, turn over the top edge 1in. on to the

lining side of the curtain and press down. Attach gathering tape following the method given on pages 35-36.

Making your own 'four-poster'

A standard bed which has a head and foot-board can be made into a kind of 'four-poster' by constructing a tall, four-legged frame to be placed over the bed (Figs.1-4).

The legs of the frame should be about 6ft high and made from 2½in. (63mm) dowel. The upper part should be the same size as the bed, made from 2in. x 1in. (50mm x 25mm) battening.

The frame can be simply made by using butt joints at the corners (Fig.2). Secure the joint with pva glue and two 1½in. screws. Place the dowels into the angles of the frame and secure with two 2in. No. 6 screws on the long side of the frame and one screw of the same size on the short side of the frame. A decorative knob can be screwed to the top of the dowel.

Paint the frame and legs and then place it over the bed, screwing the legs to the legs of the bed or the divan base, preferably on the inside so that the joins cannot be seen. Fix the pelmet and curtain track to the battening on the outside of the frame. If the top of the frame shows signs of 'skewing' out of shape, you can square it up by stapling on pieces of fine wire, such as piano wire, from corner to corner across the top pulling the frame straight as you staple the last corner. Alternatively, cut triangles of hardboard and pin these to each corner.

Make the curtains following the method above. Instructions for making a valance were given on pages 60-63.

Curtains without posts

If you would like the effect of curtains but without the posts, this can be done by fixing a frame to the ceiling over the bed from which the curtains can be hung. To make the frame, use lengths of 2in. x 1in. (50mm x 25mm) battening and screw them to the ceiling so the 2in. sides are vertical.

Paint the battens, then fix the curtain track to the outside of the frame.

Throwover bedspreads

The focal point of a bedroom should be the bed—and the bedspread is the finishing touch. A throwover bedspread is one of the quickest and easiest pieces of soft furnishing to make and, if you team the fabric with your wallcovering and curtains, it will give the room an immediate co-ordinated effect.

Calculating the amount of fabric

Measure the bed with its bed clothes and pillows as shown in Fig.1. For the width: measure from the floor on one side, up and across the bed to the floor on the other side. For the length: measure from the top of the pillow to the floor at the foot of the bed. If you wish to tuck the bedspread around the pillows, add an extra 12in. to the length.

As furnishing fabrics are usually 48in. or 54in. wide (plus selvedges), you will need to join two fabric widths for a 3ft single or a small double (4ft 6in.) bed, so double the length measurement to calculate how many yards you should buy. Six yards is usually ample for an average single or double bed 6ft 3in. long. As there will be some wastage when making a single bedspread, a 36in. wide dress fabric might be more suitable here.

If your fabric has a large design or motif, add on extra to the overall length in order to match it at the seams or to position it to best advantage on the bed—the additional amount could vary from an extra half pattern to as much as two patterns (known as repeats). Ask your retailer for advice if in doubt, because so much will depend on where the first measurement is taken on the fabric roll. Choose a time for buying the fabric when the store is quiet and take a note of the bed measurements with you. Ask to have the fabric unrolled so you can

Above right. For beds with footboards, cut away the corners of the bedspread so the bottom hem can be tucked in. The side hems can be finished by stitching on a fringe by hand. It will disguise the machine stitching of the hem and also give the side panels extra weight so they hang well.

examine the design fully and decide how you would like it positioned on the bed.

If you want the first repeat to come on the pillows, for example, allow about 6in. above this (towards the cut end), and start measuring the length of the bedspread from this point. For the second length, move down the roll to the next complete repeat, start 6in. above it, as for the first length, and measure as before. This ensures a matching design when you seam the lengths together. With a particularly large pattern, there will be some wastage (at the beginning and between the lengths), but this is unavoidable.

Making the bedspread

To avoid having an ugly seam down the centre of the bedspread, cut the fabric across into two equal lengths and then cut one of these pieces in half lengthwise, thus making one full

width of fabric for the centre panel and two half widths for the sides. Allowing a total of 4in. for seams and side hems, with 48in. wide fabric, the bedspread will have a minimum finished width of 7ft 8in. With 54in. fabric the finished width will be 8ft 8in.

If your double bedspread is to be narrower, cut off the excess equally from each half width (take it from the raw edges rather than the selvedges if this does not affect the matching of the pattern at the seams). For a 3ft bed, however, this would mean that the seams run along the side of the bed, rather than the top, and the panelled effect is lost. To avoid this, cut off the excess from the full width, rather than the halves (the leftover piece could be used for cushion covers). If the fabric is plain the excess can be taken from one side of the centre panel, but if the pattern runs centrally down the fabric, divide the excess and take off an equal amount from each side.

Joining the panels

To join the side pieces to each side of the centre panel, place the 'right' sides of the fabric together, selvedge to selvedge. Make sure the pattern is matched and the fabric runs the same way on each panel. Pin and tack about ½in. from the edge (more if the selvedges are wide). If you allowed extra on the length to match the pattern, cut off the excess fabric now (remember to allow 1in. at top and bottom for hems).

Machine stitch the seams, using a medium length stitch, following the tacking line. Remove the tacking. Clip (cut into) the selvedges at intervals if they are tight (this helps the seam to lie flat), and press the seams open. Neaten the raw edges by oversewing by hand or overcasting by machine if any fabric was cut off the centre panel.

Square corners

Make ¾in. hems down the long sides of the bedspread as follows: fold over the raw edge ¼in. on to the wrong side of the fabric. Make a second fold ¾in. deep, so the raw edge is now enclosed. Tack and machine stitch through the three thicknesses, along the first fold. Remove the tacking and press the hems. Turn under ¾in. hems at the top and bottom, making the corners square. Tack and machine stitch them, taking the line of machining over the machined line of the side hems (Fig.2). Remove the tacking and press the hems and then the finished bedspread all over.

Rounded corners for divans

Join the panels as above. Position the bedspread carefully on the bed and pin a curved line where the fabric touches the floor at the corners of the foot of the bed. Take off the bedspread and use a large plate or something similar as a guide to neaten the curve. Cut away the excess fabric, 1in. outside the line of pins—enough for a ¾in. hem (Fig.3).

Turn under the hem at the foot and along the sides of the bedspread, easing in the fabric at the corners. Tack and machine stitch the hem, remove the tacking and press the hem. Make a hem the same depth at the top of the bedspread, leaving the corners square. Press the bedspread all over.

Fitting around bedposts

Join the panels as above. Place the bedspread on the bed and fold back the side panels from the edge of the bed, with the fold lying just inside the posts (Fig.4). Pin a line along the fold from the corner of the bed (point A) down to the floor. Unfold the sides and fold up the foot of the bedspread in a similar way. Pin along this fold from point A to the floor (the pin lines should meet at point A).

Remove the bedspread and, using the pin lines as a guide, pin the corner as shown in Fig.5. Cut off the corner ½in. from the line of pins. Using this as a guide, cut out a similar corner from the other side of the bedspread.

Clip into the angle and make a narrow hem, rounding the angle. Press the hems. Make 1in. hems all round the bedspread, leaving the corners square. Press the bedspread all over.

Above right. Make a feature of the seams on a plain bedspread, and cover them by stitching on braid. More braid across the foot accentuates the centre panel.

Fig. 1. How to measure the bed.
Fig. 2. For square corners, machine stitching is taken to the edges of the hems. Fig. 3. For round corners, the hem line is marked and the excess fabric trimmed off 1in. outside the line.
Fig. 4. For cut-away corners, the side panel is folded up and a guide line marked from A to the floor. Fig. 5. The corner is pinned together on the guide lines.

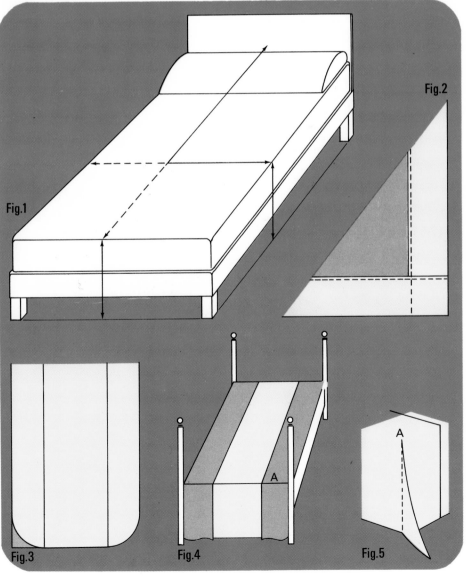

Make a bedspread with a gathered flounce

A bedspread with a gathered flounce is one of the simpler fitted bedspreads. This one has a throwover flap—sometimes called a pillow scarf—which is a separate piece of fabric stitched, 'back-to-front', to the top of the bedspread.

The bedspread is put on to the bed, the pillows are put in position on top of the bedspread and the throwover flap is folded back over them and tucked underneath. This helps the bedspread to keep its shape because if the bedspread were put over the pillows, their height would pull up the flounce at the top of the bed.

Don't use a heavy fabric for this type of bedspread, as it will not gather easily. And avoid very large patterns, because you will have wastage in matching it at seams, particularly on the flounce.

Calculating the fabric

Measure the bed with its bedclothes but without the pillows. For the **width**, measure from edge to edge across the bed and add 1in. for the seam allowance. For the **length**, measure from the top of the bed to the foot and add 1in. seam allowance. If the bed has a footboard, add 18in. to the length measurement so that the bedspread can be tucked in at the bottom. For the depth of the **flounce**, measure from the edge of the bed to the floor and add $1\frac{1}{2}$in. hem and seam allowance. (When you refer back to these measurements as you make the bedspread, always include the allowances.)

Next, put the pillows on to the bed and measure for the throwover **flap** from the bottom of the pile of pillows at the top of the bed, up and over the pillows to the other side (Fig. 1). Add on 6in. for seam allowances and so that the flap can be tucked in.

Calculate the amount of fabric needed for

NELSON HARGREAVES

Left. Piping along the top edge of the bed accentuates the lines and adds strength to the seams of this semi-fitted bedspread.

each piece separately, and then tot them up.

One-piece platform

If your width measurement is the same or less than the width of the fabric being used, the platform section (the part of the bedspread which comes on top of the bed) can be made in one piece without joins, so allow an amount equal to the bed's length.

Flounce

If the platform is made in one piece, the amount of fabric needed for a flounce with 'fullness and a half'—gathering which is neither too skimpy nor too bunchy—can be worked out in two ways, depending on the fabric. First, determine the length of the flounce by multiplying the bed's length by three—(ie. a length and a half for each side, excluding any extra length allowed for the tuck-in extension). For divans, the flounce should also go round the foot, so add on one and a half times the bed's width.

Plain fabrics

These, or fabrics with a small all-over pattern, can be used for the flounce 'sideways on', so that the selvedge threads run along the side of the bed, rather than from the edge of the bed to the floor. The fabric is split in half lengthwise, so you need half the length of the flounce.

If the flounce is deeper than half the width of the fabric, rather than buying twice as much—which would be wasteful, as it may well be a matter of only an inch or so—stitch on a fringe to give the additional depth.

Patterned fabrics

If the fabric has a definite one-way vertical pattern or pile, the flounce should be cut so that it will be the right way up when on the bed. You will have to join crosswise pieces (ie. pieces the width of the fabric) to make up the length of the flounce.

To determine the number of pieces, divide the length of the flounce by the width of the fabric. (Always work in full and half widths and take it to the width above, as any extra fabric will be used as the seam allowance for joining the pieces, or be absorbed into the gathering.)

Multiply the flounce's depth measurement by the number of pieces, and this gives the *basic* amount of fabric needed for the flounce. Allow at least one complete repeat extra to match the pattern at the seams.

For example, if the length of the flounce is 19ft 6in., and you are using 48in. fabric, the number of pieces needed would be five—two and a half for each side of the bed. For a flounce 24in. deep, you would need 10ft of fabric.

Throwover flap

This should be 12in. wider than the bed's width, so that it covers the pillows well and hangs down on either side of the bed. If you have to join pieces to make up the full width, buy twice the flap's length measurement. You will also need lining fabric of the same size.

Panelled platform

If the width of your bed is more than the width of the fabric, the method for calculating the amount of fabric economically is complicated, but worth doing if the fabric is expensive. (See Fig. 2 for a sample cutting chart.)

Allow double the bed's length measurement for the platform, so that you can add pieces of equal width to the long sides of the main piece. As some fabric will be left over from cutting the side panels, work out the width of these before calculating for the flounce.

Subtract the width of the fabric less 1in. (seam allowance) from the total platform width. Add 1in. to the remaining measurement and divide the total by two.

For example, for a 4ft 6in. bed, the total width of the platform might be 4ft 10in. (including an extra 3in. for the bulk of bedclothes, and 1in. seam allowance). If using 48in. fabric, the width of the side panels, worked out from the formula above, is 6in. (When these are joined to the main piece with ½in. seams, the platform will be the required 4ft 10in.)

When the 6in. side panels have been cut off, you are left with a strip of fabric of the length measurement and 36in. wide. If the fabric is plain, and the width of the leftover strip is twice the depth of the flounce, it could be split in half lengthwise and be used for part of the flounce on each side of the bed. Or one of the pieces could be used for the section of the flounce that comes at the foot of the bed and the other piece could be used for the pillow flap.

If the flounce is deeper than half the width of the leftover strip, or if the fabric is patterned, cut the strip crosswise into pieces of the flounce's depth. To calculate how much extra fabric will be needed for it, divide the depth of the flounce into the length of the leftover fabric This will give the number of strips that can be cut from it. Multiply this number by the width of the leftover fabric, and subtract 1in. (seam allowance) for each strip. Subtract this figure from the total flounce length, and then divide the remaining amount by the width of the fabric being used, to calculate how many more strips are needed. The number of strips, multiplied by the depth of the flounce, will give the amount needed.

For example, if the leftover piece is 36in. wide and 6ft 6in. long, and the depth of the flounce is 19½in., the number of strips obtainable is four. This number, multiplied by the width of the leftover fabric (36in.), less 4in. (1in. per strip), gives 140in. If the total flounce length is 26ft 9in. (19ft 6in. for the sides and 7ft 3in. for the foot), the additional amount needed is 15ft 1in., therefore four strips 48in. wide by 19½in. deep.

Cutting out and making up

Platform

If this can be made without joins, cut off a piece of fabric the right length and trim it to the right width, leaving seam allowances, if necessary. (If the fabric has a central pattern, cut off equal amounts from each side).

Where the fabric does have to be joined, cut out the centre and side panels as calculated above, matching the pattern. Join the pieces with a ½in. plain seam, clip the selvedges or neaten raw edges, and press the seams open.

Flounce

Divan beds

Cut out and join all the strips for the flounce with ½in. plain seams. Clip the selvedges or neaten any raw edges and press the seams open. Make ½in. hems on the short sides of the flounce, machine or hand stitch them, and press. Make a 1in. hem along the foot of the flounce, stitch and press it.

Divide the flounce into sections for the sides and foot of the bed, marking the divisions with pins. Then divide the side sections into quarters, and mark the divisions along the top edge; and mark the centre point of the foot section. Divide the platform in a similar way. Gather the flounce, using a long machine stitch or short running stitches, ½in. down from the top edge (it is advisable to stitch each division separately, as such a long length of gathering is liable to break when the thread is pulled up).

Match the divisions on the flounce to those on the platform. With the 'right' sides of the fabric facing, pin the pieces together at the division marks with the pins at right-angles to the edge. Pin the ends of the flounce to the platform ½in. in from the top edge of the platform.

Lay the platform out flat (use the floor if necessary), with the flounce on top of it. Secure one end of each gathering thread, and, leaving the divisional pins in position, draw up the other end until the flounce fits the platform. Secure the threads by winding them round the divisional pins.

Space out the gathers evenly, pin the flounce to the platform (putting the pins at right-angles to the edge at 1in. intervals), and tack, using small stitches (Fig. 3). Remove the pins and machine stitch the pieces together, with the flounce uppermost (this helps to keep the gathers from puckering as you stitch). Remove the tacking and gathering threads, and press the seam towards the platform section. Neaten the raw edges with bias binding, or by overcasting them together.

Footboard beds

Make the flounce for each side separately, and attach them to the platform section, leaving the 18in. extension free (Fig. 4). Make a narrow hem on the sides and foot of the extension.

Throwover flap

If it is necessary to join pieces to make the width of the throwover flap, calculate the width of the side panels in the same way as for the platform, but adding 6in. to each one so that it will cover the pillows fully. (If the fabric is patterned, cut the side panels so that the extra 6in. comes on the outside edge of each piece so that it will match the pattern on the platform when in position. See Fig. 5.) Join the pieces and press the seam open. Cut lining fabric to the same size as the throwover, joining it if necessary.

With 'right' sides facing, stitch the lining to the flap with a ½in. seam, leaving an opening the width of the platform along the top edge (Fig. 6).

With the 'right side of the flap facing the 'wrong' side of the platform, fit the top edge of the platform into the opening, and pin it to the flap only (i.e. leaving the lining free). Stitch the pieces with a ½in. seam (Fig. 7). Press the seam into the opening. Fold the lining over the raw edges of the seam and hem it down, enclosing the raw edges. Press.

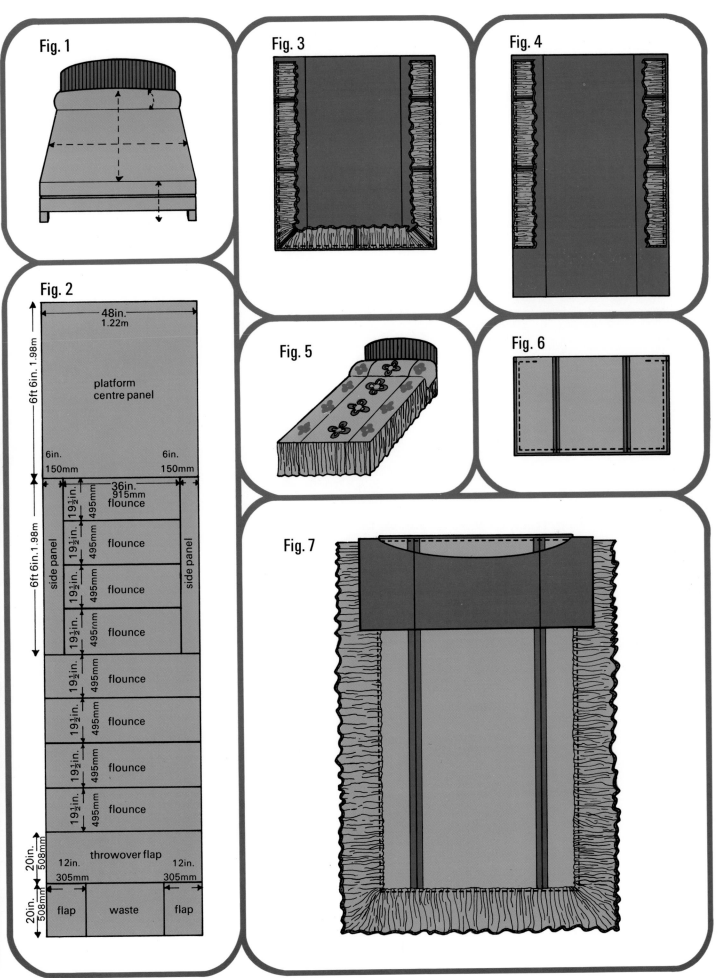

Fig. 1

Fig. 2

48in.
1.22m

6ft 6in. 1.98m

platform
centre panel

6in.
150mm

6in.
150mm

36in.
915mm

side panel

19½in.
495mm
flounce

19½in.
495mm
flounce

19½in.
495mm
flounce

19½in.
495mm
flounce

side panel

6ft 6in.1.98m

19½in.
495mm
flounce

19½in.
495mm
flounce

19½in.
495mm
flounce

19½in.
495mm
flounce

throwover flap

20in.
508mm

12in.
305mm

12in.
305mm

20in.
508mm

flap

waste

flap

Fig. 3

Fig. 4

Fig. 5

Fig. 6

Fig. 7

Day covers for divans

In most bedsitters, the emphasis is placed on the room's daytime function with an attempt to disguise its bedroom use completely. The bed is often the main seating accommodation, so it needs a smart cover which is not too 'bedspready'.

If you want to wash your bedspread, choose fabric which has been treated for crease resistance and to drip dry, because pleats are tedious to iron. Alternatively dry clean the fabric in a coin-operated machine, because if you take the bedspread out as soon as the machine stops and hang it up without folding it, it will not need pressing.

For a bedspread with a frill all round (that is, including the head of the bed) and with inverted pleats at each corner, you will need about 6¾ yards of fabric, 48in. wide. For spaced pleats all round, you need about 7½ yards fabric, or for tightly spaced pleats you will need about 8½-9 yards. If you want to make covers for pillows, allow an extra yard per case (these can be made as for boxed cushions, following the method on pages 99-101, but stiffen the box strips with iron-on stiffening).

To determine the exact amount of fabric needed, measure the bed as given below (see 'Cutting out'), and draw up a cutting chart. Allow extra fabric for matching the pattern, if necessary.

Cutting out

If the cover is to be used over bedclothes, measure the bed (without pillows) with the maximum number of blankets likely to be used during the year. The cover should fit snugly, but not so tightly that it is difficult to put on.

For the *platform,* measure the width and length of the bed, and add 1in. to each for the seam allowance (points A to B and C to D, Fig.1). If you are going to have a close-pleated frill, it will greatly help in the fitting if the length and width of the platform are an even number of inches (excluding the turning).

For the depth of the *box strip,* measure from

NIGEL MESSETT

Left. If you are using fabric with a one-way design on a bed which is placed against a wall, cut out the fabric for the top of the cover so that it runs across the bed from back to front, rather than from head to foot.

the edge of the bed to the bottom of the mattress (points B to E) and add 1in. seam allowance. The length of the side strips will be equal to the length of the platform and the length of the head and foot strips will be equal to the width of the platform (including allowances).

For the depth of the *frill,* measure from the bottom of the mattress to ½in. from the floor (points E to F), and add 2½in. hem and seam allowance. For the length of the frill, add together the length and width of the platform and multiply by two. Add on 48in. to this amount for corner inverted pleats *or* double it for spaced 2in. box pleats *or* treble it for close pleating.

Before you start to cut out, study the pattern of the fabric in relation to the position of the bed in the room. If the pattern is a one way design and the bed is against a wall, it may look better if you position it so that it runs across the bed, rather than from head to foot. If this is the case, cut the platform in sections, using a full width in the middle of the bed with part widths either side to make up the length of the platform. If the pattern has a large repeat, position it centrally on the width of the bed.

If you decide to have the pattern running from head to foot, cut off a piece the right length for the platform and trim it to the correct width, taking an equal amount from each side if the pattern should be centred.

If you are using plain fabric, or a pattern with an allover design, it can be cut lengthwise for the frill and box strip. With a one-way design, regardless of the way it runs on the platform, it should always run vertically on the box strip and frill. To calculate the number of widths of fabric you should join to make up the length of each section, divide 47 (or the width of the fabric less 1in. seam allowance) into the length. Cut out this number of strips x the depth of the section.

From the offcuts, cut out enough bias strip fabric x 1½in. wide to make two lengths of piping equal to the perimeter of the platform.

Making up the boxed section

The method for making up this section is very similar to making a boxed cushion cover. Start by joining all the box strips along their short edges to make one circular piece, with the side sections alternating with the head and foot

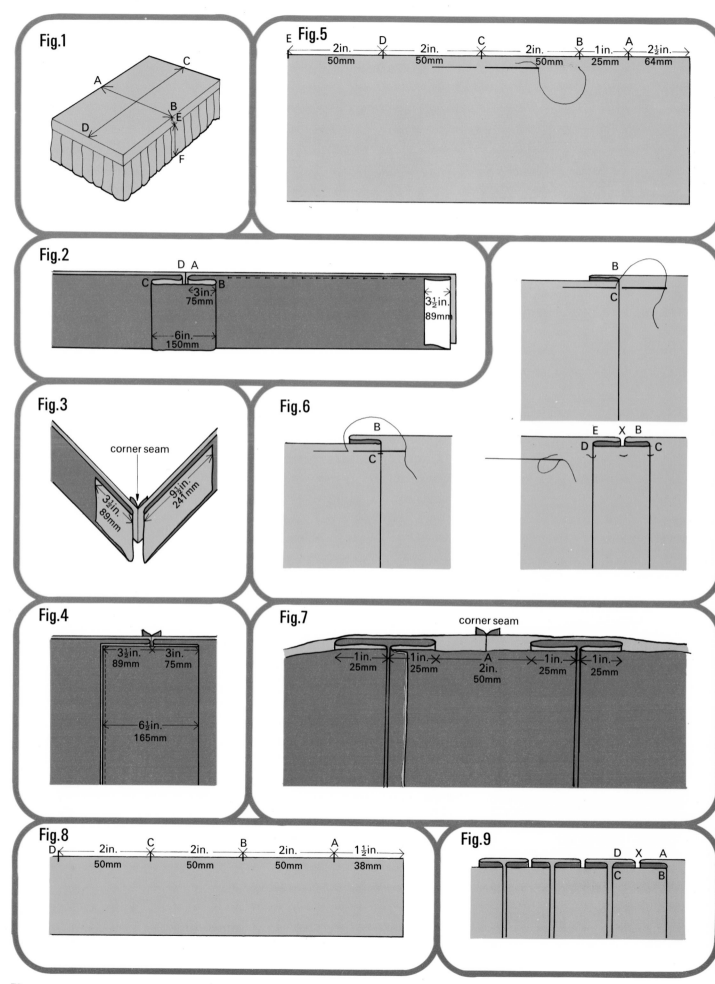

Fig.1

Fig.5
E 2in. D 2in. C 2in. B 1 in. A 2½ in.
50mm 50mm 50mm 25mm 64mm

Fig.2
D A
C 3in. B
75mm
6in. 3½ in.
150mm 89mm

B
C

Fig.3
corner seam
3⅛ in. 9½ in.
89mm 241mm

Fig.6
B
C

E X B
D C

Fig.4
3½ in. 3in.
89mm 75mm
6½ in.
165mm

Fig.7
corner seam
1in. 1in. A 1in. 1in.
25mm 25mm 2in. 25mm 25mm
50mm

Fig.8
D 2in. C 2in. B 2in. A 1½ in.
50mm 50mm 50mm 38mm

Fig.9
D X A
C B

sections. Take ½in. plain seams, and taper your stitches into the corners ½in. at the top edge of each. Press the seam allowance over to one side.

Make up the piping and join a length to each edge on the 'right' side of the box strip, with raw edges together and stitching ½in. from the edge. Join the ends of the piping as shown on pages 95-97. Snip into the piping casing at the seam lines on the box strip; do not snip into the strip itself because the tapered seams will open out eough to ease it round the corners when joining it to the platform.

Making the frill

Stitch all the pieces together, taking ½in. turnings and matching any pattern. Do not join the last seam, which would make the strip into a circular piece, yet because you may have to make slight adjustments in fitting the frill to the box strip. Neaten the seams and press them open. Turn up 2in. along the bottom edge and make a 1in. double hem. Press.

Corner inverted pleats

Turn under 3½in. at one short end of the frill. With 'right' sides together and raw edges level, place the fold to one of the corner seams on the box strip. Continue pinning the frill on the side of the strip. When you reach the next corner of the strip, fold back 3in. of the frill and pin the fold (point A, Fig.2). Make a second fold on the wrong side of the frill, 3in. from the first fold (point B), bring the fabric forward and tack both folds in position. Measure 6in. from the second fold and bring the fabric back to make a third fold (point C). Bring the fabric forward in another fold 3in. from point C, to meet the first fold. Tack all the folds firmly in position, so there is no gap between points A and D, then tack the completed pleat to the box strip.

Continue pinning the frill to the strip, making pleats at the corners in the same way. At the last corner, form the first section of the pleat as before, but to complete it join the raw edge to the edge first folded under taking ½in. turning. The seam line must fall in the fold (Figs.3 and 4).

Check that all the pleats are correctly formed, then stitch the frill to the box strip. Neaten and press all the seams.

Left, Fig.1. How to measure the bed.
Fig.2. The folds on the right side of the inverted pleat should meet exactly at the corner seams of the box strip.
Figs.3 and 4. The fabric which was folded back at the beginning of the frill forms one side of the last pleat.
Fig.5. To make the spaced box pleating easier, the frill is marked in 2in. divisions. So that a space will fall equally on either side of a corner seam on the box strip, and the joining seam is on the inside of the pleat, an amount equal to a space and half a pleat is left at the beginning.
Fig.6. How a box pleat is formed.
Fig.7. The seam joining the frill should be pressed over to one side.
Figs.8 and 9. For a frill with alternating box and inverted pleats, the divisions are marked, leaving a space for a part pleat at the beginning.

Spaced pleating

With the 'right' side of the frill uppermost and the raw edge at the top, make a mark with tacking chalk 2½in. in from the right-hand side along the top edge (Fig.5, point A). Make another mark 1in. from this (point B), and another one 2in. from this (point C). Continue along the top edge marking at 2in. intervals.

Using a long length of buttonhole thread, or regular thread used double, and knotted at one end, insert the needle into the frill at point B from the 'wrong' side ½in. from the top. Pull the thread through to the 'right' side. Pick up a small stitch at point C, then pull up the thread so that points B and C meet in a fold. Fold the fabric between B and C flat and to the left to form the first half of the pleat. Stitch through the three thicknesses of fabric and make a small backstitch to secure the fold.

At the next division mark, fold back the fabric to meet the 'inside' fold (point X) on the back of the frill. Secure it with a backstitch as before. With the needle on the 'right' side of the fabric, insert it on the edge of the finished pleat (point D), pass the thread along the back of the frill and bring it up at the next division mark. Pass the thread along the front of the frill and make a tiny stitch at the following division to form another pleat as before. Continue making pleats in the same way.

When you have made enough pleats to fit one side of the box strip, pin point A to a corner seam and fit the frill to the strip to check whether the middle of a space will fall at the next corner seam. If it does not, you may have to cheat slightly on the amount you fold under the pleat. Try to do it so that the actual size of the pleat which shows on the front of the frill is the same, but you can vary the amount of the space at the corner by as much as ½in. each side.

Continue making the pleats and adjusting the spaces to fit the corners for all sides of the box strip. Finish the last pleat by joining the short ends of the frill so that the seam falls in the inside fold of a pleat (Fig.7).

Close pleating

With the 'right' side of the frill uppermost and the raw edge at the top, make a mark with tacking or chalk 1½in. in from the right-hand side along the top edge (Fig.8, point A). Continue marking the top edge at 2in. intervals for half the length of the frill.

Above. A bedcover with a pleated frill, and made in a brightly-coloured fabric, will turn a divan into a smart day bed.

Using a long length of buttonhole thread, or regular thread used double, and knotted at one end, insert the needle into the frill at point A from the 'wrong' side ½in. from the top. Pull the thread through to the 'right' side. Pick up a small stitch at point B, then pull up the thread so that points A and B meet in a fold. Fold the fabric between A and B flat and to the left to form the first half of the box pleat. Stitch through the three thicknesses of fabric and make a small backstitch to secure the fold.

At the next division mark, fold back the fabric so that points C and D meet and the fabric between forms a fold (Fig.9, point X). Secure with a backstitch as before. With the needle on the 'right' side of the fabric, insert it on the edge of the finished box pleat (point C), pass the thread along the front of the frill and bring it up at the next division mark (point E). Pull up the thread so that points C and E meet. Fold the fabric flat and to the left, as before. Stitch the fold made at points C and E so that it touches the edge of the first pleat formed, thus making an inverted pleat.

Continue forming the pleats in this way, alternating box and inverted pleats, until you have enough to fit one side of the box strip. Pin the fold A-B to a corner seam and fit the frill to the strip to check whether the centre of an inverted pleat will fall at the next corner seam. If it does not, unpick some of the stitching of the last pleats formed and cheat slightly on their size in order to make them fit.

Re-adjust the marking of spaces if necessary, and continue making pleats to fit the remaining sides of the box strip, positioning inverted pleats at all the corners. At the last corner, join the short edges of the frill, positioning the seam so that it falls on the inside fold.

Finishing off

With 'right' sides together, pin the box strip round the edge of the platform, placing the seams at the corners. Machine stitch, taking ½in. turnings. Neaten the seams by overcasting or with seam binding. Press all the seams.

Press all the pleats carefully, making sure that the straight grain is level with all the folds. Stitch the frill to the box strip, neaten and press all the seams.

Padded bedheads

If you have an ugly bedhead, one way of smartening it up is to pad and cover it with fabric to match your bedspread or the other soft furnishings in the room. The cover may be a loose one, so that it can be removed for cleaning, or you could make it more permanent if it can be cleaned in position.

In either case, the bedhead should have a simple outline because with anything that has an elaborate shape it will be difficult to achieve a good fit. If you do want to pad an elaborate bedhead, it is usually better to inset the padding, leaving a border of wood all round. Bedheads with struts can also be padded.

Making the padding

Use 2in. thick polyether foam cut 1in. larger all round than the area to be padded. If the foam would make the bedboard so deep that the mattress would stick out at the end of the bed, leave an unpadded section of the same depth as the mattress at the bottom of the headboard.

If your headboard is shaped, the simplest way to cut the foam is to place the board on top of the foam and trace the shape round its edge. Mark another line 1in. from this for the cutting line.

The foam is attached to the bedhead by strips of tape or calico. One edge of the tape is stuck round the perimeter of the foam and the other edge is wrapped round to the back of the headboard where it is tacked down. This gives the padding a domed effect and keeps the edges of the foam level with the edge of the board. The foam should never protrude over the edge of the board because this would spoil the shape.

Cut pieces of 4in. wide tape or calico to fit round the sides of the foam, making them long enough to overlap 1in. at each corner. If the bedhead is curved, you will need to cut several short pieces of tape to fit it. Fold the tape in half lengthwise and apply an adhesive suitable for use with foam (such as Bostik I) on one half of each piece (from the edge up to the crease) to within 1in. of each corner. Mark a border 2in. wide round the edges of the foam on one side and apply adhesive to this section.

When the adhesive is tacky, put the tape, adhesive-side down, on to the foam border so that the half of tape which was not applied with adhesive protrudes all the way round and

overlaps by 1in. at each corner. Press down firmly to make sure the adhesion is complete. Place the foam on your work surface with the tape-side down, remove the headboard from the bed and place it front-side down on to the foam so that there is a 1in. border of foam showing round the edges (or along the top and sides only if an unpadded section is being left).

Squash up the edges of the foam so that they are level with the edges of the headboard, bring the tape at the top of the board over on to the back and secure with temporary tacks at 6in. intervals. Still keeping the tape tight, but without allowing the foam to come over the edges of the board, tack down the bottom tape in the same way if the board is completely padded, or simply into the lower line of padding if a section is being left.

Next, beginning at the centre and working out to the sides, completely tack the top and bottom edges, placing the tacks about $\frac{3}{4}$in. apart and $\frac{1}{2}$in. in from the edge. At the corners, slash the overlapping tape level with the sides of the board to the corner of the wood, and then to the front edge of foam. Open the slashed portion out and refold it the other way so that it now wraps round the sides and some extends at the top or bottom (Fig.4.) Tack it down and trim off the surplus tape flush with the edges of the board.

Tack down the side tapes in the same way. To finish off the corners, slash and wrap round the tape as before and tack or stick down.

Making a calico inner cover

Cut a piece of calico 5-6in. longer and wider than the headboard, and place it centrally over the foam. Tack it temporarily to the back of the board in the centre at the top and bottom. Keeping the grain of the fabric completely square, tack along the top edge to within 2in. of the corners.

Working from the tacked side to the bottom of the board, smooth the calico across the foam and tack it to the back of the board so that it is taut without being strained. Keep smoothing the fabric across before placing each tack. This procedure will make the padding into a dome.

Right. An old wooden bedhead can be brought up to date with padding which is covered in fabric to match the other furnishings. The padding can be inset to show off the carving.

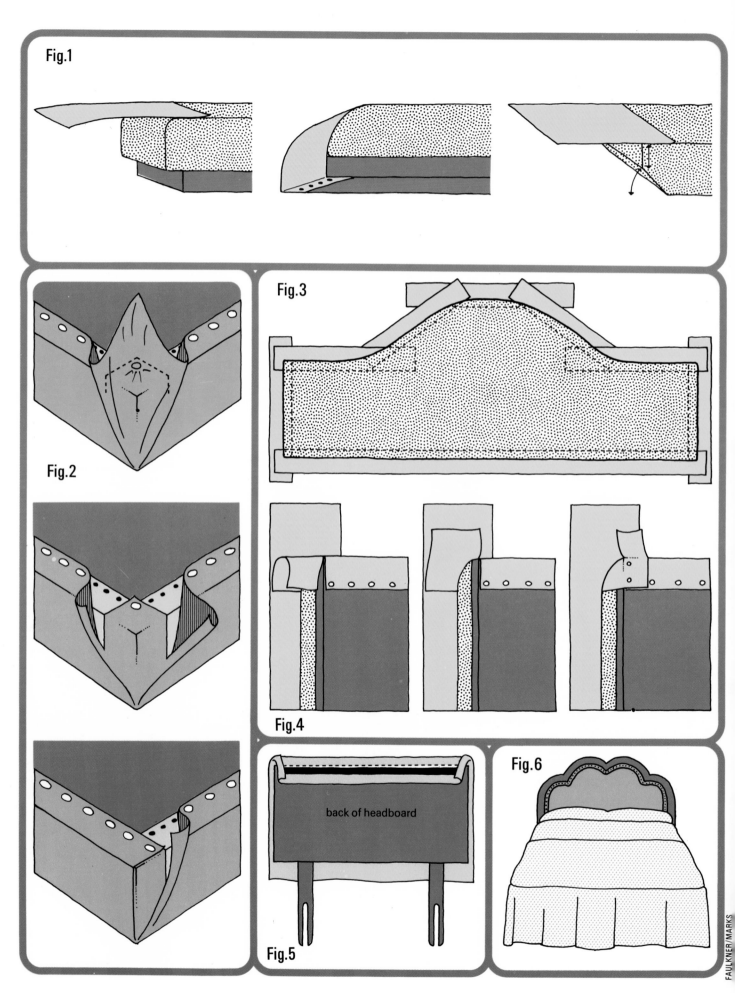

Fig.1

Fig.2

Fig.3

Fig.4

Fig.5

back of headboard

Fig.6

Tack down the sides in the same way, making sure that the calico is smooth and taut and that the grain is not distorted.

With the back of the board facing upwards, pick up the points of the calico at the corners and pull them tautly on to the back of the board. Tack down $\frac{1}{2}$in. from the corners of the wood. Fold in the excess fabric on both sides to meet in a double fold, and press down firmly to make creases. Open out the fabric and cut away some of the excess fabric to within $\frac{1}{4}$in. of the creases to reduce bulk. Trim off the point of the corner to within $\frac{1}{4}$in. of the tack. Replace the folds and tack down on the back of the board (Fig.2).

Fitted top cover

Cut out a piece of cover fabric to fit over the bedhead and round to the back. If it is not possible to cut it from one piece, cut a section for the main centre piece from the full width of the fabric and join two narrower strips of equal width to each side.

Tack it to the headboard, following the method used for the inner cover, placing the tacks about $\frac{3}{4}$in. from the edge so they will not fall in the same line as those of the inner cover.

To finish the back, cut a piece of sheet wadding or thin foam to the exact size and shape of the board and tack temporarily in place. Cut a piece of calico the same size, plus 1in. on each side for turnings.

To attach the calico, start by backing-tacking it to the top edge of the board, or to the bottom edge if the top edge is not straight. Put the calico on your work surface and place the headboard face down on top so that a border of calico equal to 1in. plus the thickness of the bedhead shows on the side to be back-tacked, and 1in. shows at the sides.

Remove the tacks holding the wadding on that edge. Turn the calico over to the back of the board so the raw edge comes 1in. below the top. Cut a piece of cardboard the same length as the width of the board and 1in. wide, and place this level with the edge on the back of the board. Tack the calico and cardboard to the

board, placing the tacks outside those already in position. The cardboard helps to keep the edge of the calico from looping down between the tacks, and gives a smooth edge.

Bring the calico completely over to the back of the board, turn in the remaining edges so that the fold is about $\frac{1}{8}$in. from the edge. Either slip stitch to the cover fabric, using curved needle, or tack into position using decorative upholstery pins.

Making a loose top cover

The method for making this is not unlike that for making a boxed cushion cover. It can be pulled over the padding and fastens under the bottom of the board with tape.

For the front and back panels, you need two pieces of fabric the same size as the bedhead, plus $\frac{1}{2}$in. at the top sides and 1in. at the bottom for turnings. If possible, cut the fabric in one long piece to fit the width of the headboard (ie, on a double bed the threads which run parallel to the selvedges would be horizontal when in position on the board). Where the fabric has a one way design which must run vertically on the board and it is not possible to cut the panels in one piece—as on a double bed, for example—cut a main centre section from the full width of fabric and join two narrower sections to each side.

If you want the panels on the back and front of the board to be reversible, cut the back panel in the same fabric as the front one. Alternatively, the back panel could be cut from calico for economy.

You will also need a long piece of fabric for the box strip, the depth of the bedhead including padding, plus 1in. for turnings x the length of the sides and top plus 1in. For the piping, cut enough bias strips 1$\frac{1}{2}$in. wide to make two lengths of casing the same length as the box strip. You will need only one casing if the cover is not to be reversible. (If you are short of fabric, the piping casing could be made from a contrasting fabric.)

Make up the piping casing following the method given on pages 95-97. Join strips

to make up the length of the box strip if necessary, then attach the piping casing along both edges on the right side, or along the front edge only if the cover is not reversible.

With right sides together, pin the box strip to the sides and top of the front panel, taking a $\frac{1}{2}$in. turning. Snip into the seam allowance at the corners if necessary to make a smooth outline, then machine stitch the seam. Neaten the raw edges if they are likely to fray much.

Join the back panel to the other edge of the box strip in a similar way and press all the seams.

Turn up 1in. at the bottom of the cover and make a $\frac{3}{4}$in. hem. Stitch on pieces of tape at the same positions on the front and back panels.

Making an inset cover

This looks best if the padding is inset leaving a border of at least 2in. at the top and sides. The lower edge should come the same amount above the mattress.

Use 2in. thick polyester foam cut to a shape to complement the shape of the bedhead and $\frac{1}{2}$in. larger all round than the area to be padded. Using scissors, cut the edges so they taper out at an angle of about 45° from the back of the foam to within $\frac{1}{2}$in. of the front (Fig.1). This will give the padding a good rounded shape.

Place the back of the foam in position on to the front of the bedhead as above. Cut the fabric to the shape of the padding plus $\frac{1}{2}$in. all round. Turn in the $\frac{1}{2}$in. allowance, clipping the edges if necessary to make a good shape, and press down. Place it over the foam and tack or staple it along the top edge, placing the tacks $\frac{1}{4}$in. from the fold and tucking the bevelled edges of the foam under the edge of the fabric.

Smooth the fabric to the bottom, tuck in the edge of the foam and tack down the fabric working from the centre to each side. Smooth out to the sides and tack down these, keeping the fabric completely taut and wrinkle-free.

Cover the tacks with decorative braid, applied with adhesive. Mitre the corners of the braid to give a neat finish. Alternatively, use decorative tacks instead of plain tacks and braid.

Left, Fig.1. To give the padding a curved edge, the foam is cut over-size and the sides are tucked under and held down by calico strips. For a softer curve, some foam can be cut away from the under side.
Fig.2. How to finish off the corners of the inner and top cover with a double pleat.
Fig.3. For a shaped bedhead, the calico strips have to be pieced round the curve.
Fig.4. The strips are tacked to the bedhead and the overlaps finished at the corners by wrapping them round the other way.
Fig.5. To make a neat finish on the back of the bedhead, the calico is back-tacked along the top edge. When it is brought over to the back of the board, no tacks show at all. A cardboard strip is used to give the edge a clean line.
Fig.6. Where padding is inset, braid is used to hide the edges and tacks of the cover.

Right. The top cover of the bedhead can be fitted permanently over the padding like upholstery, or it can be loose for cleaning.

PAF INTERNATIONAL

Traditional padded and buttoned bedheads

For a really luxurious bedhead, you cannot beat the traditional padded and buttoned headboard. It is comfortable when you sit up (the buttons sink so deep into the padding that you don't feel them), and it looks attractive in all sorts of settings.

The board

If you have an old wooden bedhead which is simply shaped, this can easily be used as the base for the new one. You will, however, not be able to use it unpadded again because of the holes you will have drilled in it for the buttoning. Alternatively, shaped plywood boards can be bought quite cheaply from DIY shops. Choose a shape which has easy curves, because with anything too intricate you will have difficulty in cutting the foam padding and achieving a smooth line with the upholstery. Check also that it has the right fittings for your bed.

The padding

Use 2in. to 2½in. thick polyether foam in a low density, soft grade, cut in the same shape as the area to be padded, but 1in. larger all round. For really luxurious deep buttoning, 3in. thick foam can be used, but this is more difficult to work with.

If the thickness of the padding would make the headboard so deep that the mattress would stick out at the end of the bed, leave an un-padded section, of the same depth as the mattress, at the bottom of the board. The mattress can then slot in underneath. To check on the exact point that the padding should end, put the unpadded bedhead in position at the top of the bed. Put the mattress up to it and mark on the wood where the two meet. Leave an extra ½in. to give clearance and to allow for the thickness of the covering fabric.

The fabric

This is not the type of cover which can be removed for cleaning, so use a fabric which does not show marks and can be cleaned easily while it is still in position.

Seams joining the fabric look particularly ugly with this type of bedhead, so if you are making one for a double bed—where standard 48in. wide fabric would be too narrow—choose one which can be used sideways (with the selvedges running horizontally, rather than vertically, as usual). Unfortunately, this means that you

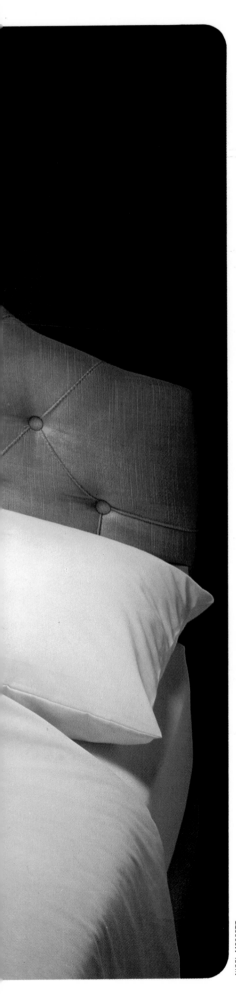

Left. With the development of sponge-clean fabrics, such as Dralon velvet, padded bedheads are back in fashion and are a decorative feature in any bedroom.

NIGEL MESSETT

cannot use patterns with one-way designs, although you can use velvet because this looks all right with the pile running sideways.

You will need enough fabric to fit over the headboard and padding, and round to the back, plus about ½in. in length and width for each row of buttoning. Allow about ¼yd extra fabric for covering the buttons. If you are leaving an unpadded section at the bottom of the board, you will need a straight strip of fabric to cover this. Allow the same amount of calico for the lining, plus enough to cut 4in. wide strips to fit round the perimeter of the foam.

If you do have to join the fabric to make up the right width, it is possible to do so invisibly by a method known as 'vandyking' (see below). This is quite tricky to do, so you should only attempt it if really necessary.

Other materials

Adhesive with a latex base, such as Bostik 1, for attaching the calico strips to the foam.

Buttons always look best if in the same fabric as the cover. These are quite easy to make yourself if you use the metal button moulds with a shank that are sold for the purpose. Templates for cutting out the fabric to the right size are given on the back of the card supplied with the buttons. Usually, the ½in. or ¾in. diameter sizes will be most suitable.

Before you make the buttons, try the fabric over the mould to see whether the metal shows through. If it does, cut a second circle of fabric the exact size of the button, and stick this on to the mould with adhesive before putting on the main button cover.

Twine is used for attaching the buttons. Use the type sold for upholstery buttoning because it is much stronger and less bulky than ordinary string.

A mattress needle is used with the twine. These were sold in various lengths, and have a point at each end, although only one eye. A 10in. or 12in. needle is most useful because it can be used in other types of upholstery work. ¾in. *fine tacks* for attaching the cover to the board, and ⅝in. *tacks* for the buttoning; a *hammer*, for use with the tacks; *wadding and sateen lining fabric*, for finishing the back of the board; and a *curved needle* and *thread to match the lining*, for stitching this in position.

Preparing the board

Before the padding can be put on to it, holes in the position of each button should be drilled in the board. The buttons are usually arranged in an elongated diamond pattern, in alternating rows about 4–5in. apart vertically, and 5–6in. horizontally. A plain border of about the same

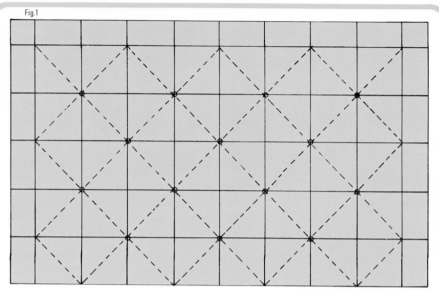

Fig.1

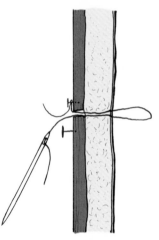

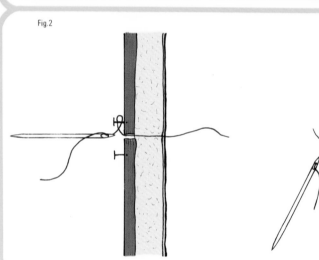

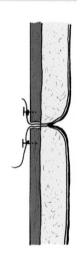

width should be left all round the edge of the area being padded.

To find the positions of the holes, start by marking the area of the board to be padded. Mark the centre of each side of the area, and draw one line on the wood from centre top to centre bottom, and another one joining the centre points of each side. Then mark a line all round the edge for the plain border.

To calculate the distance to be left between the vertical rows of buttons, measure from the centre vertical line out to the side border line, and find a measurement between 4in. and 5in. which will divide exactly into it. If necessary, the width of the outer border can be adjusted if this makes it easier, but it should never be less than 4in. wide. Repeat this process for the horizontal rows.

Draw rectangles of the size you have decided, working from the centre lines out to the edges. Mark with a cross the positions for the holes

Fig.2

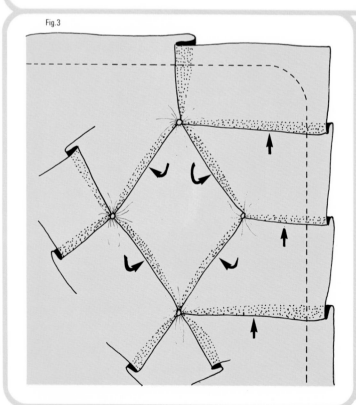

Fig.3

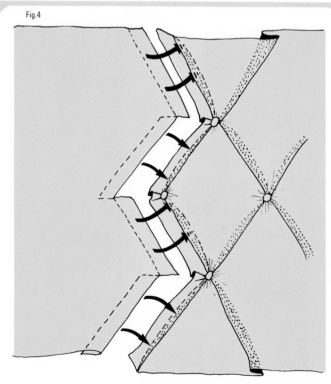

Fig.4

at each alternate intersection (Fig.1). Drill the holes, using a No.8 ($\frac{3}{16}$in.) drill bit.

On the back of the board, hammer a $\frac{5}{8}$in. improved tack halfway in on either side of all the holes.

Preparing the foam

This must be marked out in exactly the same way as for the board. Find the centre of each side and draw lines across the middle to correct the points as before. Working from the middle, draw the rectangles in exactly the same size as those on the board. You will have a wider border on the foam, because it has been cut 1in. larger all round.

Stick the calico strips to the marked side of the foam, and attach it to the board, with the marked side facing out, following the method given on pages 78-81.

Preparing the fabric

This too has to be marked out, but because it will be pulled down at each button, the rectangles should be drawn $\frac{1}{2}$in.–$\frac{3}{4}$in. larger each way. For example, if the vertical lines on the board and foam are $4\frac{1}{4}$in. apart, they should be $4\frac{3}{4}$in.–5in. apart on the fabric.

Cut out both the calico lining and cover fabric to a rectangle on the straight grain, allowing the extra $\frac{1}{2}$in.–$\frac{3}{4}$in. for each row of buttoning on the height and width, as given above, and positioning any pattern centrally.

Place the fabric with the 'wrong' side facing up, mark the centre of each side and draw lines in pencil across the middle as before. Draw the rectangles to the larger size, and put in crosses to indicate where the buttons are to go (remember that this will be reversed, because the fabric has the wrong side towards you). Mark the calico lining in the same way.

Attaching the lining

Lay out the board with the foam facing up and the top of the board furthest away from you. Put on the calico lining with the marked side down and match the centre to the centre of the foam. Make absolutely sure that the grain of the calico is straight because if it is even slightly distorted, the buttoning will be spoiled.

Cut off about 11in. of twine and thread one end into the needle. Starting at the centre, pass the needle and twine through the calico and foam to the back of the board, so that it comes out through the hole. As soon as one end of the twine is through, unthread the needle and withdraw it completely, leaving the twine with one end on each side of the bedhead. Wind the end which has been pulled through round one of the tacks and tie it. Hammer the tack down.

Go back to the front of the board and thread the needle with the end of twine still on that side. Re-insert it into the foam about $\frac{1}{4}$in. from the last place and pull out through the same hole at the back of the board. Pull quite tightly, so that the foam is compressed, but be careful not to pull so hard that the twine breaks through the fabric. Wind this end round the other tack, tie tightly and hammer the tack down (Fig.2).

Thread the needle with another length of twine and insert it into the fabric in the next button position below the one already done. (You can easily see where the needle has to go

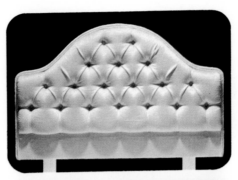

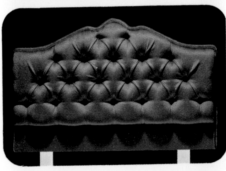

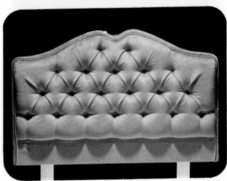

ROYAL PRIDE

Above. *The basic shape of the headboard should be simple with gentle curves, but this still gives scope for variety. The mattress fits against the unpadded section at the bottom.*

by lifting the fabric so that you can see the marks.) Then put the needle into the correponding position in the foam and pull through, as before. Finish the whole process, and then repeat it for the two button positions on each side, thus completing the diamond shape.

You will now see that there is fullness between each point of the diamond. This is neatened by forming it into pleats, all of which must face down, with the extra fabric tucked under and pointing to the top (Fig.3). You will probably find it easiest if you use a special tool called a regulator, or failing that, a spoon handle, to form the pleats, rather than your fingers.

Continue working from the centre outwards in this way, forming one complete diamond at a time before moving on to the next one. When all the button positions are formed, the fullness which will have come round the edge can be neatened into pleats. Make them so that they lie facing outwards from the centre top and, therefore, downwards on the sides.

Smooth the edges of the fabric on to the back of the board, but without pulling it so tightly that you lose any pleats, and tack down with the $\frac{3}{8}$in. fine tacks.

Attaching the main cover

This is put on in exactly the same way as the calico lining, the only difference being that the $\frac{5}{8}$in. tacks should be placed above and below the holes. Before re-threading the needle, a button should be slipped on to the twine so that this can be pulled into place.

To cover the unpadded section at the foot of the board, cut a piece of wadding 2in. wider and 1in. deeper than the area. Tack it on, wrapping it round to the back of the board at the sides and bottom.

Cut a piece of cover fabric of the same width but 1 in. deeper than the wadding. Back tack it along the top edge as explained on page 81, so that you cover the raw edge and tacks of the buttoned fabric, and wrap the sides and bottom edge round the back of the board and tack down neatly.

Finishing off

The back of the board should be finished with wadding and lining in the same way as for the fitted cover on pages 78-81.

Vandyking

In this method of joining the fabric, no sewing is actually done, because the fabric is cut in a zig-zag shape so that the edges can be concealed under the pleats of the diamonds. The fabric is held in place by the buttons.

Although you may not have to make any joins in the calico lining, as this is available in such wide widths, it is a good idea to make one in any case because it will be good practice and may avoid a disaster on the outer cover.

Start buttoning with a full fabric width, working from the middle of the headboard out to the sides, as in the method given above. When you have done as many rows as possible with this width, trim off any excess fabric at the sides to within $\frac{1}{2}$in. of the folds, following the zig-zag shape line of the diamond shape.

Lay the second width on to the part still to be covered, so that the grain of the fabric is absolutely square and with the edge overlapping the centre of the last diamonds made by about $\frac{1}{2}$in. Try to match the pattern as far as possible. Cut this edge in a zig-zag pattern like the other one, and clip into the angles for $\frac{1}{2}$in.

Fold under the edges on the sides which come at the top of each diamond on the new piece for $\frac{1}{2}$in., and lay them over the top edges of the last diamonds of the first piece, so that the folds are quite level. Tuck the edges of the sides which come at the bottom of the diamond on the new piece under the folds at the bottom of those in the first piece.

Continental quilts

A Continental quilt is really an extra large eiderdown which takes the place of the traditional bedclothes of upper sheet, blankets and standard quilt. The weight difference is considerable — bedding with wool blankets can weigh as much as 20lb whereas most Continental quilts weigh about 3½lb-4lb.

Instead of forming a tent round the body as do normal bedclothes, the quilt drapes round it and it is not tucked in at the sides. Because of the filling which insulates the body, it is just as warm in winter, yet cool enough in all but very hot or humid weather. You still use a bottom sheet and pillows but, instead of a top sheet, the quilt should have a removable cover which can be washed. You can make the bed very quickly—you simply smooth the bottom sheet, plump the quilt and smooth it down, before putting on a bedspread. Because of its bulk, a throwover bedspread usually looks better than a fitted one.

Down—the undercoat of waterfowl—is the traditional filling for Continental quilts but, because of the difficulty in separating it from feathers, it is very expensive. It is more usual for a proportion of feathers to be left with the down, and fillings described as 'down and feathers' should contain 51 per cent or more of down, and those described as 'feathers and down' may be mostly feathers but must contain at least 15 per cent of down. Down is much lighter than feathers and only 30oz of pure down is needed for a single-sized quilt, as compared with 2½lb if using a down and feather mixture, or 3lb for feathers and down.

The snag about using down and feathers for making your quilt is that they are not readily available, and they are not easy to handle. The filling from an old eiderdown may be used, but often this is inadvisable because they become less efficient at a rate of about one per cent a year (usually because of dust percolating through the cover). If you do use an old eiderdown, it is worth buying some extra filling to mix with the old, and bulk it up to the required amount. Quilts made with this filling cannot be washed.

Another snag about using down and feathers is that the primary cover must be made from downproof cambric to prevent the filling from escaping and dust filtering through (feather-proof ticking is not good enough). Because this is usually available in a 48in. width only, the cover has to be pieced to make up the total size.

The primary cover may be made like a simple bag and divided into channels down its length by stitching the sides of the bag together or alternatively—and this is the method used professionally because more filling can be inserted—the bag is divided by fabric partitions which are inserted in seams down its length. This is tricky and tedious to do at home, and it is worth buying the bag ready made if possible.

Terylene fibre filling, of the type known as P3, makes an excellent filling for home-made Continental quilts because it is light, washable, readily obtainable and not difficult to work with. It is cheaper than down and feathers, also better for hay-fever sufferers. It is sold in large sheets, sandwiched between muslin, and looks like thick cotton wool. The measurements of the wadding sheet should be slightly larger than the finished quilt. The fabric used for the primary cover may be a closely woven sheeting in cotton, cotton/Terylene or a cotton/polyester mixture. These are sold in 70in. and 90in. widths.

Calculating the amount of fabric

The finished quilt should be at least the same length as your bed, and at least 18in. wider. A good size for a single quilt is 54/55in. wide x 78/79in. long, or 78/79in. square for a double quilt. Because these quilts rest simply on top of the bed and are not tucked in at the sides, two single ones are often more comfortable than one large one for a double bed. You should make

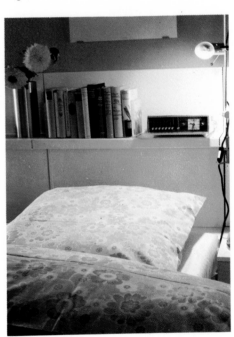

Above. Sheeting made from a cotton/man-made fibre mixture is the best to use for quilt covers because it is crease-resisting.

two types of cover: a primary cover to enclose the filling, and a couple of secondary covers which are the same size and can be taken off for washing.

Making the primary cover
Feather fillings

If you are making your own simple cover from 48in. wide cambric, you may find that it is worth drawing a cutting chart to work out the best way of piecing the fabric to calculate the total amount most economically. Basically, the cover fabric should be twice the length of the quilt, plus 2in. seam allowance x the width of the quilt, plus 1in. seam allowance.

For example, if you are making a single quilt to the size above, you will need about 5½yd cambric. From this you would be able to cut two 80in. lengths and the rest of the fabric can be cut in half from selvedge to selvedge, and then joined along the selvedges which can be trimmed to make a third much narrower length (see Fig.1).

For a double quilt, it would be simplest to allow four times the length because, although there will be some wastage, to cut it more economically would be so complicated as to make it not worthwhile. Too many seams would create weak spots, from which the filling could eventually leak. Alternatively, you could reduce the width of the quilt to just under 6ft and allow only three times the length.

Leaving one end open, join all the pieces to make a case the size of the quilt. Take ½in. plain seams, allowing at least 12 stitches per inch, and make a second line of stitching ⅛in. outside the first for extra strength. Press all the seams and turn the case 'right' side out. Turn under and press down the seam allowance along the opening (Figs.2 and 3).

Mark evenly spaced —between 9-12in. apart —parallel lines down the length of the case. Pin and then machine stitch the sides of the case together down these lines to divide it into channels (Fig.3).

When you fill the case, allow at least an hour without interruption. Work in a place which is small, uncluttered and draught-free, such as the bathroom. Close the windows and remove anything to which the filling might cling. Have handy your needles, thread, scissors and some clothes pegs or bulldog clips. It is also advisable to cover your hair and, if you suffer from hay fever, your nose and mouth.

Place the bag of filling in a larger, stout polythene bag to catch any spills, and slit the top of the bag. Place a handful of filling in the first channel of the case and close the opening with a clothes peg or clip. Shake the case vigorously to move the filling to the other end of the bag. Repeat this procedure for the other channels. When all the channels have had one handful of filling, start again in the same way, until the filling has been distributed evenly. Machine stitch the opening together, with two rows of stitching as before.

If you are transferring the filling from an old eiderdown, slit open one quilted division at a time and transfer the filling to the new case, putting one handful in each channel. Clear each section of the old quilt before you slit open the next. If you are mixing it with new filling, alternate the handfuls of old and new filling and shake the case thoroughly to mix them.

Terylene filling

Use the 90in. wide sheeting for both sizes of case because, although you can use the 70in. width for the single size, there is more wastage than if you use the 90in. 'sideways' on for the length of the quilt.

Cut out two pieces of fabric, both equal in width and length to the finished quilt, plus 1in. seam allowance. Place newspaper on the floor if it is carpeted, lay out one of the cover pieces 'wrong' side up and completely flat, and place the Terylene wadding on top of it. Bulk up the wadding slightly so that its edges, and those of the muslin 'sandwiching' it, are flush with those of the fabric, and pin the wadding to the fabric. Tack it loosely and then machine stitch, allowing at least 12 stitches per inch (Fig.4).

Below. *If you use a patterned fabric for your quilt covers, buy some extra to make pillow cases which will co-ordinate the effect.*

Pin the 'right' side of the other cover piece to the sheet side of the wadded piece and stitch them together round the edge, leaving an opening on one side. Turn the case 'right' side out and close it with machine stitching (Fig.5).

Measuring in from one long side, use pencil or tailor's chalk to mark the stitching line down the length of the case in panels of 9-12in. wide. Using 5 stitches per inch, machine or backstitch the panels through all the thicknesses.

Secondary cover

These may be made from sheeting (old 'redundant' sheets are ideal), or any easily washable, and preferably drip dry, fabric. The basic dimensions of the case are the same as the primary cover but, to allow enough fabric to make the pocket to enclose the quilt at the opening end (as for a pillow case), add 10-18in. to the length of one of the sides of the cases. (The exact amount for the pocket can be determined by the width or length of the fabric being used—if using 90in. fabric 'sideways' on,

the pocket would be about 10in. deep.) If you also want to add a flap to the cover which may be tucked in at the foot of the bed to anchor the quilt in position and prevent it from riding up, add the same amount to the length of the other side of the case.

Cut out the sides for the cover, including a seam allowance of $\frac{1}{4}$in. all round on one piece and of $\frac{3}{4}$in. all round on the other. Make narrow hems along the bottom edge of both pieces if the edges are raw and then turn down the remaining amount allowed for the pocket on the narrower piece. Press down $\frac{1}{4}$in. turnings on to the right side of the other three sides of the wider piece. With right sides together, place the narrower piece on this one, so there is a $\frac{1}{2}$in. margin showing on the side and top edge (Fig.7). Fold the margin over the narrow piece and stitch through all thicknesses. Repeat this along the sides, and continue this mock French seam in the form of a hem along the sides of the flap (Fig.8). Press the seams and turn the case right side out.

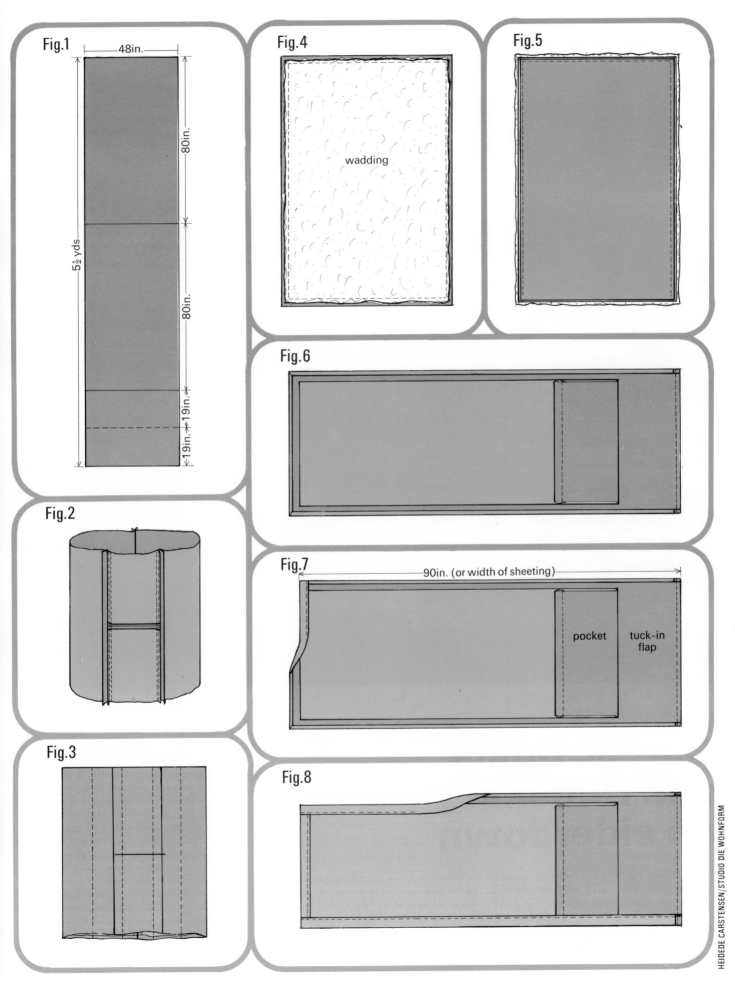

Fig.1

48in.

5½ yds

80in.

80in.

19in. 19in.

Fig.2

Fig.3

Fig.4

wadding

Fig.5

Fig.6

Fig.7

90in. (or width of sheeting)

pocket

tuck-in flap

Fig.8

HEIDEDE CARSTENSEN/STUDIO DIE WOHNFORM

Classic quilts and remaking an eiderdown

If you haven't been converted to using a Continental quilt and still prefer the traditional sheets and blankets, a good old-fashioned quilt is probably an essential addition in cold weather. You can make one much more cheaply than they cost to buy—and you can choose the fabric, size and weight of filling.

Making a quilt is much easier than it used to be because of the development of Terylene wadding. This looks like cotton wool and is sold in sheet form in different sizes and weights. In the old method of making a quilt, the cover was made up and divided into pockets which were stuffed with down. This was a difficult job, because down is very light and flies away.

Above. A large, puffy quilt is ideal for a chilly night! With Terylene filling you do not need quilting stitching to hold the layers together which tends to give a formal look.

Terylene wadding, however, is simply sandwiched between the two sides of the cover. For a traditional looking quilt, the three layers can be held together by quilting stitching or tying. Or you can leave it unstitched for a bulky, 'puffy' quilt. The composition of the Terylene is such that as long as it is held by the outer seams, it does not actually need quilting to hold it in place.

A quilt made with Terylene weighs about the same as one filled with pure down, or it may be lighter than one filled with a mixture of down and feathers. Other advantages of Terylene are that it does not need a special inner cover to prevent the filling from leaking, as do feathers; it can be washed in a machine and it

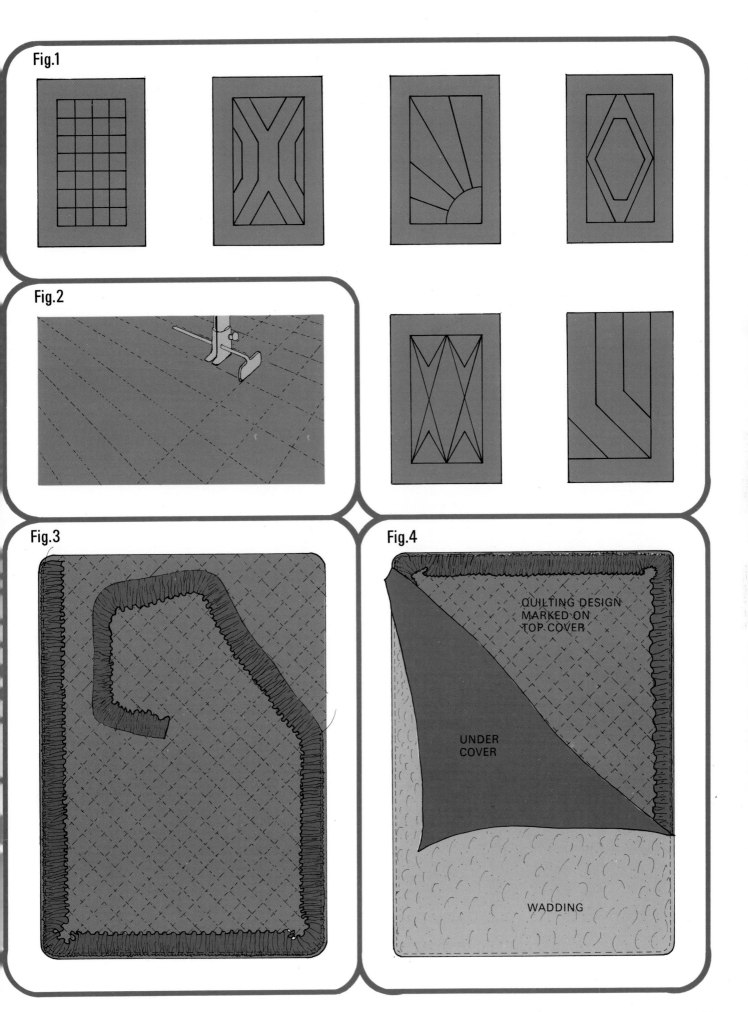

Fig.1

Fig.2

Fig.3

Fig.4

QUILTING DESIGN MARKED ON TOP COVER

UNDER COVER

WADDING

should not affect hay fever sufferers. It is also more readily obtainable than down in most places.

Calculating the amount of fabric

Make the quilt the same width, or slightly narrower, than your bed and long enough to reach from the foot to within 2-3in. of the pillows. Choose cover fabric which is lightweight and preferably crease resisting and drip dry, but not slippery if you also want to use it on the underside of the quilt. Alternatively, the underside could be covered in a fabric like brushed nylon.

For each side of the quilt, allow enough fabric to cut a panel the same size as the Terylene sheet. Allow extra if you want a piped edging. Dress fabric which is 36in. wide is ideal for both single (3ft wide) and double (4ft 6in. wide) quilts. It can be used full width for the single quilt because, although you will lose 1in. from the width in turnings, this can be made up by the edging. On a double quilt it is the right width for the centre panel (to make up the full width strips are joined to each side to form a border—see page 94).

Although 48in. wide furnishing fabric can be used, it is more wasteful because fabric would have to be trimmed off for both sizes of quilt. This can be used for the edging, particularly a frilled one because with piping made from bias strips it would need several joins.

Choosing the quilting design

Designing a quilt used to be a craft practised on a scale similar to patchwork and, like patchwork, it originated from a necessity to be thrifty. Old, worn blankets, knitted clothes, even raw wool which could not be spun, would be saved and stitched between two pieces of fabric and held in place by all-over hand stitching.

Gradually the craft became an art, and beautiful quilting designs—often made up with traditional emblems and symbols—were incorporated. For convenience of working, the fabric was stretched over a frame and the whole family would take turns at stitching. The finished quilting was used for warm clothing and bedding.

Nowadays, a lot of quilting is done by sewing machine and, although most modern machines can be adjusted to move freely enough to stitch curves and other shapes, the patterns tend to be limited in their design. The most common machine quilting is like a grid, made up from squares, diamonds or ogees (linked lozenges). Once the lines of the quilting have been marked, the actual stitching is easy and quick. Fig.1 shows some variations on straight stitching.

One way of giving a lift to this basic quilting is to use a fabric printed with a geometric or regular repeat design. The stitching of the quilting can be done following the lines of the design to extremely good effect.

Marking out the design

Some sewing machines have a special attachment which can be used for quilting regularly spaced straight lines, and all you have to do is mark the first line. When the quilt is made up, you stitch the first line, decide how far apart the next lines should be and place the work in the machine as if to start stitching the second line. The attachment is then set at the side of the machine foot so that it runs level with the first line. By keeping it level as you stitch, the second and subsequent lines will be straight and evenly spaced (Fig.2).

If you have no such attachment, the lines can be marked by using a straight edge or template and tailors' chalk or a dressmaker's tracing wheel and special transfer paper sold with it. The marks made usually brush out easily. Or for a more intricate design you could use an embroidery transfer which is ironed on to the fabric.

Making the quilt

Cut out the fabric to the same size as the Terylene, joining on the borders for a double quilt following the method shown on page 94. Mark the quilting design on the right side of the top cover, leaving a border ½in. wide all round the edge. Make up the piping or frilled edging (see below), and attach it to the top cover so that the stitching is ½in. from the edge (Fig.3).

Next, pin the Terylene to the wrong side of the under cover so that all the edges are level and tack all round. With the right sides of the fabric together, stitch the top cover to the under cover and Terylene on three sides only, taking ½in. turning. Turn the quilt right side out, poke out the corners with a pencil and press round the edges carefully. Turn in ½in. on the fourth side and stitch firmly together to close the opening (Fig.4).

Doing the quilting

To prevent the fabric from puckering and slipping during the stitching, tack the layers together using long stitches and placing the rows about 6in. apart across the work in both directions. Start each row from the same side as an extra precaution against puckering.

For the quilting, use regular sewing thread but with your sewing machine set with a fairly long stitch and fitted with a hinged foot. Place the quilt in the machine with the right side uppermost, and start and finish each line of stitching as close to the edging as possible. Stitch slowly, smoothing out the fabric as you progress. Secure the ends with a few reverse stitches or by taking the threads to the underside and knotting them together.

Tying the layers together

As an alternative to quilting, the layers can be tied or knotted together. This is quicker than stitching rows, and is much easier if the wadding is so thick that machine stitching is not practical.

Tack the layers together in the same way as for quilting. Mark out the position for the knots, spacing them in rows 4-6in. across the quilt in both directions.

To make the knots, spread the work out on your work surface so that it is completely flat and with the underside facing up. Using strong thread and a long needle, make a small stitch through the three layers. Pull the thread through, leaving an end about 2in. long. Make a back stitch, inserting and withdrawing the needle in the same places as the first stitch, and draw up the thread firmly but not so tightly that the fabric puckers. Knot the ends of the thread together in a reef knot, pull them tightly and cut off ¼in. from the knot.

Making a frilled edging

Cut out and join enough 3in. wide strips of fabric to make one circular piece equal in length to twice the perimeter of the quilt. Fold the strip in half lengthwise and press it.

Put marks in the raw edges of the frill to indicate where the corners of the quilt will fall (each section is twice the length of the quilt's sides) and mark the centre of each section. Mark the centre of each side of the top cover.

Insert a gathering thread ½in. in from the raw edges of the frill (do this in sections to avoid breaking the thread when it is pulled up). Place the frill on to the top cover with raw edges level and with section and centre points matching. Pin the frill at these points, placing the pins at right angles to the edge.

Pull up the gathering threads to make the frill fit the cover, and distribute the gathers evenly. Secure the gathering threads by winding them round the divisional pins. Place the other pins at right angles, so any slight adjustments to the gathers can be made easily. Tack and machine stitch the frill to the cover, then remove the gathering threads.

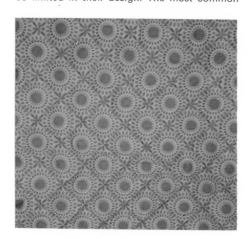

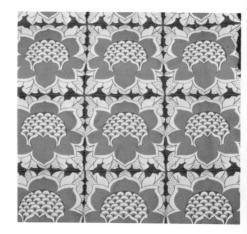

Left and right. Quilting stitching done in straight lines only may seem unimaginative, but with a sewing machine it is far easier than stitching intricate curves. It can also look very effective if the stitching follows the lines of the fabric's pattern.

The filling of an eiderdown—a down-filled quilt—loses efficiency at the rate of about 1 per cent a year. Its cover will need to be replaced more quickly, but it is no good simply putting the new fabric over the old because this will make it too bulky. You should remove the old one first—which can be more tricky since you don't want to lose the filling at the same time!

If you suspect the feather filling of the quilt is leaking, for the top side of the new cover use fabric which is light and downproof, such as a good quality sateen or cambric. Alternatively, use any lightweight fabric and interline it with downproof fabric. Do not use a heavy furnishing fabric, even if it matches your other furnishing, because it will crush the feathers and impair rhe quilt's insulating qualities.

For the underside of the cover, use a down-proof cambric or sateen because this will both prevent leaks and stop the quilt from sliding off the bed.

With 48in. wide fabric, you will need 2yd for each side of the cover for a 5ft–5ft 4in. long single quilt, or 4yd for a double quilt. Allow about ½yd extra for a piped edging.

Preparing the old quilt

Most quilts are made with an inner, down-proof cover and an outer, decorative cover. Usually the outer cover covers both sides of the quilt, but sometimes it may just be on the top side. The purpose of the stitching on the quilt is functional as well as decorative because it divides it into pockets for the filling, which trap the air and make the quilt warm. It is important to keep these pockets intact when re-covering the quilt, and even if you do not like the design, you should modify it rather than actually altering it. Never unpick any of the stitching to change the design because the filling can leak through the holes which are left.

To prepare the quilt for its new cover, start by stripping off the old outer cover from the top. This is most easily done by cutting away the outer fabric as close as possible to the quilting stitching. Any remaining fabric caught by the stitching can then be pulled away. If you accidently snip the inner cover, immediately iron on pieces of adhesive tape or even dressmaker's bonded stiffening, and restitch any broken stitches with close, firm tacking.

If the outer cover extends to the underside, cut this off too. Then cut away the edging.

Replenishing the filling

The easiest way of bulking up the filling if it has become a little thin is to unpick some of the stitching surrounding the centre pocket and push a little filling into it from the next pocket. Replace the stitching with small, firm tacking and bulk up the next pockets in the same way.

To fill the depleted outside border pocket, unpick 2-3in. of the edge seam and push in new feathers by the handful. Stitch up the opening firmly. Alternatively, convert a double quilt into a single one by cutting off the border after the feathers have been transferred to the inner pockets. Stitch round the new outside edge firmly before cutting.

Re-covering a single quilt

Cut out the fabric for the top and bottom pieces to the size of the quilt, plus 4in. each way to allow for turnings and the bulk of the filling.

Mark the centre point of the quilt on both sides and lay it out flat on your work surface with the top side facing up. Fold the cover fabric in four to find the centre, then lay it on the quilt with the 'right' side facing up and centre points matching.

Working from the middle out to the sides, smooth the fabric lightly over the quilt, moulding it to the shape of the quilting. Pin the fabric to the quilt in several places to secure it, then pin it completely following the stitched lines of the quilting exactly. Try to keep the fabric straight on the quilt, without pulling it too tightly. Tack the fabric to the quilt along all the pin lines and then mark the outer stitching line by tacking the outline of the quilt on the cover fabric. (But do not actually tack the edge of the quilt to the fabric.)

Prepare the new piping or edging and tack this to the fabric so that the stitching line of the piping falls on the tacked outline. Place the bottom cover 'right' side down on to the top cover so that the edges match, and tack and machine stitch them together along three sides on the previous stitching line, still leaving the quilt unattached to the cover fabric at the edges. Machine stitch the piping to the top cover along the fourth side.

Trim off the excess fabric on the turnings and turn the quilt right side out. Turn in the edge of the bottom cover and stitch the opening together along the piping line.

Smooth the bottom cover over the quilt, and pin and tack along the quilting lines as for the upper side. This process may seem tedious, but it will prevent the bottom cover from puckering and pleating when the quilting is machine stitched.

With the right side uppermost, and working slowly from the outside to the middle, machine stitch along the tacked lines. If you want to modify the design, simply omit some of the lines. Remove all the tacking.

Below. *If you put your quilt on top of the bedspread, cover it in fabric to match.*

SANDERSONS

Re-covering a double quilt

This is done in much the same way as for a single quilt, but because 48in. fabric is too narrow it will look best if the main piece of fabric is cut to fit the inner section of the quilt, and strips of fabric are joined on all round to make the border pocket.

Cut the fabric for the main piece, allowing an extra 4in. each way for turning and bulk. Pin it to the quilt as for the single quilt. Without catching the edges of the fabric to the quilt, tack the stitching line of the border round the edge of the fabric. Cut two strips of top cover fabric the length of the quilt x the width of the border plus 1in. each way. Cut two more strips the width of the quilt x the width of the border plus 1in. each way. Cut strips of the bottom cover fabric to the same sizes.

Mark the centre on both long edges of all the border pieces and on each side of the main piece. With right sides together and centre points matching, pin the border strips to the corresponding edges of the main piece and join along the stitching line, beginning and finishing each seam at the stitching of the adjacent side.

To mitre the corners of the border, fold over one top corner of the quilt diagonally so that the right sides are together and the top edge is flush with the side (Fig.3). Working on a line from the inner corner of the border (point X) to the outer corner (point Y), pin and stitch the top border to the side border. Repeat this at the other three corners, then machine stitch carefully, so that the stitching exactly meets the seam lines of the main panel and border, and does not overlap.

(You may find this easier if you unpin the fabric from the quilt.)

Trim off the suplus fabric at the corners and press open the seams. Open out the border and mark the outside edge of the quilt on the cover fabric with tacking. Stitch the piping along this.

Join the border pieces to the main panel of the bottom piece, in the same way, but before tacking it to the quilt. Take care that all the pieces are exactly the same size as the top piece. Attach the whole piece and finish off the stitching as for the single quilt.

Above. Re-covering an eiderdown is not difficult, but you do need patience in marking out the quilting lines.

Fig.1. (below). The new fabric is tacked to the quilt along the original quilting line.
Fig.2. Border strips are added to each side to make up the size of a double quilt.
Fig.3. The easiest way to mitre the border strips is to fold over one side level with an adjacent side. The stitching line (X-Y) is an extension of the diagonal fold.

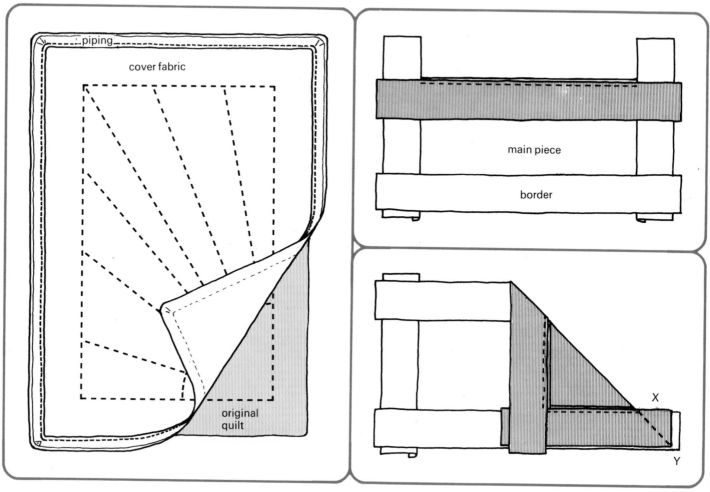

piping

cover fabric

original quilt

main piece

border

X

Y

Simple cushions

Cushions should be decorative as well as functional. Make them in fabrics to match your curtains, to tone with your covers, or to add splashes of colour to an otherwise subdued colour scheme.

Fillings

Cushion fillings fall basically into two types - squashy and firm. Down makes the most luxurious kind of squashy filling, but it is also the most expensive and difficult to obtain. Feathers make a slightly cheaper alternative, and ready-filled pads in different sizes can be bought at departmental stores. If you are able to buy these fillings by the lb (usually from poultry farms who will prepare them), $\frac{3}{4}$lb down, or 1-1$\frac{1}{4}$lb mixed feathers and down, or 2lb

feathers, are enough for a cushion to be 18in. square when finished.

Kapok, a buff-coloured, vegetable fibre, is cheaper still and very easy to obtain. It tends to go lumpy after a while, but it is ideal for garden cushions as it does not absorb moisture. Terylene, a white, man-made fibre filling, is also fairly inexpensive, and is non-absorbent and washable. One pound of either kapok or Terylene fibre is enough for a 18-20in. square cushion.

For firmer cushions, latex and plastic foam foundations can be bought in a variety of shapes and sizes. They are ideal because they never lose

Below. *A pile of cushions, picking out colours of the bedspread, offset an unusual bedhead.*

their shape and are clean, light and almost indestructible. Latex or plastic foam chips are also easily obtainable and cheap, and they have most of the properties of pads, but the finished cushion is squashier and the surface not quite as smooth.

Making the inner case

Squashy cushions. If using down for the filling, make the inner case from downproof cambric, as used for down quilts, because this has a particularly close weave. If using feathers, buy plain (not striped) featherproof ticking, such as is used for pillows. Calico, sheeting, or cambric can be used for foam chippings, kapok or Terylene fibre, as there is no danger of these fillings breaking through the case, as would feathers and down.

With any of the 'loose' fillings, the inner case should be $\frac{1}{2}$in. larger all round than the outer cover. This ensures that the cushion looks well filled and that the corners are kept in shape.

When cutting the inner case for an 18in. square cushion, for example, the pieces should be 19$\frac{1}{2}$ inches square, allowing $\frac{1}{2}$in. for each seam. Machine stitch the pieces together on three sides, leaving an opening about 4-6in. long on the fourth side. Turn the case inside out and press it.

Stuff the case with the filling, making sure the corners are well padded but without cramming it too full, which would make it hard. (It is advisable to wear a large apron for this process.)

Sew up the opening securely by hand.

Firm cushions. Use a light-weight fabric for the inner case. Add on only ½in. seam allowance all round to the finished measurement of the cushion when cutting out the case, as it should fit the pad exactly. Make the case as above, but leave a larger opening in order to insert the pad easily.

Making the outer cover

Materials. For cushions up to 17in. square, you can cut both sides of the outer cover from the width of 36in. fabric, so for each cover buy a length equal to the measurement of one side of the cushion, plus 1in. for seams. For larger cushions, you will have to double this amount (any wastage can be used for cutting bias strips for piping). With 48in. fabric, covers up to 23in. can be cut from the width. In both cases you will need extra fabric if the pattern is large, in order to position the design centrally on both sides of the cushion.

If the cover is to have a piped edge, buy four

Cut two square pieces of fabric, each side of which is 1in. longer than the finished size of the cushion (Fig.1 shows the cutting plan for an 18in. cushion from 48in. fabric. Fig.2 shows the same size cushion being cut from 36in. fabric).

From the leftover fabric, cut bias strips 1¼in. wide for the casing if using piping, and join the strips (for instructions on making bias strip casing, see below).

Lay the piping cord centrally along the wrong side of the casing and fold the casing over the cord so the raw edges are level. Tack the casing together firmly, as close to the cord as possible, to within 2in. of each end. Pin the casing all round the 'right' side of the cushion top, so the piped edge faces in and the raw edges are flush with those of the cover. Clip ½in. into the outer edges of the casing at the corners of the cover to ease the piping round and make it lie flat (Fig.3). Tack in position to within 2in. of the ends. Join the casing and piping cord (see instructions below).

Place one half of the zip, wrong side up,

cover (this gives the corners a good shape).

Pin and tack the other half of the zip (wrong side up) centrally to the 'right' side of the cushion back, and machine stitch close to the teeth (diagram 5). Remove the tacking.

With the 'right' sides of the cover facing, tack the pieces together (leaving the zip open), and machine stitch over the previous stitch line of the piping. Neaten the raw edges, and finish off the ends of the zip by stitching them together securely. Press the cover, turn it right side out and press again.

If not making a piped edge, attach the zip to the cover in the same way, and stitch the sides of the cover together. The zip can be inserted like a dress zip, after the sides have been joined, but by doing it first no stitching shows on the outside of the cover.

Making a bias strip casing

Casings for piping should always be cut on the bias grain of the fabric (diagonally to the selvedge and crosswise threads), as this has a

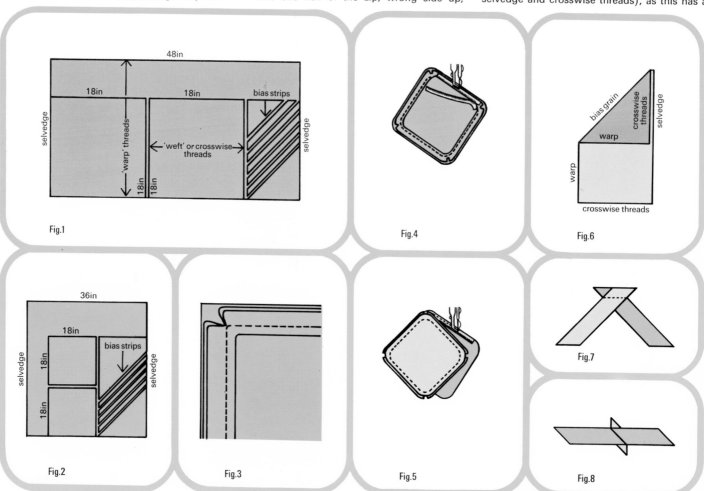

Fig.1

Fig.2

Fig.3

Fig.4

Fig.5

Fig.6

Fig.7

Fig.8

times the length of one side of the cushion, plus 1in., of No. 2 (⅛in. diameter) piping cord. If the cord is cotton, buy extra and pre-shrink it by boiling and drying it before cutting off the length you need.

A zipped opening is the neatest type for a square cushion cover which will need frequent washing or cleaning. The zip should be 1in. shorter than the length of one side of the cover.

Making up. Cut off the selvedge if this is tight (it would pucker if used as the seam allowance).

centrally on one side of the cushion top, on top of the casing. The outer edge of the zip teeth should be level with the outer edge of the piping, so that the stitching can come close to both the inner edge of the piping and the teeth of the zip. Pin and tack the zip in position.

Fit a piping or zip foot to your sewing machine so that the needle is nearest the piping, and stitch all round the cover as close to the piping as possible (Fig.4). Remove the tacking and trim away the excess fabric at the corners of the

stretching quality which makes the piping 'sit' correctly at corners and around curves. To find the true bias, fold the fabric diagonally as in Fig.6 so that the warp threads (selvedge) lie parallel to the weft (crosswise to the selvedge). Crease this fold without stretching it, and cut along the crease. Use tailors' chalk to mark off strips of the required width from this edge. If necessary, cut the ends of each strip parallel to each other and on the straight grain (either warp or weft – each strip should be a parallelogram).

BRIAN MORRIS

Above. Brightly coloured, comfortable cushions can be the finishing touch to any room.

Fig. 1 (opposite). How to cut 48in. fabric. Fig. 2. How to cut 36in. fabric. Fig. 3. Clipping the casing eases the piping round corners. Figs. 4-5. Stitching the zip to the 'right' sides of the cover. Fig. 6. Folding the fabric on the bias grain. Fig. 7. How to join bias strips. Fig. 8. The protruding corners should be trimmed level with the strip.

Join the strips together with $\frac{1}{4}$in. seam as shown in Fig.7. Press open the seams and trim off the corners that protrude (Fig.8). This method of cutting and joining the strips ensures that the seams lie on the straight grain, and keep the stretch quality. If the stitching comes on the bias, this quality is lost.

Joining piping

After pinning the piping casing in position on the cushion cover, unfold the untacked portions

at both ends and overlap them for $\frac{1}{2}$in., trimming off excess fabric (cut on the straight grain, and parallel to the other edge). Join the strips on the straight grain, as before making sure the casing fits the cover.

Overlap the cord for 1in. and cut off the excess. Unravel 1in. of both ends of the cord and cut 2 strands from one end and one strand from the other. Overlap the remaining ends of the cord and oversew them firmly together. Fold over the casing and tack in position.

97

Boxed cushions

Ready-made covers for boxed cushions —whether for scatter cushions or the larger cushions on armchairs and settees —are expensive and not often available in a wide selection of fabrics, shapes and sizes. Make your own—it is not at all difficult and you will spend a fraction of the amount you would pay to have them made to measure.

The foundation for all these cushion shapes (shown left) may be a soft pad (filled with down and feathers), or a foam biscuit.

Plain square box cushions

For the top and bottom cover pieces, measure the width and length of the pad, and add on ¾in. seam allowance. For the box strip, measure the depth of the pad and add 1in.

If your fabric is wider than twice the total width of the pad, you can cut both sides of the cover from it, so buy an amount equal to the length, plus three times the total depth of the strips. If you can cut only one side from the width, buy double the length of the pad and allow extra if you are not able to cut the box strips from the waste.

If you are having piped edges, for the amount of piping cord and bias-cut casing fabric, measure the perimeter of the pad and double it, allowing an extra 4in. for joining. As a guide to the amount of fabric needed for the casing, 1yd of 48in. wide fabric will make about 28yd of bias strip 1½in. wide.

Making up

Cut out the fabric, on the straight grain and including the seam allowance, for the top and bottom cover pieces. If the fabric has a large motif pattern, position it centrally on both pieces. Next, cut two box strips equal in length to the pad's width, and in width to the pad's depth, including seam allowances. Cut two more box strips of the same width and equal to the length of the pad. For piped edges, cut and join enough bias fabric to make two casings, each 1½in. wide and equal to the length of the pad's perimeter, plus 2in. for joining. (See pages 96-97 for piping details.)

Make one continuous strip by joining all the box strips along their short edges with ½in. plain seams; taper the stitches into the corners ½in. from both ends on each seam (Fig.1).

Attach the piping to the 'right' side of the box strip along both edges, so that the stitching line is ½in. from the edges (Fig.2). With the 'right' sides together, pin one edge of the box strip round the edge of the cover top, positioning the seams of the strip at the corners of the cover (Fig.3). Clip the casing at the corners; the

tapered seams will give enough ease to go round smoothly, so these need not be clipped. Stitch the pieces together and neaten the raw edges if the fabric is likely to fray.

Attach the bottom cover to the other edge of the box strip in a similar way, but leave a large opening in the side which will fall at the bottom of the cushion when it is in position. Turn the cover right side out and press it. Insert the cushion pad and finish the opening either by inserting a zip fastener or by slip stitching the edges together. (These stitches can be unpicked easily for removing the cover for cleaning.)

Round box cushions

For the main cover pieces, measure the diameter of the pad and add on 1in. seam allowance. For the box strip, measure the circumference and depth of the pad and add on 1in. seam allowance to both.

If your fabric is wider than twice the diameter, allow a piece the same length, plus the depth of the box strip including seamage (allow twice the depth if you will have to join pieces to make a strip equal in length to the circumference). For piped edges, allow enough fabric to make two 1½in. wide bias-cut casings equal to the circumference, plus 2in. for joining. If you can cut only one side of the cover from the width of the fabric, allow double the amount and cut the piping casing from the waste.

Making up

Using half the total diameter as the radius, make a paper pattern following the method below. Use this to cut out two circular pieces for the main pieces of the cover. Then cut out (join pieces if necessary) the box strip, making its length equal to the circumference of the pad and its width equal to the total depth .

Make both lengths of piping and, taking ½in. turnings, stitch one to the edge of each of the cover pieces.

With 'right' sides together, pin one edge of the box strip over the piping around the edge of the cover top, taking ½in. turnings. Clip the seam allowance to ease it round smoothly. When the strip fits the circle exactly, join its ends together (Fig.4). Stitch all the seams, then press them. Join the other edge of the strip to the cover bottom, leaving an opening large enough to insert the pad. Press the seams and neaten all raw edges if you intend to wash the cover. Turn the cover right side out and insert the pad. Finish the opening together with a zip fastener or by slip stitching.

Bolster cushions

For the main piece of the cover, measure the length and circumference of the pad and allow

Above. A heap of cushions in different shapes, and picking out the carpet colours, are gay and turn a divan into a comfortable settee.

Right top. Boxed cushions on dining chairs have the two-fold function of adding height and comfort.

Above. Boxed cushions often form part of the upholstery on settees and their covers are made in the same way as for scatter cushions.

a piece of fabric 1 in. longer and 1 in. wider. For *plain ends,* measure the diameter of the pad, add 1 in. and allow a piece of fabric the same length and twice as wide. For *gathered ends,* cut two rectangular strips, both equal to the circumference plus 1 in. in length, and to half the diameter plus 1 in. in width. For piping, you need two lengths of bias-cut casing, both equal to the circumference plus 1 in. for joining.

Making up

Cut out the fabric for the main section of the cover and make it into a tube by joining it along its long sides (Fig.5); leave a large opening in the middle of the seam and insert a zip fastener.

Plain ends. Using half the diameter plus $\frac{1}{2}$in. as the radius, make a paper pattern (see below) and cut out two circular pieces of fabric. Attach the piping around the edges of the circles on the 'right' side. With the 'wrong' side of the tube facing out (and with the zip undone), join the circles to each end, allowing $\frac{1}{2}$in. turning and clipping the edges of the tube to ease them round. Neaten and press the seams and then turn the cover 'right' side out. Insert the cushion pad.

Gathered ends. Cut out the two strips of fabric to the size given above and make each one into a tube by joining it along its short ends with $\frac{1}{2}$in. turnings. Turn over one raw edge for $\frac{1}{2}$in. on each tube and make a line of gathering stitches $\frac{1}{2}$in. from the fold. Attach the piping to the other edge of the tubes (Fig.6) and with 'right' sides together, join these edges to each end of the main tube, taking $\frac{1}{2}$in. seams (Fig.7). Insert the pad and draw up the gathering threads to fit the

ends tightly. Secure the ends and then cover the edges with a large covered button.

Sun 'button' cushions

Measure the cushion pad as for plain round covers. Calculate the measurements of the box strip in the same way. For the centre section of main cover pieces, double the width of the strip (less seam allowance) and subtract this from the diameter of the pad. Add on 1 in. seam allowance to the remaining figure and then, using half this amount as the radius, make a paper pattern and cut out two circular pieces.

Cut out the box strip as for the plain round cover and then cut two more strips of the same size. Make two lengths of piping, both equal in length to the circumference of the cushion, and stitch it to the 'right' side of the box strip along both edges (Fig.8). With the 'right' sides together, join the other strips to each side of the box strip, over the piping (Fig.9), and then make the whole piece into a tube by joining the short ends together (Fig.10).

Trim off $\frac{1}{2}$in. from the outer edge of the paper pattern and use it to cut two more circular pieces from stiffening (use canvas or the dressmakers' bonded kind). Place the stiffening centrally on the wrong side of the fabric circles and turn in the seam allowance on to the stiffening. Clip the edges of the fabric to keep the circles a good shape, and tack the fabric down (Fig.11).

Run a gathering thread $\frac{1}{2}$in. from the edge round both ends of the tube and then insert the cushion pad, positioning it so that its edges are

level with the edges of the box strip. Draw up the gathering threads to fit the pad and secure them (Fig.12).

Pin the prepared circles, 'right side' out, centrally over the raw edges of the gathering and oversew them neatly in position. Then, with a long needle and doubled sewing thread, draw the circles together by working through the cushion, from side to side, and drawing up the thread tightly (Fig.13).

Cutting a fabric circle

Cut a large piece of paper into a square, each side of which is a little longer than the radius (half the diameter) required. Use a pair of compasses set to the radius or tie one end of a piece of string around a pencil and measure the radius from the pencil along the length of string. Mark the measurement by pushing a drawing pin through the string. Lay the paper on a flat surface and push the drawing pin into the top left-hand corner. Hold the pin firmly with the left hand and, with the pencil held upright with the other hand, draw an arc from the top right-hand corner to the bottom left-hand corner. Cut along the pencilled line.

Cut out a square of fabric, each side of which is equal to the diameter. Fold the fabric in half and then in half again, making a square with each side equal to the radius. Pin the paper pattern to the fabric so that its square point is in the corner of the fabric where the folds meet. Cut through the layers of fabric along the curved edge of the pattern only. Do not cut along the folds.

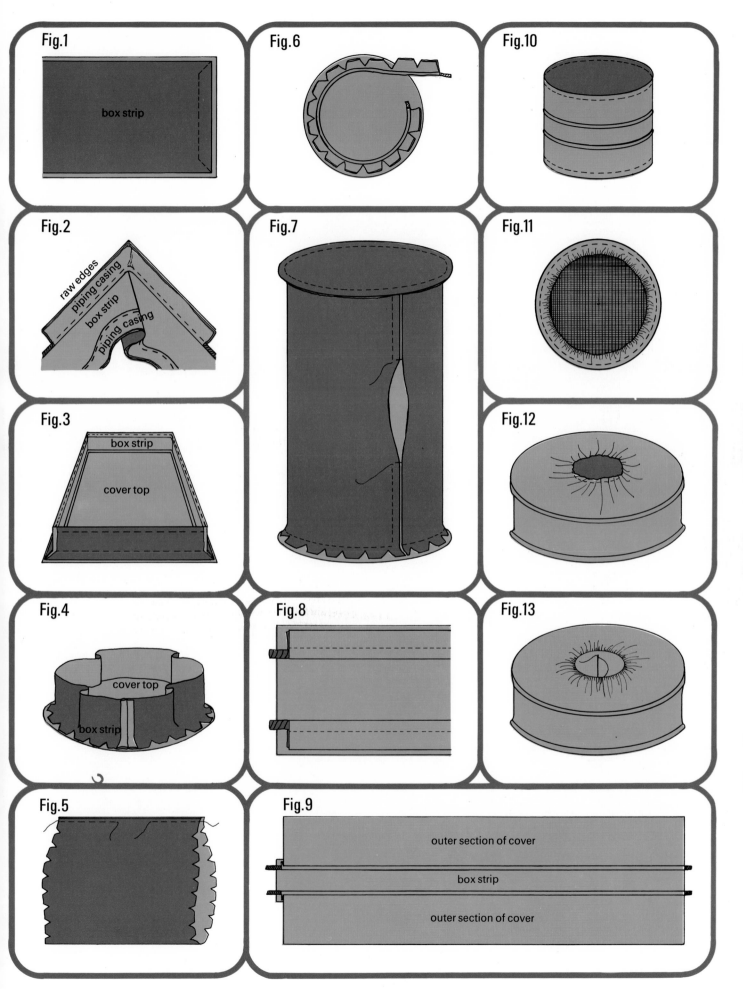

Fig.1

box strip

Fig.2

raw edges
piping casing
box strip
piping casing

Fig.3

box strip

cover top

Fig.4

cover top

box strip

Fig.5

Fig.6

Fig.7

Fig.8

Fig.9

outer section of cover

box strip

outer section of cover

Fig.10

Fig.11

Fig.12

Fig.13

Smocked
cushions

Smocking has long been a favourite method of decorating children's clothes, but it is rarely used for other things. Yet it can be adapted easily to give an unusual finish to curtains and cushion covers.

With traditional smocking, about three times the required width of fabric is used and gathered, in several regular rows, to the correct size. The gathers are then held in place by very simple embroidery which is worked on the 'right' side of the fabric. This gives the finished smocking an elasticity which is ideal for children's clothes, but it is not so suitable for household things.

However, the effect of smocking can be achieved simply by drawing points of fabric together. By this method, only about $1\frac{1}{2}$-2 times the required width of fabric is used. The stitching can be carried out on the 'wrong' side of the fabric, thus giving a pleated finish, or it can be worked on the 'right' side for the more decorative honeycomb smocking.

Choosing the fabric

Most fabrics can be used for smocking, but it stands out best on either plain or checked ones. Velvets and satins are very suitable for cushion covers made with the back smocking method.

For front smocking on square cushions or a curtain heading, cut the fabric about twice the required width, plus an allowance for turnings. No extra fabric, apart from a turnings allowance, need be added to the length. For back smocking, cut a piece of fabric about $1\frac{1}{2}$ times the required width and length, plus an allowance for turnings.

For a back-smocked round cushion, cut a rectangular piece of fabric whose length equals $1\frac{1}{2}$ times the circumference of the cushion and width is $1\frac{1}{2}$ times its diameter plus its thickness. For a bolster, cut a rectangular piece of fabric $1\frac{1}{2}$ times the circumference of the bolster pad x the diameter of one end plus the length of the pad. These measurements for both the round and bolster cushions are generous, so after working three-quarters of the smocking, fit the fabric on to the cushion to check exactly how much more you need to work.

Preparing the fabric

With all but regularly checked fabric, you should mark the points to be joined. This can be done with a printed transfer, which is ironed on to the fabric, or else you can mark the fabric lightly with a pencil. This distance between the points should be the same horizontally and vertically, forming an even grid, and can vary between $\frac{1}{2}$in. and $1\frac{1}{4}$in.

Smocking transfers, called smocking dots, can be bought in varying sizes, but because these are really designed for preparing the fabric for gathered smocking, you may have to adapt them. In some cases, for example, the space between the horizontal dots may be $\frac{3}{8}$in. and between the vertical dots it may be $\frac{1}{2}$in. Since

Left. For really luxurious cushions, try back-smocking on velvet. It gives a stunning effect and is quick and easy to work, especially since the back of the cushion can be left plain.

the difference is only $\frac{1}{8}$in., this will not affect the smocking adversely. If you are not able to buy widely spaced dots, you may have to make do with, say, $\frac{1}{2}$in. spaced ones and use alternate rows.

If you are using checked fabric, let the size of the checks determine the size of the smocking by using the intersections of the lines between colours as a substitute for the dots.

It is always wise to test a small piece of transfer on an offcut of fabric first. Cover your ironing board with paper or an old cloth to protect it and set the iron at medium (wool) temperature. If this temperature is to high for the fabric you are using, put a thin piece of cotton fabric over the paper and iron it.

Place the fabric on the board with the side to be smocked facing up, and put the transfer printed, or rough, side down. Iron over the paper, moving the iron to and fro for a little while to get a good register—be careful not to move the paper while you are ironing or you will have a blurred result. Remove the paper when the dots are transferred to the fabric.

With both methods of smocking, the dots should not show on the finished item, but in any case they will wash out.

Honeycomb front smocking

If you are making a curtain, first make the side and top hems. If you are making a cushion, leave the edges raw.

Iron on the transfer, leaving a margin of about 1in. unmarked all round the edges of the fabric. With the 'right' side of the fabric facing up, start at the first dot in the top right hand corner and work in a straight line across the fabric from right to left.

Using a long length of mercerized crochet cotton or 6 strands of embroidery cotton, knot the end of the thread and make a tiny stitch at the first dot. Pass the thread along the front of the fabric and make another stitch at the second dot. Pull the thread tight, thus drawing the first and second stitches together. Make a small back stitch to secure it. Make another half back stitch to pass the needle through to the back of the fabric on the right-hand side of the stitches (Fig.1).

Keep the needle on the back of the fabric and pull it out at the third dot. Keeping the thread flat between previous stitch and here, make a small back stitch to secure the thread. Then pass the needle along the front of the fabric and make a small stitch at the fourth dot. Pull the thread tight to draw the third and fourth dots together. Secure with back stitches as before, then move on to the next dot. Always keep the thread on the back of the fabric completely flat.

When the first row is finished, start the second row in the same way, but miss out the first dot, so you are joining the second and third dots together, the fourth and fifth and so on. When that row is finished, **work** the third row exactly as for the first. Work all the following rows in the same way, but alternately missing the first and last dots.

When all the rows have been worked, you will find that pleats have automatically formed at the top and bottom. If you are making a cushion cover, pin down the pleats evenly and

tack them in position. Stitch the seams of the cushion with the pleats 'closed'.

Lattice back smocking

If you are making a square or rectangular cushion with smocking covering the whole of one side, iron on the transfer leaving a margin of about 1in. unmarked all round the edges of the fabric.

For a round cushion cover, which is still worked on a rectangular piece of fabric, leave an unmarked margin of about 1in. at the top and bottom, and one equal to half the diameter of the cushion at each side. When on the cushion, the smocked section forms a band round the edge, with pleats on the top and bottom.

With this type of smocking, all the stitches are worked on the 'wrong' side of the fabric in rows from top to bottom. Each line of smocking is worked across three vertical rows of dots. The thread is kept mostly in the middle row, and the dots on each side are pulled in to meet it.

For ease of working, the dots are numbered as shown in Fig.2. It may seen very confusing as you start to work, but after the first few smocked pleats are formed, you will get into the rhythm.

With the 'wrong' side of the fabric facing up, start at dot 1 on the left hand side. Using a long length of buttonhole thread, knot the end and make a small stitch at dot 1. Pass the thread along the fabric and make another small stitch at dot 2 (Fig.4).

Go back to dot 1, make another small stitch over the one already there, and then pull dots 1 and 2 together. Knot them tightly by making a loop of the thread above the stitches and passing the needle under the stitches and through the loop. Be careful as you pass the needle under the stitches not to catch the material, which will show on the right side.

Pass the thread along the fabric to dot 3 and make a small stitch. Keeping the fabric quite flat between dots 1 and 3, make a loop of the thread above dot 3 and slip the needle under the thread between the dots and above the loop to make another knot. Do not draw up the thread between the dots.

Pass the thread along the front of the fabric to dot 4, make a small stitch, go back to dot 3 and make another small stitch Pull dots 3 and 4 together and knot them as for dots 1 and 2. Move down to dot 5 and knot, keeping the fabric flat, as at dot 3. Pick up a small stitch at dot 6 and join it to dot 5 in the same way as before.

Continue down the whole line in this way, picking up a dot on the left, moving down to the next dot in the middle row, and then picking up a dot on the right.

If you want to make a plaited effect, move to the fourth row of dots and work the second line of smocking over the third, fourth and fifth rows, so that it overlaps the first line (Fig.3). For a more ruched effect, move to the fifth row of dots and work over the fourth, fifth and sixth rows (Fig.2).

When all the lines of smocking are complete, you will find that pleats have formed all round the edge. Pin these down evenly and tack them in position, making sure that the opposite sides

CHRIS LEWIS

Above. Gingham is an ideal fabric for smocking because you can use the corners of its checks as the foundation and it automatically forms its own colour pattern.

of the cover are the same length. Straighten out the tucks in the smocking so that no stitches shown on the 'right' side at all, and press very lightly if necessary (Fig.5).

Finish off a square cushion as above.

Finishing off a round cushion

With the 'right' sides facing, pin together the top and bottom edges of the fabric taking a $\frac{1}{2}$in. turning. To check that the ends of the tube fit the circumference of the cushion, turn the tube right side out and insert the cushion so that it lies level with the smocked band. Adjust the seam if it does not fit snugly.

Keeping the cushion inside the tube, measure the fabric from the top edge of the cushion to the edge of the tube. If it is more than the diameter of the cushion plus $\frac{1}{4}$in., trim off the excess. Do the same at the bottom edge.

Turn under the raw edges $\frac{1}{4}$in. and draw them in to the centre of the cushion in deep pleats. You may find this easiest to do if you run a gathering stitch round the edge, taking tiny stitches, on the 'right' side of the fabric and longer stitches on the 'wrong' side. When pulled up, this will form into pleats (Figs.6 and 7). Stitch a button to the centre.

Using gingham

If you are using gingham to form a plaited effect, you will achieve the best colour contrast if you place dot 1 at the bottom right-hand corner of a pure colour square (traditional

gingham is made up of alternating squares of three types—usually plain white, a colour and a blend of both which separates them).

For dot 2, go to the top left-hand corner of the same square. For dot 3, go down to the bottom right-hand corner of the next blend square and for dot 4, go up to the top right-hand corner of the adjoining pure-colour square.

Making an inset panel

To make a cushion with an inset smocked panel, allow 2-3 in. extra above the basic $1\frac{1}{4}$ times the required fabric for the smocking, so you will have a margin for adjustment as the end if necessary.

Leave a wider border unsmocked all round, and work the smocking as above. Pin in the pleat round the edge but do not tack them yet. Mark the position of the seam line on each side of the panel, positioning it so that the finished panel will equal a complete number of squares and the major part of the unsmocked border is outside.

To calculate the width of two of the plain strips which will frame the smocking, subtract the width of the finished smocking (measuring between seam lines) from the required width of the cushion cover and divide by 2. Add 1in. for turnings. The length of the strip is equal to the length of the cover, plus 1in. for turnings ($\frac{1}{2}$in. allowance on each side). Try to cut the strip so that its seam lines correspond with the lines of the check.

Fold under the seam allowance on one long side of the strips and mark the centre points. Mark the centre on each side of the smocked panel and lay the panel flat on your work surface with its 'right' side facing up.

Above. Front honeycomb smocking makes a pretty heading for curtains. Standard pocketed curtain tape can be stitched to the back, but left ungathered, to hang them.

With their 'right' sides also facing up, place the strips on opposite sides of the panel so that the folded edges are level with the seam line of the panel and the centre points match. Pin in position.

Cut two more strips about 2-3in. wider than the first pair and 2-3in. longer than necessary to fit the remaining sides of the panel between the other strips. (The extra fabric is allowed so that you can adjust them if necessary to match the pattern).

Fold under the seam allowance on one long side of both strips and mark the centre points. Place them on to the remaining sides of the panel with the folds level with the seam line, and the centre points matching. If necessary, move the strips sideways to match the pattern with the adjoining strips. If this does not work, you may have to work some more smocking on the extra border you allowed.

When you are satisfied with the matching of the pattern, make any necessary marks along the seam line and at the corners, so you will be able to fit the pieces together again easily, then unpin the borders from the panel completely.

With the 'right' sides facing, repin the shorter borders to the panel, matching at the guide marks. Tack and machine stitch, trim the seam allowance to $\frac{1}{2}$in. and press it on to the border. Pin and stitch the longer border strips, to the panel and the short sides of the other strips. Trim the seam allowance to $\frac{1}{2}$in. and press it on to the border.

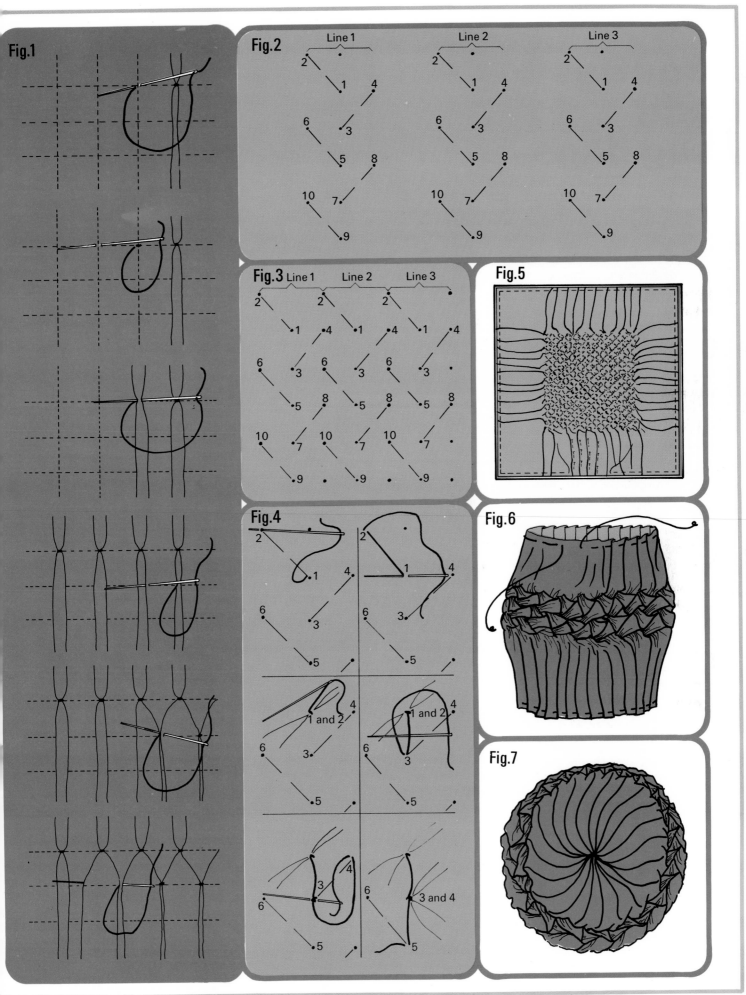

Fig.1

Fig.2

Line 1   Line 2   Line 3

Fig.3   Line 1   Line 2   Line 3

Fig.4

Fig.5

Fig.6

Fig.7

105

Pouffes and sag bags

A pouffe is a useful piece of furniture which can double as a seat, footstool or table. The sag bag is a larger, modern version, with a special filling, and is comfortable enough to sleep on.

The best filling for the traditional 'humpty' pouffe is wood shavings. These should be from machine-planed wood (obtainable from a timber merchant) and should neither be too coarse nor composed entirely of sawdust. Foam chippings can be used, but they are not as cheap as wood shavings and do not make as firm a filling.

There are no standard measurements for this kind of pouffe, but it should not be made too high or it will become lop-sided if it has not been firmly enough stuffed. If the pouffe is made in two sections, and waisted in the middle, a good size is 16in. high and 16-18in. in diameter. If it is in one section only, make it about 1ft high.

Use strong hessian or calico for the inner cover. If making it in two sections, allow enough fabric to cut four circles of the required diameter, including 1in. seam allowance. You will also need to cut two borders, equal in length to the circumference of the circles plus 1in. seam allowance, and equal in width to the height of the sections, plus 1in. seam allowance.

If you are making it in one section, allow enough fabric to cut two circles of the required diameter, plus seam allowance, with one border equal in length to the circumference of the circle, plus 1in. seam allowance, and equal in width to the height of the pouffe, plus 1in.

For the outer cover in both cases, allow enough fabric to cut two circles the same size as those of the inner cover, a border equal in length to the circumference of the circles, and in width to the total height of the pouffe, plus about half a yard for cutting bias strips for making the piping casing. For the amount of piping cord, allow twice the circumference of the circles, plus 6in. for joining. To pad the top of the pouffe, allow enough $\frac{1}{2}$in. thick foam to cut a circle the exact size of the required diameter.

Cutting out and making up

If you have a dinner plate or tray the same size as the required circles (including allowances), use this as a template for making a paper pattern for cutting out the top and bottom pieces. Alternatively, draw a circle following the method described on pages 144-145.

Before joining the short ends of the border, fit one of its long sides round the edge of one circle by pinning. Determine the exact position for the joining seam on the short sides of the border, then unpin the border from the circle and

double stitch the joining seam. Divide the circles and both edges of the border into quarters, and mark the divisions with tailor's tacking.

Pin the border to the circles, matching the division marks. Tack and then machine stitch twice, leaving a large opening on one side (Fig.1). Fit the foam into the circle to come at the top of the pouffe, and then stuff the case with the wood shavings, making it really firm. Stitch up the opening tightly.

If making a waisted pouffe, make the second section in the same way. Place the top section, with the foam side uppermost, on top of the other section and stitch the two together, using strong thread and a circular needle (Fig.2).

Making the outer cover

For one-section pouffes, make the outer cover in the same way as the inner cover, but stitch piping round the edges of the circles before joining on the border. (For details about piping, see pages 95-97). Leave a large opening right along the bottom edge so that the base can be inserted.

The outer cover for two-section pouffes can be made in a similar way, with cord tied round the middle to accentuate its waist. Alternatively —and with this method it is easier to stitch up the opening—cut two borders the same size as for the inner cover. Join them together along one long side, leaving a large opening. Stitch the piping round the edges of the circles and join on the borders (without leaving an opening). Insert the base through the opening in the border, and stitch the seam together firmly. Cover the seam with thick cord.

Making a 'sag bag'

The best filling for the floor-cushion type of pouffe is polystyrene granules. These, if not packed too tightly, move about within the cover, enabling the pouffe to be moulded to different shapes to suit the user. The pouffes can be circular (made following the method for a one-section humpty), or pyramid shaped. This can be used upright, but it is more comfortable with it lying on its side. You will need about 12 cu ft of filling.

To make a hexagon-shaped pyramid, 47in. long and graduating from 18in. high and 36in. wide at the back to 9in. high and 18in. wide at the front, allow $3\frac{1}{2}$yd very strong fabric (use canvas, pvc-coated fabric or imitation leather). Lay out the fabric flat, with the wrong side facing up. Using a ball-point pen and long straight-edge, mark off the sections directly on to the fabric, following the plan in Fig.3.

Cut out two hexagon-shaped paper patterns (see the method on pages 208-211), making the sides of one hexagon 10in. and those of the other 19in. In order to make most economical use of the fabric, cut the paper pattern for the smaller hexagon in half and cut out the fabric for it in two sections, adding on $\frac{1}{2}$in. seam allowance to the sides where the pattern was halved (see Fig.3).

With the 'right' sides of the fabric facing and with all the 10in. sides of the wedge-shaped pieces at one end, paperclip the pieces together along their long sides to make a large open-ended pyramid. Set your sewing machine with a long stitch, reduce the pressure on the presser foot and loosen the tension slightly, then stitch the seams, taking a $\frac{1}{2}$in. seam allowance and using strong thread. Put tissue paper between the fabric and the presser foot if the fabric sticks.

Join the half hexagons together, inserting a long, heavy duty, open-ended, zip fastener into the seam. Fit the 10in. ends of the pyramid round the edges of the smaller hexagon, positioning the seams of the pyramid to the corners of the hexagon. Machine stitch all the seams. Open the zip and join the 19in. sides of the pyramid to the larger hexagon (Fig.4).

Turn the pyramid 'right' side out, poke out the corners with a pencil, and pack with the polystyrene granules. Close the zip fastener. Lay the pouffe out on its side, with the larger hexagon at the back, and try it out for shape and comfort, adding or removing filling if necessary.
Pyramid 'sag bag'

This type of pouffe uses more fabric than the hexagonal one, but it is slightly easier to piece together and is better if you are using 36in. wide fabric. You will need $5\frac{1}{2}$ yds.

Cut out the pieces to the sizes shown in Figs.5 and 6. Cut the pieces for the seat, back and base through the double fabric, as shown. Cut the sides and front band through a single thickness, and dovetail the sides only if you have reversible fabric (otherwise you will end

Left and *opposite page.* The chief characteristic of the sag bag is its filling of tiny polystyrene granules. These should be packed loosely so they can move about inside the cover and enable the pouffe to be moulded to the shape of the user.

BILL MACLAUGHLIN

up with two right-hand sides).

Stitch the pieces together with right sides facing and taking $\frac{1}{2}$in. turnings. If your sewing machine works well with extra strong thread, use this. Otherwise stitch every seam twice with regular thread for maximum strength, and begin and end with 1in. reverse stitching.

Start by joining the 12in. sides of the seat and back, and join the 36in. side of the seat to one long edge of the front band. Then, working from the top down, fit the sharp point of the side pieces into the angle made by the join of the seat and back (Fig.7), and stitch on both sides (leaving the 5in. side free). On the back seam, taper the stitching into the corner $\frac{1}{2}$in. from the bottom. When these seams are finished, check that there is no gap left at the top (through which the filling might escape) and restitch if necessary. Press all seams.

Next, stitch the 5in. edge of the side pieces to the short edges of the front band, tapering the stitching into the corner $\frac{1}{2}$in. from the bottom. Finish off by stitching on the base. Pin and stitch it with the other pieces facing upwards so that you can see where the stitching lines should meet. The tapered seams of the other pieces will open out at the corners of the base, so there is no need to clip them. Leave an opening of 16in. in the back seam and insert a heavy duty zip fastener.

Fill the pouffe with polystyrene granules and try it out for comfort, removing or adding filling as necessary. Make sure that the zip fastener is completely closed.

An inner case is not used for this kind of pouffe because it would be difficult to insert it into the outer case when full, and because you may need to add more filling from time to time as the polystyrene becomes packed down with use. However, it is essential that there should be no gaps in the joins or at the zip through which the filling might escape.

Above left and *left. The cover for a traditional pouffe is made like a boxed cushion but, to make it firm enough for sitting on, the filling should be tightly packed wood shavings.*

Below. The hexagon sag bag can be used lying on its side when it is very comfortable for watching television. Or it can stand on one end to make a high seat.

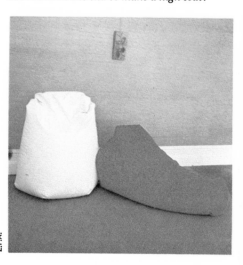

108

Fig.1

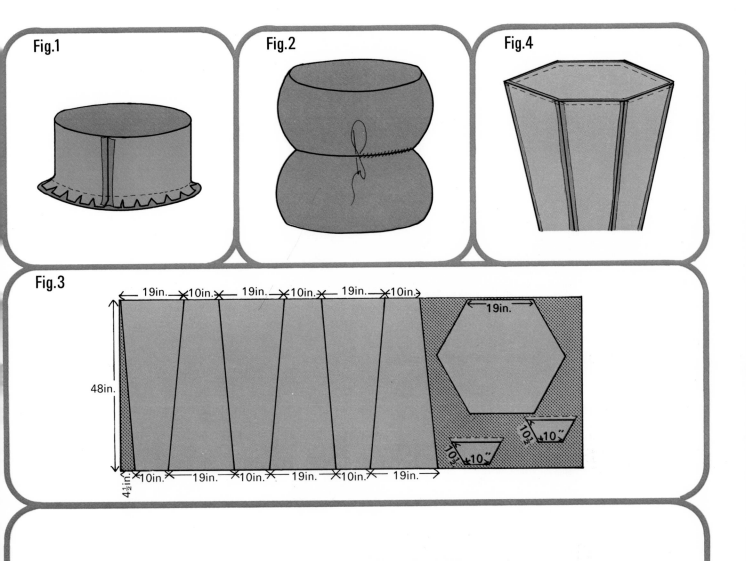

Fig.2

Fig.4

Fig.3

19in. ×10in.× 19in. ×10in.× 19in. ×10in.

48in.

19in.

10½"
10"

10½"
10"

4½in.

10in.× 19in. ×10in.× 19in. ×10in.× 19in.

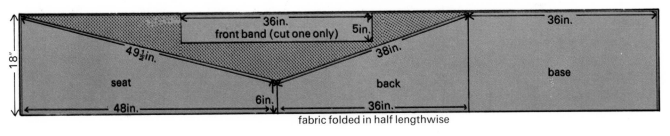

18"

36in.
front band (cut one only)
5in.

49½in.

38in.

36in.

seat

base

back

6in.
48in.
36in.

fabric folded in half lengthwise

Fig.6

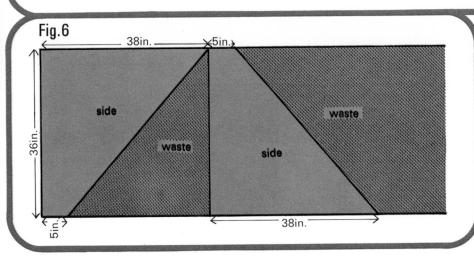

38in. ×5in.×

side

waste

waste

side

36in.

side

5in.

38in.

Fig.7

back

seat

side

Cushions
for kids

Soft cushions in brightly coloured, gaily patterned fabrics can transform a dull playroom into something much more fun. As well as the usual rectangles and circles, try making some different shapes which can then double as extra playthings.

If the cushions are likely to be used as ammunition in pillow fights, it might be a good idea to take the extra precaution of making an inner cover from a strong calico, which should prevent the filling from leaking if the outer cover gets ripped.

Game cushions

For each 11in. cube, you need 23in. of 36in.-wide main fabric and 11½in. of 36in.-wide contrast fabric. Use felt scraps for the motifs.

Cut out four 11½in. squares from the main colour and two 11½in. squares from the contrast fabric. Cut out the playing card motifs or dice circles to the shape shown in Figs.1 and 2 and stick or sew these on to a side of each cube.

Taking ¼in. seam allowance, join the main colour squares to make a circular strip. Taper the stitching into the corners ¼in. from the beginning and end of each seam. With the 'wrong' side of the strip facing out and the 'wrong' side of one of the contrast squares facing up, fit the square to one side of the strip, matching the corners of the square to the seams. Pin and tack in position, taking ¼in. turnings. The tapered seams of the strip will open out as you do this, so there is no need to clip the turnings. Stitch the seams and overcast the edges if the fabric is likely to fray. Press carefully.

Still with the 'wrong' side facing out, turn the strip so that the open end is uppermost. Fit the last square to this side, matching the corners to the seams as before. Stitch, leaving an opening on one side which is large enough for you to insert your hand. Press the seams, then turn the cube 'right' side out. Poke out the corners carefully with a pencil.

Fill the cube really full with foam chippings or Terylene wadding, making sure the corners are a good shape. Oversew the sides of the opening together by hand.

Sunflower cushion

For the centre segment, which is a hexagon with 9½in. sides and 1½in. border, you need ¾yd 36in.-wide fabric. The circle can be cut from a felt scrap. For the other segments, which match the sides of the hexagon and are 6½in. long with 1½in. borders, allow ½yd fabric.

Cut out a paper pattern for the segments, following the chart in Fig.3. Cut the fabric for the centre segment in half lengthwise, and then fold each piece in half lengthwise. Place the paper pattern on to one of the folded pieces so that the side marked with a dotted line is level with the fold. Cut out through the double thickness of fabric. Unpin the pattern, re-pin and cut it out from the other piece of fabric in the same way.

Right. *Playing card motifs can be cut from felt and stuck on to the sides of cubes to make solid cushions. Alternatively you could cut circles and make 'dice' (see Fig.2).*

TRANSWORLD

Above. *Animal cushions can easily be made by using regular shaped cushions for the bodies, with smaller shapes for the arms, legs and tails, which are oversewed to the main cushion. The eyes and noses of the animals can be made from buttons, and the hair and whiskers from wool or string. Use Terylene wadding for the filling because this will give a smoother surface than foam chippings for the small sections of the animals.*

From the remaining fabric cut 6 border strips, 2in. wide x 10in. long. Cut a felt circle to the size given in the chart and stick or stitch this to the centre of one of the hexagons.

Join all the border strips together along the 2in. sides to make one circular strip, taking ¼in. turnings. Taper the stitching into the corners ¼in. from the beginning and end of each seam.

With the 'wrong' side of the strip facing out and the 'wrong' side of one of the hexagons facing up, fit the hexagon into the strip so that the corners match the seams. Pin and stitch them together, taking ¼in. turnings. Press.

Fit the other hexagon to the other side of the strip in the same way, but leave an opening of about 3in. in one side. Press carefully and turn the cushion the 'right' side out, poking out the corners with a pencil. Fill with foam chippings or Terylene wadding, making sure you keep the hexagon a good shape, and oversew the sides of the openings together.

Fold the fabric for the semi-circle segments in half *widthwise* (so that the fold runs along the weft, rather than the warp as usual). In this way you will be able to cut out three pairs across the width of the doubled fabric. Cut three more pairs of semi-circles (making six pairs in all), then use the remaining fabric to cut the border strips. For each segment you will need 1 strip, 2in. wide x 10in. long, and 1 strip 2in. wide x the length of the curved edge (you can measure this with a piece of string).

Join the border pieces for each segment together, taking ¼in. turnings. With the 'wrong' side of the border strip facing out and the 'wrong' side of a semi-circle segment facing up, fit the semi-circle into the strip, matching the corners to the seams.

Pin and stitch the pieces together, taking

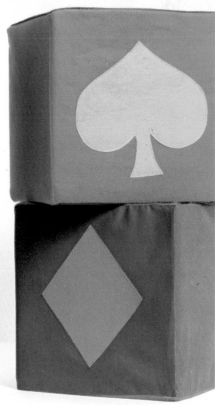

PAF INTERNATIONAL

111

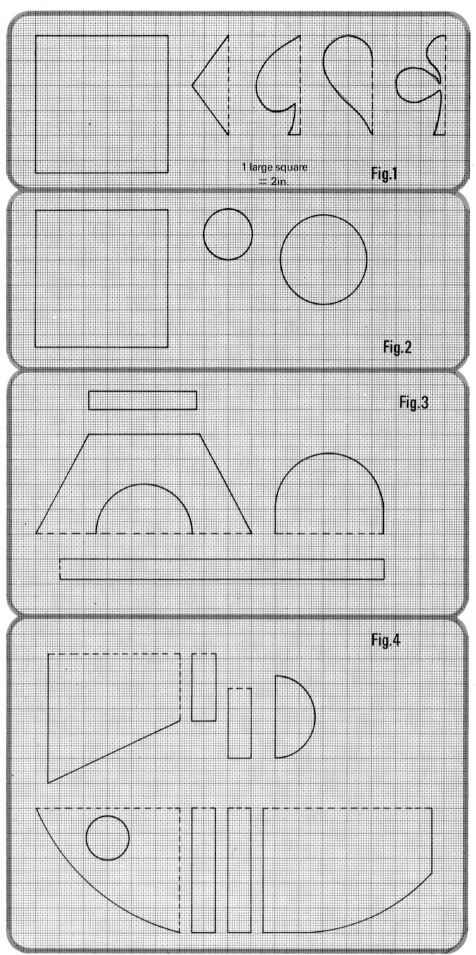

1 large square = 2in.   **Fig.1**

Fig.2

Fig.3

Fig.4

$\frac{1}{4}$in. turnings. Press. Fit another semi-circle to the other side of the strip in the same way, but leave an opening of about 3in. in the straight side. Press again carefully and turn the segment the 'right' side out, poking out the corners with a pencil. Fill it and then oversew the sides of the opening together.

Fish cushion

For each cushion, which is made in three sections and totals 30in. long x 16in. wide, with a 1in. border, you need a yard of 36in. wide fabric. The scales and eye can be cut from felt scraps, using the chart in Fig.4.

Make a paper pattern for the segments of the fish, following the chart. Cut the fabric in half lengthwise and then fold each piece in half lengthwise. Place the paper pattern on to one of the folded pieces so that the side marked with a dotted line is level with the fold. Cut out through the double thickness, but do not cut along the fold. Unpin the pattern, re-pin and cut out from the other piece of fabric in the same way.

Stick or sew the scales and eyes on to the right side of one of the pieces of the centre and front segment, as shown in the photograph.

From the remaining fabric cut out strips 1$\frac{1}{2}$in. wide x the length of each side of the segments. Taking $\frac{1}{4}$in. seam allowance, join the strips for each segment to make circular strips. Taper the stitching into the corners $\frac{1}{4}$in. at the beginning and end of each seam.

With the 'wrong' side of the strips facing out, fit one piece of each segment into the appropriate strip so that its 'wrong' side is facing up and the corners match the seams of the strip. Pin and tack in position, taking $\frac{1}{4}$in. turnings. Stitch the seams and overcast the edges if the fabric is likely to fray. Press.

Still with the 'wrong' side facing out, fit the other piece of the segments to the open side of the strips, matching the corners to the seams as before. Stitch, leaving an opening on one straight side of each segment which is large enough to insert the filling. Press the seams and turn the segments the 'right' side out. Fill with foam chippings or Terylene wadding and oversew the sides of the opening together.

Sitting snake

This is basically a very long fabric tube filled with polystyrene granules. The granules should be packed loosely so they can move around inside the cover and enable the snake to be moulded to the shape you want.

The outer cover of the snake shown in the photograph is knitted, but it could equally well be made from any strong, pliable fabric. A stretch jersey would be ideal because this 'moulds' well and can be bought in wide widths. For a snake with an 18in. diameter you will need fabric which is at least 56in. wide, and for one with a 20in. diameter, the fabric should be at least 63in. wide.

The inner cover can be made from calico. Buy a fairly heavy, closely woven grade in the widest width available (70-72in.). You will need about $\frac{1}{2}$yd more calico than outer cover material.

Start by cutting out the circles for the ends of the inner tube (the method for cutting accurate circles, if you have no compasses large enough,

Above. *Complicated shapes can most easily be made by putting more simple ones together —an idea which should appeal equally to the maker and to the user. There is more sewing involved this way, but the cutting out is much more straightforward (see Figs. 3 and 4). Making the cushions like this also gives you the chance of using up scraps of fabric.*

Right. *The 'sitting snake' has a filling of polystyrene balls which allows the snake to be moulded and twisted into different shapes.*

is given on pages 144-145). Trim down the rest of the calico so that the width equals the circumference of the circles, plus 1 in. for turnings, and join the long edges, taking ½ in. seams, to make a long tube. Leave a large opening in the middle of the seam.

Keeping the tube with its 'wrong' side facing out, clip the turnings at both open ends. Fit a circle to each end and stitch round, taking ½ in. turnings. Turn the tube 'right' side out and fill with granules. Stitch the sides of the openings together firmly with small oversewing.

Join the long edges of the outer cover to make an open-ended tube. Turn 'right' side out and press the turnings at the openings to the inside. Fit the stuffed calico tube into it. Put the ends of the inner tube together to make a circle and join it by stitching on the calico. Do not catch the outer cover in this seam. Next, pin the folds of the outer cover together and stitch, not catching the inside tube. (This will give a smoother finish than if you try to complete the joining in one big operation).

Cushions for furniture

Tables, chairs, beds and playthings—cover blocks of foam with hard-wearing covers, and you have cushions that can turn into virtually any kind of furniture your children need. Compare the variety of uses—and the cost—with that of more conventional children's furniture and you'll be surprised at what you gain—and save. Floor cushions are so good an idea you may even find yourself making-up some for your own lounging area.

Above. If your instinct leads you to choosing bright, primary colours for the covers, beware —these will show every mark (including muddy footprints). Play safe with dark colours.

If you have an old foam mattress which is in reasonable condition—perhaps after buying a new mattress for your own bed—this is ideal for making floor cushions. You can cut it to the size and shape you want with a fine-toothed hacksaw, a really sharp, long cook's knife or an electric carving knife.

If you have to buy the foam, choose a polyether one with a high density with a minimum of

1.5lb per cu ft—anything lower than this will not be strong enough. The density of this type of foam does not affect the feel of it, and from a large stockist you can buy a variety of thicknesses in a variety of 'feels'. For this purpose, a fairly hard foam between 4-6in. deep is usually best, particularly if the cushions will also be slept on.

The other measurements of the pad are

obviously up to you but, when you are deciding, it is worth bearing in mind the width of the fabric you are using for the cover. For example, if you are making it by the boxed method, it is simplest and most economical if you can cut the fabric in half lengthwise and use one piece for the top and the other for the bottom.

Making the cover

This sort of cushion is seen from all sides and so the most logical way to use the fabric—even if it is patterned—is with the selvedge threads running along the length of the pad. This way you should not need any joins on the main panels. However, if you are making the cover by the boxed method (see below), the pattern on the box strips must run from the top of the cushion to the bottom when in position, rather than on its side round the edge, so you may have to join fabric here.

If the foam is latex, rather than polyether, it is worth making a non-removable inner lining cover from calico. This will act as a barrier for the fragments of foam which tend to work loose, and cling to the cover fabric.

Make the inner cover by the second method given below, and finish the opening with oversewing, rather than a zip fastener because this will be flatter and cheaper.

A tailored cover for a foam pad with square sides can be made by one of two methods. The first method should be used if you want a piped edge, if you are using a patterned fabric with a one-way design (see above), or if the pad is an irregular shape.

The cover should fit the pad tightly and smoothly, so if you cut it slightly smaller than the foam this will be permanently under compression and stretch the cover into clean lines without wrinkles.

Boxed method

Add ¾in. to the length and width of the pad

Below. Use a stout furnishing fabric or a stretch dress jersey for the covers, because either of these will stand up to the rigours of a floor cushion.

and cut two rectangles of fabric, on the straight grain, to this size. For the box stripes, which are inserted between the main sections, cut three strips ¾in. wider than the depth of the cushion, and long enough to fit the front and two sides plus ¾in. Join the side strips to each side of the main strip along the short edges, taking ½in. turnings. Taper the stitching into the corners ½in. from the beginning and end of each seam.

Cut another strip 1in. wider than the others and long enough to fit the back of the cushion, plus ¾in. for turnings. Cut this strip in half lengthwise and re-join it for ¾in. at each end, taking ½in. turnings. Insert a zip fastener into the remaining opening. Stitch the short ends of this strip to the short ends of the other one, take ½in. turnings and tapering the stitching as before.

If you are having piping, attach this round both edges of the now circular strip, taking ½in. turnings. Clip the piping casing fabric in line with the joining seams of the strip.

With the wrong side of the strip facing out and the top of the pattern towards the top edge, fit the panel for the top of the cushion on to the top edge of the strip, matching the corners to the seams. Stitch in position and overcast the edges of the fabric which otherwise is likely to fray. The tapered seams of the strip will open out as you do this, so there is no need to clip into the

corners. Press carefully.

Still with the wrong side fabric out, turn the strip so that the open end is uppermost. Fit the fabric for the bottom of the cushion to this side, matching the corners to the seams as before. Press and turn right side out.

Two-panel method

Double the depth measurement of the pad, add this to both the length and width, and add on ¾in. each way for the turnings. Cut a piece of fabric on the straight grain to this size.

Measure in from the corners in both directions the depth of the pad, plus ½in. and mark. Fold over the adjacent sides at each corner, matching the marks, to make a dart, and stitch up from the marks to the fold on the straight grain of the fabric. Trim off the excess fabric to within ¼in. of the stitching.

Cut a second piece of fabric to the size of the bottom of the pad, plus ¾in. each way for turnings. With the wrong side of the fabric facing outwards on both sections, fit the smaller piece to the open side of the other piece, matching the corners to the darts. Stitch on three sides, taking ½in. turnings and clipping them where necessary on the main section for a smooth finish. Press and turn right side out. Finish the opening with a zip fastener.

A carpet style for every room

Carpeting is one of the most expensive and—in proportion to its cost—perhaps the least durable floor coverings. It is not very suitable in a hot, humid climate, where a cold surface like marble or one of the ceramics would be more comfortable and not susceptible to mildew. Nor, in a more temperate climate is it desirable in rooms like the kitchen or combined bathrooms, where hygiene, durability and ease of cleaning are more important than luxury.

But although in some ways carpet is the most expendable floor covering, it is the most widely used type in the home because it is the most comfortable. It is warm and soft; it absorbs sound; and it is not tiring or slippery to walk on. Carpet also adds to the decoration of a home in a way that other floor coverings cannot, because it combines the widest variety of colours, textures and patterns.

Choosing for style

When choosing a carpet for its style—the impact it will have in your home—you need to use a mixture of common sense, personal taste and foresight. Even if it is chosen correctly from a technical sense (see pages 121-123), what seems right for your needs now may be wrong later on because your way of life and tastes have changed.

A carpet should last for at least 10 years, and in that time a family can alter substantially. For example, the carpet which was the right grade for a spare bedroom will not stand up to the treatment it is likely to receive when the spare bedroom becomes a nursery and eventually a playroom for an eight-year-old toy-train fanatic. Similarly, a carpeted bathroom and a shaggy living-room carpet—both of which gave the right touch of luxury and sophistication to the home of a newly married couple—may not survive the sort of punishment inflicted by children who enjoy water fights or who like playing with scissors. And for many families it is at this stage that their budget can least afford new carpets.

Although it may seem boring, it would have been more practical to start off with a plastic-type flooring in the bathroom, and for the living room to have a carpet with a close-cut pile which is probably the most versatile sort, because it can be both luxurious and serviceable in several situations.

Whether a carpet should be plain or patterned, fitted or unfitted, is the next question, and there are points in favour of each.

Plains v patterns

This may seem just a matter of personal taste, but it should also be determined by the size and shape of the room, by your furniture and other decorations. Plain carpets are simpler to furnish to, are easier to live with over a number of years, and allow for changes in decoration. But pale colours show marks, and dark colours show bits of anything light coloured—drawbacks in households where there is a likelihood of frequent spillages, or where there are pets, or activities like sewing. So from this point of view a patterned carpet is more practical.

Apply the principles of the use of colour, pattern and texture (see pages 8-15 and pages 16-19) to your choice. Use a plain carpet in a receding colour, or a small-scale patterned one in a subtle combination of colours, to make a room look larger. To make one look smaller (in the unlikely event that you have a living room like a hotel lounge), have a plain carpet in a

Left. Wall-to-wall carpets are luxurious but on long staircases they can be very wasteful, and runners are often a more sensible choice and easier to lay.

strong colour, or a patterned one in contrasting colours. Avoid a carpet with a large pattern if there is a lot of furniture, because it may make the room look cluttered or bitty.

If in doubt about either colour or pattern, play safe. Leave experiments to less expensive materials which can be changed more easily. An unobtrusive carpet in a darkish, neutral colour—charcoal grey, moss green, earthy brown—will marry happily with all kinds of styles of furnishing and decoration. Or a colour you might not choose for the walls may look good on the floor (dark green, brown, maroon or navy blue, for example) because the floor gets more light than the walls.

As a general rule, the carpet should be one shade darker than the walls if of the same colour, or a darker shade of the main furnishing colour should be used to give stability to a fairly light scheme.

The carpet is also a good way of introducing texture to a room. Strong textures should be chosen with care so that they do not 'fight' with other textures in a room (shaggy pile with a velvet sofa, for instance). The chunky piles, made from high-twist curly yarns, or those made from

Below. A large-scale pattern would be overpowering in a large area, but in a rug it can be highly decorative and even become the focal point of the room.

a mixture of yarn heights and thicknesses, are hard wearing and give visual interest without being obtrusive in the way a definite pattern can be.

While the same carpet throughout the house can be as dull as having the same curtain fabric at every window, in a small house or flat it can give continuity between the rooms and create an illusion of extra space (this can be achieved more cheaply if the carpet is of the same colour throughout, but of a grade suitable to each room). Equally, a different pattern in each room and in the hall can be visually jarring if the doors are open, particularly if the colours do not go well together.

Of all places in the house, the hall is one that really benefits from having a patterned carpet because it is practical and gives interest to what can be an empty-looking area. It looks best if the same carpet is used for the hall, stairs and landing but, whatever is chosen, avoid large brightly coloured patterns on stairs because these can be distracting and may cause accidents.

If possible, base the colour and pattern of the hall carpet on those of the carpet in the rooms adjoining it. For example, if the sitting room carpet is red and the dining room carpet is turquoise, a hall carpet linking them should combine both colours, perhaps on a neutral background. Where both the sitting room and

dining room carpets are patterned, however, you will have to compromise on the hall carpet. If you feel that a plain one would be impractical, have one with a mottled effect which will not quarrel with either of the others.

Fitted v. unfitted

At one time, close-fitted or wall-to-wall carpeting was only for the rich, but the development of the tufted carpet, which came with the development of synthetic fibres, has reduced the cost, and the building of houses with smaller rooms means that less carpet is needed. Nowadays more and more people are having all their carpets close-fitted but, luxurious as this may seem, it is not always the best and most practical choice.

Fitted carpets are more expensive than carpet 'squares' because there is inevitably some waste and it takes more time to lay professionally. Although fitted carpets make a room seem larger, it can seem a pity to cover up a good wooden floor, such as parquet, and senseless to cover a fitted carpet with heavy furniture. They can also be inadvisable with underfloor heating.

On the other hand, you are more likely to trip on the edge of an unfitted carpet and more likely to slip on an uncarpeted surround—and there is more housework involved here. All that is necessary with fitted carpets is regular vacuum cleaning; with an unfitted carpet you will have to clean and polish the surround too, if it is to be kept looking good.

It is possible to fill in the surround quite effectively with carpet strips. The strip could be in a lighter-duty quality than the main section or, if it is in a 'traffic' area, it should be of the same or even a heavier-duty grade. If the main carpet is plain, the surround could be patterned, or vice versa. The fibre composition of the strip, however, should be the same as the main piece, so that they will behave in a similar way in use. The strip must be joined carefully to the main section so that it is level with it, because any step between the pieces could cause people to trip.

An unfitted carpet can be turned around without too much trouble to distribute wear equally, and for families who move home frequently—and as far as carpets are concerned, this could mean every five or ten years— unfitted carpets and carpet tiles are more flexible. (If you do want fitted carpets, but will be moving some time in the future, it is worth having the same carpet in more than one room, especially if in a small house. This can then be pieced together quite effectively for re-use in another room. Also, of course, it is often possible to sell the carpeting with the house.)

Saving on a carpet

It is wise to reduce the area you cover with carpet if, in order to have carpet throughout, you would be forced to have a less good quality than you need. The living room and the bedroom are usually the places where you need carpet most. Except for occasional mats, you should avoid carpet in the kitchen and it is not essential in the bathroom or the hall—in all these places one of the cheaper floor coverings can look just as good

and need not seem institutional. If they would make the stairs too noisy, compromise by covering only the treads with carpet (the pieces must be securely fixed, though). Further economies can be made in the dining room and in the children's bedrooms—and here you may be doing both yourself and the children a good turn by not using carpet.

The floor is probably the most important area of activity in a child's room because it is used for sitting, running, jumping and general play; when the children are older it will be used for homework, dressmaking, woodwork and dancing. Although a carpet may seem the most comfortable and warmest covering for the floor, it is certainly not the most durable for all these different activities. Even with the easy-to-clean synthetic fibre carpets, it is sometimes impossible to remove sticky messes, ink and paint spills and these mishaps occur even in the best regulated families.

Vinyl—and linoleum and cork if properly sealed—are all good floor coverings with resistance to stains and are not too hard or cold (of three types, cork, or lino with a high cork content, is the most sound-deadening). They are better used in sheet form, rather than as tiles, in order to reduce the number of joints, as these show most wear when subjected to frequent soakings by washing or other spillages.

A few rugs will cover up the worst damage and make the room seem less spartan when the children get older—but rugs should not be used when the children are very small as they can be dangerous.

Saving with rugs

However well chosen the carpet is for the area it serves, there are inevitably spots which show dirt and wear out more quickly than others —by doors and beds, and in front of a fire or armchairs. It is always worth putting an occasional rug, perhaps made from the offcut of a fitted carpet, in these places, but they must be made non-slip to prevent accidents.

Ideally the rugs should be put down before the wearing begins but, as long as it is in a logical place, they can also be a good way of disguising a bad patch.

As well as being functional, rugs can be very decorative, even to the extent of becoming a focal point of the room. They are also a good way of introducing a patch of colour or strong texture where an allover carpet in the same material would be overpowering or too expensive.

Far left. In a dining area a patterned carpet is more practical than a plain one because it will not show marks.
Below left. Pale colours need not be impractical with carpet tiles, which can be taken up singly and washed.
Right. A shaggy pile carpet is the height of luxury for a bedroom— provided its occupants are not scissor-happy children.
Below right. 'Plastic' floor coverings are ideal in the children's bedrooms because they are so easily cleaned. A rug will make them seem less spartan.

HEIDEDE CARSTENSEN/STUDIO HUELSTA

TINTAWN CARPETS LTD

The which, where why of choosing carpets

Choosing a carpet is not as easy as one would think, because new methods of manufacture, the introduction of new fibres and the creation of new textiles have resulted in a bewildering array of carpets of all types, in a variety of designs and colours to suit any taste and almost any budget.

Before a carpet can be chosen with any degree of confidence, it is necessary to understand some of the simple mechanics of manufacture. There are basically four different methods: Wilton; Axminster; tufted; and non-woven. Wiltons and Axminsters are not brand names, but are generic terms for methods whereby each tuft is *woven* with the backing (the names come from the places where carpets were woven by these methods centuries ago.) The difference between these two is in the type of weaving and, from a practical viewpoint, the methods make little difference to the length of 'service' of the carpet. However, because of the difference, Wiltons tend to be available in a wider variety of colours, with a limited choice of pattern, and Axminsters in a wider variety of pattern.

A tufted carpet is made in an entirely different way. The tufts are inserted into a pre-woven backing, which is then coated with latex. A secondary backing is added to increase stability and secure the tufts. The process is faster than weaving, so retail prices are

Left. The blend of 80% wool and 20% nylon is one of the most successful for carpets. Here it is used for a Wilton, one of the oldest types of carpet manufactured. Background to this page. A woven shaggy carpet in all wool.

lower. However, there is less variety of colour and pattern.

Non-woven carpets, as their name implies, are made on a different type of machine whereby a mass of fibres are interlocked together by a 'needling' process which compresses them into a tough, flat surface. There are many types of non-woven carpet, most of them having a flat non-pile surface. Some—mostly loose-lay carpet tiles—have a brushed directional pile.

Because Wiltons and Axminsters are traditional methods of manufacture, a myth has grown up around these carpets and a lot of people think that Wiltons are better than Axminsters—or vice versa—and that both are better than tufted and non-wovens. This may have been true many years ago, but there are good and bad modern carpets of all four types. It is more important when selecting your carpet to concentrate on the other essential factors—what is the pile or surface of the carpet made of, and how much wear your carpet is likely to get in any given place.

How long will it wear?

Understandably, this is the most-asked question by people buying a carpet. But you should not simply ask 'How long will it last?' but 'Will it give lasting wear *and* keep its appearance at the same time?' There is little advantage in a carpet that lasts for ever if, at the same time, it looks awful. This is largely determined by the type of fibre used for the pile.

Carpet pile or surface fibres fall into five categories: natural fibres (wool, cotton, etc.); acrylics; cellulosics; nylons; and polypropylenes.

Natural fibres

Wool is the most important and widely used

of the natural fibres, either in 100 per cent form or blended. It varies a great deal depending on the breed of sheep and the conditions under which they are raised, and the best carpet wools come from sheep raised in high and hilly country.

All wools and wool blends possess most of the properties required in a carpet—they are lasting, resilient, and keep their appearance well. A medium domestic Wilton, for example, might last as long as 20 years in a living room, and the only reason you might change it is because you are tired of it. Wool is less flammable than most synthetics, does not show soiling readily and is warm. It is, however, expensive and it is for that reason, more than any other, that synthetic fibres have been developed to such an extent.

At opposite ends of the natural fibres' spectrum are silk and cotton. Silk is used for luxury, very expensive, Oriental carpets; cotton is used mainly for bath rugs because it absorbs moisture well, dries quickly and can be washed easily. It is made into cheap floor covering by some European manufacturers, but it tends to flatten and soil quickly.

Coarse, inexpensive carpeting fibres are obtained from sisal and other plants. Sisal fibre tends to be stiff and inflexible but strong and hard wearing. It absorbs moisture readily, so stains are more difficult to remove but it dyes well to a wide variety of colours. Sisal is mostly used for flat and bouclé carpets, mattings and rugs.

Jute comes from the inner bark of plants of the genus Corchorus, and is a brown fibre which can be bleached to shades of cream or white. It is mainly used as carpet backing or in underlays, but it is sometimes blended with viscose rayon to make inexpensive cord pile carpets.

Hair from various animals is used for cord

Above. *Woven loop with shag in wool and nylon.*

carpets and carpet tiles. It makes durable, rather harsh floor covering. It is sometimes blended with wool or viscose yarn, which makes it softer.

Acrylics

These are the nearest in feel and appearance to wool. They are resilient, and have greater durability and are less prone to static than other synthetics. At the same time, they are readily cleanable from stains because they do not absorb liquids. Best known trade names include Acrilan, Orlon, Courtelle and Dralon. Modacrylics are claimed to be less flammable than acrylics, with improved resistance to soiling. Best known trade names are Teklan and Verel. They are often blended with the acrylics.

Cellulosics

This group, produced from wood pulp or cotton linters, includes viscose and modified rayons. These are bulky fibres which are not particularly resilient and tend to flatten, but are not prone to static. The best known trade name in Britain is 'Fibro', and improved versions

Below. *All wool cut-pile Wilton.*

are known as Evlan and Evlan M. The great advantage to viscose rayon is its cheapness.

Nylon

This is characterized by its toughness and good abrasion resistance and, although it tends to show soiling, it is easily cleanable. It is not readily flammable and melts to a hard mass when exposed to flame. It is used extensively in less expensive carpets which still produce satisfactory wear. Its chief disadvantage is that it can generate static but this can be overcome by occasional light spraying with water. Some well known trade names are Bri-nylon, Blue C Nylon, Du Pont 501, Celon, Perlon, Enkalon, Lilion, Brilion, Allyn 707.

Polypropylene

This is one of the newer synthetic fibres and is used in various forms. Carpets made from polypropylene are durable, generate little static and are usually easily cleaned. Brand names include Meraklon and Fibrite.

Blends

One of the most reliable blends is 80 per cent wool and 20 per cent nylon. This combines all the advantages of wool with the tried durability of nylon. It produces a hard-wearing pile which is now standard in the carpet trade.

For inexpensive carpets, 80 per cent Evlan

Above. *Tufted all-nylon with foam backing.*

with 20 per cent nylon produces a pile with a good resistance to flattening and, although it is susceptible to soiling, it does have a reasonable performance.

A clever combination of yarns that gives a pile with a warm 'handle' is $42\frac{1}{2}$ per cent wool with $42\frac{1}{2}$ per cent Evlan and 15 per cent nylon. The wool content helps the blend to keep its appearance and, although it is fairly easily soiled, it is a blend that enables the manufacturers to produce carpets for the mass market.

There are a number of other blends, such as 50 per cent Courtelle with 50 per cent Evlan, that are being developed and tried to produce good-looking and reasonably priced carpets.

Buying for the location

Always look for the manufacturers' recommendation on the label when choosing because it means what it says, and it is not just the manufacturers' trick of getting you to buy a more expensive carpet than you need. For example, one labelled 'for light domestic use' will be perfectly adequate for a bedroom that is

Below. *Natural wool, with looped pile.*

Above. *Non-woven, deep-pile, loose-lay tile.*

used purely as room to sleep in. You can afford to worry less about how easily the carpet soils and, because the room is only used intermittently, it will not need such a hard-wearing carpet as some other areas in the home. If, however, the bedroom is used as a bed-sitting room, the carpet should be one labelled 'medium domestic use'. Other areas for which a light domestic carpet would be suitable are normally bathrooms and dining rooms.

Buying a carpet for a living room however, is a different matter, as it depends so much on the amount of time the room is occupied and the habits of the occupants. The living room in the home of a large family with pets will obviously get a great deal of wear and tear, and the carpet should be one labelled 'heavy domestic'. On the other hand, the living-room carpet of a childless couple, both of whom work, could be a 'medium domestic'. (Heavy duty carpets have more yarn to the square yard than lighter duty carpets.)

Other areas likely to get heavy wear are hallways and any area leading straight into the house from outside. Whether you choose a 'medium domestic' or a 'heavy domestic' quality depends on how many people walk over the area and how often. A carpet for a stairway needs to be chosen with special care as on the wrong sort the pile will 'grin' or separate on the stair nosing. To avoid this, the carpet should have a close, tightly woven pile, a short twist (or curly pile), one with a looped pile, or be of a cord type.

Saving money

Beware of buying in a hurry—it is always worth shopping around because many shops offer discounts and 'come-on' facilities, such as free or good, very inexpensive fitting. If buying in a sale, or from a mill or warehouse, make sure you know exactly what you are getting, and that the measurements are right because mistakes cannot be corrected and there may be no after-sales service.

If you are on a small budget, it is a completely false economy to try to save money by not having Axminster and Wilton close carpeting laid and fitted by experts or on a proper underlay (see below), as the carpet will not give the service expected, even if it has been chosen correctly.

Below. *Tufted hard twist with foam backing.*

Underlays

A separate underlay should be used under all carpets except those which have an underlay built in, such as rubber-backed carpets. The heavier the underlay, the more it helps prolong the life of the carpet by providing a cushion between it and the floor, thus absorbing the 'shock' caused by people walking over it. It makes the carpet softer, retards the crushing of the pile by pressure from furniture, eliminates slight unevenness in the floor, and increases the effectiveness of vacuum cleaning by causing pockets of air, which the machine draws through the fabric. It also gives an extra layer of sound and heat insulation.

Underlays can be made from jute, hair or wool felt, rubber, foam rubber backing with a hair felt surface. Hair or wool felt is best for carpets with joins, as these help the seams 'bed down' so they do not show so much, or wear quickly. Felt is also suitable for stair pads, to give protection to the stair nosings. Jute can be used in these places, but it tends to crush down more than hair or wool felt.

Although felt can be used for seamless carpets, if there is underfloor heating a latex-coated embossed underlay is a better choice because it allows the air to circulate underneath.

ALAN DUNS

Making your own rugs

Although you can buy rugs in all colours, shapes and sizes, too often you cannot find precisely what you want. Try making your own—you don't need any elaborate equipment, yet you can produce a rug which will last a lifetime.

Rugs can be woven, knotted, hooked and stitched, or even plaited, crocheted and knitted. In the traditional method, the foundation is woven on a loom and the pile threads are knotted on to the warp threads by hand. The

method is not difficult, but to do it at home demands a lot of time, space and equipment. It is much simpler to buy a pre-woven canvas and insert the pile into it.

This is most easily and quickly done by using cut wool and a latchet hook, which produces a thick, hard-wearing rug. The latchet hook, which is rather like a crochet hook, is the only specialized tool needed; it is not expensive and can be bought from the same shop as the rug wool. It has a wooden handle and a hinged latchet which closes round the end of the hook

to prevent the hook from being caught in the ends of the wool and canvas as the knot is formed. It can be used for making either short-pile or rya (long-pile, shaggy) rugs.

Short-pile rugs. For making a short-pile rug, a special coarse 6-ply wool—often called Turkey wool—should be used. You can buy it in skeins and cut it to the length you want on a wooden gauge, or it can be bought in packs of 320 pre-cut pieces, 2¾in. long. Each piece makes 1 knot with 2 strands of pile about ¾in. long, and one pack of cut wool covers just over three 3in. squares on standard rug canvas.

Rya rugs. Here the wool should be a twisted 2-ply, sold for this purpose in pre-cut packs containing 168 pieces, 7in. long. Three pieces are used in each knot, making 6 strands of pile about 2¾in. long. On standard rug canvas, one pack would cover slightly more than one 3in.

square.

Standard rug canvas can be bought in different widths from 12in. to 48in. Buy a piece 4in. longer than the length you want the rug to be, to allow for turnings. With rya rugs, the finished rug is usually 2-3in. longer than the basic canvas because of the length of the pile.

Choosing the design

In the same way as for embroidery, it is possible to buy canvas already printed with a design. It is usually sold in a kit, complete with the amount of wool needed in each colour. You simply place the knots in the right colour as shown on the canvas. Although this may not seem particularly creative, for a rug with a complicated Oriental design, the kits are worthwhile.

Alternatively, you can buy a design printed on a chart. These are slightly more complicated to work with because you have to count up the squares on the chart which indicates the parts of the pattern, and mark the canvas in a similar way. However, they do give you the chance to adapt the design and to choose your own

Above. A beautiful rug looks good anywhere! Before the days of proper upholstery, people in Oriental countries sat on rugs on the floor (and many still do). Rugs also make good bedcovers and wallhangings.

colours.

Other attractive rugs can be based simply on subtle blends of colour which do not form a definite pattern, particularly rya rugs. It is usually a good idea to rough out a scheme in advance, because the rug should be worked in straight lines from one end. If instead you work patches of colour separately all over the canvas, and then join them up, the finish is likely to be uneven and you may miss out squares because of the thickness of the wool.

Starting off

For a rug with straight sides, place the canvas on a table with the selvedges on your left and right, and with its full length away from you. To make a neat strong edge, turn up the cut end nearest you for about 2in., with the holes matching the holes underneath. Tack it down in

position. The first few rows of knots should be worked through the double thickness.

Missing one square at the bottom and on each side of the canvas, start working the knots from left to right, or right to left if you are left-handed.

For a circular rug, leave an unworked 1¾-2in. border round the edge. The quickest knot to do is the 4-movement Turkish knot (Figs.1-5). When completed, the tufts of the knot lie towards you. If two people are working on the rug from opposite ends, one person should do the 5-movement knot, in which the tufts lie away from the worker, so the pile will run in the same direction down the length of the rug.

With a short-pile rug, a knot should be made in every square. For a rya rug, however, you should use three strands of wool for each knot, work a complete horizontal row, miss the next row, then work another complete horizontal row. This gives the rug its characteristic shaggy look—the tufts are so long and thick that the gaps between rows are unnoticeable. In fact, when the rug is completed, it does not look as though it has been worked in rows at all.

Step by step rug-making

Fig.1. *All you need for making your rug.*
Fig.2. *On a straight rug, turn up the end of the canvas for about 2in. and work the first few rows of knots through the double thickness. On a circular rug, leave a 2in. border of canvas unworked.*

The quickest knot consists of four movements.
Fig.3. *Fold the cut length of wool in half and loop it round the neck of the hook below the crook and latchet.*
Fig.4. *Holding the ends of the wool between the thumb and index finger of your left hand, insert the hook under the first of the weft threads (those running from left to right, across the canvas).*

Fig.5. *Turn the hook a little to the right, open the latchet and place the ends of the wool into the hook.*
Fig.6. *Pull the hook under the thread and through the loop of wool. As you pull, the latchet will close to prevent the hook from getting caught in the canvas.*

Fig.7. *Pull the ends of the wool tightly to make the knot firm.*
Fig.8. *The tufts of the knot will look like this.*

When two people are working from opposite ends, one person should use the five-movement knot so the pile will lie in the same direction.

Fig.9. *Insert the hook under the first weft thread. Fold the cut length of wool in half and, holding the ends between your thumb and index finger, loop it over the hook.*
Fig.10. *Pull the hook back through the canvas.*

Fig.11. *Push the hook through the loop of wool until the latchet is clear and the loop is on the neck of the hook.*
Fig.12. *Place the cut ends of wool into the crook of the hook from below, so they are enclosed by the latchet.*

Fig.13. *Pull the hook back through the loop of wool until the ends are clear.*
Fig.14. *Pull the ends of the wool tightly to secure the knot.*

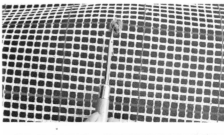
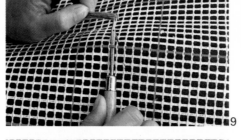
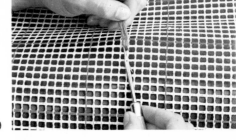

Finishing off rugs

Among the many advantages of making a' rug as on pages 124-126 are that you can alter its size, modify its design or even mend it later if necessary. Although these rugs are strong enough to last a lifetime, the first place they may wear out is along the edges.

When all the knots have been worked in the canvas, it is a good idea to add strength to the edges by neatening them firmly. On square or rectangular rugs, all four sides can be finished by stitching or crocheting in one of the methods given below. Alternatively, two opposite sides—preferably those worked through the double layer of canvas—can be edged with a fringe. On a semi-circular rug, the straight edge should be finished by stitching and the curved edge in the same way as for a circular rug (see below).

The rugs should never be backed—the open construction of the canvas is not visible from the pile side, yet allows any grit on the surface to work its way through to the back of the rug where it can be easily cleaned (see below). Adding a backing would trap the dirt and make it much more difficult to clean.

Making a fringe

On rugs made by the classical method of weaving, the warp threads of the foundation (usually cotton or silk) are secured at each end by knotting them together about 4-6in. from the ends in groups of four or five. You can achieve a similar effect on a canvas foundation by adding a fringe to the unworked thread at each end of the canvas, using a latchet hook.

The fringe can be made from natural-coloured or white cotton (use the type sold for knitting dishcloths), or from the wool used to finish the other edges. A multi-coloured fringe can be very effective, but on a rug with a strong pattern a plain one from one of the darker, background colours usually looks best.

The simplest method of cutting the lengths of yarn for the fringe is to find a book which is twice as deep as the required length of the fringe. Wind the yarn round it from top to bottom and cut through the threads along both edges.

Place the rug on your work surface with the pile facing up and the edge to which you are adding the fringe towards you. Weight the other end to prevent the rug from slipping.

Working from left to right, insert the hook under the first thread of canvas. Take three lengths of yarn and, treating them as one piece, fold them in half and loop them round the neck of the latchet hook. Complete the knot as for the four-movement Turkish knot (see page opposite), and pull the ends tight to secure it.

When all the knots have been worked, brush the ends towards you and trim off any uneven threads.

Finishing off a circular rug

The only satisfactory method of finishing the edges of a circular or shaped rug is by binding it

Left. If you would like to design your own rug, simple geometric shapes are a good starting point. Work out a pattern on squared paper and then transfer it to the canvas.

with matching 2in. wide carpet braid. You need enough to fit round the edge of the rug, plus about 2in. for turnings.

Start by trimming the unworked border of the rug to 1¾in., then press this section down on to the 'wrong' side of the rug, notching it where necessary to make it lie flat.

Pin on the carpet braid to cover the border on the 'wrong' side of the rug, so that the outer edge of the braid is slightly inset from the edge of the carpet. Make darts on the inner edge of the braid where necessary (Figs. 1 to 3).

Using strong carpet thread, oversew the tape to the canvas along both edges. Stitch down the darts.

Stitched edge

If you are finishing all the sides by stitching, work the ends which have the doubled canvas first and then do the selvedges. For all the methods of stitching you should use a carpet needle with a large eye and skeins of Turkey wool in a shade to match or blend with the colour at the edge or in the background of the rug. You cannot use the standard ready-cut packs of wool for this.

Oversewing or plaited stitch

This can be worked from left to right (Fig.4), or right to left.

To work from left to right, have the back of the rug facing up and the edge you are stitching away from you. Darn in the end of the wool and work a few oversewing stitches in the first hole and over the outside thread of canvas. Pull the wool through the hole towards you, move to the

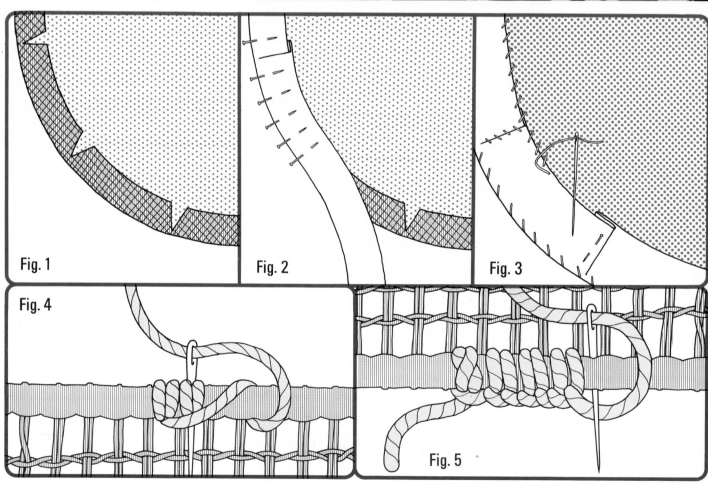

Fig. 1

Fig. 2

Fig. 3

Fig. 4

Fig. 5

fourth hole, taking the wool over the outside canvas thread, and through the hole towards you again. Take the wool over the canvas thread at the top of the fourth hole, go back to the second hole and pull the wool out towards you. Take the wool over the canvas thread and insert in the fifth hole, pull out towards you, take it over the canvas thread and insert in the third hole. Continue along the whole side in this way.

To work from right to left, have the pile side uppermost and the edge you are stitching away from you. The needle should always pass from the back of the canvas to the front.

Insert the needle into the first hole from the back of the rug and pull the wool through, leaving a tail of about 3in. lying along the top edge to the left. This will be covered by the stitches as you work. Holding the tail with your left hand, take the wool over the outside canvas thread to the back and insert it into the second hole. Pull through the wool, take it over the edge to the back of the canvas and insert it through the first hole again.

Take the wool over the edge and insert the needle from the back into the fourth hole. Take it over the edge to the back and insert it into the second hole again.

Continue working in this way, forward three holes and back two holes each time. To go round a corner, go back two holes, forward two, back one, forward one, then continue on the second edge as for the first one.

Left. *A simple idea for a large rug is to design several motifs, all with the same colours, and then link them with one colour.*

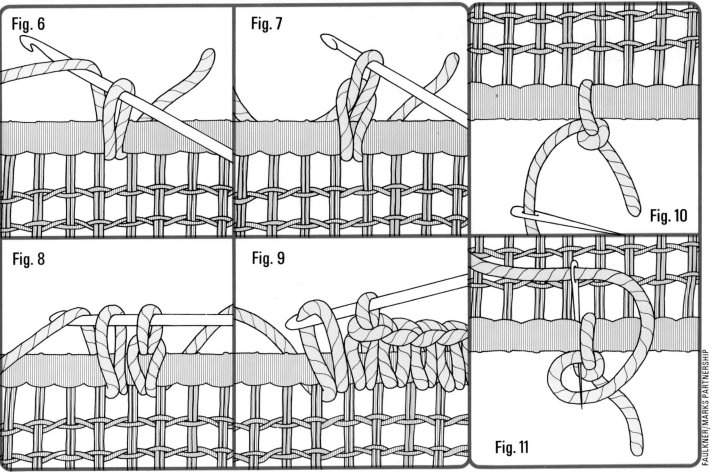

Blanket stitch

This is worked from left to right with the edge placed nearest to you and the pile side uppermost. Make two stitches in each hole (Fig.5).

Insert the needle into the first hole from the pile side and pull through to the back of the carpet, leaving a tail of wool about 3in. long. Hold the tail to the right so that it will be covered by the next stitches, then insert the needle into the same hole from the pile side. Pull it out, taking it under the outside canvas thread from the back of the rug and through the loop of wool. Pull tightly to secure the stitch.

Cable stitch

This is like a reverse blanket stitch. It is worked from right to left, with the edge placed nearest to you and the pile side uppermost.

Insert the needle into the first hole from the pile side and pull through leaving a tail of about 3in. long. Hold the tail towards you with the needle on its left. Bring the needle over the tail to the right and insert it through the loop of wool made at the edge of the canvas. Still holding the tail, pull up the wool to secure the stitch. The tail can now be left free to be darned in later, or you can continue holding it to the left to be covered by following stitches.

To make the second stitch, make a loop by holding the part of the wool which is nearest the first stitch over to the left. Insert the needle into the hole from the pile side and pull it out, taking it under the outside canvas thread from the back of the rug and through the loop of wool. Pull up the stitch firmly (Figs.10 to 11). Make all the following stitches in the same way.

Below left. For rugs with classic designs, you can buy a kit, complete with the printed canvas and wool. Or you could buy a chart and adapt it for the right size and colours.

Above. On a large rug, it is often more convenient to make it in segments which can be joined later. A simple design like this is ideal for that, and looks most effective.

Crochet edging

This is worked from right to left with the pile side uppermost and the edge placed away from you. One stitch is made in each hole.

Using a No. 6.00 (ISR) crochet hook, push the hook through the first hole and pull through a loop of wool, leaving a long tail to be darned in later. Keeping this loop on the hook, catch the wool from the back over the edge of the canvas and pull through the loop. Keep the loop thus made on the hook. To make the second stitch, put the hook into the next hole from the pile side, catch the wool from the back and pull it through the hole. Keeping the loops on the hook, catch the wool again over the edge of the canvas and pull it through the two loops on the hook. Push the hook through the third hole and repeat the second stitch (Figs.6 to 9). Make all the following stitches in the same way.

Cleaning the rug

The best way to clean both short and shaggy pile rugs is to take them outside, hang them on a line and beat them in the old-fashioned method. Alternatively, grit can be removed by using a suction tube on the back of the rug—never use a vacuum cleaner on the pile side, particularly with a shaggy rug because the pile could get caught up and pulled away.

To remove stains from the pile side, use a damp, not wet cloth, wrung out in a mild detergent solution. Do not let the rug get too wet, and do not try to wash it in a machine. The rug can, however, be dry cleaned in a machine.

PATONS & BALDWINS

Stitch-made rugs

Rugs which are beautiful and hard-wearing can be very costly to purchase. By making your own, you can both save money and add something unique to your home.

This method of making rugs using embroidery stitches is very similar to other kinds of tapestry work. You can make cushions, stool tops and wall hangings in the same way, and in designs which will suit any setting.

The design

With stitch-made rugs, you can either make a pile surface or a flat surface. Both wear well and take about the same time and skill to make, but a pile surface uses about one more ounce of wool per square foot on coarse canvases. A pile

Above. Bright colours and a simple, geometric design, developed from the pattern of the floor, make a stunning cross-stitch rug.

rug is more traditional and, for some people, more luxurious, but a smooth-surfaced rug gives more opportunity for variety because different stitches can be used and so it may be more interesting to make.

As with any other kind of tapestry work, you can buy kits consisting of canvas printed with designs together with the right amount of wool. This is the easiest way if you want to make a rug with a traditional or complicated pattern, but it is also the most expensive.

Alternatively, you can buy a chart which shows the formation of the design, and adapt it proportionally to fit the size of the rug you want. This involves using squared paper—normally one-quarter of the size of the rug, but full-size in the case of asymmetrical patterns—so you can work out precisely how the pattern will fall. This

method gives you the chance of choosing your own colours, and also of saving money by buying the wool direct from carpet factories.

You should always be careful to buy enough wool of each colour, because if you run out you may not be able to get the same colour later. In fact, slight changes of colour are characteristic of many valuable Oriental carpets, and in other types are often deliberately introduced to give variation to a large area, but this sort of thing is usually better planned in advance.

If you feel like designing your own rug, for your first attempts it is wisest to start with a very simple geometric pattern or perhaps adapt an existing one. Buy paper printed with small squares which correspond to the size of your canvas (see below), and use coloured pencils to sketch in your design. Work out several roughs of the main pattern first before you design the whole rug.

Since carpets are normally seen from all directions, you will probably find that a strictly symmetrical design is the easiest type to start with, because you need design only a quarter of it. The pattern should be reversed for each of the remaining quarters.

In a room where you do not want a rug with a pattern, you can add interest to a plain one by combining different stitches, or by alternating pile and smooth surfaced sections. Often you can add depth to a carpet by combining two shades of the same colour, particularly in those cases where you are using two strands of wool in the needle together.

The size of rug you make will obviously depend on where you will be putting it, but for rectangular ones you will usually find that it is easiest to base the width on one of the standard widths available in the type of canvas you are using, and to make the length one-and-three quarter times this size.

The wool

Woollen yarn only should be used for rug-making because it is hard-wearing, does not attract the dirt quickly, is available in the right sort of thickness and has an advantage over man-made yarns in that its hairy texture helps to cover the foundation canvas.

The thickest type of wool available is 6-ply Turkey wool. Carpets made with this are very strong, but also heavy and rather coarse. They are the quickest to make, but are also the most expensive because so much wool is needed.

For a finer carpet, you should use 2-ply carpet wool, This is thicker and coarser than 2-ply knitting wools, and is sold at needlework shops. It is often possible—and cheaper—to buy it in the form of *thrums* from a carpet mill. This is the leftover yarn which the mill cannot use. It tends to vary slightly in thickness, so you may have to use two strands, instead of one, in some cases.

Two-ply crewel wool, which is often used for other kinds of tapestry work, should not be used for carpets because it is too soft to withstand

133

Fig.1

Fig.2

Fig.3

Fig.4

Fig.5

Fig.6

Fig.7

Fig.8

Fig.9

Fig.10

Fig.11

Fig.12

Fig.13

Fig.14

Fig.15

continual friction. If you do want a finer yarn than 2-ply carpet wool, it is better to use Brussels thrums because this is stronger and more hairy. This is often supplied in loose twists of several strands, which should be separated before use.

The canvas

Rug canvas, which is the foundation on which the stitches are worked, is available by the yard in a variety of widths, and with 3, 4, 5, 7, 8, 9, or 10 holes to the inch. It is essential that the correct canvas is chosen for the type of wool being used, because if too thick a wool is used for the size of hole, the stitches will be difficult to work and will distort the shape of the finished rug, so that it will not lie flat. On the other hand, if you use too fine a wool, the rug will be floppy and the threads of the canvas will show through.

As a guide, 6-ply Turkey wool should be used only on canvas with three holes to the inch. On the intermediate sizes, with 4, 5 or 7 holes to the inch, it would be too thick but one strand of 2-ply is not enough, so here you should use two strands. On the finer canvases, use two or three strands of Brussels thrums.

Except on the very finest canvas, the mesh is formed by two threads each way which separate the holes into which the needle is inserted. Except in certain stitches, these threads should be counted as one, and the stitches worked over both. It is possible to buy single-mesh canvas which corresponds to the sizes above, but it is more difficult to use because the stitches have to be worked over two consequent threads, and it frays quickly.

Preparing the canvas

To prevent the canvas from fraying during the working and to strengthen the edges when the rug is finished and in use, it is essential to prepare it correctly, and a minimum of 4in. extra canvas should be allowed in the length.

The stitches are normally worked in rows across the width of the canvas from selvedge to selvedge, and start at one of the cut edges. A 2in. turning should be made by folding over this edge along a weft thread, so that the holes correspond with the holes underneath. The edge should be firmly oversewed in postion with matching sewing thread.

The opposite edge should be prepared in a similar way, although the sewing can be less

Figs.1 and 2. Surrey stitch consists of two basic steps which form the knot. Fig.3. The loop between the knots is cut to form the pile. Figs.4-6. The knot in Turkey stitch is formed by passing the needle twice between the double bars of the canvas. Fig.7. To work cross stitch horizontally, bring the needle out in hole 3 of the previous stitch to start the next. (Hole 1 is where the stitch begins, hole 2 the next hole the thread goes through and so on.) Fig.8. To work diagonally, bring it out in hole 2. Fig.9. To work vertically, bring it out in the hole below hole 1. Figs.10-12. In Soumak stitch the point should always lie along the warp threads of the canvas, and towards the worker. Figs.13-15. Gobelin stitch is like two rows of overlapping oversewing stitches.

neat here because you may have to adjust the width of the turning later to fit the pattern.

The selvedges can be finished, following one of the methods described on pages 127-130 before you start the main stitching but it is usually safer to complete them afterwards. This is particularly so with smooth-surfaced rugs because the type of stitching used tends to pull the canvas out of shape and this is easier to correct if the edges have not been finished.

Starting off

Before you plunge into making a full-size rug, it is always worth working a sampler. This will give you a chance to try out the various stitches and wools, and it will not matter if you have to unpick anything and distort the canvas in the process. If the sampler is a success, it may make a very attractive cushion or stool cover.

For pile rugs, the canvas should be arranged so that the folded edge is towards you, with the raw edge uppermost, the selvedges on your left and right and the unworked length of canvas stretching away from you. Start working the stitches in the first hole from the fold on the left-hand edge (left-handed people may prefer to start at the right-hand edge). Work a complete row across the canvas, changing colour where necessary.

Don't be tempted into working blocks of colour instead of complete rows, because you may find that by doing so you miss holes or make other mistakes. To save time, however, and to avoid wasting lengths of wool, it is a good idea to have several needles threaded with the appropriate colours.

For smooth-surfaced rugs, arrange the canvas so that the folded end where you are starting work is away from you, with the cut edge on the underside and the unworked length towards you. The only exception to this rule is if you are using Soumak stitch (see below). With these types of rugs, you can generally work in blocks of colour most efficiently, and this will save on the number of joins necessary.

Start off with a 18in.—24in. length of wool in the needle. You will find that it will be used up quickly, particularly with a pile rug, but don't use longer lengths in order to avoid joins, because with the constant friction caused by pulling the wool in and out of the canvas, it will start to fray and may eventually break.

With pile stitches, the ends of each length form part of the pile on the front of the rug, and do not need any special methods of securing because the formation of the stitch is enough. With smooth-surfaced stitches, however, the end should be held along the underside of canvas, and caught in the stitches.

If you are using two lengths of wool in the needle, make sure that these lie flat side by side on the canvas, and are not twisted.

The stitches

One of two stitches can be used to make a carpet with a pile: Surrey stitch (Figs.1-3), so named because it was devised by a member of a Surrey Woman's Institute, and Turkey or Ghiordes stitch (Figs.4-6), which is similar in formation to the knot used by Oriental workers.

The two stitches give a very similar appearance on the front of the carpet, but Surrey

stitch is stronger and gives a neater finish to the back, although it does take longer to work.

The length of pile made by either stitch is optional, but a length of ¾in. on canvas with three or four holes to the inch is most satisfactory; a shorter pile should be used on finer canvases. There is no need to use a gauge or guide to keep the loops a consistent length because they can always be trimmed evenly later, and you will soon find that with practice you can make them the same size. Cut the loops after each row is worked.

The best stitches for smooth-surfaced carpets are those which are worked diagonally across the mesh of the canvas, because this helps ensure that the threads are completely covered. Variations of cross sittch are most commonly used, but many other traditional embroidery stitches are also good and an interesting effect can be made by combining them. Other popular stitches are Soumak stitch and Gobelin stitch.

A rug made with Soumak stitch (Figs.10-12) looks like a loom-woven Oriental Soumak rug. The method of working it is different from other stitch-made rugs in that the unworked canvas is held to your left-hand side with the selvedge running sideways. Regardless of the direction in which you are working—from side to side, top to bottom or diagonally—the V made by each stitch should always have its point lying along the weft of the canvas and towards you.

The stitch is fairly tricky to work until you get the knack, because the point of the V is made by inserting the needle between the double weft threads and each stitch interlocks with those above and below. This makes unpicking difficult, although the resulting surface is very strong and does not use much wool.

Gobelin stitch is a much simpler interlocking stitch which is formed by working a row of stitches across the canvas from right to left, and then another row, which overlaps the first row, from left to right. It is a very quick stitch to work, but is best kept for plain or striped rugs because it does not work well for intricate designs (Figs.13-15).

Finishing the rug

Most rugs need stretching to show them off to best advantage, and this is particularly important with smooth-surfaced ones which may have become distorted.

The easiest place to do this is on a bare boarded floor, where you can follow the lines of the boards as a guide. With its right side facing up, tack one long edge of the carpet to the floor, keeping the side completely flat, but without stretching it. The tacks need not be very close together at this stage. Then tack down one of the adjacent sides, making sure that it is at right angles. Pull the fourth corner so that the other long side is also at right-angles to the short sides, and so that it is the same length as the opposite edge. Tack this down as well, then insert further tacks all round so that the carpet is completely surrounded by tacks about 1in. apart.

Cover the rug with sheets of blotting paper and soak these thoroughly with cold water. Using a hot iron, press carefully all over, including the side edges. Leave the rug for a few days until it is completely dry.

How to lay carpets

The estimating and laying of wall-to-wall carpeting can be a tricky job in a large or awkardly shaped room, and here it is probably best left to the professional. But in many average-sized, simply shaped rooms, it is practical—and more economical—to tackle it yourself.

Carpets with a foam backing, whether of the tufted, bonded or needle felt type, can all be successfully fitted by an amateur. Those with a heavy foam back—medium or high density—are particularly easy because they can be loose laid : simply cut to shape and placed in position without any securing at the edges.

Carpets without foam backing are much more difficult to lay, because often the edges need binding to prevent fraying and, if the carpet is of the woven type (Wilton or Axminster), the carpet must be stretched during the fitting. This stretching is done in order to make the backing really taut, thus keeping the pile up-right—essential if the carpet is to look good and wear well. Stretching is an art and requires skill (and developed muscles) if it is to be done well. For this reason many carpet manufacturers will not recognize complaints about the performance of their carpets unless they have been fitted by a professional. However, since expert fitting is costly, there are occasions when you may want to tackle it yourself.

To stretch the carpet fully and evenly over a large area it is worth hiring a professional carpet stretcher, known as a knee kicker. For smaller areas, it is possible to make a form of kicker (see

below), or even to use the prongs of a garden rake or fork.

The edges of unbacked carpets have to be secured in position. This can be done by turning them under and tacking them down, in which case the carpet should be 3in. wider and longer than the area being covered. This method, however, cannot be used on concrete floors. Alternatively (and this way is more efficient, but also more expensive), tackless gripper may be used. This is a wood or metal batten—in 4ft lengths— which is fixed round the perimeter of the room, and has two or three rows of prongs on the upper side to grip the backing of the carpet. The carpet should be $\frac{3}{8}$in. wider and longer than the area being covered.

With either method of fixing, the underlay should be approximately 3in. shorter and narrower than the dimensions of the area to allow for the width of the batten or turn.

Home-made knee kicker

To make a carpet stretcher, you will need: a 12in. or 300mm length of timber 4in. x 3in. or 100mm x 75mm; a piece of plywood 6in. x 3in. x $\frac{3}{4}$in. or 150mm x 75mm x 19mm; 55 1in. nails; 4 1$\frac{1}{2}$in. No. 8 screws; padding (foam or rubber) to cover the end of the timber; tacks to secure the padding.

On one side of the plywood mark a frame 1in. in from the edge. Inside the frame mark a grid of $\frac{1}{2}$in. squares. Make holes for the screws (Fig.2). Then at the corners and intersections of the grid, hammer the nails through the plywood so that the points of the nails project $\frac{1}{4}$in. on the other side.

Lay the timber flat with the 4in. side as the base. Place the plywood on the timber as in Fig.2, with the points of the nails facing uppermost. Position the edge of one of the 6in. sides of the plywood level with the short end

of the timber, and centre it on the timber's width so that 1in. of plywood extends on either side (Fig.2). Screw the plywood to the timber. Tack the padding over the other end of the timber.

Measuring and estimating

Even if you are having the carpet fitted for you, or are fitting it yourself but getting the store to estimate the quantity, it is worth making a plan and making your own estimate as a double check. Often the store may be able to save on the amount needed, but if their estimate exceeds yours by a great amount it is advisable to recheck your own and then query it with the store.

To make a really accurate plan, use paper drawn up in 1in. squares, each square representing 1ft. Measure the room carefully with a steel tape and then draw the shape to scale on the paper. Mark all recesses and projections,

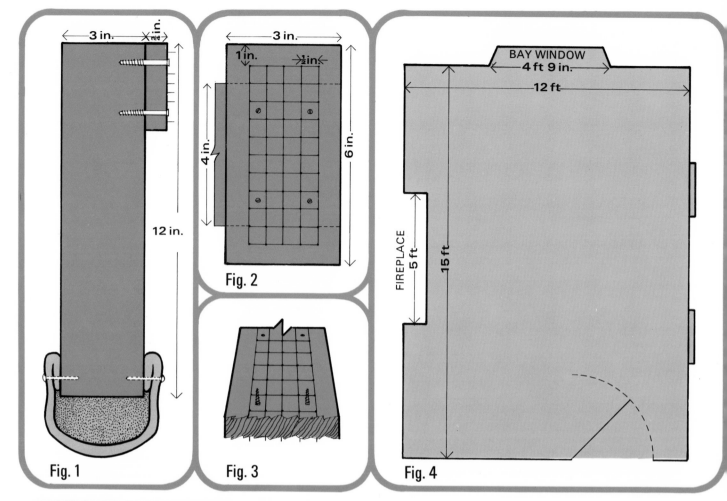

Fig. 1

Fig. 2

Fig. 3

BAY WINDOW
4 ft 9 in.
12 ft
FIREPLACE
5 ft
15 ft

Fig. 4

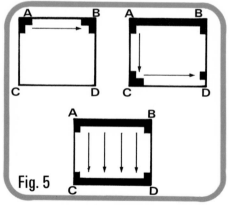

A   B   A   B

C   D   C   D

A   B

C   D

Fig. 5

Fig.1. A home-made knee kicker may be used to stretch small areas of carpet.

Figs.2 and 3. The grid marked on the plywood gives the positions of the nails, which are knocked right through the wood. Their tips grip the carpet when it is being stretched.

Fig.4. In this room, it would be best to buy a 12ft x 15ft carpet 'square', and use the offcut from the fireplace for the bay recess.

Fig.5. To stretch a carpet, secure it at corner A, stretch to B, and secure along the wall between. Stretch to C and then to D. Stretch from wall A-B and secure wall C-D. Then secure wall A-C, stretch to wall B-D and secure that.

Opposite page (Fig.6). The underlay should butt up to the edge of the gripper batten.

Fig.7. The knee kicker is used to push the carpet over the prongs of the batten, which grip the carpet backing firmly.

Fig.8. The edge of the carpet is poked down into the gulley between the gripper and the wall.

Fig.9. To join carpet, fold back one piece and mark a line at a distance of half the tape's width from the edge of the other piece.

Fig.10. Fold back this piece and stay tack it. Position the tape with one edge butting the marked line and tack it down at each end.

Fig.11. Press both the carpet pieces firmly down on to the tape.

and then measure the diagonals of the room to check on the squareness of the corners (they will be equal if the corners are true right angles). Then decide on the width of carpet you are going to use, and where pieces cut out—for a fireplace or bay, for example—could be used to fill in elsewhere.

Broadloom carpet is made in seven standard widths: 6ft, 7ft 6in., 9ft, 10ft 6in., 12ft, 13ft 6in. and 15ft. It is the easiest type to lay in simply shaped square or rectangular rooms because joining is not necessary. You simply buy the length required in the nearest width beyond that of the room.

Body carpet is made in two standard widths: 27in. and 36in. In an oddly shaped room with alcoves and projections it can be more economical than broadloom because there is less wastage, but as seaming the joins can be

tricky it is often better in the long run to use broadloom for the main area of the room and buy matching body carpet to fill in alcoves.

In all cases, the width of the carpet should go across the width of the room, and the length— and therefore the pile and pattern—should run down the length of the room towards the door, if this is in one of the short walls. Any join in a doorway should be along the line of the door when it is closed, and never at right angles to it.

Laying the carpet

Remove the furniture and doors. Sweep the floor and remove any old tacks. Nail down loose boards. If the boards are very uneven, cover the floor completely with sheets of hardboard and nail this down. To prevent dust from working through, cover concrete floors with tarred paper and floorboards with felt paper.

Rubber-backed carpet

Unroll a little of the carpet to check on the direction of the pile and pattern, turn it and start at the opposite wall if necessary to get them running in the right direction without rerolling the carpet.

With the edge of the carpet butting up to the wall, unroll the carpet evenly. Tread it out flat as you progress, but without pulling the edge away from the wall. If it starts to go out of line, reroll the carpet and begin again. If you discover that the corners are out of true, let the edge of the carpet run up the wall slightly and trim it to fit afterwards. Do not attempt to adjust a large area of carpet when it is rolled out because its weight makes it almost impossible to do so evenly.

When the carpet is almost in position, trim off any excess with a metal straight edge and sharp knife. To make a clean cut, press the straight edge into the carpet between the tufts of pile and run the knife along its edge in one continuous motion. When large areas have to be cut out, mark the line with chalk, allowing an excess margin of 1in. Cut out the main part, fit the carpet back into position and trim off the margin to fit it exactly.

To make a join, fit both pieces of carpet in position and check that the pattern fits, that the pile is running the same way, and that the edges butt exactly. If they do not, overlap the pieces and cut through both, using the straight edge as a guide. Then roll back the edge of one piece and stay tack it to hold it back. Measure the width of the carpet tape, and mark a line with chalk on the floor at a distance of half the tape's width from the edge of the carpet piece still in position (Fig.9).

Roll back this second carpet section and stay tack it back. Cut off the right length of adhesive tape and position one edge on the line so that the tape is on the side of the *second* piece that you rolled back. Stick the tape down or anchor it at each end with tacks. Replace one of the carpet pieces and press it down firmly on half of the tape. Unroll the other piece and press it down carefully so that the edges butt firmly and the pattern, if any, matches exactly.

Next, slide the joined edges towards each other, making a slight peak and thereby exposing the cut edges. Apply a thin bead of joining cement along one side and then flatten out the carpet again. Remove any excess joining cement with cement solvent and leave the seam to set for about an hour.

Unbacked carpets

If using the gripper method of fixing the carpet, nail, screw or glue the battens to the floor at a distance from the wall of slightly less than the carpet's pile height; the points of the gripper should be slanting inwards to the wall. Fix battens right round the perimeter of the room, and not just where the ends of the roll will be.

Fit the underlay in position (rubber-backed hessian should have the hessian side uppermost). If you are turning and tacking the edges of the carpet, the edges of the underlay should be 1½in. away from the wall on all sides. If you are using gripper, the underlay should butt up against the inside edge of the batten. Staple or stick (with latex based adhesive) the underlay in position and join it on the underside with adhesive tape where necessary.

Turn and tack method

Unroll the carpet as above, but position it so that a 1½in. margin overlaps on to the wall on each side. Secure it temporarily in one corner with a tack and stretch the carpet taut (see Fig.5). Retrim the margin to 1½in. if necessary, and coat the edges on the backing with latex adhesive to seal them and prevent fraying.

Turn under the margin, press the folded edge against the skirting board and then tack it down, using ½in. tacks at approximately 5in. intervals. Use 1in. tacks at corners, where there is extra thickness.

Gripper method

Unroll the carpet as above, but position it so that ⅜in. margin overlaps on to the wall at each side. Secure the carpet temporarily in one

corner with a tack and stretch the carpet taut (see Fig.5.). Retrim the margin to ⅜in. if necessary and coat the edges on the backing with latex adhesive to seal them and prevent fraying. Use the knee kicker to push the edges of the carpet over the prongs of the gripper and down into the gully between the batten and the skirting board (a screwdriver will make this job easier).

Finishing off

All carpets should be well secured at doorways to prevent both accidents and wear. This is most easily and neatly done with a binder bar, which should come immediately under the door when closed. One kind of binder bar is a 'cove' of metal which is screwed to the floor. The edge of the carpet is fitted into the recess and secured on to the prongs on the bottom lip. The top of the binder bar is then hammered down (with a wooden mallet) to close it over the edge of the carpet.

A simpler form of binder bar is a metal strip which is placed over the edge of the carpet and screwed into the floor. With both kinds, it is possible to secure the edges of an adjoining carpet at the same time.

When the bar is in position, check that the door will open and close smoothly over the carpet. If necessary, plane off just enough of the bottom of the door to make it clear the carpet without rubbing it. Rule the line to which you intend to plane, rather than guessing, and always plane 'from sides to middle' so that the plane does not rip off the edge of the door. Be careful not to plane off too much or you will create a draught problem.

6

7

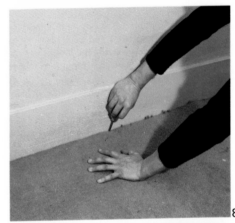
8

9

10

11

Carpeting your stairs

To look good, last well and, just as important, be safe, a stair carpet must be laid correctly. Given below are the methods for laying it on both straight and winding stairs.

Stair carpet is made in four standard widths: 18in., 22½in., 27in. and 36in. If your stairs do not fit one of these, you can either buy a narrower size and leave a border uncarpeted on each side or—and this looks nicer and is easier to clean, although more expensive—you can buy a wider size and cut it or fold under the excess at each side to fit.

To calculate the length of carpet on a straight staircase, measure in inches the depth of a tread and the height of a riser (see Fig.1). Add together the two measurements and multiply the amount by the number of stairs. Add 18in. to allow for the carpet being moved later to distribute wear and, if your underlay is very thick, add on some more to allow for this. Divide the total by 36 to give the number of linear yards.

For a curving staircase, measure the depth of each *winding* (angled) tread separately at its widest point and add it to the height of the riser. Tot up all the figures with the amount needed to cover the straight length and divide by 36 as above.

Another method of measuring—and one which is useful as a double-check—is to lay a tape measure down the stairs, following the contour of the treads and risers as in Fig.1.

Choosing the fittings

All types of carpet must be well secured on stairs for safety. This can be done by stair rods which fit over the carpet in the angle at the back of the tread and slot into eyelets at each side, but this is suitable only for carpet runners which are not fitted at the edges and tends to look old-fashioned.

The modern method of securing stair carpet—and which shows it off to best advantage—is to use *gripper battens* which hold it from behind. These are L-shaped pieces of metal nailed on the crotch (inside angle) of each straight stair. Alternatively, two flat wooden gripper strips of the type used for fitting carpet in rooms can be used. One should be nailed at the back of the tread, and the other at the base of the riser, to make an angle.

The carpet is laid on top, pressed into the angle and held in place by the angled teeth on the gripper. On curving stairs, flat pieces of gripper are used to make the darts which 'lose' the excess carpet (see below).

This type of fixing is not suitable for foam-backed carpets because the teeth would tear it, so instead you should use a system such as Copydex's Foamgrip. Here two separate flat strips are nailed to the back of the tread and the base of the riser and the carpet is held by the angle between them. The distance between the sections should be at least one and a half times the thickness of the carpet (including the pile), but no more than twice the thickness. For example, if the carpet is ½in. thick, the gap should be about ¾in. A smaller gap could damage the carpet, a larger gap would not hold it securely.

With either type of fixing, the width of the strip should be the same as, or just less than, the carpet.

Using an underlay

A separate underlay should be used under all stair carpets except those which have one built in, such as foam-backed ones, because it will both protect the carpet and help deaden the noise of people walking up and down. It can be in the form of a complete runner or separate pads which are fitted to each tread, leaving the riser free. Both types are good, but on a long staircase the pads are more economical, and on curving stairs they are easier to fit. If you are using gripper fittings, it is more advisable to use pads because you will get a firmer fixing.

The length of an underlay runner should be the same as the carpet. Pads should be deep enough to butt against the riser on one side and extend 2in. over the tread *nosing* (outer edge) on the opposite side. In most cases the width of the underlay should be the same as, or slightly less than, the carpet. Anything narrower will produce ridges which will quickly show wear. However, where you are close fitting a woven carpet on stairs which are narrower than a standard width, the excess can be turned under an equal amount on each side. The underlay in this instance should be cut narrower so that it meets the turned-under edge of the carpet. For example, if your stairs were 33in. wide you would have an excess margin of 3in. which would be turned under for 1½in. at each side. The underlay should therefore be 30 in. wide.

Most manufacturers advise on the type of underlay that should be used with their carpet, and it is worth following their advice because you will get the maximum service from the carpet in this way.

If you are using rods and an underlay runner, lay this down the staircase smoothly and pressing it well into the crotch of each stair. Hold it in place with a few carpet tacks on each step.

If you are using underlay pads, cut these to the shape of the stair if necessary. Either tack them in position, or if you are using grippers, nail this in position first, butt the pad up to the edge and secure with tacks. Use the angled sort of gripper for straight stairs and flat pieces (with the points towards the crotch) on winding stairs.

Fitting straight stairs

Professional fitters always lay stair carpet from the bottom upwards, because in this way it is easier to get a really tight fit—this is very important on stairs. However, if you think it would be easier, on a straight staircase it is possible to work from the top downwards. In all cases, the pile of the carpet must run down the stairs. If you are unsure about the direction of

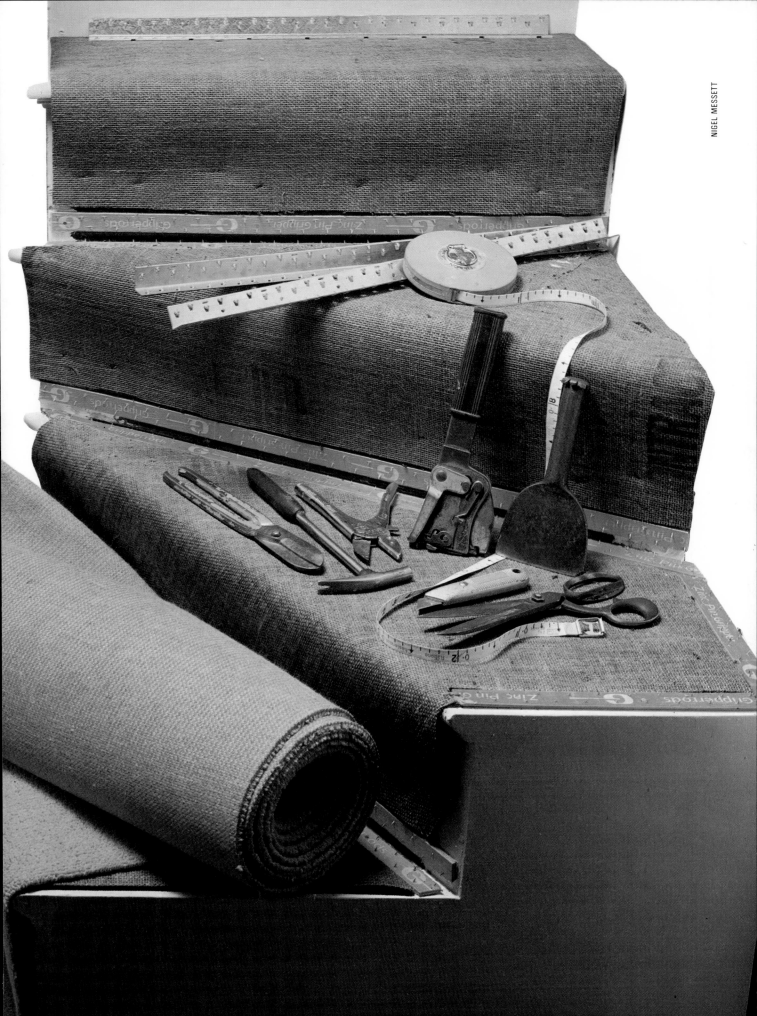

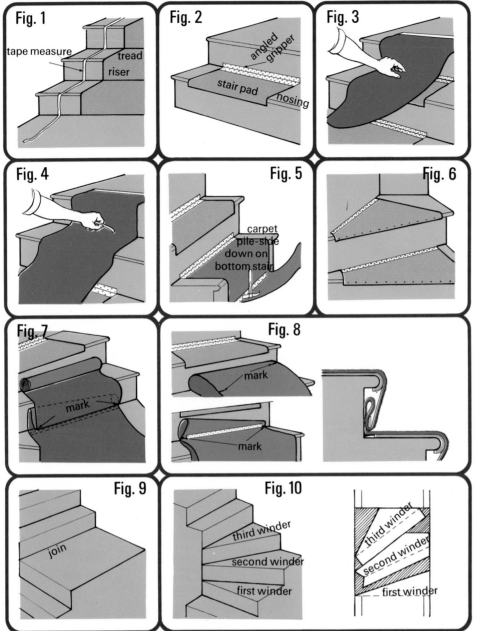

Fig. 1 tape measure tread riser

Fig. 2 angled gripper stair pad nosing

Fig. 3

Fig. 4

Fig. 5 carpet pile-side down on bottom stair

Fig. 6

Fig. 7 mark mark

Fig. 8 mark mark

Fig. 9 join

Fig. 10 third winder second winder first winder

third winder second winder first winder

Fig.1. *To estimate the length of stair carpet you need, add the depth of the tread to the height of the riser, and multiply by the number of steps. Add on extra to allow for easy fitting and for the carpet to be moved.*
Fig.2. *Stair pads should be butted up to the edge of the gripper fitting and tacked down.*
Figs 3 and **4.** *When laying carpet from the top downwards, secure the edge with a binder bar and smooth it over the top step and riser. Press it well into the angle of the gripper with a broad chisel or piece of hardwood.*
Fig.5. *When laying carpet from the bottom up, extra length so the carpet can be moved to distribute wear can be lost at the bottom. The carpet is placed pile-side down on the first step, fixed with gripper, and then turned up the stairs.*
Figs 6-8. *On winding stairs, where you do not want to cut the carpet, nail flat pieces of gripper to the tread. Make a dart in the carpet to take in the fullness on the turn, and hold this in place with another flat gripper strip nailed to the riser.*
Fig.10. *On a half landing, the best place for joining the carpet is at the bottom of the riser on the first step of the second section.*
Fig.11. *Where you have to cut separate pieces on winding stairs, you can economize on carpet by dovetailing the sections.*

If you are using gripper, fix a flat strip to the tread of the first winder and hook the carpet to it. Put the carpet roll on to the next step and swing it round to follow the turn.

You will find you have made a pocket which is larger on the inside than the outside. Smooth this down to the bottom of the riser and mark the base of the fold on the back of the carpet on each side.

Turn the carpet back, keeping the marks at the crotch of the stair. Using longer nails, fix another flat strip over the fold, through the carpet and into the base of the riser. The points of the gripper must be pointing downwards towards the step.

If you are using the special fixing strips for foam or carpet rods, the method for making the dart is very similar, but you should nail it in position using carpet tacks.

Moving the carpet

So that the carpet on the treads does not get worn out long before that on the risers, it is a good idea to move the carpet 2-3in. up or down about once a year. The usual way of doing this is to allow an extra 18in. on the length and 'lose' it at the bottom of the staircase.

The best way of moving the carpet is to remove it from its fixing down the entire length, roll it up and start laying it again from scratch. This may sound tedious, but in the long run it will be quicker and give a smoother result than if you are trying to slide it up or down without removing it entirely.

To remove the carpet if you are using gripper, carefully roll it away from one half of the angle and lift it clear from the other.

Set the end of the carpet in its new position, filling the space left on the bottom tread with a strip of underlay. Trim off some of the underlay at the top and fold under the excess carpet.

the pile, stroke it along the length of the carpet in both directions. The direction in which it feels smoothest is the way the pile runs.

If you are close fitting the carpet, you will probably find it easiest to trim off the excess amount before you put the carpet on the stairs.

If you have allowed extra carpet so it can be moved to even out the wear, you should start laying the carpet at the bottom and work upwards. The extra amount is 'lost' on the bottom tread, where it takes the place of the underlay. (Keep any pieces of underlay which you cut off, because you will need them when you move the carpet later).

With the pile side facing downwards, put the end of the carpet up to the crotch on the first tread. Secure it in place with gripper in the same way as for a stair pad. Smooth the carpet over the first tread and down the riser below, and nail a flat strip of gripper, with its pins pointing downwards, through the back of the carpet into the base of the bottom riser. Then bring the carpet up, stretching it tightly over the first nosing, and press it into the angle gripper which

is holding the edge. Move up the stairs in this way, keeping the carpet roll a couple of steps above.

If you are laying the carpet from the top, secure the end with a binder bar, pull the carpet tightly over the first stair nosing and down the riser, and press it firmly into the angle of the gripper with a mason's *bolster* (broad chisel) or wedge of hardwood. Continue working down the stairs in this way, making sure each tread is firm and tight.

If you are using rods, smooth the carpet over each stair as above, press it well into the crotch and engage the rod in the eyelets.

Fitting on curving stairs

The easiest method of turning a carpet on curving stairs is to cut out wedge-shaped pieces where necessary and to stitch the edges together again, and this method is a perfectly good one for runner underlays or on carpets which will not be moved. On carpets which will be moved, you should try to avoid cutting if at all possible and make large darts in the carpet instead.

Round tablecloths

A square cloth on a round table is like the proverbial square peg in a round hole – it doesn't look right. A round tablecloth is not difficult to make – the only slightly tricky part, you might think, is cutting it out. But if you make a simple paper pattern first, even that problem is overcome.

Measuring for the cloth

First measure the diameter of the table, then decide on the depth of the cloth's overhang (measure from the edge of the table to where you think the bottom of the hem should come). For a small occasional table, the cloth might look best if it goes down to floor level, in Victorian style. For a dining table, however, a drop of 9-12in.—just clearing knee height when people are sitting at the table—would be more practical. Double the measurement of the overhang and add it to the diameter of the table. Add on 1in. ($\frac{1}{2}$in. on each overlap) for the hem, and the total will give you the diameter of the unfinished cloth.

A circular tablecloth is most easily cut from a square of fabric, each side of the square having the same measurement as the diameter of the cloth. Some specialist needlework shops sell fabric suitable for tablecloths in wider than usual widths (up to 90in. for pure linen or a Terylene/cotton mixture), which means that the cloth can be made in one piece, without a join. You simply buy a length of fabric equal in length to the diameter. Make the paper pattern and cut out the cloth as for the panelled method (see below).

If you have to join more fabric to the main piece, there are two methods of doing so. In the panelled method, the full width of the square is made up by joining two pieces of fabric to the

NELSON HARGREAVES

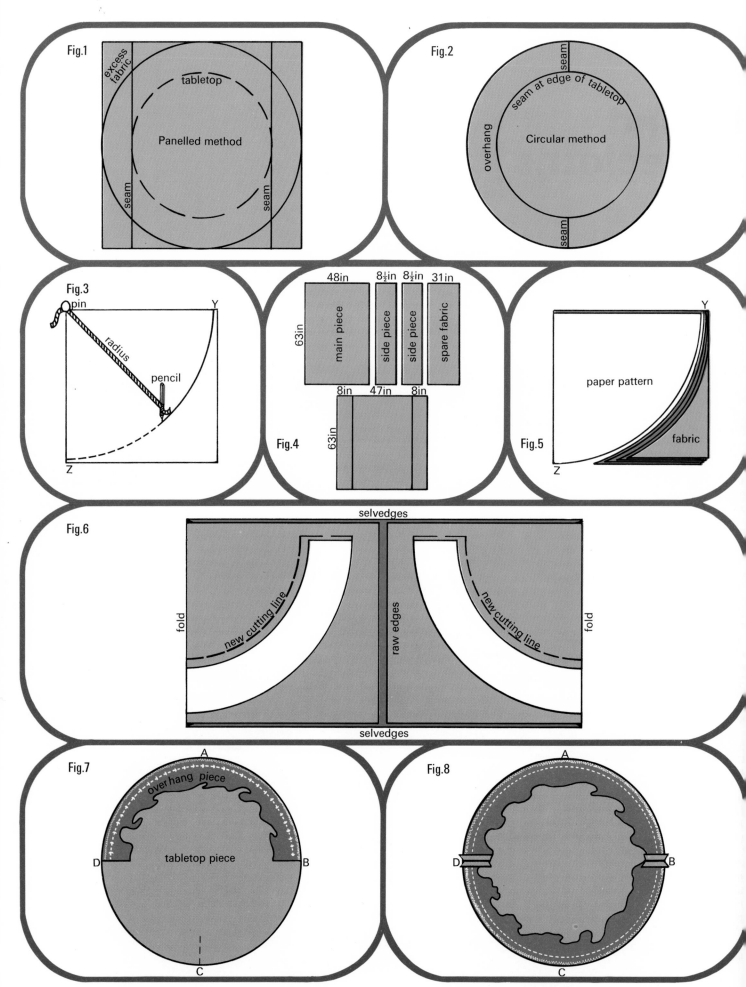

Fig.1

excess fabric

tabletop

Panelled method

seam

seam

Fig.2

seam

seam at edge of tabletop

overhang

Circular method

seam

Fig.3

pin

radius

pencil

Y

Z

Fig.4

48in

8½in

8½in

31in

63in

main piece

side piece

side piece

spare fabric

8in

47in

8in

63in

Fig.5

Y

paper pattern

fabric

Z

Fig.6

selvedges

fold

new cutting line

raw edges

new cutting line

fold

selvedges

Fig.7

A

over hang piece

tabletop piece

D

B

C

Fig.8

A

D

B

C

144

SYNDICATION INTERNATIONAL

ong sides of the main piece (Fig.1). This method is more suitable for a patterned fabric, as the seams—which fall in an uneven arc on the overhang when the cloth is in position—are less noticeable than in a plain fabric.

For a plain fabric, it would look better to use the circular method, in which a semi-feature is made of the main joining seam. The fabric is cut to fit the tabletop, two semi-circular pieces are joined to it for the overhang, and the main seam falls around the edge of the table (Fig.2). This method, however, uses more fabric, and there is some wastage.

Panelled method: to calculate how much fabric to buy, determine the diameter of the unfinished cloth as above, and double it (allow extra for matching the pattern—see page 68). *Circular method:* double the diameter of the unfinished cloth, and add it to the diameter of the tabletop, plus 1in. for turnings.

Making a paper pattern

To achieve an accurate shape when cutting out the tablecloth, make a paper pattern first. Cut a large piece of paper into a square, each side of which is a little longer than the radius of the cloth (half the diameter). Tie one end of a piece of string round a pencil, and measure the radius from the pencil along the length of string. Mark the measurement by pushing a drawing pin through the string.

Lay the paper on a flat surface and push the drawing pin into the top lefthand corner of the paper. Hold the pin firmly with the left hand and, holding the pencil upright with the other hand (with the string taut), draw an arc with the pencil from point Y, Fig.3, in the top righthand corner, to point Z, at the bottom lefthand corner. (Reverse the corners and hands if you are left-handed.) Cut along the pencilled line.

If making the cloth by the circular method,

Stitch lace to the hem of a floor-length tablecloth to give it a Victorian touch.

draw a second smaller arc with a radius the length of half the diameter of the tabletop, plus ½in. for turnings. Cut along this line.

Making the cloth
Panelled method
Cut the fabric across into two equal pieces. Then cut one of these pieces lengthwise, as shown in Fig.4, into panels of the right width to make up the full width of the cloth when these are joined to the centre panel.

To calculate the width of the side panels, subtract the width of the fabric, less 1in. seam allowance, from the diameter of the cloth. Add 1in. to the remaining measurement and divide the total by two.

Match the pattern on the panels carefully, and join the side panels to the centre panel with a ½in. plain seam. Trim the length down to the same measurement as the width if necessary. You should now have a square of fabric with each side equal to the diameter of the cloth.

Fold the fabric in half and then in half again, to make a square, each side of which is equal to the radius. Pin the paper pattern on to the fabric so that its square point is in the corner of the fabric where the folds meet.

Cut through the layers of fabric along the pattern edge from point Y to point Z, Fig.5. Do not cut along the folds. Unpin the pattern and unfold the fabric.
Circular method
Cut off a square of fabric, from the main length, with each side equal to the diameter of the tabletop, plus 1in. for turnings. Fold this square in half and in half again. Pin the triangular pattern piece (for the tabletop) to the

fabric as for the panelled method, and cut out. Do not cut along the folds.

Before unfolding the fabric, mark the straight grain four times at opposite points on the cloth by making a few tacking stitches in from the edge along the folds. These stitches will act as guide lines when attaching the overhang, and will ensure that the grain runs straight on the pieces, so the cloth 'hangs' properly.

Lay the remaining length of fabric flat on the floor. Fold over the raw edges so they meet in the middle. Pin the circular pattern piece (for the overhang) on the fabric so that one straight edge is on one of the folds.

Using tailor's chalk, mark on the fabric the cutting line for the inner edge of the overlap 1in. from the inner edge of the pattern. Mark another line ½in. from the straight edge of the pattern which is not on the fold of the fabric (see Fig.6). Cut along these lines and along the outer edge of the pattern. Do not cut along the fold.

Unpin the pattern and pin it to the fabric at the other fold. Mark the cutting line along the inner edges as for the other piece, and cut out. Unpin the pattern. Clip ⅜in. into the inner edge of both overhang pieces at 1in. intervals. With the 'right' sides of the fabric facing, and with the overhang uppermost, match the centre of the inner edge of one overhanging piece to one of the tacking guide marks on the tabletop piece (Fig.8, point A). Working from this point outwards to the straight edges of the overhang, pin the pieces together ½in. from the edge (the clips cut in the overhang will open out).

Pin the second overhang piece to the tabletop piece in a similar way, matching its centre to the opposite tacking guide mark on the tabletop (point C). Where the overhang pieces meet at points B and D, pin their raw edges together— the seam line should fall ½in. in from the edge but adjust this so that the overhang fits the tabletop exactly, and the seam lines correspond with the tacking guide marks at points B and D. Tack and machine stitch these seams. Press them open and neaten the raw edges.

Tack and machine stitch the overhang to the tabletop. Remove the tacking and press the entire seam allowance down on to the overhang. Overcast the raw edges together.

Making the hem
The easiest way to finish a circular hem is with bias binding, as this will give the right amount of ease to go round a curve smoothly. To decide exactly how much bias binding to buy, multiply the diameter of the cloth by 22 and divide the total by 7. This gives the circumference of the cloth (allow a couple of inches extra for overlapping the binding).

Unfold one of the pressed edges of the binding, and place the edge to the edge of the tablecloth, 'right' sides facing. Pin and tack it to the cloth along the crease line of the binding. Neaten the ends by turning them under ¼in. and overlapping them. Machine stitch all round the hem, following the tacking line.

Press the binding over entirely on to the wrong side of the cloth. Tack the binding to the cloth along the outer folded edge of the binding, and machine stitch. Press the hem and then the finished cloth.

Made-to-measure table linen

Ready-made tablecloths tend to come in a few standard sizes which look all wrong if your table is not a standard size too. Try making your own—then you can decide both size and cost.

Measure the length and width of the table top and add 9-12in. for the overhang on each side (9in. will bring the cloth down to about knee-level). If the cloth is to have a plain hem, add another 2in. to each side. If you can buy fabric wide enough—usually from a specialist needle-work shop—you will only need one length. If you have to join the fabric to make up the width, you may need twice or three times the length, depending on the width of the fabric and the table, and on where the seams are to fall.

Because a centre seam would look ugly, the best method is to join pieces of fabric of equal width to the long sides of the main piece. Ideally the main piece should, when in position on the table, cover the table top entirely and overhang the sides, so that any seams are part of the overhang and do not interrupt the smoothness of the top. If, however, the fabric is narrower than the table top, rather than having the joining seams so near the edges that they could upset the balance of the place setting, it might be better to make the centre panel narrower still, with the seams 9-12in. from the edges (**Fig.1**).

In either case, work out the width of the panels (following the method described on page 144) before you buy the fabric, as you may well find after cutting there will be some fabric left over which can be used for napkins.

For example, for a table 3ft 6in. wide, the tablecloth—with a 9in. overhang and 2in. hem allowance—would be 64in. wide unfinished. With 48in. fabric, you would need an amount twice the length of the table. The full width of the fabric can be used for the centre panel, which is cut from one 'length', and the side panels—each 9in. wide, including seam allowance—are cut from the second 'length'. The leftover fabric from this would be 30in. wide.

With 36in. fabric, you might decide to make the centre panel 18in. wide (19in. including seam allowance), so that the seams come 12in. in from the edges. Adapt the formula (see pages 144-145) so that you start by taking the width of the centre panel from the width of the tablecloth. In this case, each side panel, including allowances, would be 23½in. wide, so you would need fabric three times the length of the table. There would be two leftover lengths, 12½in. wide.

Left. 'Wedge' shaped mats are not difficult to make and are ideal for a round table.

ALAN DUNS

Making up the panels

Cut out the panels, including ½in. seam allowance on each side of the centre panel and on the inner edge of the side panels. Join them with a plain seam or—if the cloth is to be washed frequently—a machine fell seam in which the edges are enclosed, making the seam flat and easy to press.

Machine fell seam. Make a plain seam, but stitch it with the *wrong* sides of fabric together. When the seam is pressed open, trim one side of the seam allowance, press the other side over the trimmed side, turn under ⅛in. and press flat. Tack and machine stitch through all thicknesses, near the fold (**Fig.2**).

Making the hem

For plain 1½in. hems, mitre the corners before stitching, as this will give a flatter and neater effect than lapped corners.

Mitred corners. On adjoining sides of the cloth, fold over the raw edges ½in. on to the wrong side, and press. Make another fold 1½in. from the first folded edges and press again. Open out the second folds and turn in the corner on a diagonal line going through the point where the fold lines meet, and at an equal distance from the corner on both sides (**Fig.3**.) Leaving the first folds turned in, trim off the corner ¼in. outside the diagonal crease, cutting firmly through the folded edges (**Fig.4**).

Find the centre of the diagonal line, then fold the corner, with right sides facing, at this point so that the sides of the cloth are level. Stitch along the diagonal line, and then turn it right side out, gently easing out the point with a knitting needle (**Fig.5**). Press.

Make the other corners in the same way, then stitch the hem, using the lines of the folds already made.

Trimmed edge

Turn over the fabric ½in. on to the wrong side, and pin and tack the trimming to cover the raw edge (mitre or lap the corners of the trimming, depending on the type). Stitch along the top and bottom of the trimming.

Napkins

Dinner napkins traditionally tended to be of a good size, not only to cover laps from possible spills but also because they used to be folded into elaborate shapes. Lunch napkins were slightly smaller because these were not necessarily folded elaborately. Nowadays, when most people fold napkins simply into four, a practical size—making best use of fabric widths—is 16-18in. square. Tea and cocktail napkins can be 12in. square, or even smaller.

Above. *Colourful mats and napkins can turn a picnic into a sophisticated meal.*

Below. *By making your own tablecloth you can match it with other covers.*

Right. *Instead of using bias binding to finish the edges of shaped mats, cut scallops —using a semi-circle cut from cardboard as a template—and then overcast the raw edges.*

Finish napkins with plain hems and mitred corners, as for the tablecloth, but turning over the first fold for ¼in. and the second fold ½in. Stitch by machine, or with small, firm slip stitching.

Place mats

These tend to be more informal than a tablecloth and are ideal for tables with a surface which you want to 'show off' but protect from scratches. If you also want to protect it from heat, choose a heavy-weight fabric, in cotton or linen, or use a mat under lightweight ones. If you plan to 'fray' the edges in order to make a self-fringe, use a fairly coarse cotton, rather than linen, as cotton will keep its appearance better when washed.

A practical size for rectangular place mats is 13½in. x 18in. (12in. x 16½in. finished), but this should be adapted according to the width of the fabric. For plain edges, make hems with mitred corners as for napkins (above). For a frayed edge, remove the threads parallel to the edges to the depth of the fringe required (Fig. 6), then overcast the edges to secure them from further fraying.

Rounded place mats

For round tables, mats which are curved at the outer edge and taper towards the centre of the table can make more economical use of the space (Fig.7).

In order to make the curve on the mats 'parallel' to the curve of the table, cut a triangular paper pattern to fit the table top, following the method on pages 144-145. Then measure an equal amount in from the straight sides—judge the amount by eye to get the size mat you want—and draw straight lines parallel to the sides, and to the required depth. Join the lines at the top and then cut off the excess paper, allowing ¼-½in. hem allowance (Fig.8).

Cut out the mats so that the grain on the fabric runs parallel to the sides of the mats (otherwise they may stretch and buckle). Finish the edges with bias binding, so that the binding is completely on the wrong side of the fabric when the mats are finished.

The corners can be mitred following the method above, or by a simpler method which can be used here because the binding is not bulky and the wrong sides of the mats are not on show.

Unfold one of the creased edges of the binding, and, starting in the middle of one side, pin it to the mat, with edges meeting and right sides together. Clip the binding diagonally at the corners of the mat to ease it round. To join the binding, overlap it at the ends, turning under the raw edges to make a neat join. Tack and machine stitch the binding in position, and then press it over completely on to the wrong side of the mat. Tuck under the excess binding at the four corners, making a diagonal fold. Tack the binding down to the mat along the outer fold, and machine or hem stitch. Stitch the folds and join with small hem stitching.

Fig. 1

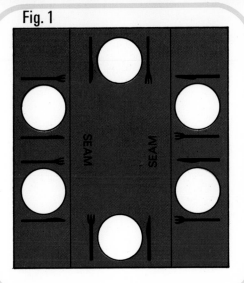

SEAM   SEAM

Fig. 2

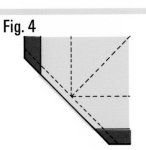

Fig. 3

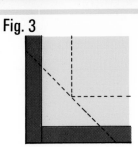

Fig. 4

Fig. 5

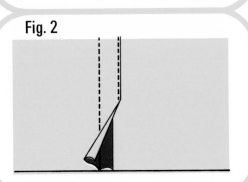

Fig. 6

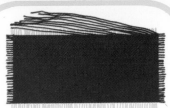

Fig. 7

Fig. 8

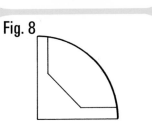

Tablecloths to your own design

By combining simple embroidery with plain sewing, you can design an unusual tablecloth which makes an attractive feature of functional seams.

A tablecloth in its simplest form is a piece of fabric hemmed all round the outside edge to prevent it from fraying and to give it a neat finish. It is very quick and easy to make, the only difficulty being that many fabrics are not wide enough for most dining tables.

It is possible to buy fabrics suitable for tablecloths up to 90in. wide, but these are fairly expensive and not available in a wide range of colours and patterns. This means that if you choose a 36in. dress fabric or a 48in. furnishing fabric, you will probably have to join pieces to make the right width for your table.

The method for making a panelled tablecloth, whereby a centre panel of the full width of the fabric has two narrower strips joined at each side by a plain seam, was given for a round cloth on pages 143-145, and for a square cloth on pages 147-149. This gives a perfectly satisfactory finish, although it is rather functional and plain. If you would prefer a more decorative effect, the panels could be joined by faggoting or insertion stitching. The panels need not be confined simply to long strips but extra seams could be incorporated to give added interest (Fig.1).

In this method of joining fabric, the edges of the pieces to be joined are placed about $\frac{3}{8}$-$\frac{1}{2}$in. apart. The faggoting stitches are worked alternately from edge to edge, joining the pieces and also giving a decorative finish.

Many of the stitches used in faggoting are common embroidery stitches but, although they are simple to work, their success depends on keeping their size and the spaces between them absolutely even. Some of the stitches also catch the hems of the panels, and with others you should slip stitch the hems first.

Use regular sewing thread and a fine needle for slip stitching, but for the embroidery use Anchor stranded embroidery cotton. This is made up from six strands which can be split into fewer strands for lightweight fabrics.

Preparing the fabric

Cut out the fabric for the panels, allowing $1\frac{1}{2}$in. on the sides which will eventually form the outside edge of the cloth and $\frac{1}{2}$in. for turnings on all other sides. Try to adjust the

Left. If you have to join pieces of fabric to have a tablecloth large enough for your table, make a feature of the seams by faggoting. The stitches are simple and quick to work.

sizes of the panels so that the seams will fall on the tabletop, rather than on the overhang, so that they will be displayed to full advantage.

Turn under the $\frac{1}{2}$in. turnings and make narrow hems. Tack them down, and slip stitch them if necessary (see below). Cut along $1\frac{1}{2}$in. wide strips of firm paper for each seam.

With the wrong side facing the paper, tack the fabric to the strips, leaving a gap of about $\frac{3}{8}$in. between the edges (Fig.2). This gap can be made slightly wider or narrower, as you prefer. In any case, the finished seam will be a little narrower than the gap because the stitching tends to pull the edges together.

Order of seams

Try to plan the order of working the seams so that you will end up with as many long seams as possible when joining the final pieces; this will give an even finish to the cloth. For example, if you are making the tablecloth in nine pieces as shown in design B, you should join the small corner squares to the long borders first and then join the remaining border pieces to the centre square. The three composite strips can then be joined by two long seams.

With design E, it would be best to make three strips by joining two large squares to the long sides of a narrow strip, and the small centre squares to the short edges of the remaining narrow strips. These could then be joined together by two long seams across the cloth.

Finishing the cloth

Leave the brown paper in position until all the seams have been completed, then remove them and press the cloth.

The outside hem of the cloth can be finished as described on pages 147-149, or if you feel really ambitious, you could finish it by hemstitching, which is a simple form of drawnthread embroidery. This looks particularly good on plain fabric which has a fairly coarse weave.

Hemstitching

On a classic hemstitched edge, some threads parallel to the edge to be hemmed are pulled out of the fabric, leaving an open band of threads running at right angles of the edge. The hem is turned under and tacked down so that its inner fold falls exactly along the outer edge of the open band. In stitching the hem, the remaining threads in the band are split into groups, thus giving an attractive finish. In many hemstitched edges, another line of stitching can be worked along the opposite side of the open band.

The number of threads you withdraw ob-

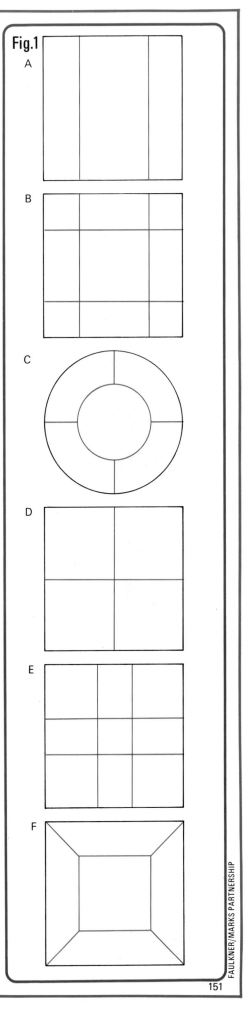

Fig.1
A
B
C
D
E
F

FAULKNER/MARKS PARTNERSHIP

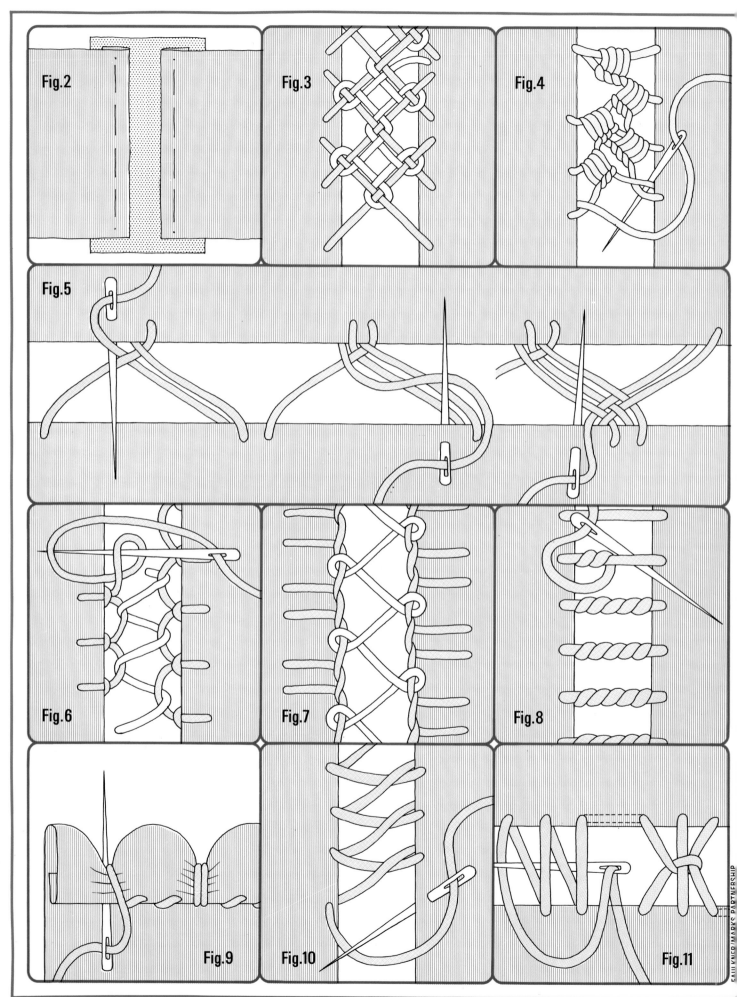

Fig.2

Fig.3

Fig.4

Fig.5

Fig.6

Fig.7

Fig.8

Fig.9

Fig.10

Fig.11

Fig.2. To keep the distance between the edges even, the prepared fabric is tacked on to strips of firm paper.

Fig.3. Interlaced insertion stitch. The second line of thread weaves through the first stitches and does not catch the fabric.

Fig.4. Italian buttonhole insertion stitch.

Fig.5. Plaited insertion stitch. The first rows of stitches also catch the hem.

Fig.6. Laced insertion. Use a firm thread to lace the edges together.

Fig.7. Cretan and buttonhole insertion. The first rows of stitches also catch the hem.

Fig.8. Bullion bar insertion.

Fig.9. A simple, but decorative way of finishing the outer edge of the cloth.

Fig.10. Half cretan insertion.

Fig.11. Faggot bundles. The stitch linking the bundles is hidden inside the fold of the hem.

Fig.12. Buttonhole insertion. Take care when moving from one edge to the other that the linking thread is tight, otherwise the effect will be uneven when the paper is removed.

Fig.13. Twisted insertion. The needle picking up the edge of the fabric always enters from the back. This stitch can also be worked with one twist, as shown on page 150.

Fig.14 Knotted insertion. This also catches the hem adequately.

Figs 15 and 16. How to remove threads for hem stitching. The threads to be removed should be cut about 1in. from the inner edge of the border, so that the ends left can be turned back and caught down under the hem.

Fig.17. At the corners of the drawn border, where there is a little square with no threads, work in buttonhole stitch. This will catch the hem securely and will not look too different from the hem stitching.

Fig.18. How to do hem stitching. Its success depends on the same number of threads being caught in each group and being picked up at the edge. A second row of stitching can be worked on the other edge of the border.

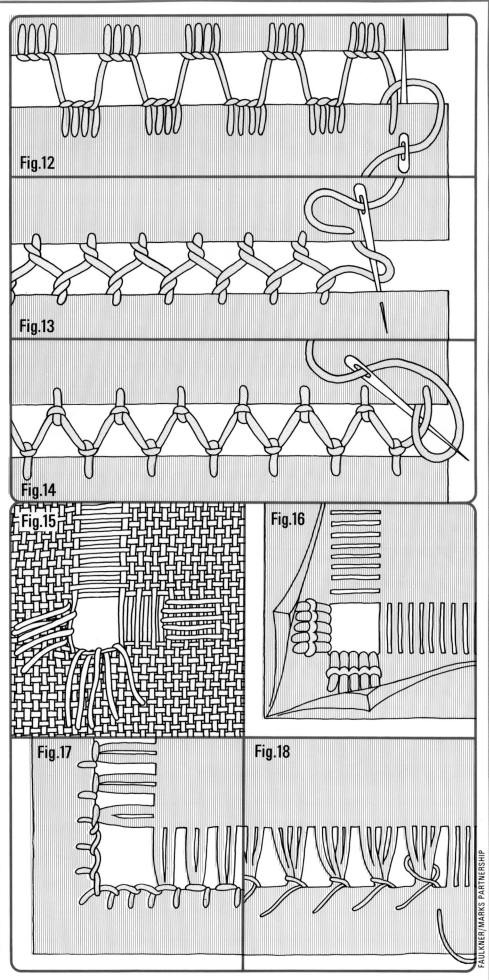

...viously depends on the weave of the fabric and the effect you want to achieve; the width of the band can vary from 1/16in. to $\frac{1}{4}$in. On something like a tablecloth, however, you should take care to pull them out from each side so that you leave in the ends of the threads where they will be part of the hem (Fig.15).

For example, where you have a 1½in. hem allowance, which will make a 1in. finished hem, mark the outer edge of the border all the way round the cloth 2½in. in from the edge. Start drawing out the threads 4in. away from each corner. The easiest way to do this is to loosen the thread by inserting a pin under it, and then cutting through it. Cut it at the other end too. Use the pin to help free a long enough piece of thread so you can pull out the whole length easily. Continue withdrawing threads all round the cloth in the same way until the border is the right width. To finish the threads which are hanging loose, turn them back on to the hem allowance and tack them down. They will be hidden by the finished hem (Fig.16).

Complete the hem, mitring the corners as shown on pages 147-149, and tack down. Work hemstitching along the hem side of the border first, then work along the other edge.

FAULKNER/MARKS PARTNERSHIP

Left. Loops, formed by two closely worked rows of chain stitch, are a simple idea and look most effective in contrasting colours on a plain, bright background.

although they seem very modern, it is a style that has been used by children for centuries. The basic shapes are simple and figurative, and their effect depends on the colours used, rather than the portrayal of the subject. This means that even if you think you cannot draw, you will be able to design something unusual and pleasing.

Another advantage with this sort of embroidery is that all the stitches are very quick and simple to work, and you do not have to use an embroidery frame.

Choosing the design

Simple flowers or geometric shapes are the most effective and easiest patterns, and usually appeal to adults and children alike. For table linen specially for children, you could include animals—cats, dogs, elephants, fish and butterflies are all easy outlines to work.

If you decide on flowers, think of the way children draw them and start from there. Sometimes you may just wish to include the head of the flower, arranged in clusters. Or you might draw the whole flower and arrange several radiating from one point.

If you think that geometric shapes are more in your line, sketch out several shapes until you find one that you like. Here again, the shapes don't have to be accurate, with equal angles and so on—much of the beauty in embroidery comes from its individuality.

Choosing the colours

The colours you choose are just as important to the design as the shape. With this type of embroidery, strong colours look best, but they need not all necessarily be bright. The colours should go with the other colours in the room and with your tableware and, if as so often happens, these are different, you can combine the colours in the embroidery.

Don't be afraid of putting unusual, or even normally discordant, colours together because the effect can be stunning providing you have a main colour as the anchor. For example, if your room has pinks and purples as its decorative scheme, and your tableware is orange, you may find that the three colours can be combined as the embroidery on a dark fabric such as brown or black.

Once you have an idea of the colours you would like to use, check in your needlework shop that the fabric is available in the right colour. If you have decided to team it with your tableware, make sure that it really is a match, and test it in day and artificial light if possible; if it is slightly different, you may find this a continuing source of irritation. You can afford to be less critical if you are matching it to the curtains or carpet because these usually will be further away.

If you cannot obtain the right colour, you might consider buying some white fabric and dyeing it (see pages 217-219). Alternatively, choose another colour which will go in the room and base the colours of the embroidery on those of your tableware. Embroidery threads are

Modern embroidery for table linen

For any good meal, an attractive setting is important as the natural complement to the food being served. Traditionally this has meant a snow-white cloth laid with shining cutlery and glassware, and it was the task of every bride-to-be to embroider several cloths for her bottom drawer. Nowadays, although this tradition has died out, embroidered table linen can still transform an ordinary meal into something special.

Specialist needlework shops have a large range of patterns and designs for this kind of embroidery, but they normally tend to be of a classic design—ideal in a traditional setting but not so suitable for the clean-cut lines of modern design. They also usually demand some skill in their execution. If you would prefer something more modern—and less time-consuming—why not have a go at designing on the lines shown in the photographs here?

The designs are a kind of abstract art but,

Fig. 1

Fig. 2

Fig. 3

Fig. 4

stem stitch

chain stitch

daisy stitch

satin stitch

available in such a wide range that you will have no problem there.

Sketch out your main motif on paper with coloured crayons, drawing in the actual shapes of the stitches over part of the pattern so you can get an idea of the balance between the colours. You may find that you should modify the juxtaposition of some colours, or introduce some more. Try the motif in a solid colour and then in combinations of colour. If you are using flowers in, say, yellow and orange, try one with a yellow centre and orange petals and then one the other way round. You may find that this alternation of the colours works and you will want to use both in your overall design.

This operation need not take a long time, but it is worth doing it because you will get a far better idea of the finished result than by just holding a few skeins of embroidery thread together over your fabric.

Finalizing the design

When you have decided on your motif, the next step is to work out its placement on the fabric. To show off the embroidery to its best advantage, you should position it so that for a tablecloth it will be on the tabletop, not the overhang, and on a mat so that it will not be covered by the plate.

If you are making a tablemat, calculate its final size and cut a piece of squared paper to fit. Put on the largest dinner plate you will be using and mark the space left over on each side. This will be the area for your embroidery.

If you are making a tablecloth, a symmetrical design looks best, so calculate the overall measurement as given on pages 147-149, and cut a piece of squared paper to a quarter of this size. Mark on the paper the area of the cloth which will fall on the tabletop.

With a circular cloth, you can complement the circular shape by starting the design from a circle in the middle of the table and work out towards the sides, placing the motifs in concentric circles or spaced lines radiating from the centre. The first way can be done with a pencil, string and a pin, the second by folding the paper in half and then in half again, until the segments are the size you want. You can then place a motif on each crease line.

Transferring the design

There are two simple methods of transferring the design to the fabric.

Carbon Paper. Sheets of carbon paper are sold specially for this purpose in needlework shops and the marks made will disappear after the fabric is washed. Lay out your fabric completely flat on a firm surface and, if it is a tablecloth, folded to the same size as the squared paper. Lay the carbon paper on top of the fabric, with the waxed side facing down. Place the squared paper on it with the design facing up, and anchor it with a few pins to prevent it from moving about. Go over your design with an ordinary pencil, pressing quite hard.

Transfer pencil. Cut greaseproof paper to the same size as the squared paper and trace your design on to it with the transfer pencil. Lay out your fabric completely flat on an ironing board, folding it if necessary to the same size as the squared paper. Place the greaseproof paper on

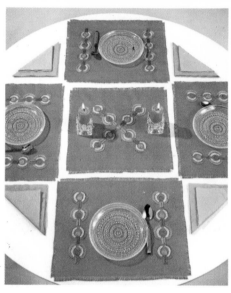

PAF INTERNATIONAL

Above. All of the outlines are simple to draw, but their success relies on the choice of colour and placement on the fabric so they are displayed to the full.

Previous page, Fig. 1. *Overlapping concentric circles can be developed into different designs.* **Fig.2.** *A pattern for a square cloth looks best if it is symmetrical, so only a quarter of the design is worked out. The bands are formed by working lines of chain stitch.* **Fig.3.** *A simple flower motif, which could be adapted for mats or cloths.* **Fig.4.** *How to do the stitches. All of them are quick and easy to work.*

the fabric with the design side facing down. Heat the iron to a warm temperature and go over the paper firmly. Leave for a few seconds and then remove the paper.

You will find that by this method you will get a mirror image of the design. In most cases this will not matter but, if it does, turn over the squared paper and trace the design through the

back. If the paper is too thick for this, trace the design first with one sheet of greaseproof paper and an ordinary pencil, and turn this over and trace it again with another sheet of greaseproof paper and the transfer pencil.

Starting off

Instructions for making a basic round tablecloth were given on pages 143-145, and for tablemats and square cloths on pages 147-149. Use a linen or cotton fabric because these will have similar properties to the embroidery thread and will react in the same way when washed. Embroidery also seems to 'sit' better on these fabrics. Any embroidery thread can be used, although you will probably find a stranded cotton gives the softest result.

The stitches used in this type of embroidery are all very simple : stem stitch which borders the motif ; chain stitch which quickly fills in the centre when worked in rounds or rows ; daisy stitch for single petals, etc. ; and satin stitch for more solid areas.

Loose covers for fireside chairs

The term 'loose cover' is a slight misnomer because the cover should fit the chair like a glove, and be 'loose' only in that it can be removed for cleaning. Many modern chairs are made with covers which can be removed but, if they cannot be, it is often worth fitting loose covers on top to protect them. In true Victorian tradition, the loose covers can be removed on special occasions!

The other advantage of loose covers is that they can make an old suite blend in with new furnishings. They can also disguise shabby upholstery, although they should not be used where the 'innards' of the upholstery need repair. They do not 'sit' successfully on chairs with leather or plastic covers, and should not be used with velvet because the pile sets up a resistance to the cover fabric which makes it wear badly.

For your first attempt at making covers, choose a simple fireside chair—the type which has wooden arms. The cover should be fitted actually on the chair, following the method below, and never made to match old covers which may have stretched.

Calculating the amount of fabric

Choose fabric which is tough and hard-wearing, firm in weave, colourfast and non-shrink. Avoid very thick fabrics, as these will be difficult to work with. Medium-weight furnishing cottons and linens treated for crease resistance are ideal. Don't be tempted to use dress fabric, because this will not be strong enough. 30in. wide fabric is the most economical to use for chairs, but if you do have to buy 48in. wide, the offcuts can be used for making the piping casing.

Like any other kind of soft furnishing, it is worth making a simple cutting chart showing the measurements of each section. You will then see where the pieces can be dove-tailed, and how much fabric you will have left for the piping casing. The warp threads of the fabric—those running down the length parallel with the selvedge—should run vertically on all the upright sections of the cover, and on the seat they should run from the back to the front, rather than across.

Start taking your measurements by putting pins in the padding of the chair on the seam line of the existing upholstery at the top of the back in the centre, and in the seam behind the arms at the widest part of the back, so that the inside and outside measurements are taken from the same point.

Inside back. Measure from the pin at the top (Fig. 1, point A) down to where the back and seat meet (point B). Add on 1in. for the turning at the top and 5in. for the turning and tuck-in at the bottom. For the width, measure between the pins at the sides (points C to D), and add 1in. on each side for turnings.

Outside back. Measure from the pin at the top (point A) to the bottom of the seat (point E) and add 1in. for the turnings at the top and 5in. at the bottom for the turning and tie-under. For the width, measure from C to D (but on the outside of the chair), and add 1in. on each side for turnings.

Seat. If the seat has a removable cushion, the cover for this should be made using the method described on pages 99-101. In order to cover the section below this if it is upholstered, or the seat if it is a fixed one, measure from the back of the seat at point B, to the front (point F). Add 5in. for the turning and tuck-in at the back and 1in. for the turning at the front.

Seat border. For the depth of the seat border, measure from point F to the bottom of the seat (point G). Add 1in. at the top for turnings and 5in. at the bottom for turning and tie under. For the width of the *front border,* measure from one arm, round the front of the seat to the other arm, and add 1½in. on each side. For the width of the *side borders,* measure from the arm to the back of the chair and add 1½in. to the front edge and 1in. to the other edge (allow double the amount of fabric, since two side bands are needed).

To calculate the amount of piping cord and bias-cut casing fabric needed for the piping, measure the perimeter of the seat and the chair back (from the back leg, up the side, across the top and down the other side to the leg). As a guide, 1yd 48in. fabric will make about 28yd bias strip, 1½in. wide; 1yd 30/31in. fabric will make about 24yd bias strip.

All the turnings given are generous because this allows easy fitting, and also makes the seam allowance less likely to fray too near the stitching line. It is always advisable to overcast the seams of loose covers, especially if you will be washing them by machine.

If your chair is different in design from that shown in the diagrams, cut the loose cover sections to correspond with the original upholstery, placing the seams in the same places. In the chair shown in Fig. 2, for example, there is an extra piece between the inside and outside back sections, and this is in two sections because of the arm.

Fitting the cover

Cut out all the pieces, including allowances, taking care to position any pattern on the fabric the right way up and, where possible, centrally on each piece.

Find the centre of each section of the chair and mark a line with pins on the padding up the outside back, down the inside back, along the seat and border.

Fold all the pieces of fabric in half lengthwise, with wrong sides together. Place the piece for the inside back on the left-hand side of the chair, with the fold level with the centre pin line. Arrange the fabric so that 1in. projects at the top and then pin the fold to the chair all the way down. Smooth the fabric out to the side of the chair and pin along the top, following the seam line of the original upholstery.

If you have not inserted a strip between the front and back pieces, to fit the fabric round the arms, fold back the edges of the fabric level with the inner edge of the arm. Mark another line with pins on the fabric from the centre of the arm out to the raw edges (Fig.3). Cut along this pin line from the raw edges to within 1in. of the arm and then snip into the corners of the arm (Fig.4). Fold under these turnings, level with the arm, remove the pins which hold the fold down and smooth out the fabric to the side of the chair.

Bring the lower piece under the arm to the outside back and pin along the seam line of the original upholstery. Bring the upper piece over the arm and pin. Check that this section fits smoothly and exactly follows the contours of the chair. Adjust the pins to improve it where necessary, and make darts to take in any fullness which cannot be disposed of without distorting the fabric.

Place the fabric for the seat section on the left-hand side of the seat, with the fold level with the centre pin line and 1in. projecting over the front of the seat. Pin the fold to the seat padding, smooth the fabric out to the side and pin it at the front and side of the seat. Pin the lower edge of the inside back section to the back edge of the seat section and push in the tuck-in at the back of the seat.

Pin the outside back section to the same half on the outside of the chair, with the fold of the fabric level with the centre pin line and 1in. projecting at the top. Pin it to the inside back fabric along the top of the chair, removing the pins which hold the inside section to the padding as you progress. Smooth the outside back fabric to the side and, working down from the top, pin it to the inside back fabric. Pin it to the padding at the bottom of the chair.

Pin the border sections to the seat fabric in the same way, but do not attempt to fit them round the legs yet. Pin the back edge of the side border to the outside back fabric. Check that all the sections fit the chair exactly, but without the weave of the fabric being stretched or distorted. Then mark with pins the outline of the legs on the border sections (Fig.5).

Carefully remove the cover from the seat and, with it still pinned together, trim the seam allowance to 1in. where necessary. Cut away the sections for the legs to within ½in. of the outlining pins. Mark the centres of each section with tacking stitches, and cut notches in the seams (use groups of one, two or three) so that all the sections can be fitted together easily. Also mark the points where the seam joining the inside and outside back section divides, and where the seat and border pieces are joined on. Remove all the pins and open out all the pieces.

Facing the arms and legs

Start by finishing off the openings for the arms. Place the inside back section flat on your work surface, with the 'wrong' side facing

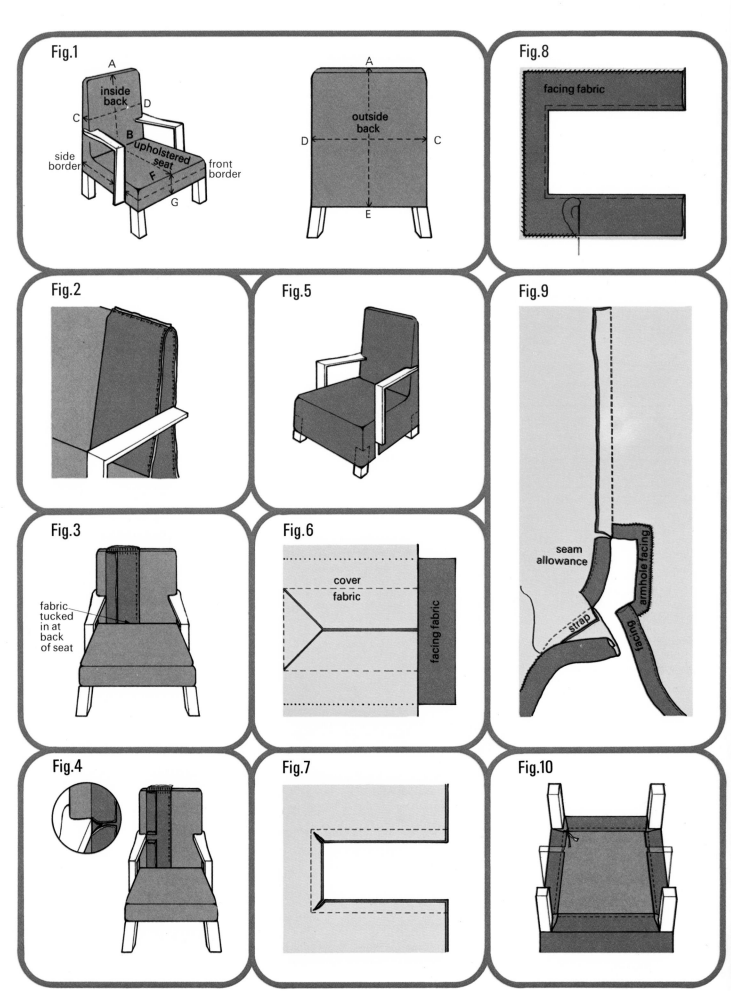

Fig.1

A

inside back

C — D

B

side border

upholstered seat

front border

F

G

A

outside back

D — C

E

Fig.8

facing fabric

Fig.2

Fig.5

Fig.9

seam allowance

armhole facing

strap

facing

Fig.3

fabric tucked in at back of seat

Fig.6

cover fabric

facing fabric

Fig.4

Fig.7

Fig.10

Opposite page, Fig.1. How to measure a chair with a rounded back and fixed seat.

Fig.2. On a chair with a square back, a strip of fabric is inserted between the back pieces. It is cut in two parts because of the arm.

Figs.3–4. Where no strip is inserted, the fabric has to be shaped round the arm. So that each side of the cover is the same, the fabric is doubled and fitted to half the chair.

Fig.5. The position of the fabric to be cut away for the legs can be marked in the initial fitting or after the main pieces have been stitched and the cover is tried on the chair.

Figs.6–8. The openings made for the arms and legs should be faced with extra fabric to give a neat, strong finish.

Fig.9. An opening has to be left below the arms on each side so the cover can be put on the chair. This is finished with a placket.

Fig.10. The cover is tied under the chair.

upwards. For the facings, cut two squares of fabric 3in. larger than the total size of the openings and place these, 'right' side facing up, under the openings. Pin and machine stitch the pieces together, following the line where the fabric was folded under level with the arm (Fig.6). Cut the facings away to within ½in. of the stitching, and snip into the corners (Fig.7). Turn the facings over on to the wrong side of the cover, tack round the seam line through all thicknesses so that none of the facing shows on the right side, and press. Turn under the outer raw edge of the facing for ¼in. and hem it firmly to the cover (Fig.8).

Face the openings for the legs in the same way.

Making up the cover

Make all the piping, following the method given on pages 95–98. Pin it to the seam line round the sides and top of the outside back section and around the sides and front of the seat section.

Pin and stitch together the outside back and inside back sections, leaving open the seam below the armhole opening on each side (this will be finished by a placket later). Pin and stitch together the lower edge of the inside back and the back edge of the seat.

Turn under 1½in. on both short ends of the front border and make hems. Turn under 1½in. on the front short ends of the side borders only, and make hems. Stitch the borders to the seat section, matching all notches carefully, so that all the leg and arm openings are still in the right places, and the tuck-in is left free.

Finishing the opening

Because the opening at the back is made up on one side of the inside back and side border, with the seat tuck-in left free in between, it cannot be fitted with a slide fastener as for most other types of loose cover. Instead it should be finished with a 'strap and facing' placket.

On the straight grain of the fabric, cut a strip for the strap 3½in. wide x the length of the opening on the outside back side (excluding the arm opening), plus 1in. for turnings. Turn under ½in. at each short end of the strap and trim the seam allowance on both sides of the opening to ½in. With the 'right' side of the strap

facing the 'right' side of the cover seam allowance, and with raw edges level, pin one long edge of the strap to the opening, along the piping line. Tack and machine stitch.

Snip the seam allowance of the cover at the top of the strap. Turn under ½in. along the free side of the strap, fold over to the wrong side and pin the edge to the other stitching line, enclosing the raw edges (Fig.9). Tack and stitch in position.

Mark the beginning of the tuck-in section, and measure the length of the opening on the inside back above the mark. Cut a strip for the facing 1in. longer than this measurement x 2¼in. wide. Turn under ½in. at both short ends of the facing, then pin it to the 'right' side of the seam allowance on the inside back, taking ½in. turnings. Tack and machine stitch. Turn the facing completely on to the 'wrong' side of the cover and fold flat. Tack along the seam line so

that no facing shows on the 'right' side of the cover. Turn under the raw edge of the facing for ½in. and slip stitch to the cover.

Make another facing for the border section of the opening in the same way. Press the strap over the facing. Sew hooks and eyes at 1½in. intervals along the placket to close it. Turn under the raw edges of the tuck-in section and armhole opening and stitch these down.

Finishing the cover

Turn under a hem to make a ½in. wide casing all round the lower edge of the cover, and machine stitch. Place the cover on the chair, insert tape through the hem casing and tie it under the chair (Fig.10).

Below. The cover for the back of this chair is really a tight-fitting bag. Openings were cut for the arms before the pieces were joined.

SYNDICATION INTERNATIONAL

Above. The advantages of a loose cover are that it protects the upholstery of a chair and can be removed for cleaning. A well-cut cover is also a good way of disguising shabby upholstery or blending it with other things.

Loose covers for armchairs

Many people, who would think nothing of making a dress in a weekend, balk at the prospect of making a loose cover for an armchair. But once you know how —and if you take your time—the method is more straightforward and you need fewer techniques.

Start by measuring the chair as given below in the sections on measuring the parts of the chair. Keep a note of all the individual measurements because these will be needed both for calculating the amount of fabric to buy and again when you cut out the fabric. If you are using a patterned fabric which will need careful

positioning on the chair, it is also advisable to add the measurements for the turnings and tuck-ins on each side of the sections separately.

Use a fabric tape measure and take all the measurements in inches. To estimate the length of fabric required, add together the lengths of the sections, including allowances.

If you are using patterned fabric with a one-way design or a large repeat, or if you are making several covers from plain fabric, it is always worth drawing up an accurate cutting chart. The way to do this is described in the section on making a cutting chart below. This will show how pieces can be dovetailed and where the repeats will fall. You may well find that you can save quite a lot of fabric in this way.

Measuring the chair

The professional way of making loose covers is to cut a block of fabric for each section as in Figs.1 and 2, and then fit it exactly. Measuring the chair gives the sizes of the blocks.

When fitting the cover for the back and seat, the fabric is folded in half lengthwise and fitted on half the chair, so that the two sides will be identical. For the arms and scrolls, the pieces for opposite sides of the chair are placed together and fitted to one side at the same time.

Because of this, it is simpler to take the initial width measurements across half the chair too, in order to save confusion later on. If you are right-handed, you will find it easier to do the fitting on the right-hand side of the chair (the side which is on your right when you are sitting in the chair). If you are left-handed, fit the cover on the left-hand side. Take the measurements on the same side that you will be fitting on.

Remove the seat cushion if there is one, then mark a line up the centre of the outside back, down the inside back, along the seat from the back to the front edge and down the front border. If you are going to fit the cover straight away, mark this line with pins, pushing them into the existing cover. If you will be taking longer and do not want to leave in pins, mark the line with tailor's chalk and then tack along it. All length measurements should be taken along this marked line.

Outside back

For the *length,* measure from the seam line at the top (point A) to the bottom of the chair. Add 1in. at the top and 6in. at the bottom for the turning and tie-under. If you are having a skirt instead of a tie-under, measure the length to the floor, add 1in. at the top for the turning and subtract 6in. from the bottom. (The standard length for a skirt is 7in. finished, regardless of the height of the chair's legs.)

For the *width,* if there is no extra piece of fabric inserted at the side of the chair between the outside and inside pieces (a side scroll), measure from point C across the back to the centre pin line. If there is a side scroll, measure from the seam joining it to the outside back piece, to the pin line.

Inside back

For the *length,* measure from the seam at the top of the back (Fig.1, point A) down to where the back and the seat meet (point B). Add on 1in. at the top for the turning and 6in. at the bottom for the turning and tuck-in.

For the *width,* measure across the widest part from the seam line (point C) to the centre pin line. Add 1in. at the side for the turning. Measure again at the bottom of the seat and add 6in. at the side for the turning and tuck-in. Use the greater of these two measurements for the calculation and cutting-out size.

Seat

If the chair has a removable seat cushion, the cover for this should be made following the method described on pages 99-101. To cover the section below this, or the seat if it is fixed

one, for the *length* measure from the back (point B) to the seam at the front (point D). Add 6in. at the back for the turning and tuck-in and 1in. at the front for the turning.

For the *width,* measure across the widest part from the side of the seat to the centre pin line. Add 6in. at the side for the turning and tuck-in.

Seat border

For the *length,* measure from the edge of the seat (point E) to the bottom of the chair. Add 1in. at the top for the turning and 6in. at the bottom for the turning and tie-under. If you are having a skirt instead of a tie-under, measure the length from point E to the floor, add 1in. at the top and subtract 6in. at the bottom.

For the *width,* measure from the inner edge of the arm to the pin line. Add 1in. to the edge for the turning.

Arms

Because the shape of the arms would distort the grain of the fabric so that any pattern would finish by slanting at the bottom of the chair, the arms should be covered in two pieces. The inside piece should start at the bottom of the seat and finish on top of the arm at its outer edge (the 'sight line'). Decide on the position of this line and mark it with pins.

The outside piece extends from this line to the bottom of the chair. This is the only piece of the cover which need not follow the lines of the chair exactly, because if you make it too tight it will be impossible to take the cover off the chair.

Inside arms

For the *length,* measure from the seat to the pinned sight line and add 6in. at the bottom for the turning and tuck-in and 1in. at the top for turning. Double the length when calculating the amount of fabric necessary to allow for the other arm.

For the *width,* measure along the top of the arm on the pinned sight line and add 1in. to the front edge and 6in. at the back for turning and tuck-in. On some chairs, the top of this piece will be shaped round to the back of the chair and joined on to the outside back, so it must be made wide enough.

Outside arms

For the *length,* measure from the highest point on the pinned sight line to the bottom of the chair. Add 1in. at the top for the turning and 6in. at the bottom for the turning and tie-under. If you are having a skirt instead of a tie-under, measure the length to the floor and add 1in. at the top and subtract 6in. from the bottom. Double the length to allow for the other arm.

For the *width,* measure across the widest part and add 1in. to each side for the turnings.

Side scrolls

For the *length,* measure from the top of the back of the chair on its side face, to the top of the arm. Add 1in. at the top and 1in. at the bottom for the turnings. Double the total when calculating the fabric necessary to allow for a scroll the other side.

For the *width,* measure across the widest part and add 1in. to each side for the turnings.

Front scrolls

For the *length,* measure from the top of the arm on its front face to the bottom of the chair. Add 1in. at the top and 6in. at the bottom for the turnings and tie-under. If you are having a skirt instead, measure from the top to the floor, add 1in. at the top and subtract 6in. from the bottom. Double the total to allow for the scroll on the other side.

For the *width,* measure across the widest part and add 1in. to each side for the turnings.

Skirt

For a plain skirt with corner inverted pleats, measure the perimeter of the chair round the bottom and add 48in. If you will not be able to cut a piece of fabric long enough without joining (and you won't with a patterned fabric) measure each side of the chair and add 12in. to each. By making the skirt in four sections you will be able to hide the seams inside the corner pleats.

For a skirt with spaced pleats, double the perimeter of the chair. For close pleats, treble the perimeter.

For a gathered frill, allow 1½ times the perimeter.

To calculate the total amount required, divide the length of the strips by the width of the fabric, and multiply this amount by the depth of the skirt.

On professionally made loose covers, the skirt is always made 7in. deep when finished. To do this, cut strips 9in. wide, which allows for ½in. turning at the top and 1½in. at the bottom for a ¾in. double hem.

Making a cutting chart

The simplest way to do this is with a ruler which gives twelfths of an inch, such as a wooden school ruler. Using a scale of 1in. to 1ft, draw on a long sheet of paper a rectangular strip equal to half the width of the fabric x the estimated length of the amount required. Mark on this the position of the pattern repeats.

Using the same scale, cut out from another sheet of paper small pieces to represent the sections of the cover. Mark the tops of the sections and which pieces should be placed against the fold (the inside and outside back, the seat and the front border). All the other pieces will be cut through the doubled fabric.

Place the chair section pieces on to the main strip of paper, adjusting them so that the repeats are central both vertically and horizontally. This is particularly important on the back, seat and front border pieces. You will then see what fabric there is left over for the smaller pieces and for cutting bias strips for piping.

If you are finishing the cover with a tie-under, you may be able to save fabric stitching on separate pieces for this and reducing the length of the outside back, outside arm, front scroll and front border pieces by 5in. each. The seam joining the fabric should come exactly at the bottom of the chair, and may be piped (Fig.6).

Cutting out the fabric

Cut out the fabric for each section, following the plan worked out on your chart. Professional cutters always cut the pieces in a set order and mark the top of each piece with a pin for quick identification. You might find it easier and safer

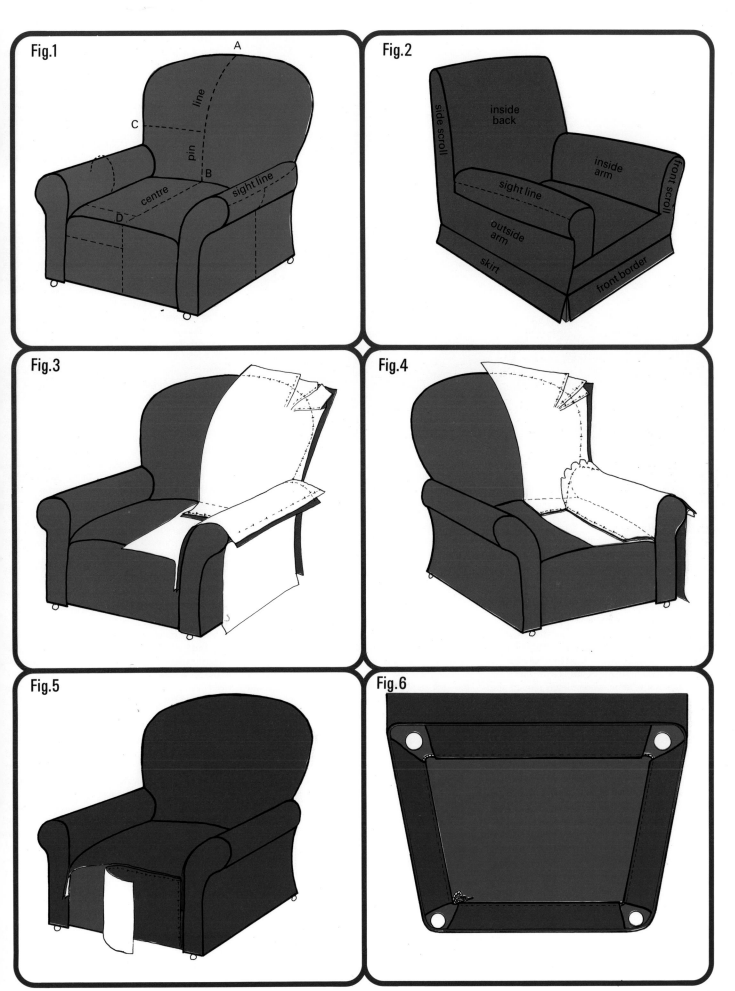

Fig.1

A

line

C

pin

B

centre

sight line

D

Fig.2

side scroll

inside back

inside arm

front scroll

sight line

outside arm

skirt

front border

Fig.3

Fig.4

Fig.5

Fig.6

163

to number the pieces in tailor's chalk, or put a tailor's tack in the top of each piece, using a different coloured thread for each. Alternatively, pin on labels.

Fitting the cover

Starting with the outside back piece, place the folded fabric 'right' side out, on to the chair. Having the fabric folded and fitting it to one half of the chair ensures that both sides are identical. Keep the fold level with the centre pin line, and position the fabric so that turnings allowed project at the top, bottom and side. Smooth the fabric out to the side of the chair and pin, keeping the grain of the fabric horizontal.

Pin on the seat piece in the same way, so that the allowance for the tuck-ins is at the back and side. When the fabric is completely pinned, fold over these allowances on to the seat for the time being.

Next, pin on the inside back piece. Pin it to the outside back piece at the top of the chair, following the shape of the chair exactly. With some fabrics you may be able to ease out any fullness by stretching it slightly; with others you may have to make small darts at the corners.

If you have side scrolls, fit these (with 'wrong' sides together) between the outside and inside back pieces. This is one of the more difficult pieces to fit neatly, so it is worth taking some time over it, and re-pinning as necessary. Always keep the grain of the fabric vertical and horizontal. In some places you may have as much as 2in. turning allowances, but this can all be trimmed off later.

If there are no side scrolls, pin the inside back piece to the outside back piece at the sides. Work from the top down, keeping the fabric quite smooth. At the arm, you will have to cut into the fabric from the side so that it can be

Above. Armchairs often vary in their design, so you should always cut the sections of a loose cover to correspond with the lines of the original upholstery.

wrapped round to the back smoothly. The fabric below this should be cut so that the allowance for the tuck-in is reduced to 1in. at the top, increasing to the full 6in. at the seat (Fig.4).

Fitting the arms

Place the pieces (with 'wrong' sides together) for the inside arm in position. Pin the front edge first so that the 1in. turning allowance overhangs the edge of the arm. Smooth it across to the back of the arm, keeping the grain of the fabric as straight as possible. Pin the bottom edge to the side tuck-in of the seat piece and cut the back edge to correspond with the shape of the inside back tuck-in. Clip into the seam allowance over the top of the arm where necessary to get a smooth fit. If it has to join the back piece, cut away fabric to form the correct shape.

Keeping the crosswise thread parallel to the ground, pin on the outside arm pieces. You will probably have to increase the amount allowed for the turning at the back of the arm, and the edge of the fabric may not stay level with the edge of the inside arm fabric. Pin the back edge of the outside arm piece to the outside back piece, but leave the front edge (Fig.3).

Fitting the front scrolls

Place these centrally on the widest part of the scroll and pin carefully to the outside arm piece, following the shape of the chair as closely as possible. Continue pinning to the inside arm as far as the beginning of the tuck-in. Mark with pins the fitting line from this point to the bottom.

Trimming the seam allowance

You will probably find it easiest to fit the front border when all the other pieces have been stitched and the tuck-in can be tucked in properly. So, if you are completely satisfied with the fit of the cover so far, trim all the seam allowances to within $\frac{1}{2}$in. of the pins. Try to keep exactly to the $\frac{1}{2}$in. since this will make the fitting together much easier. Cut notches in the corresponding seams in groups of one, two and three, so that you will be able to fit the pieces together again. Remove all the pins and open out the pieces.

Making the piping

To make quite sure that the piping cord will not shrink when the cover is cleaned, which would have the effect of tightening all the seams so much that the cover would be too small, boil and dry it a couple of times before making up the lengths of piping.

Cut out and join several long lengths of $1\frac{1}{2}$in. wide bias strips and make the piping following the method given on pages 95-97.

Pin and stitch the piping on the seam line all round the vertical and top edges of the side scrolls and front scrolls, along the top edge of the inside front piece, and along the top and back edge of the outside arm.

Stitching the cover

Start by joining the tuck-in seam at the back of the seat and bottom of the inside back pieces. Join the outside arm pieces to the inside arm pieces, then fit these to the seat and inside back pieces.

Join on the outside back piece to the inside back piece along the top edge, and one side edge if there are no side scrolls. If you have side scrolls, fit these between the back pieces.

Leave one of the back seams open for about two-thirds of the way down so that the cover can be pulled on and off the chair—try to choose the side which will be least noticeable when the cover is on the chair.

Join on the pieces for the front scrolls, continuing the seam down into the tuck in section on the inside arm piece—it must not be stitched to the tuck-in section on the seat piece.

Fitting the front border

Put the cover on to the chair with the 'right' side facing out. Tuck down the tuck-ins neatly, leaving the seam allowance protruding at the front edge. Open out the fabric for the border and place it centrally on to the chair. Pin it to the seat piece and to the seat tuck-in along the top edge, and then to the lower part of the front scroll. Trim the seam allowance to $\frac{1}{2}$in. where necessary, cut notches, then remove the cover from the chair. Unpin the border and repin and stitch it with 'right' sides together (Fig.5).

Finishing off

The opening at the back can be finished with a zip fastener or with a strap and placket as shown on pages 157-159. If you have decided on a tie-under, finish also as shown on the same pages 157-159. If you are having a skirt, stitch this on round the bottom edge, following the method given on pages 75-77, making a $\frac{3}{4}$in. double hem at the lower edge.

Loose covers for settees

A well-made loose cover for a settee looks as good as a fixed cover, and it has several advantages. It can be easily removed for cleaning and repair and, very important, it is simpler, quicker and cheaper to make.

The average life of a settee is likely to be anything from 15 to 30 years. In that time you may find that you tire of the original covering, wish to change the decorative scheme it originally matched, or need to have the settee re-covered because it has become worn and shabby.

Unless the innards of the upholstery actually need attention, it is usually not worth removing the old cover and completely replacing it, particularly if all you need is a different colour or pattern. Even if you are having it done pro-

fessionally, and almost certainly if you are doing it yourself, the new cover will be simply tacked over the old. But with much less effort, and for rather less cost, you could make a loose cover for the settee—with the advantage that when you eventually want to change this cover, it will be easy to replace.

The method for making a loose cover for a standard settee is almost the same as for armchairs, the main difference being that the width of a three-seater settee is usually greater than the fabric being used. With a plain fabric, which has no nap or pile, it may be possible to use it so that its length runs across the width of the settee, but with fabrics where the pattern or pile must run vertically you will have to join pieces to make up the full width for the seat, inside and outside back pieces and front border.

As with other soft furnishing, a centre seam

Above. *Most people would consider a pale-coloured fabric to be too impractical for the upholstery of a settee, but if you use it for a loose cover made in a man-made fibre which does not need ironing, you can easily remove it for laundering whenever necessary.*

should always be avoided because it looks ugly. Instead, you should cut a main panel from the full width of fabric and join narrower strips to each side. If you cut the width of these strips from the selvedge in towards the middle of the cloth, taking care that any pattern is level on all the pieces, it will be possible to match the pattern horizontally and it will run in a line down the back and seat pieces. The only difficulty in matching the pattern might occur where the seat has three cushions and the fabric you are using has a main motif.

Cushion covers should always be cut with the motif placed centrally, but this may not correspond with the pattern on the panels on the inside back. Here, you may find it would look better to make each of the inside back panels the same width as the cushions, so that you can centre the motif on each strip. In this case, the panels for the outside back and front border should be cut in the same way.

Calculating the width of the strips

Work out the total width required for the section, including the allowances for the turning and tuck-in as described on pages 161-164. Subtract the width of the fabric, less 1in. seam allowance, from the total width. Add 1in. to the remaining measurement, and divide the total by two.

For example, if the total width required is 66in., and the fabric is 48in. wide, the width of the strips to be cut out would be 10in. When joined to the main panel with $\frac{1}{2}$in. plain seams, the centre panel would be 47in. wide and the two smaller panels 9$\frac{1}{2}$in.

The strips should be joined on to the main panel before the fabric is fitted on to the settee.

Making up piping

Where you have a large amount of piping to make up, it is much quicker to join up a very wide bias strip and cut this into narrow lengths, rather than to cut several narrow bias strips and then join them in the normal way.

Start by cutting a rectangle of fabric, at least 9-12in. wide, on the straight grain of the fabric. Fold up the bottom right-hand corner (Fig.1, point D), so that the right-hand edge of the rectangle is level with the top edge (points A-B). Crease the fold well and then cut along it. This line is the true bias of the fabric.

With right sides together, stitch the triangle A-B-X to the left-hand edge of the rectangle so that B and A are together and C and D are together. The fabric will now be shaped like a parallelogram.

On the wrong side of the fabric, mark the width of the strips required down the fabric parallel to the slanting edges, (if you are using No. 3 or No. 4 piping cord, the strips should be 1$\frac{3}{4}$in.—2in. wide). With 'right' sides together, join the top and bottom sides of the fabric with a $\frac{1}{4}$in. seam, so that the width of one strip protrudes beyond the opposite edge (Fig.2), and the marked lines match.

Press the seam carefully, and then start cutting along the marked lines. Make up the whole length of piping by placing the cord (which must previously be boiled and dried twice to prevent subsequent shrinkage) centrally along the wrong side of the bias strip. Fold the strip over the cord so that its edges are level and pin them together.

Fit your sewing machine with a piping foot and machine tack the sides together (using a medium to long stitch), keeping the stitching as close to the cord as possible. As well as holding the piping in place, this stitching helps to prevent the fabric from fraying when it is slashed at corners.

By making up the piping by the 'sleeve' method as above, you will notice that all the joins are running in the same direction, so when you cut off a length, try to cut it in the same direction too. When you have to join edges of piping, pin the ends of the fabric together as shown in Fig.3.

To join the cord, overlap the ends by 1in. and cut off the excess. Unravel 1in. from both ends and cut off two strands from one end and one strand from the other. Overlap the remaining ends and bind them firmly together (Fig.3). Fold over the casing and tack it back in position.

Always try to avoid placing a join on the front edge of any of the cover sections, because even if correctly done, the extra

thickness of fabric may produce an unsightly ridge.

Once you have reached this stage, you can proceed in exactly the same way as with an armchair. The only differences in method will arise if you have a drop-end settee. It is a good idea, however, to add extra ties under the cover to keep it anchored in position.

Drop-end settee

This type of settee needs a slight alteration of the ordinary method, because it has one folding arm. When the arm is upright, this settee looks very similar to a normal one, but when the arm (normally the right one as seen from the front) is lowered, the settee turns into a sort of day bed.

The general method for making a loose cover for this is very similar to making one for a normal settee, but it needs some modification on the right-hand side so the arm can be lowered and raised without the cover having to be removed.

Because the cover should be smooth when the arm is lowered, the usual tuck-ins at the back and bottom of the arm are not made. The scroll or border between the outside and inside back sections is made long enough to reach the bottom of the seat (instead of the top of the arm), and an extra scroll is inserted at the back of the arm (Fig.4).

Measuring the sections

There are various methods of measuring the sections, depending on the type of fabric being used. If you are using a patterned fabric which needs careful placing, you will need to take extra care because the measurements for each side of the cover will not be the same. To make sure of this, the safest way of measuring is as follows.

With the arm upright, measure and mark the centre line down the sections and the sight line on both arms in the usual way. Then lower the arm and measure each side of the sections separately. Mark two columns on your list for the left and right sides, remembering that the right-hand side is always the side which is on your right when you are looking at the settee from the front.

If the arm which drops is on the right-hand side, as it usually is, measure up the left-hand side in the usual way, with all the normal allowances for the tuck-ins and turnings. Then measure the right-hand side as follows.

Inside Back. For the width, measure from the centre line to the side seam line and add 1in. for the turning. For the length, measure from the seam line at the top to the junction of the back and seat. Add 1in. at the top for the turning and 6in. at the bottom for the turning and tuck-in.

Outside back. As for the other side.

Seat. For the width, measure from the centre line to the junction of the seat and arm, and add 1in. for the turning. For the length, measure from the junction of the back and seat to the front edge. Add 6in. at the back for the tuck-in and turning and 1in. at the front for the turning.

Inside arm. For the width, measure from the seam at the back of the arm to the seam at the

front of the arm. Add 1in. to each side for the turning. For the length, measure from the sight line at the top of the arm to the junction of the arm and seat. Add 1in. to the top and bottom for the turning.

Outside arm. As for the other side.

Front border. As for the other side.

Front scroll. As for the other side.

Side scroll. For the width, measure across the widest part and add 1in. to each side for the turning. For the length, measure from the seam at the top to the bottom and add 1in. to each side for turning.

Back arm scroll. For the width, measure across the widest part and add 1in. to each side for the turning. For the length, measure from the top of the arm to the bottom of the scroll and add 1in. to each side for the turnings.

Cutting out

Although you have measured the sides of the settee separately, the fabric for each section should be cut out in one complete piece wherever possible. The sections which are identical for both sides of the settee can be cut through the doubled fabric in the normal way, but all the other pieces must be cut through single fabric. Cut out all the pieces that can be cut through the doubled fabric first, then lay out the fabric completely flat with the 'right' side facing up and mark a line with pins down the centre.

If the sections for the inside back and seat can be cut from the full width of the fabric without pieces having to be joined on, start from the marked centre line and measure out the widths of the left and right-hand sides, being careful that the pattern is the correct way up. Then cut out the remaining pieces, checking that the pattern is centred if necessary.

If you do have to join pieces for the inside back and seat, you will have to calculate the width of each side panel separately. Subtract half the width of the main panel, excluding seam allowance, from the width of the side being calculated. Add on $\frac{1}{2}$in. turning allowance to each side to be joined.

For example, when you are using 48in. fabric full width for the centre panel, this will actually be 47in. wide, because you lose $\frac{1}{2}$in. on each side for turning. If the right-hand side of the settee measures 36in., 23$\frac{1}{2}$in. of that will come from the main panel, and the side panel should be 12$\frac{1}{2}$in. Therefore, when cutting out, the side panel should be 13in., the extra $\frac{1}{2}$in. being added to the left-hand side for the turning.

When you cut out the panel for the right-hand side of the settee, stand so that you are looking at the fabric with the pattern the correct way up. Cut in from the left-hand selvedge for the required width, so when the seam joining the panels is formed by the selvedges of both pieces, the pattern will match. Reverse this for the left-hand panel.

Fitting the cover

Because some pieces are symmetrical and others asymmetrical, the cover must be fitted over the whole settee, rather than with doubled fabric over half as in the normal method.

Keep the fabric the 'right' side out, and match the centre marks on the fabric to the centre line

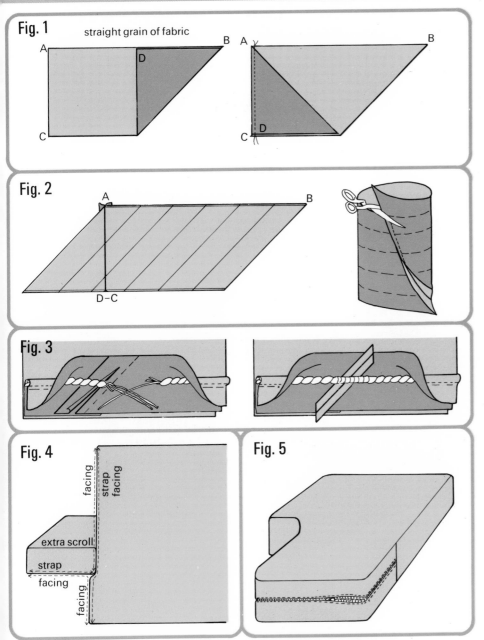

Fig. 1 straight grain of fabric

Fig. 2

Fig. 3

Fig. 4 facing / strap facing / extra scroll / strap / facing / facing

Fig. 5

marked on the settee. Pin the pieces together in the normal way, taking care that the grain of the fabric is square to the floor. Trim the seam allowances to ½in., remove the cover from the settee and re-pin and stitch the seams.

When inserting the piping, be careful to match up both sides. For example, the piping on the left-hand side scroll would come down only as far as the top of the arm, so make the other side to match, even though the scroll actually goes down as far as the seat. This is because the settee will probably be used much more with the arm upright, rather than down, so the sides of the settee should look the same in this position.

To finish the ends of the piping when it finishes 'in mid air' like this, simply cut the piping cord to the right length, cut the bias strip ½in. longer and turn this under level with the end of the cord. Slip stitch the end of the casing neatly.

Finishing the cover

The strap-and-facing opening on the drop

end of the settee should be made in two sections. On the outside back fit a strap, following the method given on pages 157-159. Fit another strap to the outside edge of the back arm scroll. Fit facings to the inside back and outside arm (Fig.4).

The drop arm is normally worked by a knob in the middle of the outside arm, so an opening should be made for this in the fabric.

Measure the diameter of the knob and mark its position on the fabric with a circular tacked line. Cut a piece of fabric for the facing 2in. larger than the circle and place it centrally on to the circle, with 'right' sides together. Machine stitch the pieces together on the tacked line, then cut away the double layer of fabric inside the circle, leaving a border of ¼in. inside for turning. Clip into the turning at right-angles to the stitching at about ½in. intervals. Turn the facing fabric through to the wrong side of the cover and press and tack it down so that none of the facing shows on the 'right' side. Turn under the outer edge of the facing for ¼in. and hem neatly to the cover.

Covering shaped cushions

Many settees have rectangular seat and back cushions, and these are quite straightforward to cover, following the method given on pages 99-101. If you have cushions which are shaped to fit round the arms, the best way of cutting the fabric for the two main sections for the top and bottom is from a paper pattern.

Place the cushion on to the paper and draw round it carefully with a pencil, keeping the point as close as possible to the edge of the cushion. Remove the cushion and draw another line ½in. outside the first one. Cut round this.

If possible, cut the top and bottom pieces at the same time through doubled fabric (folded with 'right' sides facing, so you can check on the placement of the pattern). If you would prefer to cut the pieces singly, lay out the fabric the 'right' side up and cut the first piece. Keep the fabric the same way, but turn the pattern over for the second piece, so that the shaping is reversed.

For the box strips which are inserted between the main sections, measure the depth of the cushion and cut three strips 1in. wider and long enough to fit the front and each side, plus 1in. for the turning. Join the side strips to each side of the main strip along the short edges, taking ½in. turnings. Taper the stitching into the corners ½in. from the beginning and end of each seam.

Cut another strip 1in. wider than the others, and long enough to fit the back of the cushion, plus 1in. for turnings. Cut this strip in half lengthwise, and re-join it for ¾in. at each end, taking ½in. turnings. Insert a zip fastener into the remaining opening. Stitch the short ends of the strip to the short ends of the other one, taking ½in. turnings and tapering the stitching as before.

Attach the piping around both edges of the now-circular strip, taking ½in. turnings. Then, with the 'wrong' side of the strip facing out and the top of the pattern towards the top edge, fit the piece for the top of the cushion to the edge of the strip, matching the corners to the seams. Pin and tack in position, taking ½in. turnings, and clipping the seam allowance where necessary to turn the curves smoothly. The tapered seams of the strip will open out as you do this, so there is no need to clip into the corners. Stitch the seams and overcast the edges if the fabric is likely to fray. Press carefully.

Still with the wrong side facing out, turn the strip so that the open end is uppermost. Fit the fabric for the bottom of the cushion to this side, matching the corners to the seams as before. Press and turn 'right' side out.

With some very deep cushions, you will find it easier to insert the pad into the cover if the opening is made extra large by extending it round to the sides. To do this, cut the strips for the sides of the cushion about 3in. shorter, and cut the strip for the back 6in. longer. Join them all as before, and insert the zip fastener. Fit on the main sections so that the zip fastener extends an equal amount into each side. Here you will have to clip into the turnings at the corners, so it is a good idea to strengthen them with an extra line of machine stitching ⅛in. outside the main stitching, for about 2in. at either side of each corner (Fig.5).

Re-rushing chair seats

Most households have a few old chairs whose wooden frames are sound, but whose upholstery or cane bottoms have worn out, so that the chair can no longer be used. Re-upholstering or re-caning are long jobs requiring some degree of skill, and unless the old chair is a valuable antique, you may well not think it worth the trouble. But you can easily bring the chair back into service by covering the seat with rushes.

Rushing is an easy, quick and above all cheap way of filling in rectangular frames. It gives chairs and stools an attractive rustic look that blends well with the simple lines of modern furniture.

Most four-sided frames can be covered with rushes; this includes square and rectangular frames, chair frames wider at the front than the back, and even a circular stool or chair seat, provided it has four legs. Nothing triangular or three-legged can be covered, however—at any rate, not using the normal technique. The only other unsuitable type of frame is one where the pieces vary sharply in thickness, for example if they are decorated with deeply-cut carving or turning.

Suitable materials

The classic material for rushing is, of course, rushes. These used to be grown for the purpose in Britain, but are now imported from the Middle East. Recently, however there has been a series of bad harvests which have made ordinary rushes hard to get.

A thoroughly good alternative is seagrass. This is a tough, fibrous material, shiny and pale green or beige in colour. It is bought already woven into a continuous cord, like string but unlike rushes, which arrive as bundles of single rushes and have to be tied together. Seagrass is stronger, more flexible and cleaner to use than rushes, so you may prefer to use it anyway, even if you can get rushes. It can be bought at most hobby and handicraft stores.

The third alternative is thick brown string. It is just as strong as rushes or seagrass and easier to work with, though not nearly as good-looking as the first two.

Some other materials, such as raffia, straw, reeds or basketmaking cane are not suitable because they are either too thin or too brittle. But at a pinch you could use any thick, strong, flexible natural fibre for covering a chair seat.

Preparation

No special tools or equipment are needed for the job. There are, however, some that will make the job a lot easier.

If you are using seagrass, which comes in continuous lengths, it will speed up your work if you make some wooden 'shuttles' to wind the grass on. These can then be passed through the chair frame, gradually unwinding the grass as they go. Make them out of very thin wood (orange-crates or $\frac{1}{8}$in. (3mm) ply) cut into a rectangle about 9in. x 2in. (230 x 50mm) with deep V-shaped notches in each end, so that the grass can be wound on lengthwise.

A screwdriver is useful for pushing the loops of seagrass along the chair frame to tighten them, but don't use it on rushes or they will break.

You will need few materials other than the rushes and the chair. If you are using rushes rather than seagrass, you will want some kind of packing to fill the gap between the top and bottom rows where they are separated by the thickness of the frame (this is not needed with seagrass, which can be pulled tighter than rushes). Since rushes come in awkward lengths and often break, you will be left with a lot of cut rush ends and broken rushes, which make excellent packing.

In Britain, rushes come in 'bolts' or bundles large enough to cover four chairs (but beginners should budget for one bolt to every three chairs, to allow for wastage through inexperience). Seagrass generally comes in smaller hanks; you will need two to cover a large chair.

Rushes need to be soaked in water to make them pliable. The best way to do this is to cover

them in cold water for half an hour, then take them out, spread them on a flat surface and cover them with an old towel or blanket to keep them damp. Seagrass should be soaked in the same way, but this should be done when it is wound on its 'shuttles', to keep it from shrinking. Put a weight on it to keep it under water.

To prepare the chair for rushing simply remove all traces of the old seat covering to expose the square wooden frame. If the old seat was made of rushes, there may be thin wooden strips pinned to the sides over the rushes to protect them. Remove these carefully so that you can put them back afterwards (or you can replace them with new ones, or omit them entirely). Polished chair frames should be cleaned with turpentine and re-polished before covering.

Method

The basic method is for a perfectly square frame, with all four sides the same length. It must be modified slightly for rectangular frames, or frames with sides of unequal length, so read right through this section and the next one before you start work.

The instructions given here are for right-handed people, who will find it most convenient to work round the frame anticlockwise, so that they are always passing the reeds from left to right. Left-handed people who want to work the other way should simply read 'left' for 'right' and vice-versa (but *not* 'top' for 'bottom'; these remain unchanged).

The appearance of a typical rush seat is

Opposite page. It only took slightly over an hour to cover the seat of this chair with seagrass. The strands have been pressed down level and varnished to neaten them, as well as making them more hardwearing.
Below: Fig.1. The basic knot. If this is made at each corner in turn, the seat will fill itself in quite automatically.
Fig.2. How to tie a reef knot. The second half-knot is a mirror image of the first.

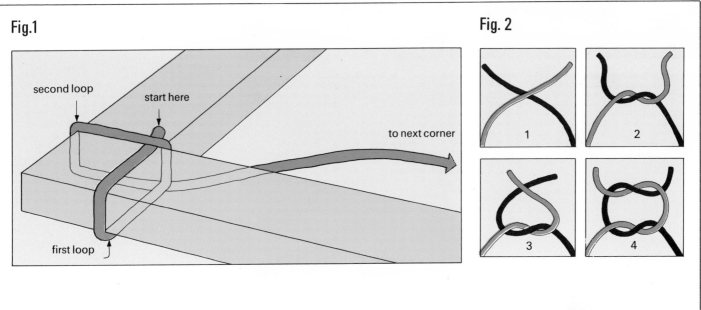

Fig.1

second loop

start here

to next corner

first loop

Fig. 2

1

2

3

4

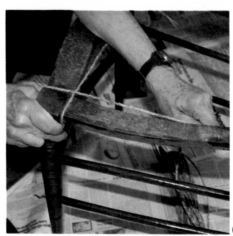

shown opposite. The rushes interlock to form a neat 'X' shape, with the arms of the 'X' running across the frame at 45°. This may appear to require complex weaving techniques, but in fact the pattern forms itself automatically as you work round the frame, as the result of a very simple knot made at each corner (see Fig.1).

The sequence of events in making this knot is shown in Figs.4-6. Start at the front left-hand corner. The first step is to hold either end of the first reed to the top of the left frame member with your left hand, a few inches from the front corner. Then pass the other end over the front member. Give the loose end of the rush a sharp clockwise twist and keep it twisted the whole time you are tying each knot. This will help to pack the rows tightly together. There is, however, no need to twist seagrass in this way. Now, still twisting the rush, pass it under the front member from front to back and bring it up again through the middle of the frame (see Fig.4). Then pass it over the left frame member (as near the front as possible) and give it a pull to tighten the loop you have made.

Complete the first knot by passing the rush under the left member and back up through the middle of the frame (see Fig.5). Pull it again to tighten it, then stop twisting the rush and take the end over to the front right-hand corner. Make the second knot at each corner in the same way (see Fig.6); you should start by passing the rush over the front end of the right-hand frame member, then twisting it clockwise and looping it under.

Carry on doing this all round the frame for four or five turns until it looks like Fig.7. When you come to the end of a piece of rush, tie a new one on to it at a point that causes the knot to be on the underside of the seat where it does not show (see Fig.8). The knot must be a reef knot or it will slip. Those who are not absolutely sure how to tie one correctly should consult Fig.2. Any unusually thin rushes should be used double; twist them lightly together and tie them on as if they were one.

Fig.3 *(top left). Seagrass should be wound on small wooden 'shuttles' to make it easier to thread through the frame of the chair.*
Fig.4. *When making the first knot, hold the end of the rush or seagrass in your left hand to stop it from slipping.*
Fig.5. *When you have looped the strand first round the front, then the left frame members, move on to the next corner.*
Fig.6. *The knot at this corner should be made in exactly the same way as the first knot, but there is no need to hold the end.*
Fig.7. *The first few rows completed. The strands have not yet been slid along the frame to tighten them, so they look irregular.*
Fig.8. *When you come to the end of one piece of seagrass, tie on the next piece so that the knot comes under the seat.*
Fig.9. *Any projecting strands that refuse to lie flat can be pulled down by looping a strand round them from underneath.*
Fig.10. *To increase the width of the front of the seat, loop alternate knots round the front frame twice. This can also be done round the sides to deepen the seat.*

Fig. 11

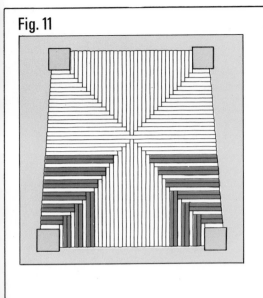

Fig. 12

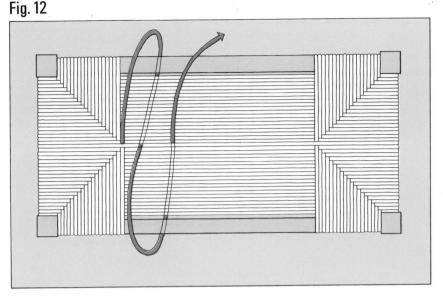

If you are using seagrass, the process is exactly the same except that you are passing a shuttle full of seagrass through the frame instead of the end of one rush. Pull the seagrass as tight as you can, and pack the rows of loops tightly on the frame sides by forcing them together with a screwdriver.

When you have gone round the frame four or five times, you will notice two things. One is that the characteristic 'X' pattern of a rush seat is beginning to form at the corners. It may not be quite straight (on a normal square frame it should lie at exactly 45° to the frame sides). If it is crooked, you can straighten it by pushing the rushes about with your fingers. You should continue to check, and if necessary straighten, the rushes every few turns as the seat builds up.

The other thing you will probably find is that your hands are beginning to get sore, particularly around the top joint of your right index finger (unless you have very calloused hands). Protect yourself from blisters by binding up any vulnerable spots with sticking-plaster (wearing gloves would make you clumsy). Do not stop pulling the rushes tight however sore your hands get. The tighter they are, the more comfortable and durable the seat will be (but if using real rushes, don't pull them *too* tight or they may break).

After you have done 10-15 rows, you will notice a hollow beginning to form around the edges of the seat just inside the frame, caused by the thickness of the frame separating the rushes into top and bottom layers. If, and only if, you are using real rushes, poke cut rush ends into this space and pack them tightly with a piece of wood. As the seat builds up, continue to insert packing in this way. It will tighten the rushes and pad the seat a little, both of which will make it more comfortable.

When you have completely filled the chair seat with rushes or grass, stop at a point that leaves the loose end of the rush in the middle of the seat and pointing downwards. Look at the seat. If there are any loose strands on top, push the end of the rush up through the middle of the seat, loop it round the loose strand and

Fig.11. (above, left). To cover a chair frame that is deeper than it is wide, and wider at the front than the back, make double loops (shown in red) on the front three sides until the space left in the middle is square.
Fig.12 (above, right). Filling the space left in the middle of a long frame is done by making a row of figure-8-shaped loops.
Fig.13 (below). The seat before varnishing.

pull it down again to tighten the strand (Fig.9).

Tie the end of the rush to any of the strands on the underside of the chair to complete the job. All you need to do now is to give the new seat a coat of polyurethane varnish, paying particular attention to the front edge, which gets the most wear. When the varnish is tacky, push down any loose strands on top to neaten the appearance of the seat.

Awkward-shaped frames

The method described above is suitable only for square frames, or frames with four curved

sides of exactly equal length. Other shapes of frame will require you to modify the method slightly.

For rectangular frames, use the method exactly as described, taking particular care to keep the X-shaped rows of knots at exactly 45°. Carry on until you have completely filled the shorter sides of the rectangle. The seat will then look like Fig.12, with a large gap in the middle. Fill the gap with a series of figure-8-shaped loops made in series from left to right; the rush should always pass from top to bottom and from bottom to top between the same two centre strands for a neat result. Finish the seat by the same knotting method as for a square frame.

Many seat frames have a wide front and a narrow back. The way to overcome this problem is to broaden the row of loops along the front. Every *alternate* time the knotting process comes round to the front, instead of looping the rush under the frame and immediately passing it to the side as shown in Fig.4, loop it round *twice* and then pass it to the side (see Fig.10). When knotting the second front corner, make the same type of double loop around the front frame member. The first time round the frame, the two front corner knots should be normal (i.e. single), the second time they should be doubled, the third time normal, and so on. As soon as this alternate double-looping process has compensated for the slant of the sides, and the gap in the middle of the seat is square or rectangular, stop doing it and carry on normally. The double-looped section will hardly show if you press the rows together tightly enough at both front and back, though there will inevitably be a slight curve in the X-shaped row of knots.

This method can also be used to make a rush seat for a rectangular frame that is nearly, but not quite, square. In this case, the double loops are made on both the two longer sides. In the chair illustrated here, which is wider at the front than at the back, and deeper than it is wide, double loops were used on both the front and the two side members, as shown in Fig.11.

Re-caning chair seats

Cane has been used for centuries as a material for making chair seats, and for decorative purposes as well. It is tough as well as attractive, and its characteristic interlaced pattern is much easier to make than it looks. Once you have picked up the knack, you will find that the range of applications for canework is endless, and that cane furniture makes an interesting addition to any decor.

Cane is most commonly used for making chair seats, but it has a huge range of other uses as well. Many chairs have cane panels in the back, and cane can also be used for making table tops (suitably protected by glass), screens and room dividers, wall panels and even false ceilings to reduce the height of tall rooms. Large areas of this type can be covered quickly and economically by using an open weave and thick cane. No doubt you will be able to think of other uses as well.

Before you tackle any large project, it is best to get a good grounding in the technique. The best way of doing this is to re-cane the seat of an old chair or stool. In most houses, there is at least one old chair with an upholstered or caned seat that is in such bad condition that it can no longer be used. Provided that the frame is sound and of the right shape (it must be level all round) this is an ideal starting-ground.

Don't start work on anything valuable, as you might make a botch of the job. And don't tackle any very large area, since not only is this harder to do, but will also take so long at a slow beginner's pace that you will probably get bored and give up. Later, when you have the necessary skills, you will be able to cover large areas quite quickly.

Buying cane

Cane can be bought at craft shops, and at some DIY shops. In Britain, it is usually sold in bundles large enough to cover a small chair seat. There are six thicknesses numbered from one, which is much finer than you would normally use for furniture, to six, which is very coarse and strong. The most commonly used grades are two, four and six.

A chair seat of normal size should be covered with grade four cane, which also has the advantage of being the cheapest type. The very fine canes cost approximately twice as much as this, the very coarse ones about one-and-a-half times as much.

Left. These attractive chairs have had their seats recaned. They were once junk but are now valuable additions to any home.

You will also need a small amount of very fine cane for finishing off the chair seat. If you are using grade four for the main job, you should use grade two for the finishing work.

Preparation

The preparation of a chair for caning is very simple. First, strip off all the old cane and pull out any small nails or wooden pegs that have been used to jam pieces of cane into the holes. Throw these away; you will not be needing them.

If you are caning a chair frame that has not previously been caned, there will be no holes and you will have to drill them. They should be drilled all around the frame from top to bottom, and should all be at exactly the same spacing, except where the corners make this impossible. It is essential that the centre front hole lines up exactly with the centre rear one, and that the side holes also line up exactly across the frame. Since chair frames are wider at the front than the back, there will be more holes along the front edge, but this is quite unimportant.

If you plan to use grade four cane, the holes should be at $\frac{1}{2}$in. or 15mm centres, and drilled with an $\frac{1}{8}$in. or 3.50mm drill bit. They must be spaced very evenly at the top, but their exact angle does not matter very much.

Clean out the holes (old or new) with a piece of wire or a nail slightly smaller than the holes, its end cut off square with a hacksaw or file. This step is important to keep the cane from sticking in the holes.

While you have the chance, clean up the chair frame with turpentine and polish it. This cannot be done properly with cane in place.

Count the holes across the front and back of the chair frame to fine the centre front and back holes, and mark these with a pencil. Then put your bundle of cane in cold water to soak for at least five minutes; dry cane is too brittle to use.

While the cane is softening, whittle down the end of some old wooden skewers or pieces of thin dowel to make three of four blunt pegs that can be jammed into the holes to hold the cane firm. These are the only tools you will need apart from a razor blade.

Weaving the cane

Before you actually insert any cane, carefully study the weaving diagram (Fig.1) and the photographs (Fig.2-10). This may well save you from going wrong part of the way through the job.

Remove the bundle of cane from the water, separate one length of cane and sharpen both ends roughly with the razor blade. Then insert one end through the centre back hole from

above and right through the frame, so that about 1in. (25mm) protrudes below it. Hold this protruding end steady by jamming a wooden peg into the hole beside the cane, then take the other end of the cane across to the centre front hole and push it through from above. The cane should not be twisted, and should have the shiny side upwards along its full length.

Pull the free end of the cane down through the frame tight enough to stop the piece crossing the chair sagging, but not actually taut, since it will shrink as it dries. Taking care not to twist the cane, pass the free end across under the frame to the next hole and up through it, then over to the back of the frame and down through the next hole to where you started. Continue to insert parallel strands across the top of the frame, joining lengths of cane as described below, until you reach the last hole before one of the rear corners.

The next strand should be strung between the next front hole and the most convenient hole on the side of the chair that will keep the strand exactly parallel to the previous one. This will not necessarily be the side hole next to the corner, though equally it may be, depending on the shape of the chair. The only important thing is to keep the strands parallel, and to do exactly the same on the left and right sides of the chair.

Insert the next strand towards the edge of the frames from its front hole to the most suitable side hole, and carry on until you have used up all the front holes. Then re-start stringing from the middle towards the other outside edge, reproducing the arrangement of the last few strands that you made when doing the previous side.

Next, string the frame from side to side. There are (or should be) the same number of holes in both sides, so you can start at the front and work straight through to the back without interruption. When caning from side to side lay the canes over the front to back strands. With diagonal canes it will be necessary to interweave with both the front to back and the side to side strands. Laying the side to side over the front to back strands provides a frame for this.

Now string the frame diagonally. Start at either rear corner and pass the strand of cane over and under the intersections of the first two sets of strands. This will make its angle exactly 45° to either of the first two sets, so it will not hit the front corner on the opposite side of the frame unless it is a perfectly square frame, but this is unimportant.

String right across the frame to the corner, passing above and below alternate intersections, then with the next strand passing below those you previously passed above (and vice-versa). When you have reached the corner, re-start on the other side of the first diagonal strand and work to the opposite corner.

Finish the weaving by stringing across the other diagonal, passing the strand below the intersections that the previous diagonal strands passed above. By the time you have finished, there will be three pieces of cane through each of the holes in the frame, except at the corners.

If the cane shows signs of drying up during the job, put the unused strands back in the water for another five minutes. This will keep the strands pliable.

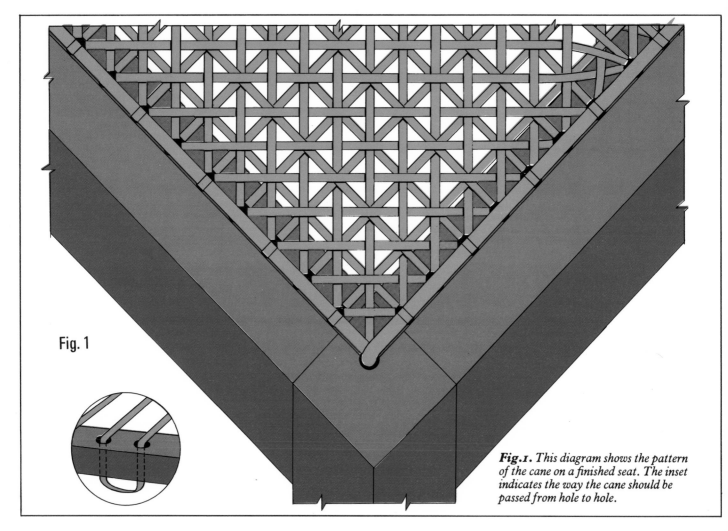

Fig. 1

Fig.1. *This diagram shows the pattern of the cane on a finished seat. The inset indicates the way the cane should be passed from hole to hole.*

Joining pieces

The beginning of each set of strands will be held firm by a wooden peg, though this can be removed as soon as another strand is passed through the hole to jam the first one in place. But pieces of cane are only of a certain length, and you will soon run out of cane and have to start with a new piece. This should not be held in with a peg, but it cannot just be tied to the first piece with a knot, as this would break the cane.

Remember, when you are joining the pieces of cane, that it can only be done under the frame on the short stretch where the cane passes from one hole to another. Pass the first cane down through its hole and hold it firm at the top with a peg. Then loop (but do not knot) the new piece around the protruding end, right up against the frame. The free end, of the new piece (which should be sharpened) is then passed up through its hole and pulled fairly tight, jamming the looped link against the frame. This joint will stay done up when the cane dries.

Finishing off

When the cane dries, it shrinks, and thus fits its holes less well. There is a possibility that it might slip when sat on, but this can be avoided by the use of cane as a reinforcement.

A piece of thinner cane (grade two should be used here) is passed up a frame hole from below, looped around the three strands coming out of the top of the hole, and passed down through the same hole. It is then taken along the underside of the frame to the next hole and the procedure repeated. This should be done all round the frame.

Sometimes nails or small wooden pegs are used to jam the strands in their holes, but they tend to come out as the cane shrinks, so their use is inadvisable.

The edge of the seat may be decorated with more cane, preferably of a thick grade such as number six, threaded all around the edge of the frame in straight lines from hole to hole as shown in Fig.1. You will have to go round twice to cover all the spaces between the holes.

Other uses for cane

Cane is not just for chair seats. A well-caned panel has an extremely smart appearance that makes it suitable for all kinds of other decorative uses.

Occasional tables can be given cane tops, which should be made of thick grade six cane for strength, and are probably best protected with glass as well. If the table frame with its top removed is an unsuitable shape for caning, you can easily make a wooden frame the same size as the original top, and paint or polish it to match the table before applying the cane.

Cane screens have a very attractive light appearance, and do in fact let quite a lot of light through, which makes them suitable for use as room dividers in badly-lit rooms. The best way of covering the rather large area involved is to make a number of identical caned frames and set them in a timber framework. The same type of frames may be used for wall panelling. Square frames are the quickest to make—a worthwhile point when you have a lot of caning to do.

Panelled doors look interesting with caned inserts made to cover the panels. This is a very good way of 'lightening' a heavy-looking door. An ugly radiator can be masked by a box frame filled with caned panels, which will let the heat through, but it is advisable to put a thick block-board shelf on top (blockboard warps least of all boards, including solid timber).

Cane headboards for beds enjoy a deserved popularity as they help to bring light to the darker room. You can 'dress up' a boring plain headboard with a caned panel shaped to follow its outline, leaving a solid-wood border showing around the outside. Quite complicated shapes can be caned by following the instructions given below.

There is no need to leave cane in its natural colour, even though this is attractive and goes with most colour schemes. It can be painted with acrylic paint (available from most DIY shops and artist's material shops); this is flexible even when dry and will not flake off. Plain colours such as black white, and red look far better than pastels; a painted cane wall or door panel should be set against a contrasting background to bring out the pattern.

174

2

Fig.2. *The holes in the chair frame should be thoroughly cleaned of all dirt and old cane by using the cleaning tool as shown.*

3

Fig.3. *Soak the cane for five minutes or so before starting the job proper. If the cane is left dry it will break easily when handled.*

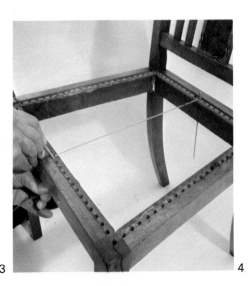

4

Fig.4. *Start caning from a hole in the back of the frame holding the cane in place with a wooden peg as shown.*

5

Fig.5. *Lengths of cane are joined together by looping the new length around the old and pulling tight against the chair frame.*

6

Fig.6. *Because there are more holes in the front than the back of the frame some strands will have to run from the front to a side hole.*

7

Fig.7. *Caning is more straightforward when working from side to side as there are an equal number of holes on each side.*

8

Fig.8. *Diagonal canes should be at 45° across the frame, and should be interwoven as shown with the existing strands.*

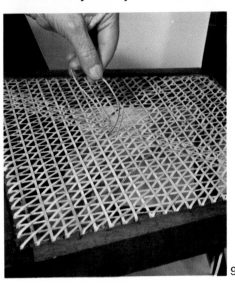

9

Fig.9. *After caning diagonally in one direction the same method should be applied in the other, interweaving in the same way.*

10

Fig.10. *The finished chair. Its appearance and resilience will be improved if the cane is coated in clear varnish or stained.*

Remaking a drop-in seat

Upholstery is really a combination of soft furnishing and carpentry and, in some simple jobs, needles and thread are not even used. Many of the tools used are similar to carpenters' tools, but have been modified for the purpose. The development of foam and other modern materials has made upholstery much easier for the amateur, although time and patience are still essential.

The best introduction for the complete beginner is to remake the drop-in seat of a dining chair. These chairs can often be bought very cheaply in junk shops, and simply need a bit of work on the seat to bring them back into everyday use.

Calculating the amount of fabric

For the main cover, choose fabric which is hard-wearing, simple to clean and easy to work with. It should have a firm, close weave and be colour-fast. Fabrics with a smooth finish will keep clean longer than those with a pile or nap (velvet or needlecord, for example) which hold dust, cling to clothes and have to be allowed for when the cloth is cut. Avoid using those fabrics which have a large pattern or motif which would have to be placed centrally on the seats, as this can be very wasteful if several chairs are being covered.

To calculate the amount needed for each chair, measure the length and width of the seat (at the widest part) and allow a piece at least 6in. longer and wider so that the fabric can be turned under the seat frame. You will also need a piece of hessian and two pieces of linen (or calico) 1in. wider and longer than the seat.

Other materials

Foam biscuit, ½in. larger all round than the size of the chair seat x 2in. deep. Old dining chairs were usually stuffed with wool on horsehair but this is expensive to buy and difficult to obtain and use, and foam padding is perfectly suitable for this purpose. Latex (rubber) foam is best to use but polyurethane (man-made) is quite adequate.
Webbing. This is placed across the seat frame in strands running both ways, and supports the padding. Most chairs have two strands each way, but the wide, early Victorian type of chair may need three each way or two by four (Fig.2). To check on the amount you need, slit open the fabric covering the underneath of the seat and buy enough to make the same arrangement. The highest grade of webbing is made from pure flax and is black and white with a twill weave. Other grades of black and white webbing are

made from mixtures of jute and cotton or hemp, and sometimes linen threads are woven into the selvedges to strengthen them. Plain or striped brown webbing is a cheaper grade made from jute, and is not recommended for dining chairs. Rubberized webbing, made by Pirelli, can be used for this job, but it is not really worth it because it is so expensive.

Above. This is a typical example of the sort of 'between period' dining chair that can be bought cheaply from a junk shop. All it usually needs is a new seat to make it usable.

Web strainer (or 'dwang'). This is the only specialized piece of equipment necessary. It is used for stretching the webbing across the seat of the chair to prevent it from sagging when the chair is sat on. The simplest type of strainer is a piece of hardwood, about 10in. x 3in. x 1in., slightly waisted for a good grip, with a groove at the end which gives leverage (Fig.1, left). Other more elaborate versions have a slot into which the webbing is inserted (Fig.1).

Alternatively, a narrow piece of hardwood round which the web can be wrapped and pulled taut is efficient if you have a strong wrist.
Tacks, ⅝in. and ¾in. long. Use the sort sometimes known as 'improved' which have wide heads.
Combined hammer and tack extractor. A small carpenter's hammer may be used.
Ripping chisel or tack extractor for removing the old tacks. An old blunt wood chisel may be used.
Mallet for use with the chisel.
Plastic wood, for filling old tack holes.
Strong tape, 1½in. wide x the perimeter of the chair seat plus 4in.
Adhesive with a latex base, for attaching the pad.
G cramps.

Stripping the seat

Cover your work surface with newspaper, remove seat from chair base and secure the seat, upside down, to the work surface with G cramps. Using the ripping chisel and mallet, start to drive out the tacks holding the bottom hessian and cover fabric. To do this, place the tip of the chisel behind the head of the tack and drive it out, working with the grain of the wood. Use the tack extractor on the hammer to pull it out completely. It is essential to work *with* the grain of the wood to prevent it from splitting. Next, turn the seat over and remove the cover and stuffing. Strip off the hessian and webbing in the same way. If there is no webbing and plywood has been used as a base, remove all the nails holding this.

As you work, note the way the webbing was placed originally, the side of the frame to which it was tacked, and the part of the frame which is uppermost when finished. Then examine the frame carefully and remove all old tacks; fill the holes with plastic wood.

Replacing the webbing

If there is an uneven number of webs, start with the centre web running back to front. Without cutting off a length of webbing, insert it or wrap it round the strainer at about the right length. Place the end of the webbing on to the top of the frame on the back side, with the cut edge of the webbing facing inwards (Fig.3). Tack it down, placing three tacks in a triangle. Turn the webbing over and tack again, using 3 more tacks in a reverse triangle, thus making two lines of tacks.

Stretch the webbing across to the front of the frame, pressing the edge of the strainer the side of the frame to give leverage. Tack the webbing again, using three tacks in a triangle (Figs.4 and 5). Cut off the webbing with 1in. to spare, turn it back over the first tacks and tack again, placing the tacks in a reverse triangle. Place the other pieces of webbing from the back to the front of the frame in the same way, then secure the side webbing (which runs across the seat), interlacing it with the other webbing (Fig.2).

To cover the webbing before attaching the padding, fold over ½in. on one side of the

Right. A deeper foam cushion has been used on this chair to make the seat a more comfortable height for writing at the bureau.

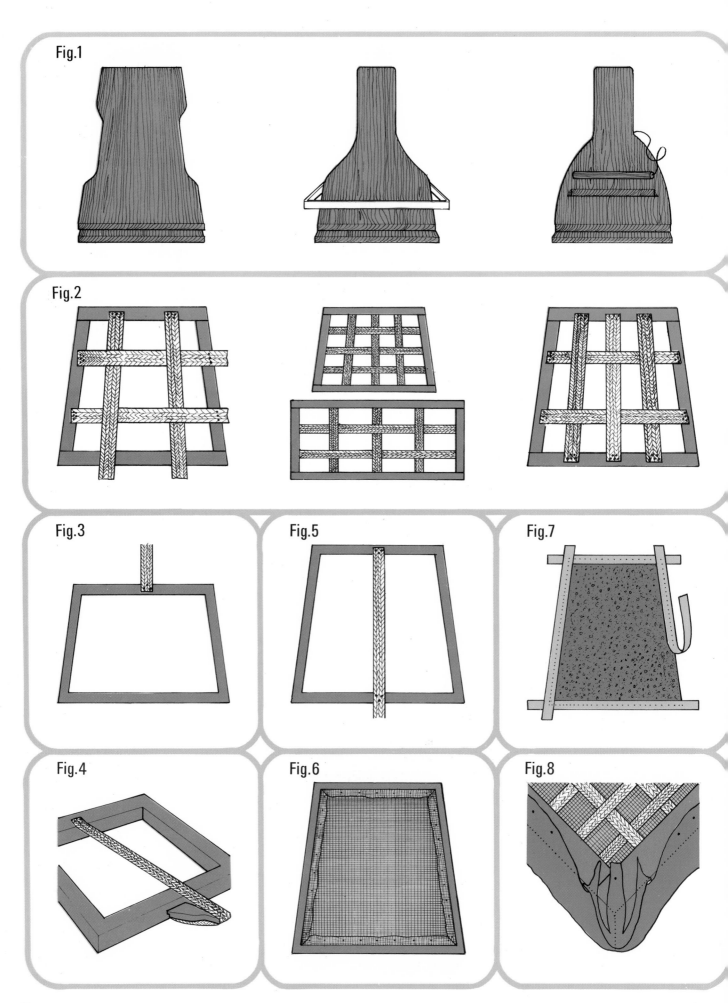

BILL MACLAUGHLIN

BRIAN MORRIS

hessian and, with the fold uppermost, tack it to the back of the seat frame with ⅝in. tacks. Strain it tightly to the front and secure temporarily with three tacks. Repeat this at the sides, keeping the grain of the fabric straight. Then, working from the centre of each side towards the corners, place tacks about 1½in. apart. Turn

up the raw edges and tack these down (Fig.6).

Attaching the padding

Cut four pieces of tape equal in length to the sides of the foam, plus 1in. Fold the tape in half lengthwise and crease firmly. Glue one side of the tape to the perimeter of the foam, placing the

crease on its edge. When this is completely dry, place the foam on the hessian and, holding it firmly in position, tack the free edge of the tape to the frame. As the foam is slightly larger than the seat, it will dome in the centre, giving a rounded shape to the finished seat.

To give a better foundation on to which to place the final cover, the foam should now be covered with a piece of calico or linen. Attach this like the hessian covering the webbing, but cut off the raw edges close to the tacks. Place the tacks below those on the tape.

Attaching the final cover

Place the cover fabric on the work surface with its wrong side facing uppermost. Place the seat, foam side down, centrally on the fabric and turn up the edges of the fabric on to the bottom of the seat frame. Tack it down in the same way as for the calico, starting along the centre back, then centre front, centre sides, and working out to the corners. From time to time turn the seat over to make sure that you are not pulling the grain out of true. It must run straight from centre back to front, with the other threads running across the seat at exactly right angles.

At the corners make a double pleat as shown in Fig.8. Start by pulling down the point tightly and tacking it. Fold the excess fabric into inverted pleats and tack these down. Cut off any excess fabric and then cover the bottom of the seat with the remaining piece of linen or calico. Fold under the raw edges and tack it to the frame, covering the raw edges and tacks of the seat fabric, spacing the tacks evenly.

Replace the finished seat in the chair frame and tap it down lightly for a good fit.

BILL MACLAUGHLIN

This page. Whether you have dining chairs of the traditional style (top), or more modern ones (left), the method for upholstering the drop-in type of seat is the same. Older chairs were originally stuffed with horsehair, but foam makes a good, easy-to-use substitute.

179

An ottoman from a whitewood box

An ordinary whitewood box can be transformed into a luxurious and useful ottoman for storage and extra seating simply by padding it with foam and covering it with an attractive fabric to match your other furnishings.

Prepare the box by removing the lid and sanding down the whole box, including the inside and lid. If you will be using the box regularly as a seat, with thick padding, drill $\frac{1}{4}$in. diameter ventilation holes in the lid in rows 3-4in. apart (this allows the air released by the foam to escape).

If the lid is recessed into the top, plane it down all round to allow clearance for four layers of fabric (see below).

If the foam for the top of the box is more than 1in. thick, pad and cover the lid for the padded bedhead (see pages 83-85). Cut out the calico inner cover and top cover larger than usual, so that the tacks can be placed well in from the edge on the inside of the lid. They should be far enough in to clear the top of the box when the lid is closed.

If you are using thinner foam cut it large enough to cover the top and sides of the lid. Stick it straight on to the lid, taking it over the edges. Hold it in place with staples until the adhesive dries.

Covering the box

To pad the outside, cut a piece of $\frac{1}{4}$in. foam to match the height of the box and go right round it. Place any joins in the middle of the back or on a side; do not put them at the corners because this will take away the rounded look and will not pad them enough to prevent the fabric from chafing.

Stick the foam in position, using an adhesive with a latex base, such as Bostik 1. The inside of the box can be padded in the same way, but should be cut to finish 1in. from the top (or 1in. below the lid, if this is recessed). Since it does not matter if the foam has a join on an inside corner, you may find it easier to handle if you cut a piece to fit each side of the box separately. Stick strips of wadding over the edges of the box and lid for extra padding.

Cut out the cover fabric, allowing an extra inch at the bottom and 2in. at the top. If you cannot cut a piece long enough to fit right round the box, cut a separate piece for each side, allowing $\frac{1}{2}$in. seam allowance on each vertical side. Alternatively, you may be able to cut a piece long enough to fit the front and sides, with a separate piece for the back.

Join the side pieces to the front piece, taking a $\frac{1}{2}$in. plain seam and leaving unstitched $\frac{1}{2}$in. at

the bottom and 1$\frac{1}{2}$in. at the top. Join on one edge of the back piece in the same way. Do not join the other back seam yet, but simply press under the turnings. The seams can be piped if you wish.

Fit the fabric round the box, positioning the seams exactly at the corners with 2in. extending at the top and 1in. at the bottom. The unstitched seam should come at one of the back corners. Hold the fabric in place with temporary tacks and pin the last seam together, with the folds butting.

Using a long length of thread and a curved needle, secure the end of the thread 1in. from the top of the join. Insert the needle into one of the folds and draw it out, taking a stitch about $\frac{1}{4}$in. long inside the fold. Insert the needle into the other fold, placing it slightly back from where it has just been pulled out, and make another stitch. Draw up the thread tightly so the two folds meet without puckering. Continue stitching the folds together in this way and fasten off $\frac{1}{2}$in. from the bottom.

Next, turn the fabric under the box, mitre the corners and tack it down. Place the tacks $\frac{1}{8}$in. in from the raw edges of the fabric and about 2in. apart. To finish the top, turn the excess fabric to the inside of the box, mitre the corners and tack it down. Cut away the fabric and turn under the raw edges to fit round the hinges.

Finishing the inside

Cut a piece of lining fabric to fit each side of the box (measure on the *inside*), allowing $\frac{1}{2}$in. for joining the seams on each side and 1in. at the top and 2in. at the bottom. Join all the pieces to make one circular strip. Cut out strips of stiff cardboard, 1in. wide x the length of each side.

Hold the lining upside down over the box with the 'right' side facing out and matching the seams to the corners. Lower it into the box, until the lower edge is 1$\frac{1}{8}$in. below the top. Staple it in a few places to hold it in position.

Still holding the bulk of lining above the box (this is where an extra pair of hands is essential), place the cardboard strips over the turnings of the lining, so the lower edge is level with the edge of the fabric and the top edge is $\frac{1}{8}$in. below the edge of the box. Tack down, placing the tacks as near to the top edge of the card as possible, to prevent it from curling.

Turn the lining down into the box, fit it neatly into the corners, and fold the excess fabric at the bottom into the middle of the box. The cardboard will give the top a clean, smooth edge and prevent it from looping down between the tacks. Stick or staple the turning at the bottom.

Cut a piece of cardboard to fit the inside bottom of the box, allowing about $\frac{1}{8}$in. clearance all round. Pad it with foam and then cover it with a piece of lining fabric, cut 1in. larger all round. Take the turnings of the lining to the underside of the cardboard and stick them down. Fit the padded cardboard into the bottom of the box.

Finishing off

To neaten the outside bottom of the box, cut a piece of hessian ½in. larger all round. Turn under ⅜in. on each side, mitre the corners and press down. Tack the hessian to the box, placing the tacks outside those of the main cover.

Replace the lid. If necessary, to make it fit well, reposition the hinges. Fill old screw holes with plastic wood and leave it to dry before drilling new holes. Fix the hinges to the lid first, aligning them carefully with each other, and only then mark the hinge positions on the box.

Making a removable cover,

If you prefer, it is possible to make the cover so that it can easily be removed for cleaning without your having to do a major upholstery job each time. The techniques used are very similar to making traditional loose covers.

Fig.1. The foam is attached to the box with adhesive. The adhesive should be applied to the wood, not the foam.

Fig.2. Hold the foam in place with temporary staples until the adhesive dries.

Fig.3. Position any joins on the foam on a side, rather than a corner.

Fig.4. Strips of wadding should be stuck over the edges of the box and lid for extra padding.

Fig.5. Then the inner calico cover can be tacked on. The fabric should be cut away and mitred at the corners.

Fig.6. For a neat finish, the felt lining is back tacked on. The strips of card give a firm, strong edge.

Fig.7. The lining is turned down into the box and tacked along the bottom.

Figs.8 and *9.* The main cover can be put on in the same way as the calico one. If you prefer, you can make it removable for easy cleaning. This cover is held in place under the box with tape, in the traditional style of loose covers. For the lid, a pocket was made which is held in place with loose cover pins.

The box is prepared in the same way as for the upholstered version up to the inner calico cover. All the lining—for the lid, inside box and underneath—is put on next. The lid can then be screwed back into position.

The outer cover is different from the upholstered one in that the fabric for the lid and back of the box are cut in one piece. The panels for the front and sides of the box are made up in a similar way to the upholstered version, although one side piece should be cut about 1in. wider to make a placket at the back seam. The back piece is stitched on one side to the regular-sized panel and is joined to the other panel by means of the placket. The placket can be fastened by hooks and eyes, press studs, a zip fastener or Velcro.

When the cover is put on to the box, the top is held in place under the lid by a 'pocket' made of strips of fabric attached to the front and sides (Fig.9). The piece for the sides and front is then wrapped round the box and fastened at the placket. It is held in place underneath by ties in the normal method used for loose covers, and at the top by upholstery tacks, which can easily be removed when necessary.

1

5

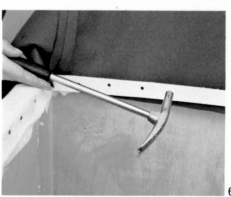

8

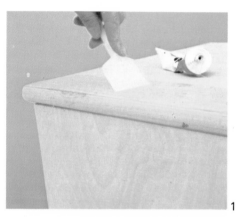

6

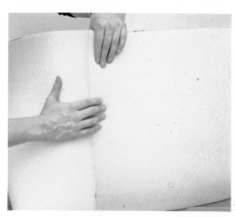

9

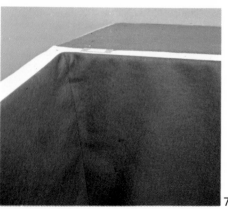

4

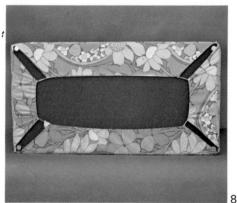

2

3

7

Upholstering deep-padded dining chairs

Re-upholstering the sort of dining chair which had a sprung seat has become much easier since the development of techniques using rubberized webbing and foam rubber. The result is just as comfortable—and a lot cleaner.

Materials

For removing the old upholstery

Ripping chisel, for removing tacks. An old, blunt wood chisel, or even a screwdriver, could be used.

Mallet, to use with the chisel.

Above. This is not the sort of cover which can be easily removed for cleaning, but many pale fabrics can be cleaned in position with a proprietary dry cleaning fluid.

Tack extractor or *lifter,* also for removing tacks. The claw end of a hammer can be used.

Scissors.

Plastic wood.

Treatment for woodworm, if necessary.

For the new upholstery

Webbing, rubber. This takes the place of the traditional webbing and springs which were probably used in the original upholstery of the chair. It is made from two layers of bias-cut corded fabric which sandwich a rubber layer. This makes it very strong and springy. It is more expensive to buy per inch than traditional

183

Fig.1 (centre). A junk-shop chair as it was—with dirty upholstery and damaged wood.
Fig.2 (top left). Allow plenty of time when removing the old upholstery because each layer is held in place by closely spaced tacks, all of which must be carefully removed.

It is also wise to cover the floor with paper. The first step is to take off the hessian which covers 'the works' under the seat.
Fig.3 (top right). If the edge of the seat was finished with braid, it should be pulled off next. Then the top cover can be removed.

Fig.4 (bottom left). Under the top cover there is an inner cover and then a thin layer of hair which can be lifted off.
Fig.5 (bottom right). To give the chair a good shape, the main layer of hair was stitched at the edge. Cut through this next.

webbing but, since it eliminates the need for springs, it is more economical in the long run. It is also easier to use and saves a good deal of time. Buy enough 2in. wide webbing to have three or four strands running from the back of the seat to the front, with one strand running across it (the gaps between the strands should be 2in.).

Polyether foam biscuit, ¾in. larger all round than the chair seat x 4in. deep.

Wadding, to cover the foam. This is cotton-wool-like material sold specially for upholstery, and gives a soft edge to the seat. Buy enough to extend under the seat if this is where the original upholstery finished.

Cover fabric. This is not the sort of cover which you will want to remove frequently for cleaning, so choose fabric which will not show the dirt or can be cleaned in position. Allow enough to cover the seat as in the original upholstery, with an extra 2-3in. all round for turnings and ease of working.

Calico. A piece of this is used as an inner cover between the wadding and top cover. Allow the same amount as for the top cover, plus enough for making 6in. wide strips to fit round the perimeter of the foam.

Adhesive, with a latex base (such as Bostik 1) for attaching the calico strips to the foam.

Tacks. Use the sort with wide heads (known as 'improved') for attaching the webbing. You will need ten, ⅝in. long, for each strand. For attaching the main upholstery, use ⅜in. long fine tacks (or ½in. long if the cover fabric is thick). Allow enough to make four rounds of the perimeter of the seat, placed at 2in. intervals.

Hammer. A special upholster's hammer, called a cabriole hammer, has a strong shaft and a small end on the head—about ⅝in. wide—which makes it easier for tacking in small spaces. The other end of the head may be larger, or it may have a claw for lifting tacks. A small carpenter's hammer may be used instead.

Gimp, or *braid*, for covering the edges and tacks of the cover fabric if this finishes part way

Fig.6 *(top left). Before the hair can be removed completely, more tacks have to be driven out. To avoid damaging the wood when doing this, the chisel blade should be held as parallel to the wood as possible and driven in the direction of the grain.*

Fig.7 *(top right). Cut the stitches which holds the springs to the hessian above, and remove this.*
Fig.8 *(bottom left). Turn the chair upside down and drive out the tacks holding the webbing.*

Fig.9 *(bottom right). Take out any tacks that are left in the frame, then clean it.*
Fig.10 *(centre). The tools and materials needed for the new upholstery. The smaller foam biscuit is needed only when the front legs extend above the seat frame.*

down the seat frame, or around the bottom of the frame if the upholstery finishes under the seat.

Gimp pins, or a clear adhesive such as Bostik 1, for attaching the braid. Gimp pins have a very small head and are available in several colours.

Black hessian, the size of the seat, to finish underneath.

Stripping the old upholstery

Cover your work surface or the floor with newspaper, because the innards of the seat will be very dusty. If the old cover was finished with braid, examine it to see if it was tacked or stuck on. If it was tacked, remove the tacks carefully

by putting the end of the chisel at an angle under the head of the tack and firmly tapping with the mallet. Drive out the tack, working with the grain of the wood, and with the chisel blade held as parallel to the wood as you can. If you hold the chisel upright, or drive against the wood, you may split the frame.

If you cannot see the direction of the grain because the fabric is covering the wood, check on the direction in which the tacks were originally driven. The head is probably slightly at an angle. Place the tip of the chisel under the highest part. It is also wise to drive away from the wood which is exposed when the chair is upholstered. Remove the tacks holding the top

and inner cover in the same way.

Cut through any twine that might be holding in the next layers and remove each one, lifting out the hair stuffing. Discard this immediately. If the seat was sprung, cut through the stitches holding the springs to the layer of hessian below the stuffing, then remove the hessian. This may release the springs to their full height, or you may have to cut through more twine which lashes them down.

Turn the chair upside down and remove the tacks holding the webbing.

Clean the frame, repair and treat it for woodworm if necessary. Fill all the tack holes with plastic wood.

When all the old upholstery has been removed and the chair frame cleaned and repaired, the interesting stage of the upholstery can begin. Although using rubber webbing and foam is easier and quicker than the traditional webbing and springs, it still pays to take time over attaching them. Keep on adjusting the tacks at the various stages until the shape of the foam is just right.

Webbing the seat

Because the rubber webbing takes the place of the original webbing and springs, it is attached to the top of the seat frame, rather than the bottom as before. Mark the position for each strand on the back, front and side rails, and sand down the inner edges of the frame so it will not cut the webbing.

Using the webbing straight from the roll to avoid waste, place it in the position of the first strand, with the cut edge just inside the outside edge of the back rail. Tack it down, using five tacks placed in a straight line $\frac{1}{4}$in. from the cut edge. Be careful to position the tacks at right-angles to the frame, and to tack them down so that their heads are completely flat on the webbing, so they cannot cut into it.

Each strand of webbing should be 9/10th the length of the distance it spans and stretched to fit; so, after fixing the strand at the back, mark this measurement on it and stretch it until the mark is in the middle of the front rail. Tack in position, placing the tacks on the mark. Cut off the webbing $\frac{1}{4}$in. outside the tacks.

Attach the other strands in the same direction, then interlace the cross strip with the other strands. Because weaving the cross strand in and out will use extra webbing, it is best to interlace it through the main webbing first, then tack one side. Mark the place where it reaches to opposite rail unstretched and measure 1/10th of the total measurement back from this. Stretch and tack down on the second mark.

Padding the seat

If the front legs are higher than the seat frame, cut a piece of 1in. foam to the size of the chair, and stick it to the frame.

Cut out the foam biscuit to the shape of the seat, plus ¾in. all round. Mark the position of the back uprights, but do not cut the foam away. Mark the centre of each side of the foam and of the chair.

Make enough 6in.-wide calico strips to fit round the perimeter of the foam, making those for the sides and front long enough to overlap at the front corners by 3-4in. The strip for the back edge should just fit between the uprights.

Fold the strips in half lengthwise and apply adhesive along them from one long edge up to the crease. Mark a 3in. wide border round the edge of the top of the foam, omitting the area of the uprights, and apply adhesive to it. When the adhesive is tacky, stick the calico to the foam, with the crease level with the edges.

Put the foam on to the seat, matching the centre points. Roll the excess foam under so that it does not hang over the edge of the seat frame and tack down the calico strips as for the padded bedhead (see pages 83-85). Then, to fit the foam at the uprights, simply slash it diagonally at the corners and wedge it between them (Fig.7).

Cut a piece of wadding to fit over and down the sides of the foam with ½in. turning, or long enough to reach below the chair to pad the edges if the upholstery finishes underneath. Tack in a few places, slashing and overlapping it at the corners.

Fitting the cover

Place the calico inner cover over the wadding and attach it as for the padded bedhead (see pages 83-85). At the back uprights, fold back the fabric diagonally so that the fold just touches them (Fig.16). Slash diagonally from the point to within ½in. of the fold. Fold under the slashed fabric, trimming off the excess, so that the folds are level with the uprights and tack the fabric down. Finish the front corners of the calico by slashing them diagonally from the corner to the edge of the foam. Fold each piece round the corner, press as flat as possible and tack down (Figs.19 and 20).

Fit the top cover in the same way, but making pleats at the front corners. If the cover finishes part way down the frame, trim the raw edge to within ¼in. of the tacks and cover with braid or gimp. If the cover finishes under the seat, tack it ½in. from the edge and trim off the excess fabric to within ¼in. of the tacks. Otherwise attach the braid around the bottom of the seat.

Finish the underneath of the seat with a piece of black hessian. Cut it to the exact size of the seat frame, turn under ¼in. on each side and place it centrally under the seat. Tack in position, mitring the corners for a really neat finish.

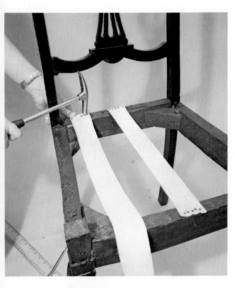

Fig.1. *To support the upholstery, webbing is placed across the seat. The gaps between strands should equal the width of the webbing.*

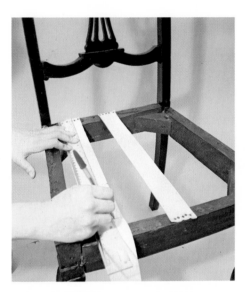

Fig.2. *So that the webbing is stretched the right amount, 1/10th of its total distance unstretched is marked in from the end.*

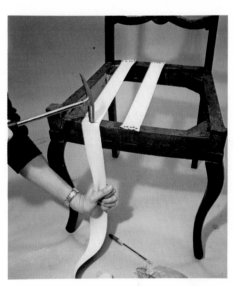

Fig.3. *The webbing can then be pulled so that the mark comes to the point where it should be tacked down. Five tacks are used for strength.*

Fig.4. *Rubber webbing is so strong that cross strands are not necessary, although one can be put at the back for extra support.*

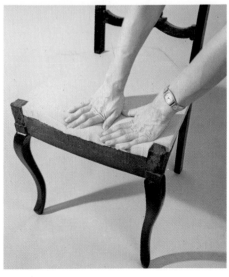

Fig.5. *To build up the frame to the level of the extended front legs, a piece of foam the exact size of the seat is stuck in position.*

Fig.6. *The main foam padding is attached to the chair by wide calico strips which are stuck to the foam and tacked to the chair.*

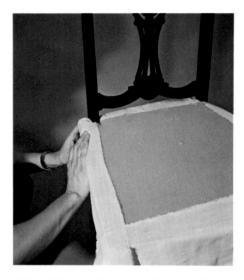

Fig.7. To fit the foam at the back uprights, it should be slashed diagonally in from the corners and wedged inbetween them.

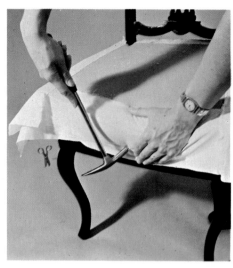

Fig.8. To get a good shape, the foam is cut larger than the seat and its sides squashed down and held in place by calico strips.

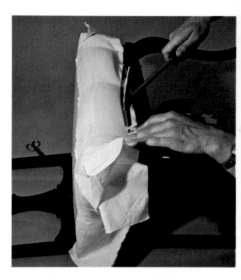

Fig.9. So that they can be adjusted if necessary, the tacks holding the strips are widely spaced and not driven right home yet.

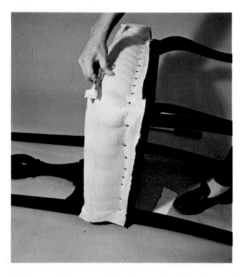

Fig.13. The excess fabric can then be trimmed off. Do not trim it too close to the tacks, however, or it may pull away.

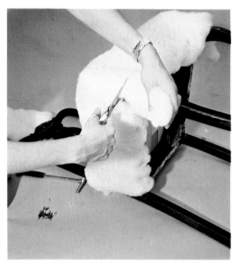

Fig.14. On a chair where the cover finishes below the seat, wadding should be tacked on to pad the edges of the wood.

Fig.15. The next step is to put on the inner calico cover. This is held in place at first by one temporary tack on each side.

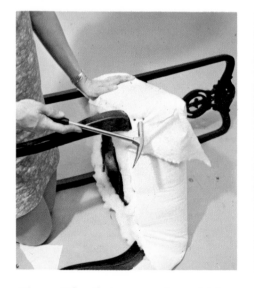

Fig.19. When the inner cover is completely taut and smooth, the fabric at the front corners can be finished off as for the strips.

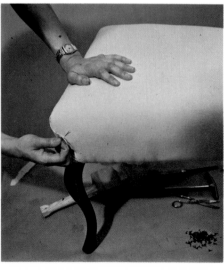

Fig.20. After the excess fabric has been trimmed off, the piece wrapped round can be stuck down or held in place with stitching.

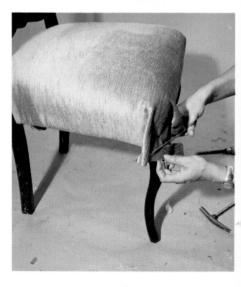

Fig.21. To finish the front corners of the top cover in a double pleat, pull down the point of the fabric and tack it in place.

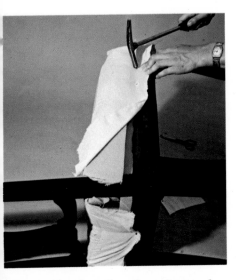

Fig.10. *After the main tacks are in on each side, more can be put in between. The sides of the foam must still be kept level with the seat.*

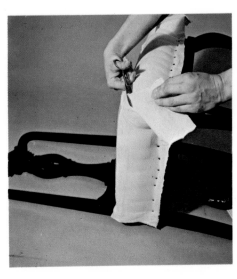

Fig.11. *To finish the front corners, the strips are cut so they can be wrapped round the other way and tacked or stuck down.*

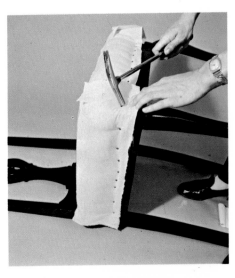

Fig.12. *The wavy line of tacks may look untidy, but it will prevent the strips from ripping along the grain of fabric through strain.*

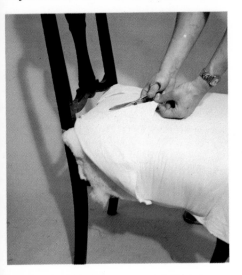

Fig.16. *To fit the inner cover at the back uprights, fold back the corner diagonally so that the fold just touches the wood.*

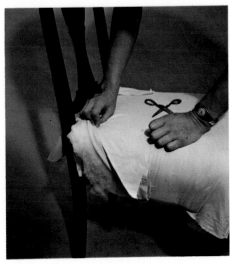

Fig.17. *Slash the fabric diagonally from the point to within ½in. of the fold. Fold it level with the uprights and trim off the excess.*

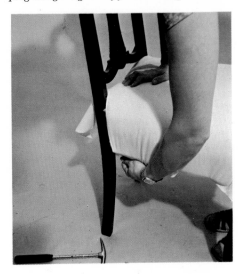

Fig.18. *Tack the fabric down, pulling it as tightly as possible at the back corners. You may then have to adjust the other tacks.*

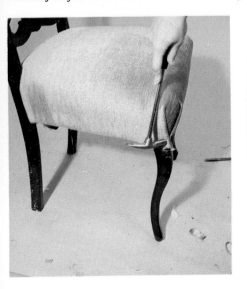

Fig.22. *Fold under the excess fabric neatly in two inverted pleats. Some fabric inside them can be trimmed away so they will lie flat.*

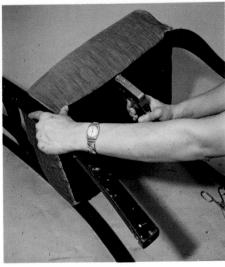

Fig.23. *To hide the 'works' under the seat, a piece of black fabric should be tacked or stapled on. Cut it away to fit round the legs.*

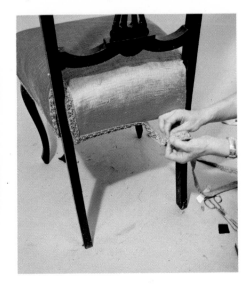

Fig.24. *The final touch is to attach braid round the edge of the seat. Stitch down the mitres at the corners for a neat effect.*

Making a footstool from an old box

A footstool is always a useful 'extra', and for many people it is an essential part of relaxing comfortably in an easy chair. You can make one very cheaply, simply by upholstering an upturned wooden box. Providing that the wood is at least $\frac{1}{2}$in. thick, it doesn't have to be anything special because it will be completely covered by the fabric.

This method of upholstery involves using hair or fibre as the padding. This is a traditional form of stuffing and, although foam rubber could equally well be used, it is possible to achieve a more pleasing shape with hair. The cost involved in both methods is about the same. If, however, you plan at some future time to re-upholster an antique piece of furniture—where it is essential to use traditional methods in order to maintain the value—it is a good idea to have had some practice in the handling of hair on a small item first.

Materials

Horsehair is the traditional stuffing material but, because it is so difficult to obtain today, and is expensive, it is often mixed with hog hair. Old hair mattresses can sometimes be bought cheaply at jumble sales or from junk shops, and if you wash the stuffing it returns to its original springiness.

Alternatively, use *Algerian fibre*. This comes from the Algerian palm tree and, provided it is teased out properly, it makes a very good, inexpensive stuffing. For a small footstool with about 3in. depth of padding, you will need $1\frac{1}{2}$lb-2lb of either type of material.

Twine, a very strong, smooth string made from flax and hemp, is used for making bridle threads round the edge of the box which help hold the stuffing in place. It is also used for stitching up the edge, another process which holds the stuffing in place.

For making the bridles you will need a *spring needle.* This is a heavy needle, about 5in. long, which is curved at one end so that it can be pulled in and out easily. For stitching the edge you will need a 10in. straight *upholsterer's needle,* which is pointed at both ends.

Another useful implement which helps form the stuffing into a good shape is a *regulator.* This is a piece of metal about 6in. long, with one pointed end and one flat end. A kitchen skewer could also be used for this, although if you are planning to do a lot of upholstery it is worth investing in the proper tool—it is not expensive.

Scrim, a loosely woven hessian with flat threads, is used for covering the base of the box to make a foundation for the upholstery, and again for covering the first layer of stuffing. Allow enough to cut one piece the same size as the base, plus 1in. all round for turnings, and another piece about 6in. larger each way to allow for the depth of the padding.

Calico is used for covering the second stuffing; you will need a piece 1in. larger each way than the second piece of scrim. *Wadding* is used over the calico to prevent the stuffing from working through and also to pad the sides of the box. Allow the same amount as for the calico, plus the depth of the box all round.

For the *main cover,* choose a dark colour in a proper upholstery grade fabric which will wear well and not show the dirt quickly. Patterned fabrics or those with a raised surface, such as moquette, are often better than plain ones. Allow the same amount as for the wadding.

To attach the various fabrics to the stool, you will need enough $\frac{1}{2}$in. fine tacks to go right round the edge once with them placed 2in. apart, and four times round with them placed 1in. apart. A proper upholsterer's hammer is the best thing for attaching these, because it is heavy and has a small head, but a small regular carpenter's hammer could be used.

Preparing the box

Sandpaper the outside of the box if necessary to make the wood really smooth. Then turn it upside down so that the base is uppermost, and chamfer the edges of the base, which will now form the top, all the way round at roughly 45°, as shown in Fig.1. This should be done with a rasp or Surform. It provides a ledge on to which the tacks can be driven and also helps prevent the covering fabric from becoming chafed on the corner.

Cut a piece of scrim, on the straight grain, to fit the top of the box (the surface which was the base), plus $\frac{1}{2}$in. turning all round. Turn under the edges, keeping the folds level with the weave of the fabric. Tack the fabric to the box, spacing the tacks about 2in. apart and $\frac{1}{2}$in. from the edge.

The stuffing

To make bridle threads for the stuffing, thread the spring needle with enough twine to go $1\frac{1}{2}$ times round the stool. The stitch used is rather similar to back stitch. Start by making a stitch in the scrim about 1in. long and 1in. from the edge. Pull it through, leaving a 3in. tail. Tie the tail in a slip knot to the main length at the point where it emerges from the scrim (Fig.5).

Go forward and insert the needle about 4in. away, but pointing it backwards. Pull it out about 3in. away from the starting point (Fig.5). Leave the stitch on top of the scrim loose enough for your hand to be inserted easily.

Continue round the whole edge in this way, making sure that a 1in. stitch falls at each corner. You may have to adjust the length of the bridles to do this. Finish off by tying a slip knot.

Take a handful of stuffing and tease it out thoroughly, removing any lumpy pieces. Put it under one of the bridle threads, working it together well to prevent lumps. Do this for all the bridles, then fill the middle with more stuffing, tease it well to make an even shape, and to overhang the edge slightly by the same amount all round.

Covering the stuffing

Cut a piece of scrim large enough to cover the stuffing and reach the chamfered edges all round with $\frac{1}{2}$in. to spare. Fold this allowance under to make a turning along one side. Place the scrim centrally over the stuffing so that the fold is level with the bottom of the chamfered edge. Put a temporary tack—one that is driven only halfway in, so it is easy to adjust if necessary—in the middle.

Smooth the scrim over the stuffing to the opposite side, turn under the edge so that it is level with the bottom of the chamfered edge and place a temporary tack in the middle. Still keeping the weave of the fabric straight, smooth it out to the sides, turn under each edge and insert a temporary tack in the same way.

Go back to the first side and finish tacking it, driving the tacks into the chamfered edge and placing them about 1in. apart. Stop about 2in. from the corners. Complete the other sides in the same way.

To finish the corners, cut away the excess fabric at the bottom and tuck the remaining corner under the stuffing. Keeping the shape of the stuffing at the corners as square as possible, form any excess fabric into an inverted pleat by pinching the corners together. Tack down.

Regulating the stuffing

During the covering you may have worked the stuffing out of shape, so this should be evened out with the regulator. Poke the sharp end of the regulator through the fabric, and ease the stuffing along to a good shape. Keep feeling it to judge where there is any unevenness. Only when you are completely satisfied should you begin stitching the edge.

Stitching the edge

This is done in two stages. The first, which is called blind stitching, pulls enough stuffing to the sides to enable a solid edge to be built up. The second stage, top stitching, forms a roll from this section of stuffing. The roll has to be really firm because the covering fabric is pulled over it, and any unevenness would spoil the shape.

To do the *blind stitching,* thread the upholsterer's needle with a good length of twine. Then, starting at a corner and working along the side of the stool from left to right, insert the unthreaded end of the needle into scrim just above the tacks and about $1\frac{1}{2}$in. from the corner (Fig.1, point A). Insert the needle into the

Right. This sophisticated footstool with its leathercloth cover was made by upholstering a beer crate.

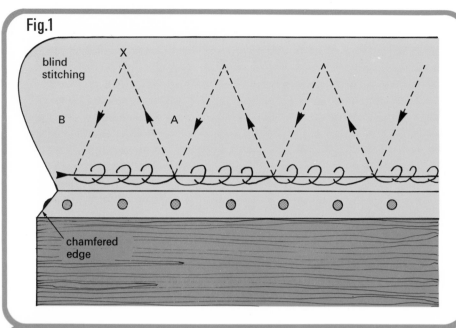

Fig.1

blind
stitching

X

B   A

chamfered
edge

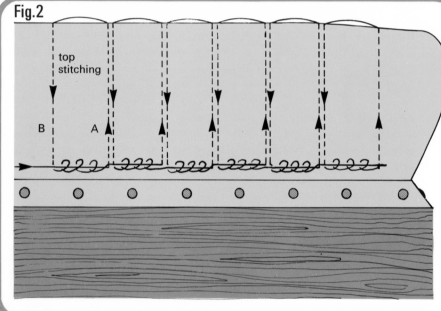

Fig.2

top
stitching

B   A

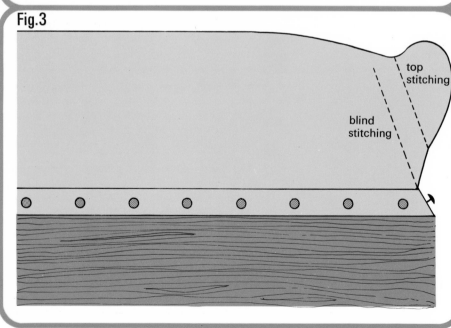

Fig.3

top
stitching

blind
stitching

stuffing at an angle of about 45° to the horizontal and with the point offset to the left, so that it will emerge on the top of the stool about 1in. in from the edge and ½in. nearer the corner (point X).

Pull the needle through, stopping as soon as you see the eye, so that it is not completely withdrawn. Push it back into the stuffing again, altering the angle so that it emerges through the side on the same level as where it first entered, but 1in. nearer the corner (point B). You have, in effect, made a V-shaped stitch in the stuffing.

Pull the twine through so that there is a tail of about 3in. left at point A. Tie it to the main length with a slip knot, and pull tight.

Insert the needle about 2in. further along the edge from point A, slanting it in the same way as before and bringing it out on the same level on top as the first stitch. Bring it down again at an angle to emerge on the side about 1in. back. Before withdrawing the needle, wind the twine which is to the left of the needle round it twice anti-clockwise. Pull the needle through completely.

Put the unthreaded end of the needle into the centre of the stool top to anchor it temporarily. Hold the edge of the stuffing with your left hand so that your fingers are on the top and your thumb is on the side, wrap the twine round your other hand and pull the stitch really tight, pressing down with your left hand at the same time.

Continue working round the edge in this way, being careful not to place the twisted section of a stitch so that it goes round a corner. To finish, knot the twine carefully and tightly.

Correct any unevenness in the stuffing with the regulator, then re-thread the upholsterer's needle with a long length of twine.

Top stitching is similar to blind stitching, the main difference being that the needle is completely pulled through on top of the stuffing so that a stitch can be made on the top. This means that the needle should be inserted straight into the scrim, and not inclined to the left as with blind stitching.

Starting at a corner, insert the needle about 1½in. away and about ½in. above the blind stitching (point A, Fig.2). Push it through so that it emerges on the top about 1in. from the edge. Re-insert the threaded end of the needle about 1in. to the left of this point, keeping it parallel to the first entry so that it emerges at point B, 1in. away from point A. Tie the end of the twine in an upholsterer's knot as before.

Insert the needle again about 1in. to the right of point A, and complete the stitch, reinserting it about 1in. to the left as before so that it is just short of the first stitch. Before withdrawing the needle completely from the second half of the stitch, wind the twine round it and pull tight in the same way as for blind stitching. Continue all round the edge in this way. The stitches on top of the stool should form a continuous line, and following the line of one thread of the scrim.

Second stuffing

Make more bridle threads round the edge and insert a second, thinner layer of stuffing under these and over the scrim. Take it right up to the roll and dome it slightly in the middle.

4

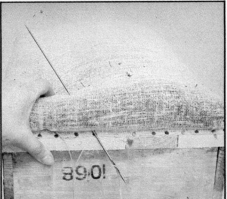

5

6

7

8

9

10

11

12

*How to turn a beer crate into an attractive footstool. **Fig.4.** The crate is inverted and a piece of scrim tacked over the base. The raw edges are then turned under and tacked down. **Fig.5.** Ties of twine, made like back stitch, are put into the scrim to secure the first stuffing. The end of twine is tied in a slip knot. **Fig.6.** The stuffing should be teased out thoroughly before it is put under the ties. **Fig.7.** The stuffing is covered by a piece of scrim which is tacked on to the chamfered edge of the box. The next stage is blind stitching, which helps form a firm edge of stuffing. Note how the needle enters the stuffing at an angle to the left.*

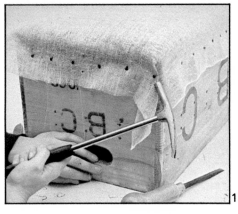

13

Figs.8 and 9. The second stage of blind stitch. Before the needle is withdrawn at the side, the twine is wound round it and pulled very tight. (See Fig.1 for a diagram of the stitch.) Fig.10. Top stitch is a combination of blind stitch and back stitch, and forms a roll of stuffing all round the edge. (See Fig.2 for a diagram of the stitch. Fig.3 shows the difference between blind and top stitching.) Figs.11 and 12. More ties are put in for the second stuffing, which fills up the hollow left by the roll edge. Fig.13. The second stuffing is covered by a piece of scrim, and the excess fabric at the corners tucked under in a neat pleat. The box is now ready for the top cover.

This layer of stuffing should be covered with calico or scrim. Cut it large enough to cover the top and come 1 in. down on each side. Without turning under the edges, place it centrally over the stuffing and put in a temporary tack on each side, as for the scrim. It should be quite smooth and tight. Tack completely along the edges to within 2 in. of each corner, placing the tacks about 1 in. apart. Finish off the corners in a double pleat as for the main cover of the dining chair on page 189.

The main cover

Both the wadding and main cover should be applied and finished in the same way as for the dining chair on pages 183-189, the tacks being placed on the bottom edge of the sides of the box.

As a final touch to the pleats, it is often a good idea to slipstitch the folds together at the bottom for a couple of inches. For this you should use a curved needle and sewing thread. Alternatively, the main cover can be made like a boxed cushion and tacked on.

Remaking a Chesterfield

A buttoned chesterfield is the aristocrat of living room furniture; and the cost of one reflects its high standing. One way of cutting the cost is to buy an old chesterfield—not necessarily buttoned—strip it down to the bare frame, and re-cover it. For a fraction of the normal price you can own a splendid piece of furniture.

Re-upholstering an item of furniture that would otherwise be scrapped can in addition be a satisfying project.

The techniques detailed below are applicable to all seating that is sprung and filled, and will enable you to convert whole suites of furniture at a fraction of the cost of purchasing them new.

A buttoned chesterfield has been chosen because it is one of the most difficult projects in upholstery. But while it is not a subject for the complete novice, it is a feasible proposition if you have had some experience upholstering sofas and chairs. Competence in buttoning and pleating is important—and patience is, too. The professional might take two weeks to do this job; it should take you at least twice as long. Do not try to rush things or invent short cuts.

Tools and materials

The essential tools required are: a mallet with a 4in. or 100mm head, a ripping chisel for removing tacks, a 6oz. claw or warrington hammer, a webbing stretcher, heavy duty 9in. or 230mm scissors, a curved spring needle, a heavy straight needle, 10in. or 250mm long, for the main stitching, a light straight needle, 10in., for buttoning, a small curved needle, 3in. or 75mm, for finishing edge joints, and a regulator, for regulating stuffing and pleating.

The quantity of materials varies with the size of the unit being upholstered, but you will need the following: webbing, to anchor the springs at the base, springs, heavy canvas, about 12oz, light canvas or scrim, about 7½oz, cover fabric, coconut fibre for the first stuffing, horsehair for the 'top' filling, upholstery wadding, upholstery tacks, 3-ply sisal cord for lashing the springs, and flax twine for stitching and buttoning.

If you are buttoning the furniture, you will also need a quantity of upholstery buttons. These have to be covered with matching fabric but this can be done by the shop you buy them from.

Left. The frame for this elegant buttoned chesterfield was made more than 50 years ago. Bought for a nominal price and re-covered, it is good for many more years of service.
Top left inset. *The chesterfield as it was before renovation.*

Stripping down

Strip the sofa down to the bare wood frame, removing every single tack and scrap of fabric. Do this carefully, using the mallet and ripping chisel to pry out the tacks. Keep any springs and horsehair in good condition as these can be used again.

At this stage some repairs to the frame will be necessary. At the very least, the holes caused by the removal of tacks will have to be filled with plastic wood and sanded down after the filler has dried. Any other defects, such as loose joints, must be attended to as well.

When all repairs have been made, treat any affected areas for woodworm. This should be left until all other repairs to the frame have been completed because using woodworm fluid first would affect the bonding power of any adhesives used on the joints. Areas so treated must be left to dry for at least a week, otherwise the fluid may spread on to the fabric.

Setting the seat springs

Turn the frame upside down and begin securing the webbing across the bottom of the rails. Start with the webbing strips that run from the back to the front. Tack the strips in place, one at a time, on the rear rail and, using the stretcher, strain the webbing over the front rail and tack in position. When these strips have been placed, repeat along the length, from side rail to side rail. Before stretching and tacking these long strips, weave them in and out.

Then turn the frame right side up and stitch each spring in position as in Fig.2, using the curved spring needle. Lace the tops of the springs down to compress them and keep them in position. First knot a length of sisal to an outer spring, at a point facing a rail. Lead the sisal to a rail and tack it to the rail bottom, then run the sisal across the springs to the opposite rail, securing each spring as in Fig.3. As each spring is lashed, compress it about 1½in. or 35mm.

Stuffing the seat

Cover the lashed springs with heavy canvas. Fold and tack the canvas along the top of the back rail, then stretch and tack it over the front rail, and finish along the side rails. Stitch the canvas to the tops of the springs in the same way as detailed for stitching the bottoms of the springs to the webbing.

Place 4in. of loose coconut fibre over the seat and cover the filling with light canvas. Stretch the canvas tightly so that it will compress the fibre down to about 1½in. or 35mm. Then tack it along the back and side rails, and stitch it along the front as detailed in Fig.24. Stitch the filling in place between the two canvases, as in Fig.7.

194

Fig.1. *The stretcher is used to pull the webbing across the frame, then held while four securing nails are driven in.*

Fig.2. *When the webbing has been stretched across the frame in a basket-weave pattern, the springs are stitched to the top.*

Fig.3. *The springs are compressed and kept in position by knotting string along the tops and securing at the edges.*

Fig.7. *After the light canvas has been laid over the coconut fibre stuffing, it must be anchored between the two canvases by stitching through, as shown.*

Fig.8. *Cutting the diagonal slits for the buttons. The coconut fibre stuffing immediately under the slits must be cleared down to the base canvas.*

Fig.9. *Horsehair stuffing is placed over the second seat canvas. Strands of twine are anchored to the canvas and led up through the stuffing to the top canvas.*

Fig.13. *Laying the final canvas over the seat. Skewers or pins hold the material in place while it is being stitched.*

Fig.14. *Pulling a button through. The line at the opposite end is anchored to the base canvas by a roll of webbing.*

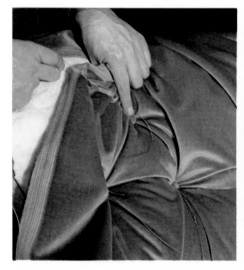

Fig.15. *Pleating and buttoning. The quantity of loose material is such that these have to be done together.*

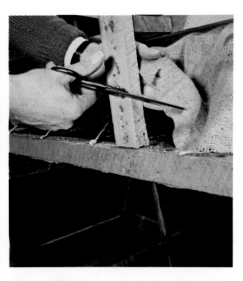

Fig.4. When the seat springs have been compressed and tied, heavy canvas is laid over and nailed to the frame rails.

Fig.5. This is the positioning for the arm and back springs. The lashing is only carried out horizontally.

Fig.6. Coconut fibre is the first filling. This is laid as shown, and compressed when the light canvas is stretched over.

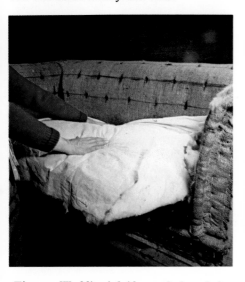

Fig.10. Wadding is laid over the horsehair and the anchored strands of twine are stitched through. The wadding prevents bits of stuffing protruding though the cover.

Fig.11. This shows the pleating and fitting procedure for the front of the arms. Pay particular attention to this point—it acts as a mould for the final cover.

Fig.12. Cutting out rough patterns. If a cheaper material is used for measuring and cutting the first pattern, expensive mistakes will be reduced to a minimum.

Fig.16. Pleating the final cover round the front edges of the arm rest. The nails in the middle are covered with a panel.

Fig.17. Running the skirting panel along the front. When stitched, the material is pleated down and nailed under the rail.

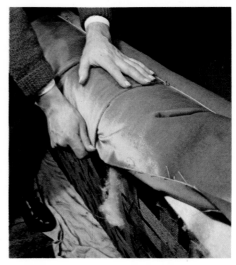

Fig.18. Fitting the top seat panel. The panel is stitched along the front, pleated over to the back and nailed along the back.

Back and side springs

Weave the webbing along the back and arms and tack and stretch into place in the same manner described above. Place the springs in position on the webbing and stitch in place as illustrated in Fig.2.

Lash the spring tops, as described above, but do so only along the length of the sofa, not up and down. Cover the lashed springs with a heavy canvas, stretch and tack in position, and stitch to the springs.

Back and side fillings

Place coconut fibre over the back and arms and cover it with light canvas as described above. Then tack the canvas in position along all edges except the arm fronts. At this point the fabric is stitched as described in Fig.22, and the filling is tied to the 'sandwich' canvases.

Button preparation

Mark out the eventual positions of the buttons on the light canvas. With the scissors, cut a diagonal 1½in. or 35mm slit where each button will be placed. Open out the filling by clearing a 'shaft', 1¼in. in diameter, through each slit. This is achieved by inserting the flat end of the regulator through the slit, and forcing the filling away from the slit all the way down to the base canvas. This will allow the buttons to sink deeply.

The top cover patterns

Ten pieces of fabric are needed for the cover—the front border or panel, seat, inside back, outside back, two inside arms, two outside arms, and two facing panels for the arms. To work out the dimensions of each piece, measure the length and width of each of the above areas, then add 4in. or 100mm to each measurement to account for the filling and buttoning. Transfer the final dimensions to the cheap muslin and cut out. These pieces are placed over the final filling to check that the pattern fits, and are then used to outline the cutting for the final covers.

The final covering

Place 3in. of loose horsehair over the seat area and then lay the wadding over the horsehair. This prevents the horsehair ends from protruding through the cover. The wadding is tied through the horsehair to the light-canvas as in Fig.10. Cover the filling with the muslin seat pattern. If the fit is correct, cut the seat cover from the upholstering fabric, using the muslin pattern as a guide.

The seat cover is lockstitched along the front edge, stretched over the filling, compressing the horsehair to 1in., and tacked in place along the back and sides.

The back, arms and front panel are covered with horsehair and wadding, and the final fabric stretched over in the same manner. With these panels the buttons have to be placed and secured and the material pleated, before the upholstery fabric is tacked down. The arms are pleated in 'rays' (Fig.16) before tacking down.

The final covers for the back of the seat and arms, the arm fronts, and the front panel, are stitched and tacked in place.

Buttoning

To place the buttons, thread a needle and push the eye end of it (an upholstery needle is pointed at both ends) through the outside cover and through the shaft in the coconut fibre. When the eye of the needle has just pierced the base canvas, place a 1in. scrap of webbing between the twine and the needle. This will act as an anchor and prevent the twine from pulling through the canvas.

Pull the *other* end of the needle back through the canvas, out through the main cover, and

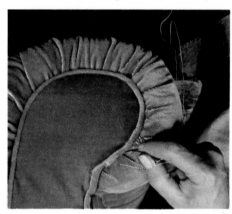

Fig.19 (above). Stitching the arm cover panel in place. Fig.20 (top right). Nailing the side cover under the bottom rail. Fig.21. Method of securing the heavy canvas to the spring tops. Fig.22. A slip-stitch.

secure the twine to the button with a slip knot. Pull the twine tight so that the slip knot forces the button into the filling, but leave the ends loose with about a 4in. or 100mm loose end. When all the buttons have been fitted, knot each length of twine, cut the loose ends to about ½in., and tuck under the button (Fig.14).

As each button is sunk into position, the fabric is pleated out to take up the excess material. The front panel is pleated vertically, and the back and side panels are diamond pleated.

Fig.23. The slip-knot is used for pulling the buttons down. Fig.24. The front edge of the seat being stitched in a roll. Fig.25. A pleating detail. Pleating is done at the same time as buttoning.

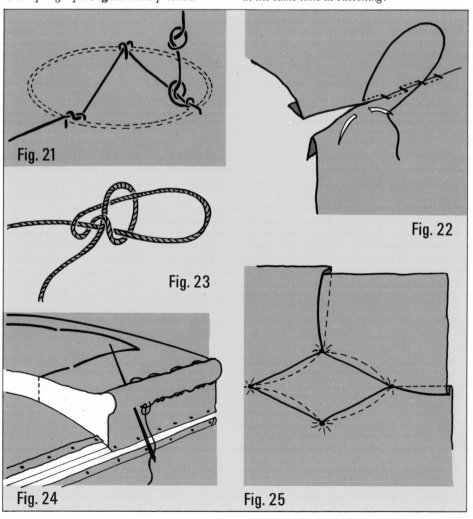

Fig. 21

Fig. 22

Fig. 23

Fig. 24

Fig. 25

Fabrics for wall coverings

Fabric has long been a popular form of wallcovering, but it can also make an attractive alternative to painting or varnishing parts of furniture, such as drawer fronts, doors, bath panels, blanket boxes, bedheads, shelves, waste baskets, lamp bases, and screens.

Covering surfaces with fabric is different from actually *making* a cover for the item because the fabric is attached by adhesive or tacks, and there is no sewing involved.

Fabrics used this way are hard-wearing and practical; they can be cleaned by brushing or vacuuming and, with the exception of felt, they can be 'refreshed' by gentle sponging with a damp cloth. Almost any fabric may be used, but some are more successful than others.

Hessian. This is made from jute and is available simply as furnishing fabric in widths up to 50in. or paper backed specially for wallcovering in a 21in. standard wallpaper roll or in pieces by the yard between 30in. and 39in. wide. It is probably the most popular of all fabric wall-coverings, and looks particularly good in alcoves and as a background for paintings. Of the two kinds, the paper backed is more expensive but has the advantage of being easier to hang because it gives the hessian body and prevents it from distorting or wrinkling much. It is not available in as many colours as furnishing hessian, but there are a variety of weaves. Some are treated with a special process which keeps the weave straight and helps to prevent fading—a snag of furnishing hessian. Both kinds can be emulsion- or gloss-painted satisfactorily.

Linen. This is made from flax and, like hessian, is available by the yard as a furnishing (or dress) fabric in a variety of widths, or paper backed and 30in. wide. It is softer than hessian and, although the unbacked kind should be hung in the same way as hessian (see below), the backed version is hung like a standard wallpaper because it is thinner.

Felt. This is available in rolls for wallcovering up to 72in. wide and in a tremendous range of colours. It is fairly easy to use, although heavy, and is particularly good as a sound insulator. (It is also good for cupboard and drawer fronts because it is firm and does not easily fray or stain from adhesive—provided the adhesive is applied carefully.) It should not be used in a sunny position, because it fades.

Silk. The most commonly used types are moiré and slub silk. Silk should always be paper backed for use with adhesive because otherwise the surface would be spoiled by the adhesive seeping through and staining. The paper backing also gives it some body when being used as a wallcovering. It is very expensive, however, about five or six times as much as a good wallpaper. Even though the 30in. wide rolls are sold with instructions, it is difficult to use because it is untrimmed—and trimming is not easy because of the natural variation in weave—and because the slightest mistake (rough handling or uneven application of adhesive which seeps on to the face of the fabric) can ruin a whole wall length. For this reason, manufacturers usually stress that it should be hung by an expert (there are many professional decorators who baulk at it), and they will often recommend specific people. It is worth following their recommendations because if anything goes wrong the silk will be replaced free of charge to you.

Grasscloth. The beautiful rough texture is achieved by sewing together dried grasses of various thicknesses which are then stuck on to a paper backing. Like silk, it is very expensive and although it is possible for a non-professional to hang the lighter kinds quite successfully, many of the same problems apply and it is worth having an expert to do it.

Cork. Not strictly a fabric, it comes into the same category because of its delicate, textured effect and because it is applied in the same way. It is made in rolls 30in. wide, specially for a wallcovering, from wafer-thin cork shavings which are pressed on to adhesive-covered paper.

Carpet. To use this as a wallcovering would have seemed ludicrous at one time—and also

CROWN WALLPAPERS (GLIDE ON)

too expensive and heavy. However, it is possible and practical with self-adhesive carpet tiles and is actually recommended as a wallcovering by the manufacturer. It would probably be too oppressive on more than one wall in a room, but it does give warmth and virtual soundproofing.

PVC fabrics. With so many vinyl-coated wall-papers available, it is not worth using pvc fabric as a general wallcovering. However, for other small areas it is very practical because it is strong and easy to clean. It is very easy to use in the self-adhesive versions, as the adhesive is 'activated' either by removing the paper backing, or by soaking in water, depending on the make.

Treated fabric. If you want to use ordinary dress or furnishing fabric to cover large areas of wall, it is worth having it specially treated by the Alphacol process. Almost any fabric—both natural and synthetic fibres—can have the treatment, which is a form of plasticizing that stiffens the fabric but without making it shiny or affecting its appearance in any other way. Any shrinkage occurs during the stiffening process, and not when the fabric is applied to the wall; the fabric can be sponged clean and will not fray. It should be used with the adhesive supplied by the manufacturer who treats the fabric. This adhesive should be applied to the wall as for other fabric wallcoverings (see below); because it is slow drying it gives more time to position the pieces but without any danger of seepage. Any bubbles can be ironed out—with a hot iron—when the adhesive dries.

Methods of attaching fabrics

Wherever it is possible (in panels for a door front or blanket box, for example), it is better to attach the fabric to the surface by tacking it down because, unless the fabric has been treated, shrinkage is one of the main hazards of using adhesive. If adhesive has to be used—for a wallcovering for example—each piece of fabric (including paper backed ones) should be cut 1in. wider and 2in. longer than the area to be covered (this extra should be allowed for when calculating the total amount). Shrinkage can be reduced if the adhesive is put on the surface being covered, rather than on to the fabric back or paper backing. To ensure that any shrinkage is even, the adhesive should be rolled on smoothly. Applying the adhesive to the surface also helps prevent the staining of the fabric through seepage.

Manufacturers of paper backed fabric wallcoverings usually recommend which adhesive should be used for their particular product. It may be a heavy-duty standard wallpaper paste, such as Polycell Plus, or a thick prepared paste, such as Clam 143. For unbacked and untreated fabrics, Clam 143 or a not-too-sloppy adhesive such as a thick pva or an adhesive with a latex base may be used. It is always wise to test it with a small piece of fabric first to make sure that it

Below. Textured fabric wallcoverings make an ideal setting for paintings and give extra interest without being obtrusive.

will bond the fabric and surface together satisfactorily, that the adhesive does not seep through, and that the fabric's colours do not run. A lot will depend on the type and weight of the fabric, how much dressing (starch) it contains, and the temperature of the room. In a cold room, the fabric will take longer to dry out and there is more chance of shrinkage.

Whatever the surface being covered—even if the fabric is preshrunk—all joints should be butt-edged following the method given below. (With treated fabrics, the edges should be butt jointed as for wallpapering.) If you are covering something with a tricky shape, make a paper pattern first and try it for size before cutting out the fabric.

Fabric as a wallcovering

You will need all the tools used for normal paperhanging, plus a heavy 6in. rubber roller and a foam-sleeved paint roller for applying the adhesive.

Prepare the walls and, if using an unbacked fabric, line the walls with a toning paper to prevent any patches showing through, particularly at the joints. To prevent fraying, use a sharp pair of scissors—or a sharp knife and a straight edge—to cut the pieces (allow the extra for shrinkage). Do not stretch the fabric or pull at any loose threads—these can be cut off later.

Next, mark with chalk a plumb vertical line on the wall for the first length at a distance from the corner of 1in. less than the fabric width.

Continue marking vertical lines along the wall at the same interval of 1in. less than the fabric width. Using the foam roller, apply the adhesive to the section of the wall for the first length of fabric only, to within 1in. of the line.

Position the first length so that one edge is level with the chalk line and there is a free 1in. overlap on the other side at the corner and at the top and bottom of the piece. Pat down the length with your hands and then smooth it down with the rubber roller, working from the centre towards the sides. Do not roll too heavily, or the fibres may become distorted, and do not trim off the excess fabric yet. If using felt, roll the length on to a batten and suspend it between two step ladders. Allow overlaps as for hessian, press it on to the wall at the bottom and work upwards.

Making a butt edge

Roll the adhesive on to the next section of wall and then hang another length of fabric, overlapping at top and bottom and on the side of the first length that you hung. Hang all the remaining lengths in the same way, leaving the overlaps loose and untrimmed.

When the adhesive is dry, flatten the loose edge on the join and, with a straight edge and sharp knife, cut through the centre of both pieces (be careful not to gouge the wall). Remove the waste strips. If you are using felt, tease the edges slightly to fuzz the join. Paste the wall immediately under the join and press the fabric down into position. Then trim the top and bottom edges, and the corner overlap, to fit. Use a seam roller with great care, as it can cause stains if pressed too hard.

Applying fabric to panels

Where fabric is being used simply for panels, it can be stuck on as for a wallcovering or it can be tacked inro position. The tacks can be covered with cut-out frames of $\frac{1}{8}$in. thick plywood, or with a beading, or with a braid edging.

Plywood frame

Use a fine-toothed panel saw to cut the plywood to the overall size wanted; sand the edges smooth. Mark the area to be cut out, and remove it with a sharp handyman's knife. Fill in any holes with cellulose filler; when it is dry, sand the edges smooth and paint the frame.

Cut the fabric to the same size as the inner edge of the panel, plus $\frac{1}{2}$in. all round for the frame to grip it firmly. Tack the fabric to the surface you are decorating with flat-headed tacks or staples. Apply a strong all-purpose adhesive to the back of the plywood round the edges and/or the surface to be covered (see manufacturer's instructions) and then cover the fabric with the frame. Use adhesive tape to hold it in position until the adhesive dries.

Beading edging

Any design of wood beading or moulding may be used, providing it has a flat base and it is wide enough to secure and hide the edges of the fabric. If the panel is on a door, the frame should be 1-2in. from the edges so the door can close. Mark out, on the surface you are decorating, the area of the frame (ie, the line to which the *inner* edge of the beading will be placed) and cut two lengths of beading the length of the frame height, plus 2in. If you have a mitre block, use it to cut off both ends of one piece of beading so that they slope inwards at an angle of 45°

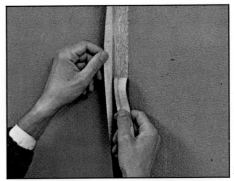
1

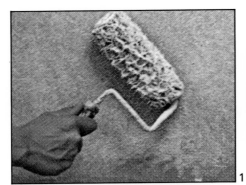

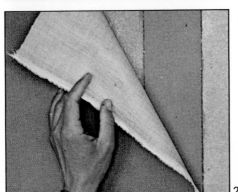
2

5

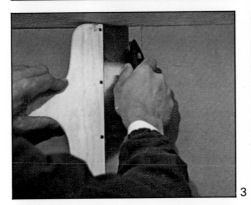
6

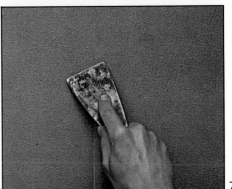

3

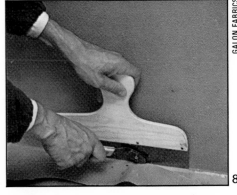
7

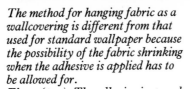
4

GALON FABRICS

The method for hanging fabric as a wallcovering is different from that used for standard wallpaper because the possibility of the fabric shrinking when the adhesive is applied has to be allowed for.
***Fig.1** (top). The adhesive is spread evenly on the wall for one 'drop' at a time, to within 1in. of the plumb line.*
***Fig.2** (second from top). The adhesive for the next lengths should be applied carefully, leaving uncovered the sections where the pieces overlap.*

***Figs.3** and **4** (third from top and bottom). When the lengths are hung and the adhesive is dry, a cut is made through the middle of the overlap, using a sharp knife (or special weave cutter) and a straight edge.*
***Fig.5** (top right). The waste strips are then removed.*
***Fig.6** (second from top). The wall under the join is pasted.*
***Fig.7** (third from top). The edges of the fabric are pressed into position.*
***Fig.8** (bottom). The excess fabric at the top and bottom of the wall is trimmed off.*

Above. Gingham fabric makes a gay wallcovering in the kitchen in places not likely to be splashed.
Below. On a plain door, brass tacks are a decorative finish to fabric panels.
Opposite, above. Panelled doors are ideal for picking out in fabric. You can achieve a similar effect with a cut-out frame.

(Fig.10). Always cut first through the top surface of a moulding. Cut the other piece in the same way and to the same length. Smooth all edges.

If you have no mitre board or bench hook, improvise a bench hook as described on page 47. Then mark the beading to the exact length of the frame, leaving about 1in. of 'waste' on each end for easy handling. Measure the width of the beading exactly, and measure the same distance in from the ends along the outer edge. At this point, mark another line—with pencil—across the beading parallel to the first line. Check that the distance between the lines is exactly the same as the width of the beading, and then mark the beginning and end of a diagonal line—this will be the cutting line (Fig.10). Hold the beading on the bench hook and then cut off the ends as above.

Lightly tack the lengths in position with three panel pins—two about 1in. from each end and one in the middle—but without driving them completely home (the gap between the beading and surface should be the thickness of the beading). Cut two more pieces of beading to match the width of the frame, plus 2in. Gently wedge these pieces in position behind the upright pieces of beading (Fig.11). Check that the frame is square by measuring the diagonals (they should be equal).

Use a handyman's knife or other sharp knife to scribe the angled cutting lines on the top and bottom pieces so that they join the side pieces exactly. Then remove all the beading, being careful not to tear the side pieces. Cut the top and bottom pieces, smooth the edges, and then paint or varnish all the pieces. When completely dry, check that the pieces still fit together perfectly and make any necessary adjustments.

Cut the fabric to the inside size of the frame, plus $\frac{1}{8}$in. To make sure edges are square, pull a thread for each side and then cut along it. Pull a piece at the opposite corner if it still is not square. Starch the fabric to give it body and then secure it smoothly in position using staples or double-sided adhesive tape. If there is a possibility of the fabric stretching, leave it for a few days and cut and re-position if necessary. Then tack down the beading to cover the fabric $\frac{1}{8}$in. all round with panel pins at 3in.-4in. intervals, and touch up the paint where necessary.
Braid edging

Mark the area of the frame and cut a length of braid to fit the perimeter, plus $\frac{3}{4}$in. Mark the position of the corners and mitre the corners (see pages 147-149), cutting off excess braid. Cut out the fabric and secure it in position as above and then, using a latex-based adhesive, stick down the braid to cover the fabric edges. Join the braid by turning under the edges and making a butt join.

Opposite (Fig.9). With a plywood frame the fabric is tacked down and its edges are covered by the inner edge of the frame.
Fig.10. If you have no mitre board, a 45° angle can be made by first marking a line parallel to, and at a distance of the beading's width, from the end. The diagonal is the cutting line.
Fig.11. To make a perfect join, mark the cutting line for the top and bottom of the frame when the side struts are in position.

Fig. 9

Fig. 10

Fig. 11

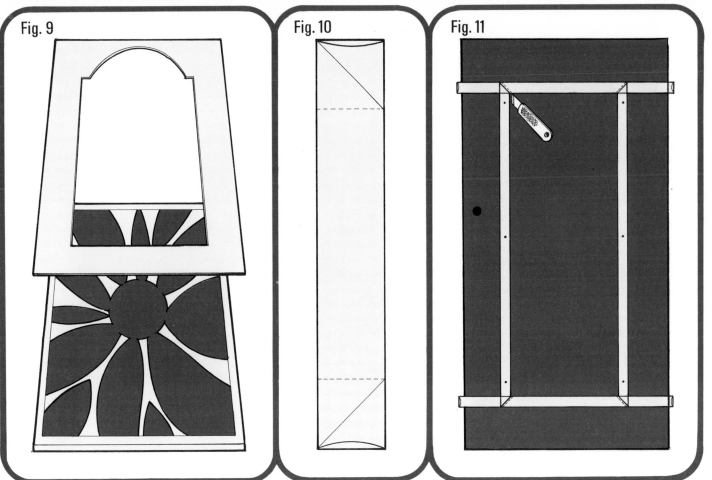

Fabrics on furniture

The uniform design and plainness of most whitewood and kit furniture may initially appear unsuitable for many people's decorating schemes. But the basic practical designs can be altered to a considerable extent by using a few simple to use and readily available materials.

The greatest advantage of this kind of furniture is its adaptability. Fabric coverings, like hessian or grasscloth, or stencilled designs, or even something as simple as brass studs, can lend a unique decorative effect both to the furniture and to the room in which it is used.

Decorating with fabric

Since most kit furniture is relatively inexpensive, it is ideal to use if you are experimenting with your own design ideas. Bedrooms are especially easy to work with. Fig.2 shows two different effects that can be achieved by combining fabric with a kit design bed unit. The all-yellow scheme at the left is achieved by using the same fabric for the bedspread, draw fronts and headboard. The scheme at the right uses tweed fabric in the same way and gives a strong, masculine-looking effect. Surfaces in the darker room are covered with small sheets of float glass, cut to size and with the edges polished.

If you intend to cover drawer fronts or similar areas with panels of material it is wise to practise with a few odd scraps first. As a general rule, it is best to use a fabric which will not ravel easily. This may, however, not be possible, especially if you want a rough-looking fabric such as hessian or grasscloth. A cotton or rayon blend is probably the least expensive and the easiest to use.

Before doing any cutting, the material (unless it is hessian, felt or grasscloth) should be washed and pressed. This will remove any unnecessary sizing in the cloth and will also allow you to test the cloth for shrinkage and for colour fastness.

Always measure the area to be covered accurately. Then allow about 1in. (25mm) all around on the fabric for possible shrinkage—if you have already tested for shrinkage, allow less.

If the cloth is likely to ravel, allow at least ½in. (13mm) all around for folding under, as well as the 1in. (25mm) shrinkage allowance. Although the glue used to fix the fabric to the surface should prevent most ravelling, it is still advisable to turn the edges under. Mitre all corners and use a fabric adhesive, such as Copydex, to hold down the folded edges.

Before actually fixing the fabric in position, hold it over the surface and mark out with a pencil any positions for handles or other protuberances. Carefully slit these with a scalpel blade just so that the handle bolts will push through the cloth; exact trimming should be done when the cloth is finally glued in position.

Actual fixing of the fabric will depend very much upon the size of the area to be covered and the weight of the material. Lightweight fabrics, or even heavy materials over a relatively small area (such as the drawer and cabinet fronts seen in Fig.2), may be fixed with any fabric adhesive. Begin by outlining the edges of the furniture surface *and* the fabric with the glue and wait 15 to 20 minutes until the adhesive looks transparent. Then carefully position the cloth over the surface, and smooth it quickly into place. It is most important that you work

Fig. 1

Fig.1. A rich mixture of warm brown in this wallsetting is enlivened by the bright colours of the scatter cushions. The cabinets are standard whitewood units.

Fig. 2

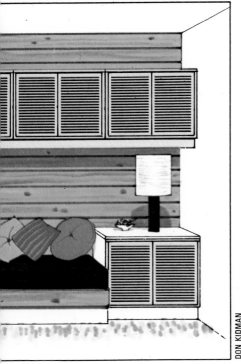

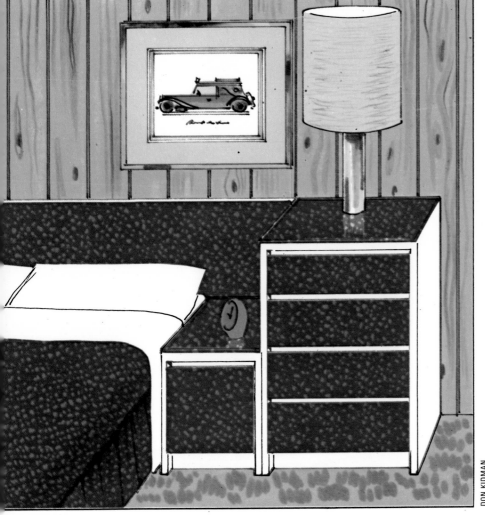

Fig.2. Left. Soft pastel fabric adds a suitably feminine touch to this bedroom . . . Right. Here the bitter chocolate and light wood effect makes a bedroom of sterner stuff !

DON KIDMAN

quickly and accurately, since once the two glued edges meet they will bond almost immediately.

Alternatively, it is possible over slightly larger areas or with very heavy material to soak the cloth thoroughly in wallpaper paste, such as Polycell. Apply the fabric on to the surface and then brush it smooth until wrinkles are removed. The result may look somewhat disastrous at first, but if the surface is perfectly smooth, the material will dry smooth and taut over it. If using this method it is imperative that you practise on a test area first to ascertain the extent of shrinkage.

If you have drawers or cupboards with detachable fronts, it may be easier to fix the fabric over the entire area. Provided that the folded over fabric is not thick enough to hinder the re-fitting of the drawer front, it can either be stapled or glued in place on the concealed side. When the drawers are re-fixed, there will be no visible edges (see Figs.6-7).

To protect finished fabric panel decorations from dirt and stains, you can apply a proprietary fabric sealer such as Fend.

Using these same basic techniques, there are any number of decorative projects you can undertake. To make a slightly padded bedhead, for example, simply cover a sheet of ⅛in. to ¼in. or 3mm-6mm thick foam, available from upholstery shops, with the material of your choice and fix this to the bedhead with Copydex.

Covering larger surfaces

Wardrobes lend themselves very well to fabric decorating. The three examples shown in Fig.3 have all been done on the same size overlap-type wardrobe door, but the finished appearances each look slightly different in proportion. The first example, at the left, has been covered in a basic brown hessian. The best way of doing this is firstly to turn under all edges and then fold the corners under to make mitres, so that the panel covers the outside of the door exactly. Glue these folded edges to the rest of the material with Copydex.

Next cover the surface of the door with a good coat of wallpaper paste, such as Polycell, and proceed to hang the hessian on to this surface in much the same manner as you would for wall-paper. Brush out wrinkles as you go and allow the material to dry. By applying the adhesive only to the door in this way, you minimize the chances of the hessian shrinking. But because unbacked hessian is a bit unpredictable, it is wise to complete one door and let it dry before tackling the next one, 'just in case'. When it is set, an inner trim of curtain or carpet tape may be applied to the door. The corners should be mitred first, and then fixed on to the hessian with Copydex.

The centre door has been covered with felt. The same procedure as described above can be used for fixing or, alternatively, the felt can be fastened to the door with small panel pins or tacks around the edges. A collage design made from odd bits of felt can then be stuck on to the backing with Copydex. This idea may be fun to try in a child's room. Notice the difference in appearance between the hessian covered door and this one; the former looks much narrower.

For a really plush look, try covering the door with a piece of imitation leather or vinyl cushioned at the back with a piece of ⅛in. (3mm) thick foam. Cut the foam sheet approximately 1in. (25mm) smaller, and the vinyl approximately 1in. larger, all round than the door. Fold under the excess vinyl and fix it to the door (over the foam piece) with either up-holsterer's nails or good quality brass head drawing pins (see Fig.4).

Overall schemes

Further variations may be considered. Bead-ing or moulding can be tacked around the edges of the door with panel pins to add further decoration and to disguise any rough edges if need be. Additional techniques and ideas of this nature are discussed on pages 199-203.

Once you have added fabric panels to the furniture there is no need to stop—curtain, bedspread and vanity skirt fabrics can all be matched to the panel coverings. Fig.5 gives one idea for decorating all over in green and blue gingham.

Often, units such as those shown are made with overlapping door fronts. The best method of covering these is simply to stretch the fabric over the doors and staple the fabric to the inside of the flange, or rim, of the door. A strip of carpet self-adhesive tape cut approximately ½in. (13mm) wide can then be used to cover the staples.

If you would rather not use fabric for all surfaces, some firms, such as Sandersons, do

DON KIDMAN

manufacture matching fabric and wallpaper. Furniture panels can be wallpapered to blend in with the room and the fabric used for bed covers, cushions, and curtains. Wallpaper can be protected by varnish, or covered with a plastic-type, transparent self-adhesive covering such as Transpaseal.

Using standard units

Plain furniture can be easily adapted to provide uncluttered storage space for any room in the house. A cosy living room or bed-sit corner unit, such as that pictured in Fig.1, makes extensive use of standard kitchen wall cabinet units in louvred pine. Tongued-and-grooved boards on the wall impart a feeling of textural unity, and a day-bed mattress set on a pine-faced base completes the picture.

One of the advantages of a unit like the one shown is that it is basically very easy to construct. The cabinets can be hung from the wall in a variety of ways, but perhaps the easiest is to use battens, No. 8 screws and cups and No. 8 wall plugs. All screws must be countersunk.

The only problem will be to see that the units hang evenly and are level, and probably the best way of doing this is to use a batten sawn lengthwise at a 45° angle. This edge of the batten fixed to the cabinets fits into the angle of the batten fixed to the wall. Fix the top section of the long batten—it should be at least ½in. (13mm) thick—across the top of the row of cabinets as they lie on the floor. Now mark out on the wall the position for the other

Fig.3. Dazzling designs or rich elegance achieved by fabric covering wardrobe doors.
Fig.4. For a really plush look, use brass head pins to fix a foam backed vinyl.
Fig.5. Green gingham used for the curtains as well as the doors makes for added impact.

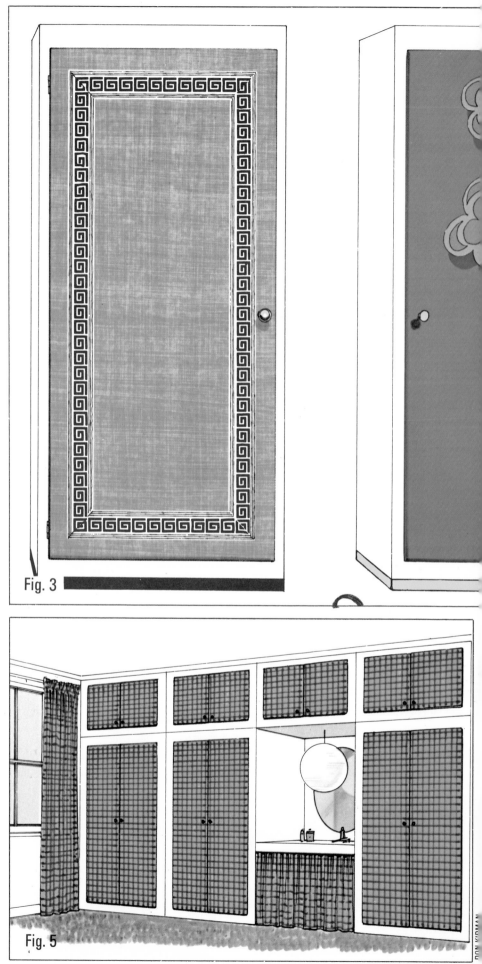

Fig. 3

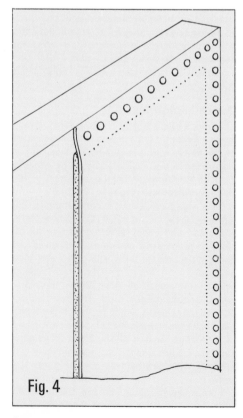

Fig. 4

Fig. 5

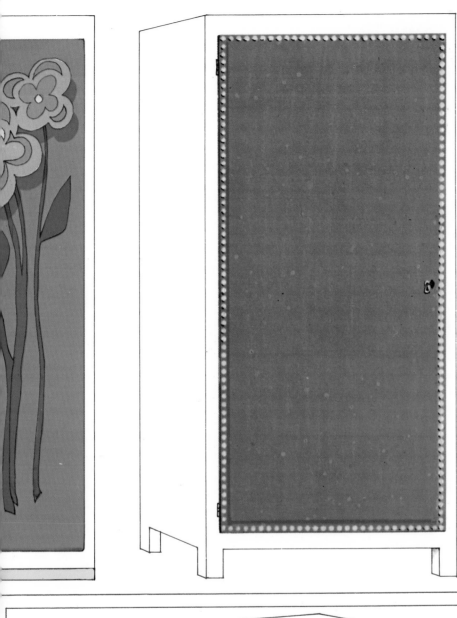

section, checking with a spirit level that it is true. If the wall is severely out of true, adjust the cabinet so that it *looks* level, even if it does not align perfectly with the wall. This batten should be screwed right into the wall using No. 8 screws and cups and No. 8 wall plugs. The cups are not absolutely essential, but they will help to prevent the wood from cracking or splintering.

Before hanging the cabinet unit onto the wall by hooking the two battens together, screw a small square-section batten, approximately the thickness of the upper batten, at the base of the unit. The purpose of this batten is to adjust the balance of the cabinet, so that it will not topple forward.

If desired, a 3in. x 1in. (76mm x 25mm) piece of timber may be fixed with angle brackets to the underside of the front edge of the entire wall unit. This will help unify the appearance of the row of units, and is extremely useful for fixing concealed fluorescent lighting.

A basic knowledge of carpentry should enable anyone to make the base for the mattress and the free-standing cabinets. The base is made up of 4in. x 1in. (102mm x 25.4mm) timber, and halving joints are employed at each of the corners. The whole mattress area will need additional rails right across the top of the base frame for support, and these can easily be placed inside the side rails. As soon as the base is assembled, the cabinets are set on top and held in position by small sections of wood glued to the bottom of the cabinet.

Fig.6. *A plain whitewood chest of drawers gains a touch of distinction with the drawer fronts covered in fabric.*
Fig.7. *Detachable drawer fronts can be covered in this 'wrap around' fashion, which produces an attractive finished effect.*

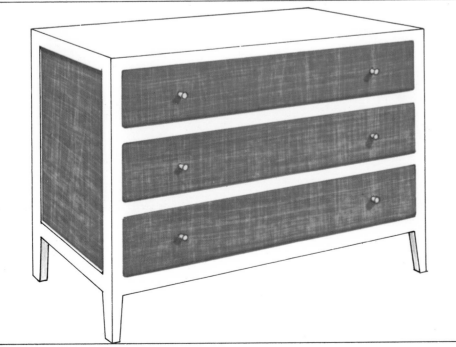

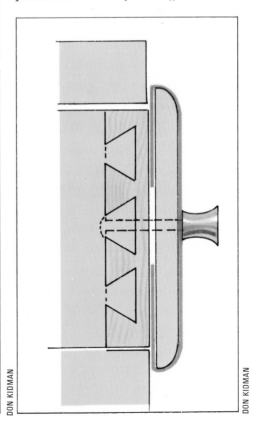

Simple patchwork

Patchwork is an old country craft, which originated from the need to be thrifty by using up offcuts of fabric and the good parts of worn clothes and household linen. New curtains, bedcovers, cushion covers and wallhangings were frequently made by piecing together patches from old ones.

The most popular shapes for early patchwork were those which were simple to cut and made most economical use of the fabric—squares, rectangles and triangles. These are the easiest shapes to use, but even with different combinations of size and shape, they are limiting in the type of design that can be produced and give a striking effect, rather than a beautiful or delicate one.

Gradually patchwork was developed into an art and reached its height of popularity from the mid-18th to the late 19th century, when it became a popular alternative pastime to fine needlework. More elaborate shapes, which could be made into subtle combinations and groupings, were developed, and some of the most popular designs can be found, with variations, in patchwork all over the world. Many are still used as a basis for patchwork today.

The prettiest patchwork is centred round definite and subtle, rather than random, selection and formation of colours and patterns. Where fabrics of widely varying colours and patterns are used, it is better to keep each type in a group, possibly against a plain background, and not jumble them all together. There are several standard groupings, such as the rosette (Figs.1 and 4) and ocean wave (see Figs.5 and 6), which can be used time after time but appear quite different in a variety of fabrics.

Probably the most versatile patch is the hexagon, which may be in the form of an equilateral 'honeycomb' an elongated 'church window' or the broader 'coffin' (see Fig.7).

These shapes are not difficult to make and lend themselves to countless variations in design. Of the three, the honeycomb is the simplest to work with because its broad angles make it easier to fold the corners neatly.

Choosing the fabrics

Ideally the fabric of the patches should be all of the same fibre and weight so they will 'react' in the same way during the making and in wear.

Cotton, with its firm weave and even texture, is the best fabric to use, because it takes a crease well and makes up easily. It is also practical, being both hardwearing and washable. Linen has many of the same qualities as cotton, although some of the coarser types are a little more difficult to make up when the patch has sharp-pointed corners.

Silk makes beautiful patchwork, but needs more skill in the making up because of its slippery nature, and it will not stand up to much hard wear. Velvet also needs skill in making up because it tends to 'creep' during the

stitching. It makes strong, but very heavy, patchwork.

Wool is not often used for intricate patchwork because it tends to be too bulky, but for simpler shapes it can be most successful—and warm if used for a quilt.

Synthetic fibres, such as nylon or Terylene, are the most difficult fabrics to use in patchwork because the quality which makes them ideal for clothes—crease resistance—makes them difficult to fold and achieve sharp angles. Many synthetics, such as rayon, tend to fray as soon as they are cut, and some types stretch out of shape.

Honeycomb patchwork

To make a really accurate shape, the edges of fabric should be folded over and tacked on to a paper base cut to the size of the required patch, which holds it firm and keeps the angles true. These bases should be made from strong brown paper or thin card (glossy magazine covers, the backs of old greetings cards or pages from company reports can be used), and their shape cut from a template.

The template may be a bought metal or plastic one, or you can make one from stiff cardboard, although this is not as durable. Of the bought templates, the 'window' type is more useful than the solid ones because you can use it for selecting the exact area of fabric to be used in each patch, and for cutting both the paper base and the fabric (Fig.8).

Home-made template

With a pair of compasses set with a radius equal to the length of one side of the required hexagon, draw a circle. Place the point of the compass at A in Fig.9 (anywhere on the circumference) and, with the same radius, draw an arc to cross the circle at point B. Set the compass at B and draw another arc. Repeat this four more times, working round the circle and the last arc will cross the circumference at A. Join the marks, using a ruler and sharp pencil. Cut out the template, using a ruler and knife. If necessary, strengthen its sides with clear adhesive tape.

The patches may be any size you like—individuality is one of the essential characteristics of patchwork—but, although you can easily combine sizes in one article if all the patches are squares or rectangles, with more complicated shapes it is simpler to keep them the same size. You can, however, combine different shapes, providing the length of the sides of the patch is the same. For large items, such as a bedspread, it is a good idea to use large patches, as there is less sewing involved.

Cutting the patches

The straight grain of the fabric should always run along one edge of the patch and, where possible, the patches should be joined with the grain running in the same direction. This improves the look of the finished work, particularly in plain fabrics with a distinctive weave, and also gives strength and helps keep the work flat.

If using a solid template, whether home-made or bought, cut out the paper patches to the same size as the template and the fabric patches

Fig.1 (left). The honeycomb-shaped hexagon is one of the most versatile patches to use and looks prettiest formed into rosettes.

NIGEL MESSETT

209

with a seam allowance of $\frac{3}{4}$in. all round. With a window template, cut the paper patches following the internal outline, and the fabric patches following the external outlines.

Place the paper patches centrally on the wrong side of the fabric ones, and secure them with one or two pins (use fine pins to avoid leaving pinholes). Clip the turnings of the fabric at the corners and fold the seam allowance over the paper as in Fig.10. Crease the edges firmly and, without knotting the thread (for easy removal), tack the turnings down.

Joining the patches

Patchwork is traditionally sewn by hand, using small, firm oversewing, but it is also possible to machine stitch it using a swing needle machine.

With either method of sewing, use a fine needle and white thread for light patches and black thread for dark ones.

Hold two patches together with 'right' sides facing, and stitch them along one edge, securing the ends of the thread firmly. Fit a third patch into the angles, making sure the corners meet exactly, and stitch it in the same way, first on one side and then on the other (Figs.11 and 12).

When a block of patches is completed, open out the seams and press firmly on both sides. Remove the tacking and paper shapes, and tack round the outside of the block to hold the turnings down.

To finish the patchwork, join all the blocks together and cut part patches to fill in round the edge.

Lining or mounting

When making a cushion cover it is not necessary to line the patchwork, but most other items should be backed to hide and protect the raw edges. The lining should be cut on the straight grain of the fabric and may be joined using the 'bag' method, by machine stitching.

When you are mounting the patchwork on to a large piece of fabric, pin it in position and slip stitch, using tiny, neat stitches, all round the edge. For large areas of patchwork, catch it to the mounting fabric at various points in the middle.

Fig.2 (above) and *Fig.3* (below). Square patches are the simplest shapes to cut, but they must be joined accurately. For small squares it is wisest to tack them on to paper bases before joining them together.

Fig.4 (below right). A bedspread will be easier to handle if you join the patches in small groups and then sew all these together at the end. It should then be backed with plain fabric to give extra strength.

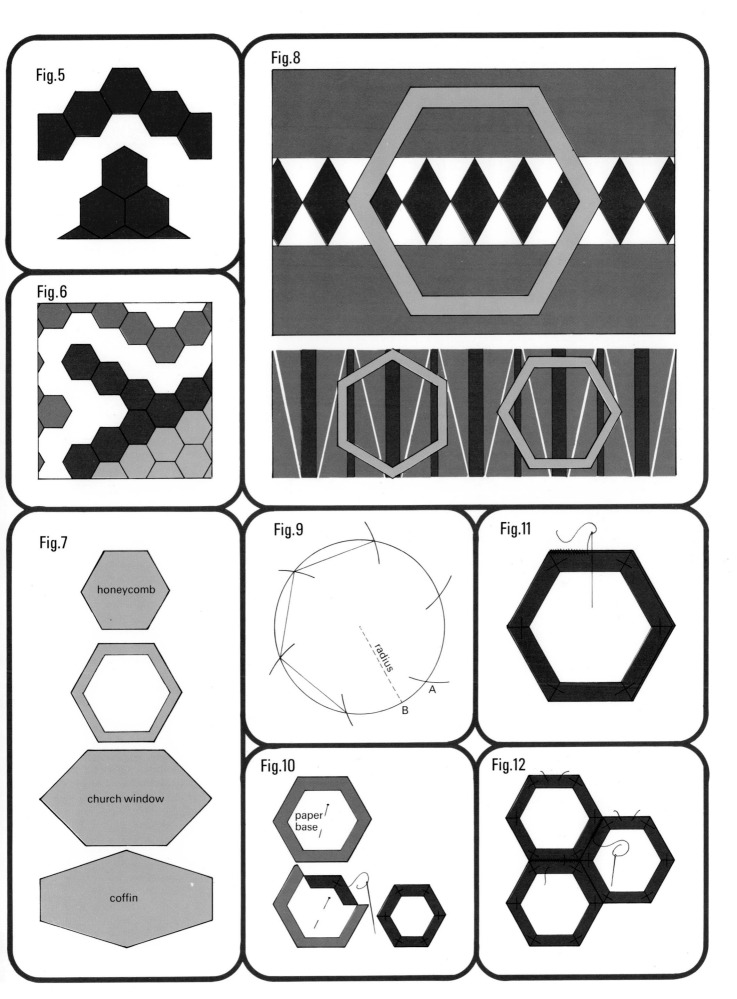

Fig.5

Fig.6

Fig.7

honeycomb

church window

coffin

Fig.8

Fig.9

radius

A

B

Fig.10

paper
base

Fig.11

Fig.12

Combining different shapes

The real skill in patchwork is in combining different shapes to make an attractive, co-ordinated design, rather than a disorganized jumble of colour and pattern.

With some forethought, squares, rectangles, diamonds, triangles, hexagons, pentagons and octagons can be combined to make interesting geometric patterns. The success of the design you choose is largely dependent on the correlation of the colours and pattern, and ideally each segment of a particular motif should be cut from the same fabric. Since this is often not possible, the same effect can be obtained with colours of the same tone, or by using plain fabric for the motif and pattern fabric for the background, and vice versa (Figs.2 and 3).

Using diamonds

Diamonds can be used most effectively by themselves, arranged in groups of three to make a box, or in groups of six or eight to make stars. They also combine well with hexagons, squares and triangles, providing the sides and the angles fit.

To cut a diamond to use with hexagons, or to make a six-pointed star, divide a hexagon as shown in Fig. 8. (The method for making a hexagon template was given on pages 209-211 in the last chapter).

The long diamond, which is used to make an eight-pointed star or to combine with squares, is more complicated to cut out if you have no commercial template. To make your own template, start by constructing an octagon, following the method given below. Each side of the octagon will be equal in length to the distance between the wider angles of the diamond.

Mark one radius from the centre of the octagon to one of the angles (Fig.9, points x-A) mark another one to an adjoining angle (point B). This gives two of the sides of the diamond.

Below. *If you have the time and patience, combining standard patchwork shapes with quite irregular ones can produce a stunning effect, particularly with bright, plain fabrics.*

Pages 214-215, Fig. 1. Diamond patches, used in groups of three, can give the three-dimensional effect of a pile of boxes. Each box should contain one light, one medium and one dark patch for the best result.

Fig.2. By using six diamond patches of the same colour, a star is formed. When placed in alternate rows, a box motif is included.

Fig.3. By placing stars directly on top of one another, with patches of another colour to link them, a different pattern is formed.

Figs.4 and 5. The diamond can be combined most successfully with the honeycomb hexagon.

Figs.6 and 7. The church window hexagon can be mixed with squares to form interesting patterns.

Fig.8. The most accurate method of cutting diamond patches to go with hexagons is actually to divide the hexagon being used.

Fig.9. The elongated diamond, which can be used in groups of eight to make a star, is most easily cut from an octagon.

Fig.10. When tacking a diamond to a paper base, the protruding fabric at the sharp points must be tucked under neatly to keep a good shape.

Fig.11. How to mark an octagon.

Figs.12-14. Octagons need square patches on each alternate side to complete a motif. The square could be from two rectangles, two or four triangles, or four small squares.

Fig.15. Honeycomb hexagons can be stitched on to square bases to give unusual effects.

Fig.16. The different shapes of the pentagon.

Fig.17. The popular Victorian motif, combining hexagon, pentagon and diamonds.

Above. Fabric with a border print can be used to advantage in patchwork if the patches are large enough. Here the centrepiece is made up of triangles, with long strips all round.

Set the compasses at the same radius and, with the point on A, draw an arc outside the octagon. Next, using B as the centre, draw a second arc. Draw lines from A and B to the point where the arcs intersect to complete the diamond.

To keep the patches a good shape, tack them on to a paper base. When folding the seam allowance over the paper, take special care on the sharp angles so that the point is not distorted. Beginning at a blunt corner, tack down the first side. At the sharp corner, turn back the long point of fabric on itself so that it lies along the second side of paper. Then fold the second side of fabric, tacking down the seam allowance through the double fold (Fig.10).

When joining the patches to make a star, join them in the same way as for hexagons (see pages 209-211), but work from the wider of the points towards the sharp ones to make sure that the sharp points are exactly together and that the star lies flat.

Using the octagon

When octagons are joined together, they automatically leave a square space on each alternate side. This can be filled by a solid square, or by square made up from two or four triangles. If this is well done and a rectangle is included, it can give the effect of framing the octagon.

To construct an octagon template, decide on

Above. Only two fabrics have been used in this patchwork, but the design worked out to use squares, triangles and church window hexagons is both simple and highly decorative.

the width of the patch (not the length of each side), and draw a circle with half the width as its radius. Mark the diameter of the circle, then draw a perpendicular line across the point where the diameter meets one side (Fig.11, point A).

Using a protractor, draw a straight line at an angle of $22\frac{1}{2}°$ to the perpendicular line from point A to cut the circle at point B. The distance between A and B is the length of one side of the octagon. Set the compasses to the same length and place the point at B. Draw an arc through the circle (point C). Place the point of the compasses at C and draw another arc. Continue round the circle in this way until the final arc crosses at A. Join all the points with straight lines. Cut out the template with a sharp knife, rather than scissors.

Using the pentagon

By themselves, lots of pentagon patches joined together automatically make a ball but, with a hexagon as the centrepiece, they can be made into a very attractive star motif. If diamonds are added, it becomes the traditional 'box and star' pattern which was very popular in Victorian patchwork (Fig.17).

The simplest method of making a pentagon patch is to cut off the sharp point of a diamond. To make an equilateral pentagon, follow the method for making an octagon (above), but use an angle of 36°.

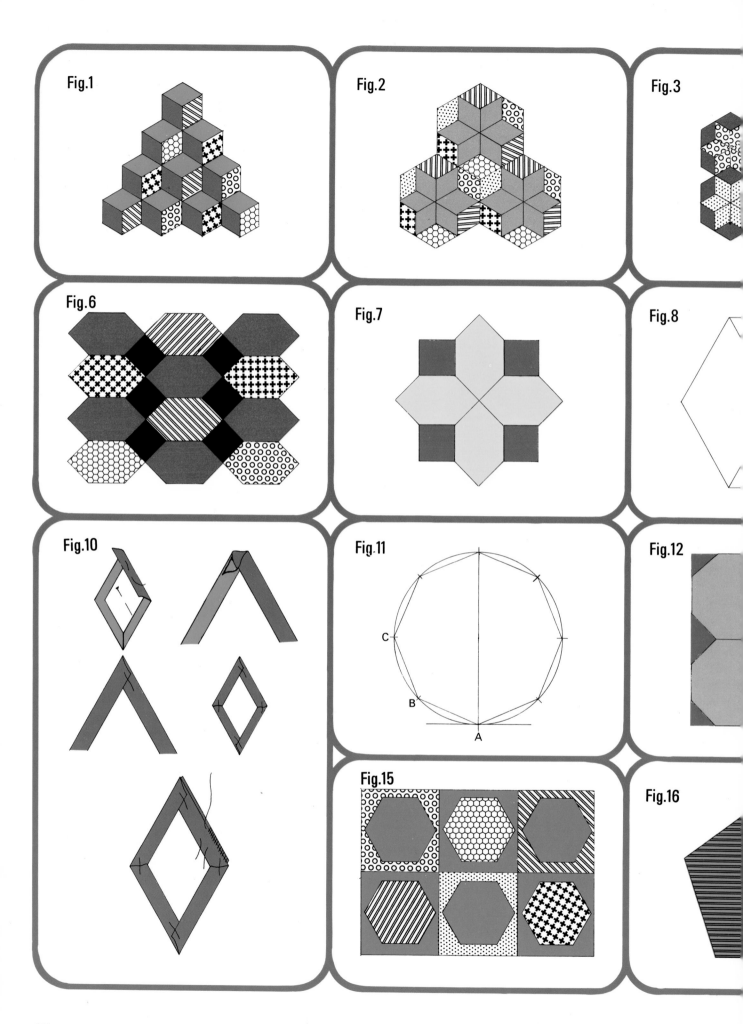

Fig.1

Fig.2

Fig.3

Fig.6

Fig.7

Fig.8

Fig.10

Fig.11

Fig.12

Fig.15

Fig.16

214

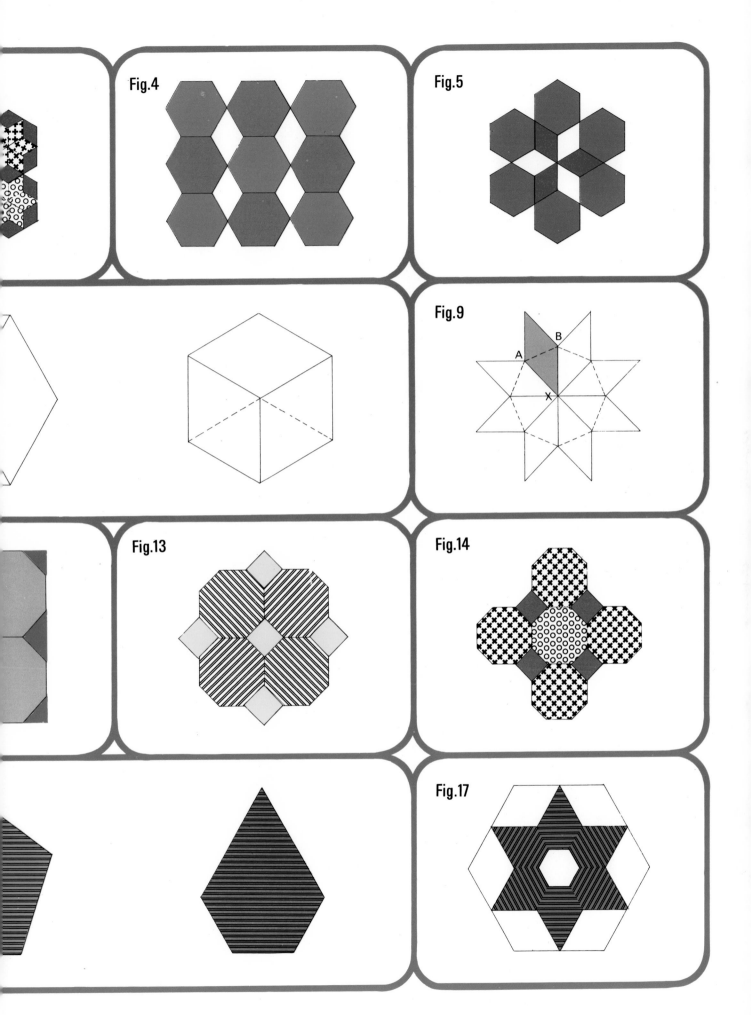

Fig.4

Fig.5

Fig.9

Fig.13

Fig.14

Fig.17

215

Dyeing

How many times have you thought of adopting a new colour scheme in your house? How many times have you thought how nice fresh curtains or furniture covers would look? And how many times have you rejected or modified a new decorative scheme because it wouldn't go with your other soft furnishings, or decided you could not afford to replace curtains or covers?

In fact there is no need to be limited at all. You can dye soft furnishings to match the new scheme—and to make them look as good as new. Curtains, bedspreads, loose covers, even carpets and lampshades, can all be dyed most successfully at home—and all at the cost of a few pence.

And in those cases where you cannot find the right fabric in the right colour, dyeing can often be the answer.

Knowing your fabric

You must know what the fabric you intend to dye is made from; some fabrics cannot be dyed successfully at home at all, and for others the type of dye may be important or there may be special instructions.

Fabrics which cannot be dyed at home are those which wholly or partially contain acrylic fibres. Unfortunately this includes fabrics like Courtelle, Acrilan, Orlon and Dralon, all of which are popular for soft furnishing. Although these fabrics can be dyed industrially, it is impossible to do so at home.

Other materials which may not dye satisfactorily are glass fibre fabrics and those which have been treated in some way—for fire proofing, or to resist dirt and creases. This does not include fabric like Terylene, where crease resistance is one of the properties of the fibre.

If you have any doubts about the fabric, you can easily check up on it by writing to Dylon International of Sydenham, London, the main manufacturers of dye in most English-speaking countries. They run a consumer advice bureau which will test the fabric for you and advise on which type of dye is most suitable. Although this bureau is based in London, they willingly deal with queries from all over the world, and if you want an exact match for a colour, they can help in this too.

Choosing the colour

Dyeing is not like painting, in that if you use enough coats you can paint a yellow wall blue. If you were to use a blue dye on a yellow curtain, it would turn green because the new dye would act on the old one to produce a combination of both colours.

The similarity between dye and paint is in the way two or more colours can be blended to make another colour, the precise shade being determined by the proportions being used. Examples of colour combinations are:

red + yellow = reddish orange
yellow + pink = coral
green + yellow = lime
pale blue + pink = lilac
yellow + brown = golden brown
dark brown + light red = reddish brown

All this does not mean that you can never transform yellow curtains to blue, as in many cases it is possible to strip out the old colour (see below), leaving a neutral foundation for the new one. Pastel-coloured fabrics, or those to be dyed in deeper tones of the same colour, do not need to be stripped first.

If after testing your fabric you find that it will not strip, it is usually still worth over-dyeing it with a hot water dye (see below). Then if you decide you don't like the new colour, it can be stripped back to the old one.

Patterned fabrics are usually vat dyed, and so may not strip. But they can often be over-dyed successfully, and with interesting results. The dye manufacturers recommend that the strongest colour in the pattern should be used to suggest the new colour. For example, with a red, yellow and pale green pattern, you should

use a red dye because this is the strongest of the three colours. Here the red would stay red, although it might alter in shade, the yellow would turn orange and the pale green would become a browny colour.

If, on the other hand, you want to lose the red, it might be worth trying a blue dye. Then the red would turn purple, the yellow would go green, and the light green would change to a greeny blue. The effect could be extremely pleasing. However, you always run the risk of being disappointed because so much depends on the exact colours you are starting with, and the exact colour you choose for the dye. For example, the red could equally well go to a plum or wine colour.

Another point you should remember about over-dyeing curtain fabric is that if it is lined with the usual off-white or beige colour, this will probably take on the new colour in its pure form. So with the red curtains dyed blue, and which are now purple, you would have a blue lining. You would get a blue lining, too, with the blue-dyed red, yellow and pale green pattern, which is now mainly purple and green.

What dyeing won't do

You should always wash and remove any stains from the fabric being dyed first, because dyeing will not cover dirt or stains and they will still show. Obviously, if you dye a pale fabric which has been stained with blue ink to a similar shade of blue, the stains will show less, but they will still appear as shadows. Sometimes the stain may act as a barrier to the dye and show up as a paler or deeper area.

The same principle applies to fabric which has faded. The faded parts will receive the new colour much more strongly than the other areas, giving a patchy or even multi-coloured result. For example, if you were to dye a faded blue curtain yellow, the unfaded areas would turn green, but the faded parts would be yellow, since there is so little blue left from the original dye to blend with the new one. Here, it would certainly be best to try to strip the fabric because the fact that it has faded at all suggests that it might strip satisfactorily.

You will also get a patchy or disappointing result if you use the wrong proportion of dye to the weight of fabric being dyed, or if the dye bath is too small to allow the fabric to move around freely in it.

Types of dye

There are basically four types of household dye.

Hot water dye. This is really a multi-purpose dye, as it can be used on all fabrics, with the exceptions given above. The range of colours available is enormous. On polyester fabrics (Terylene, Crimplene, Dacron, Tricel), however, the colours are not so deep and are called half shades.

Fabric treated with this dye should always be washed separately because the colour tends to lose its strength eventually with washing, but it will be some time before the loss shows.

An advantage of using hot water dye is that if you don't like the colour, or want to change it later, it can be stripped out.

To work properly, the dye solution has to be

kept simmering throughout the dyeing period (a maximum of 20 minutes), which can create some difficulties with items too large to fit easily into a container which can be used on a cooker safely. However, it does work perfectly in a washing machine, provided you do not dye more than half the machine's maximum load to ensure that the fabric can move easily.

Hot-water dye is available in a powder form, which has to be mixed with water, but it is also possible to buy it ready mixed. If you are using a washing machine, you can buy a specially prepared mixture of dye and detergent, such as Dylon's Wash 'n Dye, which cuts out the need for washing the fabric first.

Cold water dye. This is a completely colour- and light-fast dye, which is ideal for anything which has to be washed regularly. The drawback is that it works only on natural fibres such as cotton, linen, wool and silk, and also viscose rayon. If you use this dye, you must be sure that you will like the new colour, because it cannot be stripped out.

Dyeing with this type takes quite a long time— the fabric has to be immersed for an hour—but it is often more convenient to use because the water does not have to be kept at simmering point throughout. Once the dye is mixed, you could use the sink or bath. You can also use a washing machine. Always wear rubber gloves when using this dye.

Carpet dye. As its name implies, this is specially for carpets and should not be used on anything else. It can be used on carpets made entirely from, or from mixtures of, wool, nylon and Evlan, or mixtures of this with an acrylic such as Courtelle. It is not suitable for cotton carpets, those made from 100% Acrilan or Courtelle or shaggy-pile or foam-backed carpets.

Stripping the colour

The colour can be stripped from most fabrics, except polyesters, acrylics, those with special finishes or which have been fast (vat) dyed. Special products are made for the purpose. Some of these, such as Dygon Colour and Stain Remover, also remove stains, so before trying to remove stains strip the colour: you can do both operations in one go.

It is always worth testing a small piece of the fabric first to check that the colour can be stripped. Complete the test before going ahead with the whole article, because very occasionally it is possible for a colour to appear to strip when the fabric is wet, but then return when it dries.

If you are stripping a small article, and have a vessel large enough to be used on the stove safely, it is probably quicker and cheaper to use the 'hand' method. For larger items, it is easier to use a washing machine, though here, because of the large amount of water used in a washing machine, you may have to use more Dygon. Use a whole 3oz (85g) bottle of Dygon for each 2½-3lb (1.25-1.5Kg) dry fabric, and do not try to strip more than half the machine's normal wash load. Do not use this method for wool, although the drum could be used as a container.

'Hand' method. Weigh the fabric and then soak it in a large rust- and flameproof container with enough hot water to cover it and allow it to

move easily. Dissolve the Dygon in the proportion of one $\frac{1}{2}$oz (14gr) tin (which strips $\frac{1}{2}$lb or 0.2Kg dry fabric) to 1 pint (0.6 litre) boiling water. Lift the article, add the Dygon solution to the water in the container and replace the article, stirring well. Simmer for 10 minutes, or until the colour disappears. Rinse then wash with soap or detergent in hot water. Rinse again.

If the fabric you are stripping is wool, handle it very carefully throughout the process, and allow it to cool before rinsing in lukewarm water. Wash it in warm water, then rinse again. If the fabric is acetate rayon, do not allow the temperature of the water to rise above 60°C or 140°F.

Washing machine method. With twin and single tub machines, put in the unfolded fabric and cover with the hottest possible water. Dissolve the contents of a 3oz Dygon bottle in 2 pints boiling water, move the fabric to one side of the tub and pour in the solution. Run the machine, using the heater if possible, for 10 minutes or until the colour disappears. Rinse well in the tub, then give a hot wash with soap or detergent and rinse again.

With a fully-automatic machine, put in the fabric and run through the pre-wash cycle. Dissolve the contents of a 3oz Dygon bottle in 2 pints of boiling water, move the fabric to one side of the drum and add the solution. Set the machine to run for its hottest and longest wash and leave it for the full cycle. Then wash the fabric with soap or detergent on a warm wash cycle.

Using a hot-water dye

If you are not using a washing machine, weigh the dry fabric and then wash and rinse it. Work out the amount of dye necessary from the manufacturer's instructions (you will need more for acetate rayon and polyesters), and dissolve it in the recommended amount of boiling water.

Fill a rust- and flame-proof container with enough water to cover the fabric easily and add the dye solution. When the instructions say use salt, this is essential. It makes the fabric receptive to the dye.

Put in the wet fabric and spread it out well. For all fabrics except acetate rayon, polyester and wool, heat the water to simmering point and keep it at this temperature for 20 minutes. For acetate rayon and polyesters, heat the water to 60°C (140°F) and keep it at this point for 15 minutes. For wool, bring the water to simmering point, reduce the heat immediately and move the fabric gently in the water for about 10 minutes.

Rinse the fabric until the water clears, then wring or lightly spin, and dry away from the sun or direct heat. With wool, let the fabric cool before rinsing it.

Very often the fabric will appear to have taken the new colour halfway through the dyeing time, but don't be tempted to take it out then because it needs the full time for the colour to become fixed. The only exception to this is a fabric lampshade, which will not be washed often, and which may turn rusty if left wet too long.

Don't use more dye than recommended, or you may find that the fabric is a much deeper colour than you want. It is sometimes possible to use the left-over dye solution for something else.

Washing machine method. Although the amount of dye powder you use is dependent on the weight of the fabric to be dyed, if you are using a small amount of dye you may find the shade is not as strong as usual, because of the large amount of water used in the machine.

With twin and single tub machines, wash and rinse the fabric first and remove from the tub. Fill the tub with enough hot water to cover the fabric easily, add the dye solution and salt. Add the wet fabric, run the machine for 15 minutes, keeping the heater on if possible (you will have to re-set your machine if its wash programme is shorter than this).

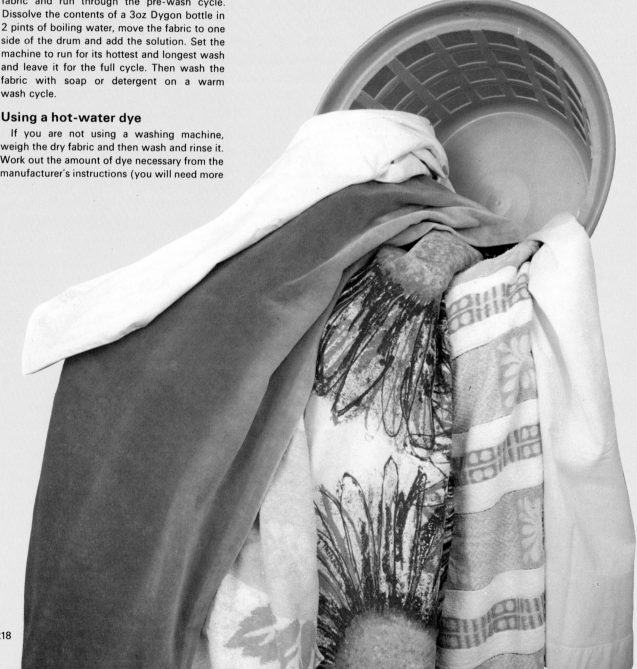

Rinse the fabric until the water is clear, using the machine tub only. Wring or lightly spin. Wipe away any spills immediately, and clean the machine by running it with very hot water, wash powder and a cupful of bleach.

With a fully automatic machine, put the dye solution and salt into the drum and add the wet fabric. Set the machine for its longest and hottest wash and leave for the full cycle. Clean the empty machine by giving it a hot wash cycle with wash powder and a cupful of bleach.

Using cold water dyes

If you are using the hand method to dye something large in the bath, remember that fabric can double its weight when wet and it may become too heavy to lift out and rinse easily.

Weigh the fabric, then wash and rinse it. Mix the dye solution, following the manufacturer's instructions, and add it to enough cold water to cover the fabric and allow movement during dyeing. Add the recommended amount of salt and soda, which fix the dye, dissolving them carefully in hot water first. Put this into the dye bath and stir well.

Add the wet fabric and steep for 60 minutes, stirring constantly for the first 10 minutes. After this, move the fabric occasionally, always keeping it fully submerged. Rinse it, then wash with very hot water and wash powder to remove any residue of dye. Rinse again until the water is clear.

Washing machine method. Wash and rinse the fabric. With a single or twin tub machine, fill it with enough cold water to cover the fabric. Prepare the dye solution, and add it, with the salt and soda solution (as above) to the machine. Agitate to mix, then add the wet fabric. Run the machine for 10 minutes, and then leave in the fabric for a further 50 minutes, agitating occasionally. Wash and rinse as above.

With fully automatic machines, the dye manufacturers recommend that you write to them, because the instructions vary.

Clean the machine immediately by running it empty with hot water, wash powder and a cupful of bleach.

Using carpet dye

If the carpet is close-fitted, cover the skirting and lower part of the wall with newspaper. For unfitted carpets, remove the underfelt and protect the floorboards with a thick layer of newspaper. To protect yourself while using the dye, wear old clothes and rubber gloves.

Go over the carpet thoroughly with a vacuum cleaner to remove the dirt and grit, then shampoo it with a liquid shampoo and leave damp. Remove any stains which did not come out.

Mix the dye solution, following the manufacturer's instructions. The solution has to be kept simmering the whole time, so you will have to transfer a small amount into another pan and take this, preferably on a tray to catch drips, to the carpet. If you work quickly enough, the dye should not cool down too much. Apply the dye to the carpet with a clean, firm scrubbing brush, working it well down into the pile. Be careful not to saturate it, or the dye may wear off. If parts of the carpet are very faded, it is a good idea to dye these areas first, let them dry, then dye the whole carpet. Let the carpet dry completely before you use it, then brush or vacuum clean it.

Don't be tempted to use a shampoo machine to apply the dye—many of these are plastic and might be melted by the solution, and in any case you will not be able to work in the dye deeply.

*Left (before) and **right** (afterwards), working from the outside in. White cotton pillowcase, dyed deep pink; faded brown velvet curtain, stripped and redyed green; patterned towel, overdyed orange; patterned curtain, overdyed blue and scarlet; striped towel, overdyed yellow; and cotton/Terylene pillow case, dyed with the same pink as the other, but taking a paler shade because of the Terylene content.*

219

Tie-dyeing

One of the most effective methods of transforming old and faded bed linen (see left), towels, plain curtains, bedspreads, cushion covers and tablecloths, is by dyeing them. You can even introduce a multi-coloured pattern if you tie up or bind the fabric first.

Tie dyeing and batik are both methods of resist dyeing—an age-old technique of creating a pattern on fabric by treating it in such a way that parts of it will 'resist' the dye when the fabric is totally submerged in it, and remain the original colour. The 'resist' parts can be formed by folding the fabric and tying it in different ways, so that the dye treats only the exposed area; or by painting on wax, so that the dye treats the unwaxed parts.

Of the two, batik needs more patience, artistic ability and elaborate equipment (see pages 225-226); both methods require a little knowledge of colour and the way they combine to make others. When the resist treatment has been made, however, the dyeing process is very similar for both methods.

Choosing the fabric

All fabrics should be white or cream, because this gives the widest variety of colours to which the fabric can be dyed. Most natural fibres are ideal for both tie dye and batik—cotton, linen, silk, and viscose rayon particularly. Wool is not really suitable for tie dye because it is difficult to remove the creases where it has been tied. Synthetic fabrics are not really suitable for batik because of the kind of dye necessary (see below). Nylon can be used for tie dye, polyester fibres (Terylene, Dacron and Crimplene) can be tie dyed to paler shades quite well, but acrylics (Orlon, Acrilan, Courtelle, Neospun) should not be used because they do not 'receive' the dye well. Treated fabrics—crease resisting or drip dry—should be avoided because their finish resists the dye unpredictably, making the results patchy.

Choosing the dye

The best kind of dye for both tie dyeing and batik is a cold water one because it is absolutely colourfast, will withstand constant washing and will not fade. Its disadvantage is that it works only on natural fibres. For man-made fibres a hot water dye has to be used but, although this is fine for tie dyeing, it should never be used for batik because the temperature of the liquid would melt the wax. This type of dye can be used with hot water, but density of colour can be achieved only by using simmering water. Even with simmering water, however,

the colour does tend to lose its strength eventually with washing—although it will be some time before the loss is apparent on the article. For this reason, the article should be washed separately and anything which will be washed regularly should be dyed with a cold water dye if possible.

All fabrics should be completely clean before being dyed and, if new, they should be boiled with a washing powder to remove all the dressing or finish. If you have any doubts about how the fabric will take the dye, try out a small piece first.

Tie dyeing

As its name implies, the pattern is made by tying the fabric in a variety of ways. This may be done by knotting the fabric, or by binding it in folds or around an object. For binding, use strong elastic bands, buttonhole thread, string, cord, raffia or even pipe cleaners. The binding must be tight and securely fastened at the ends—it is best to start off with a slip knot.

The exact pattern is determined by the amount of binding. A solid band, for example, will keep out nearly all the dye from the area; single thicknesses will make fine lines; crisscross binding will make a more random, open pattern, especially if both coarse and fine bindings are used.

Marbling is one of the simplest methods of tying. All you do is bunch the fabric into a ball and bind it at random. For a large article, bunch the fabric in sections, making a long firm roll.

A different marbled effect can be made by

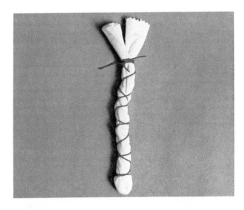

Above. *By twisting the fabric so that it coils back on itself like a skein of wool, and then binding it, you produce a marbled pattern with stripes running across the fabric (**below**).*

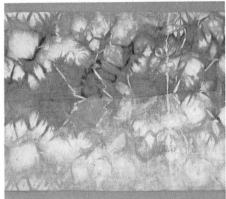

Above. *Simply bunching the fabric in a ball and binding at random gives a marbled pattern (**below**). Rearrange and rebind it before dyeing again.*

Above. *Fabric rolled round a length of string, which is then pulled up tight and bound firmly, produces a marbled pattern which has lines like wire netting (**below**).*

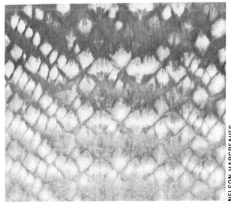

NELSON HARGREAVES

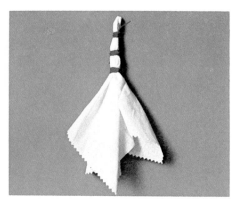

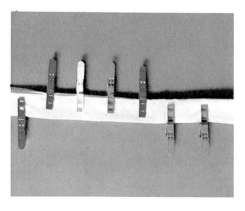

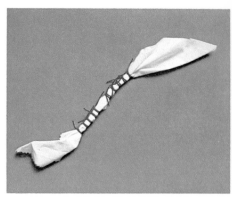

Above. Points of fabric are 'picked up', smoothed down like an umbrella, and bound to make circles **(below).** Fabric dampened before dyeing gives a sharper pattern.

Above. Fabric pleated accordian-wise and secured with clothes pegs gives a striped pattern **(below).** Move the pegs and take some off before adding another colour.

Above. Fabric furled like an umbrella and then bound finely several times makes a wavy, irregularly striped pattern **(below).** Large pieces should be folded in four first.

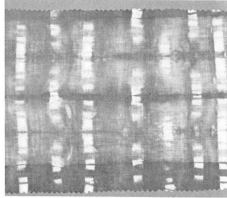

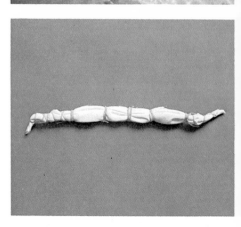

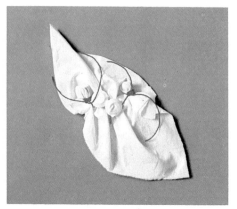

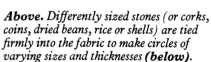

Above. Differently sized stones (or corks, coins, dried beans, rice or shells) are tied firmly into the fabric to make circles of varying sizes and thicknesses **(below).**

Above. Sheets are most easily dyed by pleating and folding, and then binding. One edge was placed in the blue dye and the other in the purple to make the stripes **(below).**

Above. Fabric folded into four, then into a triangle furled like an umbrella, before binding gives a square pattern **(below).** This is most effective on small pieces.

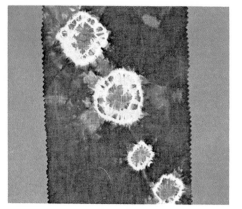

NIGEL MESSETT

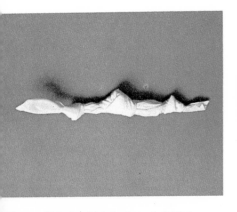

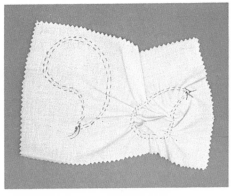

Above. Fabric which is pleated, folded or simply furled like an umbrella and then tied in knots down its length makes a pattern with broad, undyed bands **(below)**.

Above. Shapes outlined in gathering stitches in strong sewing thread, which is pulled up tight and secured firmly, gives more unusual and definite outlines **(below)**.

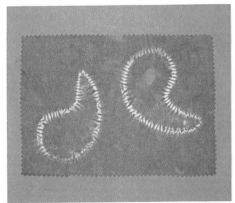

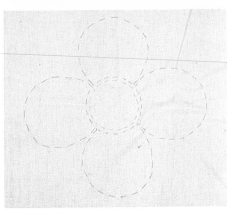

Above. Fabric folded concertina-wise and then back on itself in right-angled triangles and bound at the corners to secure it, makes a regularly squared pattern **(below)**.

Above. Here the shape of the pattern was outlined in gathering stitches which were pulled up tight. The centre was also bound and the edges were put in a polythene bag.

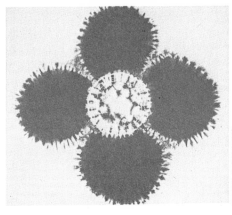

putting the fabric into a nylon stocking, a mesh cloth or bag (such as the sort used by supermarkets for vegetables and fruit). The bag should be closed tightly round the fabric, and then bound. Small pieces of fabric could even be put into a plastic hair roller, provided the ends are bound to prevent the fabric from falling out.

Circular patterns can be made by picking up points of fabric, furling them like an umbrella, and knotting or binding these. With this method, it is a good idea to mark the positions of the ties first with pencil or chalk.

Clump tying is a variation of knotting, whereby stones (or corks, coins, dried beans, rice or shells) are bound into the fabric. A more elaborate version is made by criss-crossing the clumps with the binding.

Stripes can be formed by rolling, folding or pleating the fabric and then binding it firmly at intervals. Alternatively, the folds can be secured with clothes pegs.

Random stripes can be made by pleating the fabric and tying it in knots down the length.

Diamonds, squares, and other more unusual shapes, such as squirls and hearts, can be made by sewing. Knot one end of doubled sewing thread, outline the shape with a row of running stitches, then pull up the thread very tightly and secure the end firmly.

Dyeing

Start with the lightest colour you plan to use and mix it, following the manufacturers' instructions exactly. Most dyes require an amount of salt, which makes the fibres of the fabric receptive to the dye, and cold water dyes also need soda which 'fixes' the colour, making it permanent (if this is not used, the dye will wash out immediately).

Wet the tied article first if you want the pattern to be sharply defined and then immerse it in the dye, leaving it there for the required time, and stirring frequently. Then take it out, rinse off the excess dye, remove the binding and wash in hot, soapy water. Rinse again until the water is clear.

To add another colour, refold and rebind the fabric, exposing the area you want to take the new colour. If there is a part you want to protect, but cannot arrange the fabric so that it is inside, cover it with a polythene bag and bind the opening tightly. Occasionally there is some seepage, but generally this improves the design, making the change of colour less sharp. Dye as before, and then rinse off in the same way. It is absolutely essential to rinse, wash and rinse again between each dyeing—otherwise the results will be disastrous.

Be careful when you add further colours, because eventually the combination of too many will result in a sludgy brown. For example, if you were to start with yellow on a white fabric, and then added blue, you would have a pattern of yellow, blue, green and white. If you were then to add red, some of the yellow would turn orange, some of the blue would go mauve or purple (depending on the original shade of blue), and some of the green would go brown. And here it would be wisest to call a halt—the addition of more colours would probably make the whole thing go to sludge.

223

Batik

Batik is a more artistic method of resist dyeing of fabric than tie dyeing (see pages 221-223), but you do not have to be artistic to be good at it. The skill is in the subtle use of colours and shapes rather than intricate drawing. Choose something small, with inexpensive fabric, for your first attempt and then go on to making your own designs for cushion and lampshade covers, table linen and decorative borders.

Batik, like tie dyeing, is a form of 'resist' printing on fabric which was known all over the Far East thousands of years ago. It became particularly popular with the Javanese in Indonesia, and the word 'batik' means writing or painting. Hot wax is 'written' or painted on to the fabric, which is then immersed in dye. Because wax resists the dye, only the unwaxed areas of the fabric take the colour.

Equipment

Very simple batik can be carried out using common household equipment.

Wax—this may be in the form of domestic candles or blocks of paraffin wax, obtainable from chemists and some hardware stores; or beeswax, which is more flexible and obtainable, from specialist craft shops. It is also possible to buy combined paraffin and beeswax which is ideal for batik.

Heavy pan or double saucepan to melt the wax in.

Artists' brushes for applying the wax. If you intend to do a lot of batik, it is worth buying a *janting*—a special tool which has a bowl to hold the hot wax and a spout from which the wax flows so that you can paint your design.

Frame to which the fabric is attached (an old picture frame is ideal), and some drawing pins.

Dye. The type used for batik must be a cold water dye, so that the wax will not melt when the fabric is submerged in it. With this sort of dye, only fabrics made from natural fibres may be used, because man-made fibres have to be dyed with a hot-water dye in order for the colour to be fast. Silk, linen and most types of cotton—provided they have not been treated for crease resistance or to drip dry—may be used for batik. Wool should not be used. Thin fabrics are better than thick ones, because they absorb the wax more easily, and it is also simpler to trace a design through them.

Choosing a design

Because it was against the Islamic religion to paint any living creature, Indonesian artists used stylized versions of animals and flowers, combining them with simple geometric patterns. Sometimes the wax cracks, producing a veined effect when the cracks are penetrated by the dye, and this has become an accepted characteristic of batik. Geometric or abstract designs are easiest for the beginner, since any mistake or unintentional spill can be incorporated into the overall design.

Other simple shapes can be outlined in wax by using a pastry cutter (see below). This could be the metal sort (not plastic, which would melt), with a handle if possible. On fine fabrics, such as jap silk, chiffon or lawn, uncomplicated repeat patterns can be made by folding the fabric before the wax is applied. The wax soaks through the layers of fabric which, when dyed still folded, resists the colour in the same shape on each layer.

Applying the wax

Melt the wax in the heavy pan or double saucepan over a low heat. Wax is easily over-heated and is inflammable so, if you are heating it over gas, use an asbestos mat as additional protection.

Wax tends to cool down quickly, so work as close as possible to where it is being heated, and protect your work surface with newspaper to catch any spills. It is possible to lay the fabric directly on top of the newspaper, but because this may stick to the fabric when the wax is applied, it is better to pin the fabric over a wooden frame and place this on top of the paper.

Alternatively the newspaper can be covered with waxed paper, and the fabric placed on this. The wax will not stick to this paper, but it is not possible to check that it has completely penetrated the fabric until it is peeled off and held against the light.

When the wax has melted, leave it a little longer to become really hot, but not smoking. Dip the brush into the wax and test it on the fabric. The wax must be hot and fluid enough to penetrate the fabric—it will appear transparent, and you must be able to see it on the other side of the fabric. Reheat the wax gently if it starts to solidify, or if it does not seem to be penetrating properly.

Hold a cloth under the brush as you move it to the fabric to catch any drips, and paint your design on to the fabric, covering only those areas *not* to be dyed. Work quickly, redipping your brush into the wax frequently.

To use the pastry cutter, first cover the handle with a cloth because the metal will get very hot. Dip the cutter into the wax, leaving it in for 30 seconds. Shake off the excess drips and transfer the cutter quickly to the fabric and press it down sharply. Lift it off again when the wax has formed a ring on the fabric at the foot of the cutter.

Dyeing

While the wax is hardening on the fabric, mix the dye bath according to the manufacturers' instructions. When the wax is hard, immerse the fabric for the required time, then rinse in cold water (to prevent the wax from melting), and hang the fabric up to dry. Do not attempt to speed up the drying process by heat, or the colour will seep into the wrong places as the wax melts.

Adding more colour

Like tie dyeing, it is generally best to dye the fabric only twice, or three times at the most, because this can produce a result with as many as four or five colours (see page 223).

When the fabric is completely dry from the first dyeing, add wax to the areas you wish to keep that colour. There is no need to put more wax over the original application, but you may wish to remove some of this by picking it off. Then dye the fabric again, following the process as above. For complicated designs, you may have to remove all the first application of wax (see below), and start completely again.

Left. Natural fibres—linen (left), cotton (middle) and silk (right)—are all good for batik because these can be dyed with a cold water dye which will not melt the wax.

Removing the wax

The wax may be removed by putting the fabric between two wads of newspaper and ironing until the wax melts and is absorbed by the paper (use a non-steam iron for this, because the wax can clog up the ducts of steam irons).

Or it may be boiled off, which is more economical, because the wax will solidify and rise to the top of the water. It can then be skimmed off and used again. Heat the water in a large pan and, when it is boiling, immerse the fabric in it and gently stir with a wooden spoon for about three minutes. Then lift the fabric out and drop it into a bucket of cold water. Squeeze out the water, shake off the remaining solidified wax and wash the fabric in boiling water with a detergent. Never pour waxy water down the sink—it will solidify and cause a blockage.

Below left. *Batik needs patience if more than two dyes are used because the fabric must be dried naturally before it can be dyed again. Unless you have a colossal frame, are prepared to work in rotation, or want only a border, tablecloths are probably the largest items that can be dyed easily at home by batik.*
Below right. *Often the designs formed by batik-dyed fabrics are so unusual—and unique —that they make ideal wallhangings.*

Fig.1. *The wax must be hot and fluid enough to penetrate the fabric fully. It is essential to work quickly before the wax on the brush cools down, or the resist will not be complete.*
Fig.2. *The area which was painted with wax has resisted the dye. The fine lines in the middle were made where the wax cracked.*

Fig.3. *The parts of the design which are to stay pink are treated with more wax. These areas appear a deep pink now, but they will be the intended colour when the wax is removed.*
Fig.4. *The finished design, after the second dyeing. The purple has penetrated where more of the first waxing has cracked.*

Fig. 5. *The basic outline of this stylized owl design was first traced in pencil and then painted with wax, using a fine artist's brush, A special batik tool—a tjanting—was used for the wavy lines and dots, and the larger areas were painted in with a decorator's brush.*
Fig.6. *The tjanting is being used to drop wax on to the areas which are to resist the second dyeing. The bowl of the tool contains the hot wax which dribbles out from the spout.*

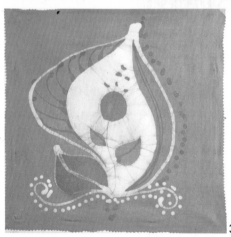

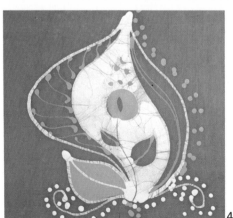

1

3

2

4

TRANSWORLD

Leather, hides, fur and fur fabrics in the home

Fur and fur fabrics are increasingly being used as a furnishing material, far removed from their association with fashionable clothing. Real and simulated furs create a feeling of warmth and luxury, while fun furs add a colourful touch to any scheme—and they need not be expensive.

Leather

Few materials are as useful and versatile in interior decorating as leather. Leather-covered chairs are fashionable and cost far less than they once used to; even sofas upholstered in leather are now available at reasonable prices. Desks with tooled leather tops, and folding screens entirely covered in leather, are smart additions to any home.

Leather is animal hide or skin that has been treated by a chemical process known as *tanning* so that it will not rot. The main types of hides or skins used in the manufacture of leather come from sheep, lambs, cattle, calves, goats and kids.

Uses in the home

The thinner leathers used for clothing are the most suitable for the kinds of articles it is possible for the amateur to make. Upholstery in leather should be left to the professional.

It is possible to buy ready-made panels for attaching to doors, walls, screens or room dividers. These panels—which are usually padded—can be plain, studded, buttoned or tooled, and are sold with complete instructions for fixing.

Cutting and sewing

Thin leather is sold by the skin in some department stores and specialist shops, and this can be cut and sewn as easily as a fabric of similar weight. You can stitch it by hand or on an ordinary domestic sewing machine, using strong thread such as silk or polyester, not cotton.

Leather has a grain, which runs along the backbone of the animal. Pieces should be cut to lie along this grain wherever possible, to keep them from splitting. Cut leather with sharp scissors. Use tape or paper clips to hold the pieces together for stitching.

If you are sewing by hand, use a glover's needle. On a machine, use a No.16 needle, fairly light tension, and 7-10 stitches to the inch. Stitch in the direction of the grain as far as

227

possible. Never backstitch, as it will cut the leather. Instead, tie the ends of the thread.

Stitch slowly and accurately, as mistakes leave holes in the leather. After stitching, press the seams open with your fingers and stick them down with rubber cement, which remains flexible.

Zips are easy to insert in leather articles, such as cushion covers, and should be placed centrally, rather than under a one-sided flap, to reduce bulk. Do not turn under the edges of the opening, as you would for fabric. To hold the zip in place while you are stitching, apply rubber cement to the fabric sides of the zip and to the leather and press them together with your fingers. Then topstitch round the placket opening $\frac{1}{4}$in. from the edge. Stitch a triangle in the leather across the end or ends of the opening to stop it from splitting when the zip is undone.

Care and cleaning

Articles made of leather need comparatively little maintenance. Wet leather articles should be dried slowly at room temperature. Avoid excessive heat, such as that produced by drying on a radiator. This distorts the leather fibres and impairs the wearing qualities of the article.

Grain upholstery leather requires the least cleaning of any type. Waxes or polishes should be applied only rarely, if ever, and only in very small quantities. Upholstery leather is best cleaned by washing with mild soap (*never* use detergent) and a little water. The soap film should then be removed with a clean damp cloth so that the leather can dry free of soap residue.

Where leather has been subjected to hard use and is excessively dry, a very light application of sulphonated oil to the *clean* grain surface (not the back) will help rejuvenate the leather.

The growth of mildew or mould on leather can be prevented by keeping it in a dry place. Leather articles should never be stored in a humid atmosphere, or where ventilation is poor.

Suede leather

Suede is not very suitable for upholstery, as it picks up dust and grease, and wears badly. It is likely to rub on your clothes, and so is not a comfortable covering for chairs. It should therefore be used more for effect than practicality.

Articles covered in suede should generally be professionally cleaned, but minor surface dirt can be removed by gentle brushing with a stiff brush. Very fine *brass* wire or stiff bristle brushes remove the dirt best, and also raise the nap, restoring the suede texture.

If the nap of suede leather has been crushed or worn off, rub it with fine sandpaper to restore the texture. Dry-cleaning fluid removes grease marks, but also takes out the colour; this can be restored with coloured chalks available for the purpose.

Hides

The term 'hide' is generally used to describe the pelts which come from cows, steers, bulls and horses, and also (less often) of walrus, bison and reindeer. The pelts of other animals are commonly called skins, for example sheepskins, goatskins and calfskins.

NIGEL MESSETT

Leather, hides, real fur, simulated fur and deep pile fabrics (fun fur) can all be used to advantage in your home. The cushions shown on the opposite page are covered in a variety of skins and furry fabrics, each of them an attractive addition to any room.

Above. *A glorious selection taken from the hundreds of colours and textures available in fur, its close imitations and fun relations.*

Key. 1 to 4. *Deep pile fabric (all from Borg Textiles Ltd.)* ***5.*** *Simulated cow hide.* ***6.*** *Simulated astrakhan.* ***7.*** *Simulated leopard skin rug.* ***8.*** *Simulated tiger (all from Lister & Co.)* ***9.*** *Fallow deer skin rug.* ***10.*** *Natural coney (rabbit).* ***11.*** *Coney stencilled to look like snow leopard.* ***12.*** *Mongolian lamb skin (all from George H. Herman Furs Ltd.)*

Uses in the home

Skins or hair on hide can be used as wall hangings or rugs and look stunning in a room with a decoration scheme based on natural timber finishes. They are quite easy to 'toggle', or suspend stretched out on a frame with cord, for wall hanging.

Stretch the hide out to its full, natural shape, and punch holes at intervals round the edge, particularly on parts that stick out. Construct a wooden frame slightly larger than the overall size of the hide. Lace the string or cord through the holes in the hide and round the outside of the frame, taking care to keep the hide stretched fully. Anchor the cord firmly to the frame at each point with pins knocked into the back.

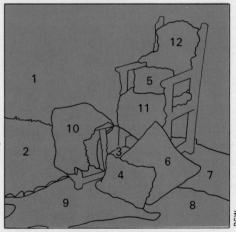

DGW

Fur

Fur is not as simple a material as it seems. It consists of a skin backing and two layers of hair. The bottom layer is thick and soft (it protected the animal from the cold) and there is a covering of longer hairs above this layer called the *guard hair* or *over-hair*. This protects the underlying fur from injury and prevents it from matting or felting. The over-hair is normally the most visible part of the fur.

The thickest, most luxuriant fur comes from animals that live in cold regions, although some wild animals living in the temperate and tropical zones also provide fur.

Fur is becoming more and more accepted as a decorative material for use in the home.

Choosing and using fur

Many types of furs and skins that once had an aura of the exclusive about them are now generally available, and make an impressive and individual addition to the decorations in your home. They are easy to use, and have a wide variety of colours and textures.

You can hang furs on the wall, scatter them on the floor as rugs, use them for cushion covers, or even bedspreads. A piece of fur thrown over the back of a sofa gives it an expensive look, and a fur rug in your car will keep you cosy in winter.

Before you choose a fur or skin from the large variety that is available, you should first give some thought to the use you are going to put it to. Not all furs are suited to the same uses.

The life span of a fur or skin depends on the curing; if it is well cured, the individual hairs will be strong; if badly cured they will come loose from the leather. Only an expert can tell if a skin is well or badly cured, but as a layman you can also choose good skins. Those with silky hair are more resistant than pieces with straw-like hairs, which tend to fall out much more quickly.

The more luxurious types of long-haired fur are not recommended for use as floor rugs because they wear out quickly. Cow, horse or similar short-haired skins are more suitable, as are the longer-haired but very tough sheep and goat skins. Skins for use on the floor should be harder and more resistant than the type used for wall decoration, bed covers and so on. Certain types of short but flat-haired fur, such as calf and pony, may not be tough enough for floor use. Shorter furs are the most practical for sitting on.

Black goat mounted on a felt backing is ideal for car rugs. It is very warm, as it has a thick pile, and practical, as it won't show the dirt like the white sheepskin that is commonly used for rugs. Beaver lamb also wears well when used in this way.

Working with fur

The fur trade remains essentially a handicraft industry, and working with fur pelts is a highly skilled job. A cutter, for example, matches pelts according to colour and quality in order to achieve uniformity of pattern and texture in the finished article. Sewing is performed on industrial machines, and is a task requiring much skill.

Many of the techniques involved, however, can be learnt and put into use by the amateur when adapting pelts and hides for use in the home.

With a little imagination, and quite a lot of time and patience, you can transform an old fur coat, a large skin bought on holiday, or even a few scraps of fur picked up cheaply in a market, into an attractive addition to your home. If you are planning to take an old fur coat to pieces, however, you must ensure that the fur is in good enough condition to be worth the trouble. If it has worn thin, it will never create a good effect or justify the time you spend on it. So examine the fur carefully and choose the best pieces to work on.

Cutting: most experts will advise against cutting fur at all, but if you are making cushion covers from an old fur coat, you will have to.

Use a one-sided razor blade, scalpel or hobby

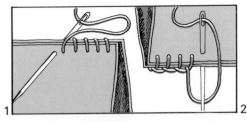
1
2

3

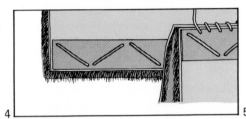
4
5

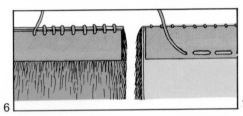
6
7

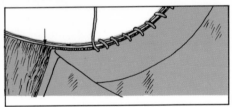
8

Above. *Fur is always sewn by hand, using a glover's needle and strong waxed thread. These diagrams show the various methods of stitching and reinforcing the seams.*

knife; it must be extremely sharp. Cut from the leather side, being sure not to cut the fur itself, as this would make the seams show. If you are marking a cutting line, use chalk, not ball point pen, as the ink might run through and stain the fur when it is cleaned.

Sewing: many fur pelts are very small, and you need to sew a large number together to make even a small floor rug. But seams in fur do not show, so it is possible to join together any number of odd-shaped pieces to create a neat-looking finished article. As no seam allowances are needed, nothing is wasted in the joining. Make sure when arranging the pieces, however, that the nap (the way the hairs lie) runs the same way on all the pieces.

Seams in real fur are always stitched by hand with a glover's needle and strong waxed thread. It is important to avoid catching the hairs in the seam; this can be managed by using a long thin needle to push the hair well down before stitching.

Sew the edges together with a close, even,

oversewing or blanket stitch (Figs.1 and 2). Be sure to sew the skin only, and use a pin to tease out any hairs that may be caught in the stitching back to the fur side. Do not stitch too close to the edge of the skin, or the stitches may tear out of the leather.

The seams can be flattened simply by rubbing with a thimble on the wrong side or, for tougher skins, by pressing the wrong side very carefully with the tip of a warm iron over a dry cloth. If many pelts have been joined together, an even appearance can be achieved by brushing the entire surface gently, always stroking in the direction of the nap.

Taping: it may sometimes be necessary to tape the seams for added strength. This can be done in two ways, both using $\frac{1}{2}$in. wide seam tape. For the first method, sew the edges of the skin together and flatten the seam as described above. Then place the tape centrally over the seam and sew it on with long running stitches (Fig. 3).

The other method involves attaching the tape before the seams are stitched. Sew tape to each edge of the skins to be joined, using long hand-worked zigzag stitches. Make sure the edge of the tape is flush with the edge of the skin (Fig. 4). Sew the seam as before, catching both the edges of the tape and the edges of the skin (Fig. 5). Then flatten the seam as before.

Edging: if the fur is going to be hung on the wall, or used as a rug or a bedspread, the edges must be finished with tape as an anchor for the backing or lining material. To do this, lay the tape along the edge of the skin on the fur side and oversew the edges together (Fig.6). Turn the tape to the wrong side and sew it to the skin with small running stitches (Fig.7).

Fur can be attached to a plain fabric, for example when making cushion covers with fur on one side and plain fabric on the other. The edges of the fur should first be taped, then joined to the fabric with oversewing or blanket stitches as shown in Fig.8.

Backing: pieces of fur should ideally be backed with good-quality felt or hessian if they are going to be used as floor rugs or hung on the wall. The edges should be taped as described above, and the backing stitched firmly to the tape by hand. An additional backing of felt cut slightly larger than the skin can be added to serve as a frame, and its edges can be pinked or scalloped for a decorative effect.

If the shape of a piece is irregular, or you want to make it slightly larger, you can stretch it out by damping it with water. Damp the leather side of the pelt thoroughly with a small soft brush or clean rag, taking care not to soak it. Allow the water to penetrate for about 15 minutes, but do not let the piece dry out. After this time, the leather will become supple, and can be pulled to an even, regular shape.

Using thick pins, thin nails or staples, anchor it round the edges to a stout board and leave it to dry. Trim off any surplus, leaving an allowance all round for turnings. If you have a particular shape in mind, you can mark this out on the board and stretch the fur over it.

Soft, flimsy skins can often be given more body by using a thick starch paste to damp them with instead of water.

Sticking: fur should be sewn wherever possible

but if you have to stick it, you can. For example, you can improve the shape of pelts with uneven edges by turning under a small amount all round to make a regular shape, and sticking the turnings down with an impact adhesive.

Storage, care and cleaning

Keep any fur article in a cool, dry, dark place if it must be stored, never in a plastic bag. Don't be afraid of moths; they only attack undisturbed furs, so you can guard against them by shaking out all fur articles regularly. Fur must, however, be protected against damp, or the leather will become hard.

Routine cleaning can be done by shaking the fur well, or using the pipe of a vacuum cleaner to remove dust. Coarse sheep and goat skins can be cleaned with a wire brush. For more thorough cleaning, and also to keep the leather flexible, all fur articles should be professionally cleaned every two years.

Never wash or soak fur in water; never use harsh chemicals, spirits or solvents on it. Should it become damp, allow it to dry naturally at room temperature. If absolutely necessary, a little carbon tetrachloride applied with a clean cloth or brush should remove light staining or marking, but test an unnoticeable area of the fur first if possible to make sure the substance will not stain it.

Simulated fur

Many species of fur-producing animal have already been destroyed; a large number are becoming scarce; and over 50 are now threatened with extinction. As a result, the import into Britain, and many other countries, of the skins of the tiger, snow leopard and clouded leopard is now banned, and the regulations covering the import of all species of leopard and cheetah have been strengthened.

This concern with the conservation of the rarer fur-producing animals has led to the production of a wide range of top-quality simulated furs. These are exact replicas of real fur but cost only about one-tenth as much, so that sumptuous feeling that fur adds to a home has been brought within more people's grasp than before—and without the risk of any pangs of conscience lessening the pleasure. The methods used to produce simulated furs are now so subtle that these give an utterly natural effect, and are often hard to distinguish from the real thing.

Uses in the home

Simulated fur fabrics are primarily produced for the fashion industry, but good simulations of most furs are now available by the yard from department stores in 54in. and 56in. widths, making them suitable for use in the home.

It is important to remember, however, that great strength is required of fabrics used in upholstery, and that none of the simulated fur fabrics that have so far come on the market is intended for this use. Their use is decorative rather than practical.

Simulated fur fabrics make excellent bedspreads, since they are both light and warm. The fabric is easy to sew if you follow the instructions given below. It can be made up into cushion covers, for example, to lend your armchairs a little simulated luxury. A length cut to the shape of the skin of the animal it is imitating can be thrown over the back of a sofa, hung on the wall, or used as a hearth rug (all modern types are flameproof).

The surface pile of simulated fur is usually made of acrylic fibre or wool, and the backing is often knitted or woven from the same material. In some types, however, the backings are quite different from the surface pile, and include cotton, foam and stiffened man-made fibre. The stiff-backed varieties are most suitable for floor rugs, and can be shampooed like carpets.

It is unwise to cover chair seats with fur fabrics because, as with the real thing, the pile usually runs one way, and will be rubbed in the wrong direction if sat on.

Instructions on sewing all types of simulated fur are given in the section on 'Fun furs'.

The shaggy mountain goat skins on the chairs and ox hide on the plain wood floor give this room a sumptuous appearance.

Fun furs

'Fun furs' are wild and colourful deep-pile fur fabrics, not intended to bear any relation to any real animal's skin. They are made from a variety of fibres, including acrylics, polyesters, and pure wool, and most have knitted backings. They are available in a wide range of textures and colours —even checks and tartans—and are particularly light and warm. All are flame-resistant, and most are spongeable or washable.

As with simulated furs, fun furs are increasingly available by the yard in larger department stores. The generous widths—54in. and 56in.— make their possible uses, and the effects they can create, almost limitless.

Uses in the home

As the length and quality of the pile of a fun fur varies, so does its suitability for certain functions. Long, shaggy fabric in wild green or orange makes a stunning rug in a brightly decorated bedroom; a brown bouclé look would make a cosy bedspread, while a baby's cot cover in a soft pink or powder blue short-piled fabric would be light, warm, safe and washable as well as attractive. A room divider or screen covered entirely in a warm-looking fur fabric will not only soften the appearance of the room, but also give a certain amount of sound insulation. A panel of fun fur hung on the

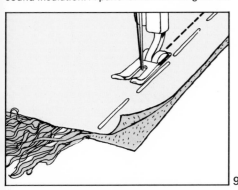

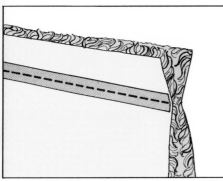

wall above a bed—perhaps matching a furry bedspread—gives any bedroom an inviting look. Many of the same limitations apply to fun fur fabrics as to simulated fur, particularly their lack of suitability for upholstery, but their use can enliven virtually any decorative scheme.

Cutting and sewing

Unlike real fur, simulated fur and fun fur fabrics can be sewn quite simply with a domestic sewing machine. Remember that prominent fur markings must be matched as carefully as a patterned fabric, and that the nap or pile must always run the same way (normally it should be arranged to run downwards). If the fabric is washable, make sure that the lining you choose is also washable.

Short-pile fabrics can be cut with very sharp cutting-out scissors, but a one-sided razor blade or hobby knife is necessary with thick fur. Cut through the backing only, and avoid cutting the pile.

When sewing fur fabrics, it is wise to test the stitching on a scrap beforehand, to check for tension. The heavier the fabric, the thicker and stronger the needle and thread will have to be. A thread with some elasticity, such as pure silk or a synthetic such as polyester, gives good results.

Plain seams are the most suitable for fur fabrics, taking the usual $\frac{5}{8}$in. allowance. If the fur fabric has a slippery long-piled surface, tack the seams carefully first. Most other simulated and fun fur fabrics can just be pinned together before sewing.

When joining simulated fur to a plain fabric, tack it securely in place to prevent it from slipping, and stitch in the direction of the nap with the plain fabric on top.

If you are using straight stitching to join the seams, you should set your machine to 8-10 stitches to the inch, with a fairly light tension. With most fur fabrics, the surface pile on the seam allowance can be shaved with a razor or sharp scissors after stitching to reduce bulk, and the edges of the seam caught back on the underside with neat loose hand stitches (Fig.10). With long-haired fur fabrics, it is easier to do the shaving before you stitch the seam (Fig.9).

Simulated furs with flexible knitted backings should be sewn with a narrow zigzag stitch. A method of seaming which eliminates excess bulk, but is not very strong, is to join the edges with zigzag stitch, taking no allowances.

Whichever method of stitching you use, make sure that as little of the pile as possible catches in the seam as you work. If some fur does catch, it can be teased out with a needle or pin after sewing (Fig.11). For seams subjected to strain, use seam tape under the stitching (Fig.12).

Most seams can be pressed open with the fingers and rubbed on the inside with a thimble to make them lie flat. Never iron pile fabrics, and do not expose them to steam.

If the fabric is likely to fray, the seams should be finished after stitching. They can be bound with bias tape, oversewn by hand or machined

Left. Simulated and fun furs can be stitched with a domestic sewing machine, but care should be taken to avoid catching the pile in the seams, as shown here.

with a wide zigzag stitch. You can also slip stitch the seam allowance to the backing, thus finishing it and holding it flat at the same time.

Zips are best sewn firmly in place by hand, as it is difficult not to catch the fur in the seam when using a machine. Shear the pile from the seam allowance before stitching to prevent it from catching in the teeth of the zip.

Cleaning

The manufacturers of some simulated furs recommend that their products should be dry cleaned by the method used for real fur; it is important that their advice should be followed, as professional fur cleaning is quite different from ordinary dry cleaning.

Many simulated furs and fun fur fabrics are spongeable, and some are washable, particularly those with knitted backings. These can be machine-washed, but it is wiser to hand wash them, taking extreme care. Once dry, the fabric will benefit from a good shake, which lifts the pile.

Above. This inviting bedspread, which spills on to the floor, is made from shaggy Chinese goat skins. It is set against a background of multi-coloured calf skins sewn together to form a patchwork wall hanging.

Real 'imitation' fur

Expensive and rare furs have been imitated with rabbit and (sad to say) cat fur for some time, generally without much success. Recently, however, the quality of these 'real imitations' has greatly improved thanks to modern techniques. So now you can get an expensive effect at low prices—and expect that your deception will pass unnoticed.

Inexpensive furs such as coney (rabbit) and kid are made up into 'plates' (pieces 24in. x 48in.) and stencilled with patterns to look like more expensive furs such as zebra, tiger and leopard. These plates can be bought quite cheaply. They are easy to make into impressive-looking cushion covers, or will smarten up a sofa if thrown over the back.

All plates of this kind are made out of real fur, and should be treated as such in cutting, sewing and maintenance.

The bolster-shaped cushion cover and the geometric flower cover (on the seat) are made from motifs which are joined together before adding a border. The sunflower cover is worked in rounds from the centre outwards.

Crochet cushion covers

Crochet has long been a favourite for tablecloths, mats and bedspreads, and it is also ideal for cushion covers, lampshades, curtains or even rugs and bathmats. Although the effect of crochet is delicate, if worked in cotton it can be very strong and the items will often last for years and become family heirlooms.

You don't have to be an expert at crochet to make up the patterns below but, if you are making the covers to fit a specific cushion, it is wise to check the tension before you start.

Abbreviations
ch—chain; st(s)—stitch(es); ss.—slip stitch; dc—double crochet; tr—treble crochet; dtr—double treble; htr—half treble; rep.—repeat.

Geometric flower cushion

Measurements: 16 inches square; 9 dc equal 1in. 4 rows dc equal ½in.
Materials: 150 gr, DMC 171 crochet Cotton; or 3 balls Twilley's Lysbet. Crochet Hook No 2.50 (ISR)
Square: (Make 9)
Make 8 ch and join into a ring with a ss.
1st round: 16dc into ring.
2nd round: * 3 dc in first st, 1 dc in each of next 3 sts. Rep from * to end. 24 sts.
3rd round: ss into first st, * 3 dc in next st, 1 dc in each of next 5 sts. Rep from *. 32 sts.
4th round: ss into first st, * 3 dc in next st, 1 dc in each of next 7 sts. Rep from *. 40 sts.
5th round: ss into first st, * 3 dc in next st, 1 dc in each of next 9 sts. Rep from *. 48 sts.
6th round: ss into first st, * 10 ch, miss 5 sts, ss in next st. Rep from * to end. 8 loops.
7th round: work 13 dc into each loop.
8th round: ss over first 7 dc of first loop, * 13 ch, ss in 7th dc of next loop, 9 ch, ss in 7th dc of next loop. Rep from * to end.
9th round: ss over first 6 ch of first loop, * 3 dc in next st, 23 dc. Rep from * to end.
10th round: ss into first st, * 3 dc in next st, 25 dc. Rep from * to end.
11th round: ss into first st, * 3 dc in next st, 27 dc. Rep from * to end. Fasten off. Press the squares and join into 3 strips of 3, then use the same yarn to join the strips to form a square.
With right side facing join yarn to one corner, * 3 dc in first st, 89 dc. Rep from * all round.
Next round: ss into first st, * 3 dc in next st, 91 dc. Rep from * all round.
Next round: ss into first st, * 3 dc in next st, 93 dc. Rep from * all round.
Next round: ss into first 2 sts, * 8 ch, miss 6 sts, ss in next st. Rep from * all round.

Next round: work 12 dc into each loop, fin. with ss to first dc. Fasten off.

Block out the crochet to the right size on your ironing board and press it on the wrong side, using a damp cloth and warm iron.

Cut out the fabric pieces for the cushion cover, making them 1in. longer and wider than the crochet. Pin the crochet to the right side of one of the pieces, allowing ½in. seam allowance all round. Using the crochet yarn, oversew it to the fabric. With the right side of the other cover piece facing the crochet, stitch the pieces together on three sides, taking ⅝in. seam allowance (the edges of the crochet should be enclosed). Turn the cover right side out, insert the cushion and stitch the opening together.

Sun-ray cushion

Measurements: 16 inches square; 2 groups of 5 dtr joined equal 2in.
Materials: 100 gr. DMC 171 crochet Cotton or 2 balls Twilley's Lysbet. Crochet Hook No. 2.50 (ISR)
Make 6 ch and join into a ring with a ss.
1st round: 12 dc into ring, ss to 1st dc.
2nd round: 2 ch, tr in same st as ss, 2 tr in each st to end. ss into 2nd of 2 ch. 24 sts.
3rd round: 3 ch, 4 dtr in same st as ss, miss 2 sts, 1 ch, * 5 dtr in next st, 1 ch, miss 2 sts. Rep from * to end, ss into 3 ch.
4th round: 3 ch, then keeping last loop of each on hook, work 1 dtr in each of next 4 dtr, yarn over and draw through all 5 loops on hook (called 4 dtr joined), 7 ch, * miss 1 st, 5 dtr joined, 7 ch. Rep from * to end, ss to top of group. (Keep the 5 dtr joined over the 5 dtr of previous round.)
5th round: As 3rd round, but missing 3 sts between each group instead of 2.
6th round: As 4th round.
7th round: 3 ch, 4 dtr in same st, 3 ch, miss 7 sts, * 5 dtr in next st, 3 ch, miss 7 sts. Rep from * to end, ss to 3 ch.
8th round: as 4th round but working 9 ch between each group instead of 7.
9th round: 3 ch, 4 dtr in same st, 1 ch, miss 4 sts, * 5 dtr in next st, 1 ch, miss 4 sts. Rep from * to end, ss to 3 ch.
10th round: As 4th round but working 6 ch between each group.
11th round: 3 ch, 4 dtr in same st, 2 ch, miss 6 sts, * 5 dtr in next st, 2 ch, miss 6 sts. Rep from * to end, ss to 3 ch.
12th round: As 4th round.
13th round: As 7th round.
14th round: As 8th round.
15th round: 2 ss in same st as ss of last round, ss in each of next 79 sts, * 3 ss in next st, ss in

each of next 79 sts. Rep from * to end.

16th round: ss in first 2 sts, 3 ch, 4 dtr in same place as last ss. * 7 dtr, 8 tr, 9 htr, 10 dc, 13 ss, 10 dc, 9 htr, 8 tr, 7 dtr, 5 dtr in next st. Rep from * to end, omit last 5 dtr, ss to 3 ch.

17th round: ss in first 2 sts, 3 ch, 4 dtr in same place, * 3 dtr, 9 tr, 10 htr, 11 dc, 19 ss, 11 dc, 10 htr, 9 tr, 3 dtr, 5 dtr in next st. Rep from * to end, omit last 5 dtr, ss to 3 ch.

18th round: ss in first 2 sts, 3 ch, 4 dtr in same place, * 9 tr, 10 htr, 11 dc, 29 ss, 11 dc, 10 htr, 9 tr, 5 dtr in next st. Rep from * to end, omit last 5 dtr, ss to 3 ch.

19th round: ss in first 2 sts, 3 ch, 4 tr in same place, * 7 tr, 8 htr, 9 dc, 45 ss, 9 dc, 8 htr, 7 tr, 5 tr in next st. Rep from * to end, omit last 5 tr, ss to 3 ch.

20th round: ss in first 2 sts, 1 ch, 2 dc in same st, 97 dc. * 3 dc in next st, 97 dc. Rep from * to end, ss to 1 ch.

21st round: ss in first st, 1 ch, 2 dc in next st, 99 dc, * 3 dc in next st, 99 dc. Rep from * to end, ss to 1 ch. Fasten off. Press the crochet and make up the cushion as above.

Bolster-shaped cushion

Measurements: 17½ inches long and approx. 16 inches round. 9 dc equal 1 in.

Materials: 200 gr. DMC 171 crochet Cotton; or 4 balls Twilley's Lysbet. Crochet Hook No. 2.50 (ISR)

Motif: (Make 18)

Make 8 ch and join into a ring with a ss.

1st round: 2 ch, 15 tr into ring, ss to 2 ch. 16 sts.

2nd round: 4 ch, * tr in next st, 2 ch. Rep from * to end, ss to 2nd of 4 ch. 48 sts.

3rd round: 5 ch, keeping last loop of each on hook, work 1 tr.tr in each of next 3 sts, yarn over and draw through all 4 loops on hook (called 3 tr tr joined), 5 ch, * 4 tr tr joined, 5 ch. Rep from * to end, 12 groups.

4th round: * 3 dc in st at top of first group, 5 dc in 5 ch loop, 1 dc in st at top of next group, 5 dc in 5 ch loop. Rep from * to end, ss to 1st dc.

5th round: 3 dc in next st, 13 dc. Rep from * to end, ss to first dc.

6th round: 3 dc in next st, 15 dc. Rep from * to end, ss to first dc.

7th round: 3 dc in next st, 17 dc. Rep from * to end, ss to first dc. Fasten off.

Half Motif: (Make 4)

Make 5 ch and join into a ring with a ss, then cont. in rows as follows:

1st row: 2 ch, 8 tr into ring, turn.

2nd row: 4 ch, tr in next st, * 2 ch, tr in next st. Rep from * to end, turn.

3rd row: 5 ch, tr. tr in next st, * 5 ch, 4 tr. tr joined. Rep from * 4 times more, 5 ch, tr. tr in next st, tr. tr in turning ch, turn.

4th row: 1 ch, dc in next st, * 5 dc in 5 ch loop, 1 dc in st at top of group, 5 dc in 5 ch loop, 3 dc in st at top of next group. Rep from * once more, 5 dc in 5 ch loop, 1 dc in st at top of group, 5 dc in 5 ch loop, dc in last 2 sts, turn.

5th row: 1 ch, 2 dc in first st, (13 dc, 3 dc in next st) twice, 13 dc, 2 dc in last st.

6th row: 1 ch, 2 dc in first st, (15 dc, 3 dc in next st) twice, 15 dc, 2 dc in last st.

7th row: 1 ch, 2 dc in first st, (17 dc, 3 dc in next st) twice, 17 dc, 2 dc in last st. Fasten off.

Join the motifs in 2 strips of 5 and 2 of 4, then

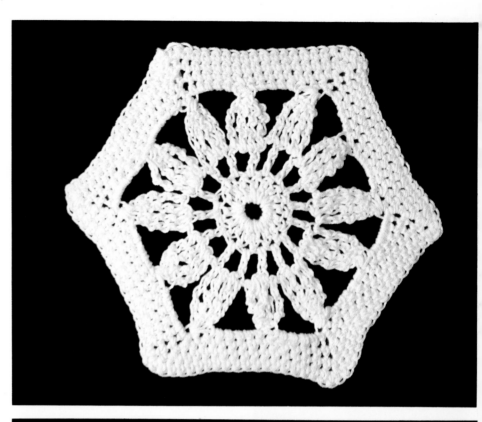

join the strips alternately, fitting the angles together with the half motifs at the ends of the short strips to complete the size above. Then work border at each end as follows:

With right side facing join the yarn to one end and work 104 dc along end, turn and work 3 more rows in dc.

Next row: 5 ch, 3 tr. tr joined, 3 ch, * 4 tr. tr joined, 3 ch. Rep from * to end, fin with tr. tr in turning ch.

Top. A motif from the bolster-shaped cushion.

Above. A motif from the geometric flower cover.

Next row: work 5 dc into each 3 ch loop, fin. with dc in turning ch.

Press work as above. Join the long sides to form a tube, insert cushion and tie a ribbon round each end.

Crocheted motifs

Beautiful tablecloths, place mats, dressing table sets, bedspreads, cushions and rugs can all be made by using a simple, but unusual, crocheted motif as the foundation.

Flexibility is the main characteristic of this type of crochet, because the size of the motif and kind of yarn used can be adapted to suit yourself. You can use up oddments of yarn and, if you change your mind about what you want to make, this is easily done by re-arranging the motifs and adding to, or reducing the number.

Making the basic hexagon

Using the selected yarn and the appropriate hook size (see below), make 5 chain and slip stitch into the first stitch to form a ring.

1st round. (5 chain, 1dc into ring) 6 times.

2nd round. (3 chain, 1dc) into each chain loop of previous round. Mark the 1st 3ch loop of this round with a small safety pin to indicate the beginning point of all the following rounds.

3rd round. (3 chain, 2dc into 3 chain loop, 1dc into next dc). Repeat 5 more times.

4th round. (3 chain, 2dc into 3 chain loop, miss 1dc, 1dc into each of next 2dc). Repeat 5 more times.

5th round. (3 chain, 2dc into next loop, miss 1dc, 1dc into each of next 3dc). Repeat 5 more times.

6th round. (3 chain, 2dc into next loop, miss 1dc, 1dc into each of next 4dc). Repeat 5 more times.

7th round. (3 chain, 2dc into next loop, miss 1dc, 1dc into each of next 5dc). Repeat 5 more times.

8th round. (3 chain, 2dc into next loop, miss 1dc, 1dc into each of next 6dc). Repeat 5 more times.

9th round. (3 chain, 2dc into next loop, miss 1dc, 1dc into each of next 7dc). Repeat 5 more times.

10th round. (3 chain, 2dc into next loop, miss 1dc, 1dc into each of next dc). Repeat 5 more times.

Table set

The set shown in the photograph is made from 3 balls of Twilleys Lyscordet, which is equivalent to a No.5 cotton. The tension should be 6dc to 1in. in width, on a No.2.50 (1SR) crochet hook.

Page 236. By using yarns and adjusting the size of the motif or joining several together, this crocheted motif can be made

If you would prefer to make the set in a finer 40 cotton, you should use a finer hook (No.1.25) and increase the number of rounds to make the hexagons the required size.

Place mat (10in. x 10in.). Work 7 hexagons, following the instructions as for the basic motif. Place one hexagon in the middle and join the remaining ones to each of its sides (Fig.1). For the method of joining, see below.

When the motifs are joined, work one round of dc, placing 1dc into each dc and 3dc into each 3 chain loop, round the outer edge.

Glass mat (5in. diameter, 2½in. sides). Work the basic motif as above, then continue for a further 3 rounds. Finish off by working a round of dc, placing 1dc into each dc, and 3dc into each chain loop.

Table centre (14½in. x 14½in.). Work 7 motifs to the same size as the glass mat. Join them as for the place mat, finishing off in the same way.

Cushion (18in. diameter, 9in. sides).

The cushion shown in the photograph is made from three 50g balls of random dyed double knitting wool, but of course plain dyed wool can be used. The tension should be 5dc to 1in. in width, using a No.3.50 (ISR) crochet hook.

Work two basic motifs as above, then continue for a further 24 rounds (34 rounds in all) on both. Finish off by working a round of dc, placing 1dc into each dc and 3dc into each chain loop.

Join the hexagons together on five sides, leaving the sixth side open for inserting the cushion pad. The opening can be finished by oversewing the sides of the opening together, or by inserting a zip fastener.

Floor cushion (18in. diameter, 6in. deep).

For a cushion of this size, you need 4 50gr balls of double knitting wool. The tension should be 5dc to 1in. in width, using a No.3.50 (ISR) crochet hook.

Work one motif as for the cushion above.

Band round cushion (6in. wide x 54in. long).

Make 26 chain.

Below. The basic motif, made in cotton. The hexagon shape is developed from a circle by the method of increasing in each round.

1st row. Work 1dc into 2nd chain from hook, 1dc into each remaining chain to the end. Turn with 2 chain. (24dc). The two turning chains always count as the 1st dc of row.

2nd row. Miss last dc of previous row and work 1dc into back thread only of each dc of previous row. (25dc). Turn with 2 chain.

Repeat 2nd row until work measures 42in. in length. If the yarn you are using is wool, press the crochet under a damp cloth, using a fairly hot iron. If the yarn is a man-made fibre, press it carefully, following the manufacturer's instructions.

Then measure the length again. This type of double crochet is very elastic, and the stitch opens out by one-third again when pressed, so you may find that you have reached the right length. If not, work two more rows, press and measure again. Sew the band to the hexagon.

To finish the cushion, cut a 6in. deep base from solid foam, making each side of the hexagon 9½in. long.

For the base of the cushion, cut a hexagon from a dark-coloured hessian, using the foam hexagon as a template. Turn under the edges for ¼in. Insert the foam pad and stitch the hessian base on the other edge of the band, being careful you position the points to correspond with the first hexagon.

Rug or wall hanging

This rug measures 34in. x 44in., and uses 21oz double knitting wool, in six different colours (four main and two as a contrast). If you prefer, you can use oddments of wool which you may have left over, although here it is usually best to link the groups by one main colour, which can also be used round the border.

Work seven hexagons in each main colour, and join them to form self-colour groups as for the place mat. Work five more hexagons in each colour, and join them in two-row, three-row self-coloured groups. Then work five hexagons in one of the contrast colours.

Using the second contrast colour, work 1 round of dc round the edge of each group and single motifs, placing 1dc into each dc of the outer edge of each hexagon.

Join all the groups, placing them as shown in Fig.2.

To finish the rug, make a border of six rounds of dc round the outer edge. Try to use the colours of the groups, starting with the second contrast colour.

To keep the edge a good shape, work 3dc into each projecting point; decrease at each inside angle by picking up the loops of the stitches at each side and working 1dc into them.

Joining the motifs

The motifs can be joined either by crochet or oversewing.

Crochet. Place two motifs together with 'right' sides facing, and so that the sides are level and the angles match. Insert the hook through the first stitch of both hexagons, join on the yarn and work a dc, treating the two stitches already on the hook as one. Continue working along the edge of the motif in this way. This forms a slight ridge, so you should join on all the subsequent motifs so that the ridge is always on the same side.

Fig. 1

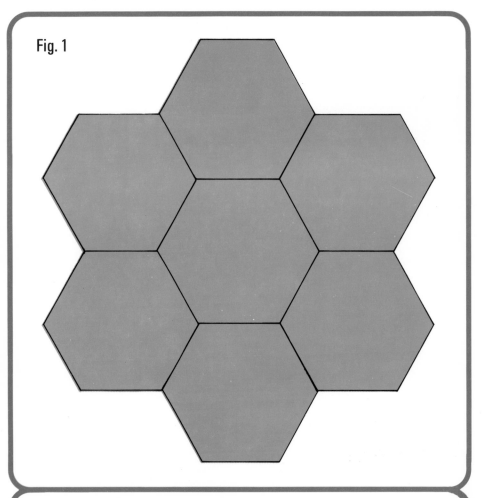

Fig. 2

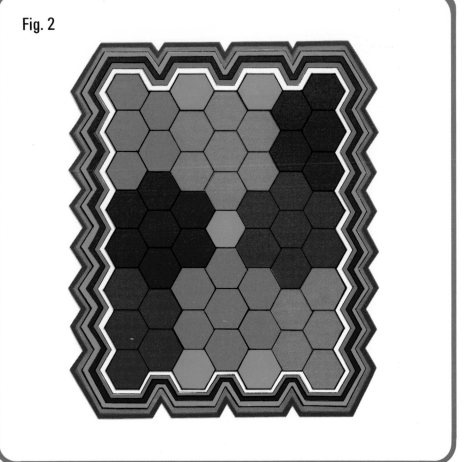

Bedspread made from motifs

A crochet bedspread may seem like an undertaking, but it is quick to grow and will last for years more than most fabric ones. The motifs could also be used to make an unusual tablecloth.

Abbreviations
ch—chain ; ss—slip stitch ; dc—double crochet ; tr—treble crochet ; dpl—double picot loop ; spl—single picot loop ; rep—repeat.

Measurements
Single bedspread : 90in. x 54in.
Double bedspread : 90in. x 72in.
Size of motif : 6in. square.
Depth of fringe : 8½in.

Materials required
Single bedspread : 54 balls Twilleys Lysbet for motifs ; 19 balls for fringe.
Double bedspread : 72 balls Twilleys Lysbet for motifs ; 22 balls for fringe.
As a guide, 1 ball will make 2½ motifs or the fringe round 2½ sides of the motifs.
Crochet hook, No. 2.50 (ISR).

First motif

Make 26ch.

1st row: Work 1tr into 4th ch from hook (1st 3ch of each row to stand for 1tr throughout).

2nd row: 3ch, *1tr into next tr. Rep from * to end. 1tr into 3rd of 3ch. Turn.

Rep 2nd row 10 times.

13th row: *6ch, 1ss into 4th ch from hook (picot made), 7ch, 1ss into 4th ch from hook, 2ch, 1dc into 6th tr. (1dpl made.) Rep from * 3 times more, working the final dc into top of 3 turning ch. Turn.

14th row: Ss, taking about 4 st including 1 behind picot, into centre of 1st dpl. *Make 1 dpl, working the dc in the next dpl over the ch. between picots. Rep from * twice. (3dpl.) Turn.

15th row: Ss into centre of 1st dpl. *Make 1dpl, working the dc over the ch. between picots in the next dpl of previous row. Repeat from * once. (2 dpl.) Turn.

16th row: Ss into centre of ch. between the picots of 1st dpl. Make 1 dpl, working the dc over the ch. between picots of 2nd dpl of previous row. Fasten off.

Turn the square upside down, rejoin the yarn to the top right corner and work the 13th row as above into the bottom loops of the starting chain of the 1st row.

Rep. rows 14-16 as above. Fasten off.

Turn the square sideways, rejoin the yarn to the top right corner and work the 13th row again into the side of the inner tr. square. Place the dc of each dpl into the base of the 10th, 7th, 4th and 1st rows of the inner tr. square.

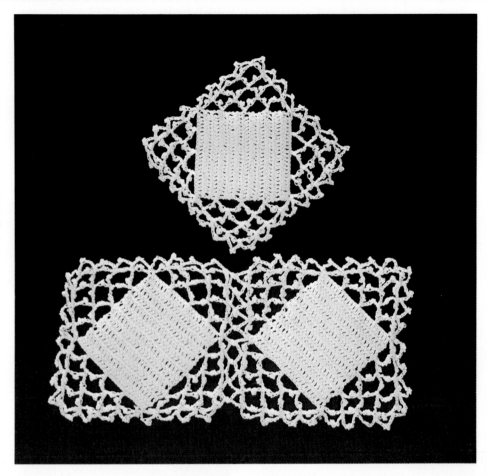

Above. *Each motif in this bedspread is made up from a small square of treble stitches and a triangle of loops is added to each side. This pattern has the advantage of joining the motifs by crochet, not sewing.*

Repeat on the fourth side of the square.

Final round: Re-join the yarn to any corner of the inner square of tr. *7ch, ss into 4th ch from hook, 3ch (spl made). 1dc into junction of 1st and 2nd rows of dpl. 1spl, 1dc into junction of 2nd and 3rd rows of dpl. 1spl, 1dc into junction of 3rd and 4th rows of dpl. 1spl, 1dc between picots of 4th row of dpl. 1spl, dc into junction of 4th and 3rd rows of dpl. 1spl, 1dc into junction of 3rd and 2nd rows of dpl. 1spl, dc into junction of 2nd and 1st rows of dpl. 1spl, dc into corner of tr square.*

Rep from * to * on other sides of motif.

Second motif

Work as for the 1st motif until the final round.

Final round: Re-join yarn to corner of tr square. 1spl, dc into junction of 1st and 2nd rows of dpl. 1spl, dc into junction of 2nd and 3rd rows of dpl. 1spl, dc into junction of 3rd and 4th rows of dpl. 1spl, 1dc into ch between picots of 4th row of dpl.

Place the first motif behind the second one with the trebles and corners matching. Holding the motifs together, start joining them as follows :

3ch, ss into first picot on 1st motif. 3ch, 1dc into junction of 4th and 3rd rows of 2nd motif. **3ch, 1ss into next picot of 1st motif, 3ch, 1dc into junction of rows of dpl of 2nd motif.** Rep from ** to ** 6 times. 3ch, ss

into corner picot of 1st motif, 3ch, 1dc between corner picots of 2nd motif. This has joined the motifs.

Finish the remaining sides of the 2nd motif as for the 1st motif.

Making up

Continue adding motifs in the same way, until 15 are joined together.

Single size. Join on 8 more rows of motifs, joining each one on two sides in the final round.

Double size. Join on 11 more rows of motifs, joining each one on two sides in the final round.

Making the fringe

Starting at any corner at the beginning of a spl, 3ch, 3tr, 1ch across top of picot. *8tr, 1ch. Rep from * all round outside.

Wind the yarn round a slim 12in. wide book. Cut along one side of loops. Take 4 strands of yarn, fold in half and, with right side of bedspread facing, loop the yarn through the first picot space and knot it with a half hitch (see below). Miss 4tr and put the next 4 strands in the next space. Repeat all round the border.

2nd round. Take 4 strands from one tassel and knot it with 4 strands of the next tassel about 1in. down. Repeat all round.

3rd round. Take the strands of the original tassel and knot together. Repeat all round.

4th round. As 2nd round.

To make a simple half hitch knot, hold the threads in your left hand. Take the ends round behind and down through loop just made. Put the wrong end of a fine crochet hook through top of loop to ease the knot into position.

A bathroom set to crochet

A crochet bath set may seem unusual, but when made in a thick cotton yarn it is as soft and absorbent (and much cheaper) as some of the very expensive ready-made sets. The pattern given below gives two colours, but the set would look just as good in one, or even three, colours.

Measurements

Bathmat: 18in. x 20in. (can be made larger).
Pedestal mat: 22in. wide x 24in. deep.
Lavatory seat cover: 17in. x 14in.

If your seat is a different size, check the foundation row against the front edge of the lid and adjust the size by adding more stitches if necessary. Keep checking the cover for size as you work. You can alter the shaping by adding to, or missing out, the increasing and decreasing rows. Make a note of the alterations and repeat them on the flap.

Materials

For bathmat: Twilleys Knitcot, 6oz main colour, 3oz contrast colour.

For pedestal mat: Twilleys Knitcot, 8oz main colour, 4oz contrast.

For lavatory seat cover: 4oz main colour, 2oz contrast colour.

Crochet hook: No. 4.50 (ISR).

Making loop stitch

Insert the crochet hook into the top of the first stitch, wrap yarn round first finger of your left hand, then put the yarn round the hook (y-o-h) and draw through one stitch. Y-o-h, draw through two stitches, then work 1 chain tightly to lock the loop into place. This chain stitch is part of the loop stitch, and does not count as a separate stitch.

Bath mat

Using the main colour, make a foundation row of 9 chain.

1st row: 1dc into 2nd chain from hook, 1dc into each of the remaining chain. (8dc made.) Turn with 1 chain.

2nd row: Work 1 loop stitch into each dc of previous row. Turn with 1 chain. (8 loops made.)

3rd row: 1dc into space at the top of each loop of previous row. Turn with 1 ch.

Rows 4, 6, 8, 10, 12, 14 & 16: repeat 2nd row.
Rows 5, 7, 9, 11, 13, 15: repeat 3rd row. Fasten off.

Left. Loop stitch is not very common in crochet, but when worked in thick yarn on a large hook it is quick to grow and makes an attractive bathroom set.

TUBBY

17th row: In contrasting colour, work 8dc into first 8 loops of previous row. *To turn the corner,* work 1dc into same loop as 8th dc, 2ch, 2dc into the side of the same stitch.

Continue the 17th row by working 1dc into the side of each previous row. Turn with 1 ch. (16dc, excluding the corner stitches, made.)

18th row: 1dc into each dc of previous row. *To turn the corner,* work 1dc into the 2ch at corner of previous row, then work 2ch, 1dc into same place.

19th row: Repeat 18th row.

20th row: Work 1 loop stitch into each dc of previous row. *To turn the corner,* work 1 more loop stitch into dc on either side of the corner chain of previous row.

21st row: 1dc into each dc of previous row. Turn the corner as for 18th row.

22nd row: Repeat 20th row.

23rd row: Repeat 21st row.

24th row: Repeat 20th row. Fasten off.

25th row: Change to main colour and repeat 21st row.

26th and 27th rows: Repeat 21st row.

28th row: Repeat 20th row.

29th row: Repeat 21st row.

30th row: Repeat 20th row.

31st-44th rows: Repeat 17th-30th rows inclusive.

45th-53rd rows: Repeat 17th-24th rows. Fasten off. (If the mat is not large enough, repeat the 25th-30th rows again.)

To finish off: In main colour, work dc into each dc of previous row. Do not turn the work, but work an extra dc into the last stitch, then 2ch, 1dc into the side of the same stitch. Continue working along the other three sides of the mat with 1dc into the sides of each row and into bottom of the foundation chain. Turn the corners in the same way.

At the 4th corner, work 1dc, 2 chain, 1dc, slip stitch into 1st chain of round.

Final round: 1ch, 1dc into each dc of previous round. Work corners in same way. Finish off.

Pedestal mat

Using the main colour, make a foundation row of 9 chain.

1st row: 1dc into 2nd chain from hook, 1dc into each of the remaining chain. (8dc made). Turn with 1 chain.

2nd row: Work 1 loop stitch into each dc of the previous row. Turn with 1 chain. (8 loops made.)

3rd row: 1dc into space at the top of each loop stitch of previous row. Turn with 1 chain.

4th-17th rows: Repeat the 2nd and 3rd rows alternately. Fasten off.

18th row: With the right side of the mat facing

up, and the loops towards you, join the contrast colour to the bottom right-hand corner. Make 1 chain, then work 1dc into the side of each row of the main colour.

At the corner, make an extra dc into the same place as the previous stitch, then 2ch, 2dc into 1st dc of top short side. Work 1dc into each stitch until 2nd top corner, 2dc, 2ch, 2dc into 2nd long side. 1dc into side of each row of the main colour. When you reach the third corner, check that the number of dc's worked on this side equals the number worked on the opposite side. Turn with 1ch.

19th row: With the right side of the mat away from you, work 1dc into each dc of previous row. *To turn the corners,* work 2dc into the last stitch before turning the corner, then 2ch, 2dc into first stitch of next side. Turn with 1ch.

20th row: Repeat 19th row.

21st row: 1 loop stitch into each dc of previous row. *To turn the corners,* work 1 extra loop stitch into the dc on either side of the corner stitches of previous row. Turn with 1ch.

22nd row: Repeat 19th row.

23rd row: Repeat 21st row.

24th row: Repeat 19th row.

25th row: Repeat 21st row. Fasten off.

26th row: In main colour, repeat 19th row.

27th-41st rows: Repeat rows 20-26. Change to contrast colour for rows 34-41. Fasten off.

42nd row: To work the shaping, have the right side of the mat facing up and the loops towards you, and rejoin the main colour to the top right-hand corner of the mat. Work 1dc into each loop stitch of previous row across top side only. Turn at corner with 1 chain.

43rd row: Work 1dc into first 23dc of previous row. Turn with 1 chain.

44th row: 1dc into each dc of previous row.

45th row: Work 1 loop stitch into first 22 dc of previous row. Miss the last stitch. Turn with 1ch.

46th row: 1 dc into each loop stitch of previous row. Turn with 1 ch.

47th row: 1 loop stitch into first 21 dc of previous row. Miss the last stitch. Turn with 1 ch.

48th row: 1dc into each loop stitch of previous row. Turn with 1ch.

49th row: 1 loop stitch into first 20dc of previous row. Miss the last stitch. Turn with 1ch.

50th row: 1 dc into each loop stitch of previous row. Turn with 1ch.

51st and 52nd rows: Repeat 50th row.

53rd row: Repeat 49th row.

54th row: Repeat 50th row.

55th row: Repeat 49th row.

56th row: Repeat 50th row.

57th row: Repeat 49th row.

58th and 59th rows: Repeat 50th row. Fasten off.

To complete the other side of the mat, miss the stitches worked in the middle of the 41st row, re-join yarn and work 1dc into each of the remaining 22 stitches. Work the 42nd-59th rows as before, but reversing the shaping, by missing the first stitch of the row instead of the last.

To finish off, work 2 rounds of dc all round the outer edge of the mat.

Seat cover

Using the main colour, make a foundation row of 9 chain.

1st row: 1dc into 2nd chain from hook. 7dc to end. Turn with 1 chain.

2nd row: 1dc into each dc of previous row. (8dc made).

3rd row: 2dc into first dc of previous row, 1dc into each of next dc, 2dc into last dc. Turn with 1ch. (10dc.).

4th row: Work 1 loop stitch into each dc of previous row. Turn with 1ch. (10 loops made.)

5th row: 2dc into space above first loop stitch of previous row. 1dc into each of next 9 spaces, 2dc into last space. Turn with 1ch. (12dc made.)

6th row: 1 loopstitch in each dc of previous row. Turn with 1ch. (12 loops made.)

7th row: Repeat 5th row. (14dc made.)

8th row: Repeat 6th Row. (14 loops made.)

9th row: In contrast colour, repeat 5th row.

10th row: Repeat 2nd row.

11th row: Repeat 3rd row.

12th row: Repeat 6th row. (18 loops made.)

13th row: Repeat 5th row.

14th row: Repeat 6th row. (20 loops made.)

15th row: Repeat 5th row.

16th row: Repeat 6th row. (22 loops made.)

17th row: In main colour, repeat 5th row.

18th row: Repeat 2nd row.

19th row: Repeat 3rd row.

20th row: Repeat 6th row. (26 loops made.)

21st row: 1dc into space at the top of each loop stitch of previous row (no increases made). Turn with 1ch.

22nd row: 1 loopstitch into each dc of previous row. Turn with 1ch.

23rd row: Repeat 21st row.

24th row: Repeat 22nd row. Fasten off.

25th row: In contrast colour, repeat 3rd row.

26th and 27th rows: Repeat 2nd row.

28th row: Repeat 6th row. (28 loops made.)

29th row: Repeat 21st row.

30th row: Repeat 6th row.

31st row: Repeat 21st row.

32nd row: Miss 1st dc, loopstitch into each of next 26dc, miss last dc. Turn with 1ch. Fasten off.

33rd row: In main colour, miss 1st stitch, dc into each of next 24 stitches, miss last stitch. Turn with 1ch.

34th row: 1 dc in each dc of previous row.

Below. The lavatory seat cover has a special flap which fits over the front edge of the lid and holds it in position.

35th row: Miss 1st dc, 1dc into each of next 22dc, miss last dc.

36th row: Repeat 6th row. (22 loops made.)

37th row: Repeat 33rd row.

38th row: Repeat 6th row. (20 loops made.)

Try the cover on the seat, and if it is not long enough, work one more row of dc then another row of loopstitch.

39th row: Miss 1st stitch, 1dc into each of next 18 stitches, slip stitch into last stitch. 1ch, do not turn work.

40th row: With the loop side facing you, work 1dc into each of row endings, across foundation chain and along other side of row endings. 1dc into each of final dc row, slip stitch into single chain at the end of that row.

41st row: Repeat 40th row, working 1dc into each of dc all round.

Flap

Using the main colour, make a foundation row of 13 chain.

1st row: 1dc into second chain from hook, 1dc into each chain to end. Turn with 1 chain. (12dc worked.)

2nd row: 1dc into each dc of previous row.

3rd row: 2dc into first dc, 1dc into each of next dc, 2dc into last dc. Turn with 1ch. (14dc worked.)

4th row: Repeat 2nd row.

5th row: Repeat 3rd row. (16dc made.)

6th row: Repeat 2nd and 3rd rows until 26 rows altogether have been worked.

Do not fasten off, but withdraw hook. Place the flap on the plain side of the cover at the front end, matching the shaping. Pin into position. Turn the work over so that the loop-side is facing up and the yarn is on your right-hand side. Put the hook through the 1st dc on the loop-side that coincides with the edge of flap. Putting the hook through the edges of both the cover and the flap, work 1dc into each dc of the cover. Continue round the edge of the flap, thus joining the two pieces together.

When you reach the other side of the flap, continue working 1dc into each dc of the cover until the 1st side of the flap is reached. Slip stitch into the 1st dc.

Last round: 1 chain, 1dc into each dc of previous round. Slip stitch into 1st chain. Fasten off.

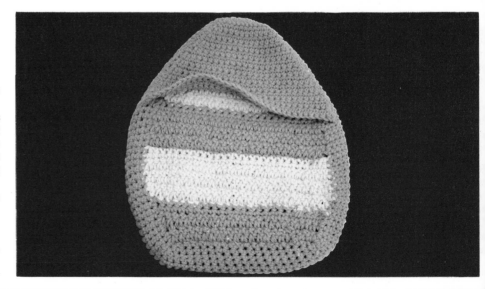

Quick-make lampshades

Where you have the choice, large lampshades are better than small ones because they give a greater pool of light and do not restrict the airflow round the bulb. Yet they can be expensive, so it is worth making your own because the materials are simple and cheap.

One of the most simple and quick ways of making a lampshade is to use a fabric which has a stiff backing. There is little or no sewing involved because the cover can be glued to the frame, and there is no need for a lining.

This type of fabric is suitable only for lampshades with straight or sloping sides because it cannot be stretched or moulded to one with curved sides. This is one of the main differences between firm and soft shades: with the latter, the fabric can be stretched to fit, but the backing in a firm shade makes this impossible.

Although standard frames with struts can be used for firm lampshades, all you actually need are the two rings which come at the top and bottom of the shade—the structure in between is formed by the rigidity of the fabric.

Using rings without struts cuts down on the amount of binding needed and, because they are available in a wide range of diameters, you can vary the exact shape and size of the lampshade to suit yourself (Fig.1). The easiest type to make is where the top and bottom rings are the same size because the cover fabric is cut to a simple rectangle. Where the top ring is smaller than the bottom one, you would need to make a paper pattern to cut out a circular piece of fabric to fit round smoothly. The top ring should also have a fitting suitable for hanging on a table lamp.

Choosing the fabric

Many stores which sell lampshade frames also sell a selection of fabrics already bonded to the stiffening. Alternatively, you can buy the stiffening separately and bond it to the fabric of your choice. There are two main types of stiffening—both white—which are suitable.

One, such as Parbond, is an adhesive parchment which is ironed on to the fabric. With this, the cover can be either stitched or glued to the frame. The other type, such as Selapar, is self adhesive. It is very stiff and so the cover can

Right. *Table lamps are a quick and easy way of adding an extra light, and their shades should be chosen to suit both the base of the lamp and the rest of the room. Dark or opaque fabrics should be backed with white so as much light as possible is reflected into the room.*

only be glued to the frame. It is not suitable for open weave fabrics because dust could stick to its uncovered parts.

To calculate the amount of fabric needed where the rings are the same size, decide on the height of shade you want, measure the circumference of the rings and buy enough to cut a rectangle of the same size, plus about 1 in. on each side.

Where the rings are different sizes, make a pattern following the method below, place it on another rectangular piece of paper so that one short side of the pattern is level with the edge of the paper, and measure across the pattern at its widest and highest points. Allow a piece of cover fabric of the same size, plus about 1 in. each way.

Making a paper pattern

If possible, use a really large sheet of squared graph paper for making the pattern because this makes drawing parallel and perpendicular lines much easier than on blank paper.

Near the bottom left-hand corner of the paper, draw a horizontal line (Fig.2, A-B), equal in length to the diameter of the bottom ring. Find the centre of the line (C) and draw a perpendicular line upwards from it to the required height of the shade (D).

At D, draw another horizontal line (E-F) equal to the diameter of the upper ring and with D as the centre. Join A-E and B-F and extend these lines upwards until they intersect at G.

Using G-E as the radius, draw a large arc from E, equal to the circumference of the top ring (the length of the arc can be measured with a piece of string). Then, using G-A as the radius, draw another arc from A, equal to the circumference of the lower ring. Add $\frac{3}{4}$ in. to the length of each arc and them join them (H-I). Cut round A-E-H-I and this gives the paper pattern.

If you prefer, you omit the graph stage by assessing the 'slant' height of the shade. To do this, lay the lower ring flat on your work surface and hold the upper ring centrally over the lower one at the required height of the shade. With a long ruler, measure the length of the slant between the rings.

To calculate the radius for the upper edge of the pattern, multiply the radius of the upper ring by the slant height and divide this by the radius of the bottom ring minus the radius of the upper ring.

Radius of upper ring x slant height

Radius of lower ring—radius of upper ring.

Add the radius of the upper edge of the pattern to the slant height and this gives the radius for the lower edge of the pattern.

BROCK

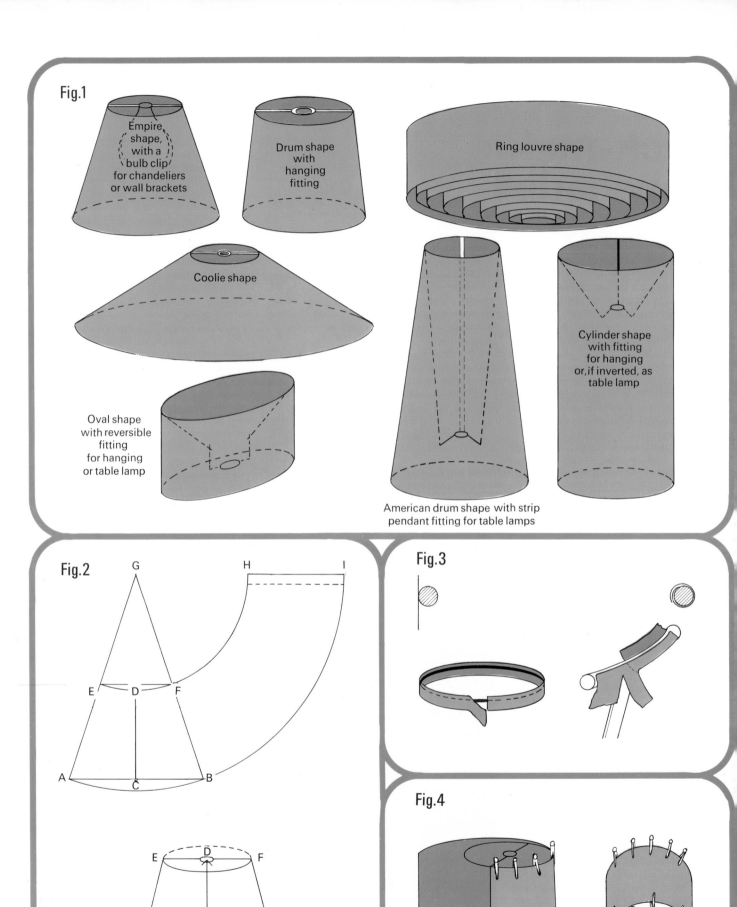

Fig.1

Empire shape, with a bulb clip for chandeliers or wall brackets

Drum shape with hanging fitting

Ring louvre shape

Coolie shape

Oval shape with reversible fitting for hanging or table lamp

American drum shape with strip pendant fitting for table lamps

Cylinder shape with fitting for hanging or, if inverted, as table lamp

Fig.2

G

H   I

E   D   F

A   C   B

E   D   F

A   C   B

Fig.3

Fig.4

SYNDICATION INTERNATIONAL

Above right. One advantage of making a shade with backed fabric is that the only framework needed is two rings for the top and bottom. The fabric forms the structure in between, eliminating the need for ugly struts.
Above left. If you want to make a shade to match wallpaper, you can stiffen it easily with an iron-on or self-adhesive backing.

If you are using a frame with struts, you can make a less accurate pattern simply by wrapping a piece of paper round the shade, pressing it over the top and bottom rings to make firm creases, and marking where the paper joins following the line of a strut. Cut out the pattern along the crease lines, try it again on the shade and make any necessary adjustments.

Preparing the frame

To prevent the frame from rusting, paint it first with a fast-drying enamel or cellulose paint and allow to dry completely.

If you are going to sew on the cover, bind the rings following the method described on pages 249-251. If you are going to stick on the cover, the binding should also be stuck on.

For this, use $\frac{1}{2}$in. wide adhesive cotton tape. Unwind enough of the tape to fit the circumference of the ring, and press the centre of the adhesive side round the inside of the ring. Overlap the ends by $\frac{1}{2}$in. and cut off. Turn over one edge of the tape smoothly on to the outside of the ring and press down all round. Turn over the other edge in the same way and press down firmly so that it overlaps the first edge smoothly on the outside of the ring. This ensures that the overlap will be secure and hidden when the cover is in position (Fig.3).

Preparing the fabric

For a lampshade where the rings are the same size, cut out a piece of fabric equal in size to the height of the frame x the circumference of the rings plus $\frac{3}{4}$in. For slanting shades, cut out the cover fabric from the paper pattern. In either case, cut out the stiffening to the same height but $\frac{1}{4}$in. narrower.

If you are using iron-on stiffening, first test it for correct iron temperature. Using offcuts of stiffening and cover fabric, place the stiffening on your ironing board with the shiny side up. Place the fabric over it with wrong side down and iron the two pieces together. Allow to cool and then check if they have adhered. If you need a high temperature to get a good bond, cover the fabric first with paper to avoid scorching.

Lay out the main piece of stiffening in the same way, and place the cover fabric on it so that one vertical side is level and the other overlaps by $\frac{1}{4}$in. Iron the pieces together and allow to cool. Check that the edges are correctly bonded and re-iron if necessary.

Turn the overlap section of fabric on to the backing and stick down with adhesive (see below). This edge should come on to the outside of the overlap when the cover is placed on the shade, giving it a neat finish.

If you are using self-adhesive stiffening, start unpeeling the protective backing from one vertical edge. Place down the cover fabric carefully and smoothly, with the edges level. It will overlap by $\frac{1}{4}$in. at the opposite edge. It often helps to roll the fabric, with its right side inside, on to a rod first. The edge of the fabric can then be placed level with the edge of the stiffening, and then unrolled smoothly on to it. Turn the overlap section on to the backing and stick down.

Attaching the cover

Although the cover can be either glued or stitched to the rings, it is usually most satisfactory to glue the overlap on the vertical seam. Use a clear adhesive, such as Bostik 1 or Uhu, because this will not stain the fabric.

Using sprung clothes pegs (not pins, which would leave holes), peg the cover round the rings as tightly as possible, allowing $\frac{1}{2}$in. overlap and placing the edge where the fabric was turned over on the outside.

If you are sewing the cover on, use strong thread to match the binding tape. Starting about 1in. from the overlap, stab stitch the cover to the tape on the rings, taking the needle out below the ring. Make the stitches small on the inside of the shade, but larger on the outside where they will be hidden by the trimming. Sew round both rings to within 1in. of the overlap, leaving enough thread to finish off.

Check that the seam is straight, then apply a little adhesive to each side of the overlapping section and press firmly together. Finish sewing round both rings.

If you are sticking the cover to the frame, remove about half the clothes pegs and spread some adhesive along the outside of the rings on the portion which is uncovered. Press the cover firmly and carefully back into position. Replace some of the pegs to hold it until the adhesive dries. Repeat this process on the other half of the shade and stick down the overlap (Fig.4).

A different way of sticking the cover to the frame may be easier where the shade is tapered. Before fitting the rings to the cover, overlap the edges of the seam for the right amount and secure with clothes pegs at the top and bottom. Peg the top ring in position so that it fits tightly—adjust the pegs holding the overlap if necessary. Fit the bottom ring in the same way.

Check that the seam is straight, then mark inside the shade the points where the fabric overlaps. Remove the cover from the rings, apply adhesive along each side of the overlapping section and press together firmly along the marked line (Fig.4).

Apply adhesive all round the outer edge of the top ring and insert it into the shade, from below, pressing it to the cover firmly. Hold it in place with clothes pegs. When dry, remove the pegs and repeat the process for the bottom ring.

Adding the trimming

Cut pieces of trimming to fit round the top and bottom of the shade, allowing $\frac{1}{2}$in. extra for an overlap. Turn under $\frac{1}{4}$in. at each end and stick or stitch down. Apply adhesive along the underside of the braid, place one of the folded edges to the seam of the shade and press the braid on to the rim all the way round, so that it covers the stitches and is level with the cut edge of the fabric, finishing with a neat butt join.

Alternatively, you could stick on the braid so half shows on the outside of the shade and the other half on the inside.

Classic, lined lampshades

Beautiful, lined lampshades, in silk or a fabric to match other furnishings, are expensive to buy, yet they are not costly to make yourself, especially if you buy sale remnants for a few pence.

The methods for making drum, straight and bowed empire lampshades are very similar. The cover is a tailored one, made in two sections, and the lining is of the 'balloon' type—fitted to the inside of the shade. Both cover and lining may be cut on the bias grain of the fabric, like the Tiffany lampshade (see pages 249-251), but by careful pinning and stretching they can be equally well cut on the straight grain, which is more economical of fabric.

Although cutting the fabric on the straight grain means that you are not restricted in your choice of pattern, the fabric must have 'give' and be strong enough to withstand pulling; it must also be non-flammable, translucent and wash well. The easiest fabrics to work with are lingerie and crêpe backed satins, tussore, muslin, ninon, silk and cotton chiffon, and georgette. Cottons may also be used but, because their weaves vary, some, such as chintz, have to be wetted in order to make them stretch. Do not use heavy furnishing cottons or damask because they will not readily mould to the shape of the shade; avoid slipper and Duchesse satins and poult because they are affected by heat and cannot be washed. If you choose a dark fabric for the cover, make the lining in a pale fabric to gain maximum light.

To calculate the amount of fabric needed, measure the circumference of the frame at its widest part and, if it is narrower than the width of the fabric, allow a piece the height of the frame, plus 3-4in.

Choosing the frame

Make sure that the frame has the right fitting for your light; one for a hanging light has one bar with a central ring across the top (Fig.1); one which can be used for a hanging or table light should have a gimbal, or tilter as it is sometimes known (Fig.2). If making a drum shade, buy the sort of frame which has struts—those with just two rings are solely for 'stiff' lampshades, made with backed fabric.

Examine all frames thoroughly to check that the struts are evenly spaced and not bent; also that they are securely welded and that the wires are strong and firm on even the smallest ones (you will be pulling the fabric tightly round the struts and unless they are thick enough, they will pull out of shape).

Prepare the frame by painting it and then binding the rings and two opposite struts (see pages 249-251).

Fitting the lining and cover

Start by fitting the lining to the outside of the frame. Fold the fabric in half, on the straight grain, and with the 'right' sides together. Place this doubled piece against half the frame and pin it to the rings at points A and B (Fig.3). Smooth out the fabric to the bound struts and if making a bowed Empire shade, put two more pins in the middle of both struts. Put one pin at the foot of each strut, smooth the fabric up the struts and pin it again at the top (these four pins are known as 'markers', and should always be placed in pairs, as here).

Right. Wild silk lampshades, in a neutral colour and with plain rouleau trimmings, enhance their beautiful bases. Silk is ideal for the curved Empire shapes because it is strong and has a natural elasticity which makes it easy to mould over the frame smoothly.

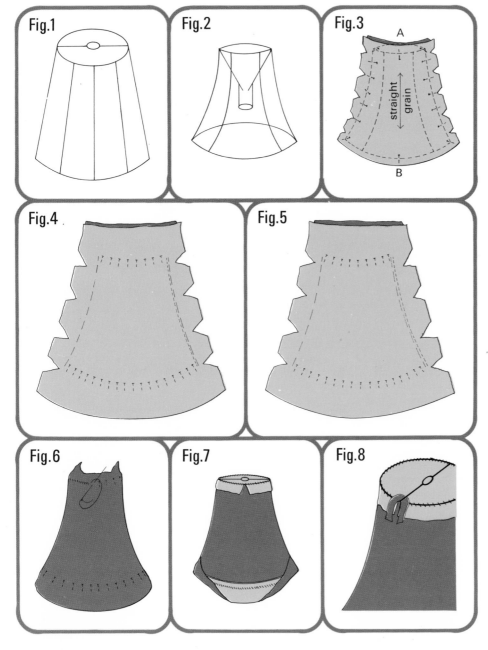

Above. *Choose the fabric of your lampshade to suit your room and its other furnishings— silk (left) for a formal living room, broderie anglaise (centre) for a pretty bedroom and chintz (right) to match the other covers in a bedroom or an informal living room.*

Above. *A tall, slim base needs a large, wide lampshade to balance the proportions.*

Empire shades. Clip the excess fabric diagonally at each side of the frame and trim it to within 1in. of the bound struts. Put in 'in-between' pins down these struts, easing the fabric across the frame as you progress. Put marker pins at the foot of each remaining strut, with in-between pins round the bottom ring. Place more markers at the top of each strut, followed by 'in-betweens' round the top ring. Continue to re-pin and stretch the fabric out to the sides until the fabric is completely smooth. Check that the fabric is not twisted— the straight grain must be in line with the centre point between the side struts (Fig.3).

Drum shades. Stretching the fabric from top to bottom and keeping the grain completely vertical, place marker pins in pairs at each strut end. Do not stretch the fabric across the frame or you will lose the round shape of the shade, and emphasise the angles instead. Slash the excess fabric at the sides and cut off any surplus, leaving a seam allowance of 1in. and then pin down the bound struts. Re-pin the fabric until it is smooth, still stretching it from top to bottom only.

Using a pencil, draw a fine line along the fabric directly over each bound strut between the pins. Unpin the fabric from the frame and

re-pin the pieces together, using the same pin-holes. Tack along the pencilled line, leaving in top and bottom pins. Because the lining should be fractionally smaller than the frame, machine or back stitch the pieces, taking the line of stitching $\frac{1}{16}$in. inside the tacking (Fig.4), and a little above and below the remaining pins for neatness at the top and bottom. Make tailors' tacks in the position of the main marker pins, trim the seam allowance to within $\frac{1}{8}$in. of the stitching and press the seam over to one side.

Make the cover in the same way, but stitch it $\frac{1}{16}$in. outside the tacking for ease when refitting it on the frame (Fig.5).

Attaching the cover

Pull the cover over the frame. Position the seams over the bound struts with the edges of the seam allowance falling to one side of the strut only, and with the tailors' tacks at top and bottom of the seams exactly level with the rings. Pin the fabric to the frame at the top and bottom of each strut, then with in-between pins round the rings. Do not put in-betweens down the struts, or you may spoil the cover by leaving pinholes. Be very careful at this stage not to prick your fingers and stain the cover.

Re-pin the fabric until the cover is completely smooth and then oversew it round the rings, easing the fabric over the rings (Fig.6). Trim off the surplus fabric close to the stitches.

Attaching the lining

Place the lining inside the frame, with the 'wrong' side facing the struts, matching the seams to the seams of the cover. Pin it to the frame at the top and bottom of each seam and then at the ends of the other struts. Put in-between pins along the rings, making a small slit in the fabric in the top at each side for the bar or gimbal. Adjust the pins all round smoothing out the fabric.

Starting at the top, ease the lining over on to the outside of the ring, completely covering the raw edge of the cover, and oversew it firmly. Stitch the bottom ring in the same way.

To cover the raw edges of the slits on the lining made for the bar, cut two small strips of lining fabric 2-3in. long and 1in. wide. Fold in the raw edges to make long, thin strips. With the raw edges underneath, slip the strips under the bar and draw the ends over on to the outer side of the frame (Fig.8). Stitch in place and trim off the excess fabric.

Attaching the trimming

Cover the raw edges of the lining with bought trimmings (see pages 249-251), or with a self trimming such as a rouleau.

To make a rouleau, cut bias strips twice the width of the required trimming plus $\frac{1}{2}$in. turning (if using chiffon or georgette, cut it three or four times as wide and fold it more times). Fold the strip in half, with 'wrong' sides together. Place the raw edges of the folded strip over the edge of the lining, so the bulk of the strip protrudes beyond the frame at each end (Fig.7). Stitch along the edges of the strip, through all thicknesses, to the frame binding, taking $\frac{1}{4}$in. turnings. Then turn the strip back over the stitching and smooth it round the frame.

Tiffany lampshades

The Tiffany lampshade, which takes its name from those designed for the American jeweller's is traditionally bow-shaped and has 12 struts. It is more of a decorative shade than a functional one, and is normally trimmed with a heavy fringe which gives it its distinctive character.

Almost any fabric, provided it looks good when seen on the cross (diagonally), can be used for a Tiffany lampshade. If the fabric is lacy, use a 'stretchy' fabric such as crêpe-backed satin for the lining. Do not use dress lining fabrics such as taffeta or lining satin, as they may split or fray. Beware of using a synthetic such as nylon, as this may scorch or melt under the heat of the bulb.

Preparing the frames

If the frame is not a plastic-coated one, paint it first, using a metal primer and a fast-drying enamel or cellulose paint to match the colour of the cover. This will prevent the frame from rusting and also looks better if the shade is unlined. Next, when the paint is completely dry, bind the rings and struts of the frame to which the fabric is to be fitted and stitched. (The traditional method whereby all the struts and rings were bound is considered unnecessary these days because it can spoil the smooth finish of the shade. In some cases now the binding is removed after fitting.)

Use ½in. cotton tape, bias binding or, if the cover fabric is suitable, cut ½in. strips of it (from the selvedge, if possible). Allow twice the circumference for the rings and one and a half times the length for each strut. If all the binding is to remain permanently on the frame, bind the struts first. If some of it is to be removed, bind the rings first. For an unlined Tiffany shade, start with the binding on the top and bottom rings, as this will be permanent, and then bind two opposite struts if the cover is tailored. For a lined shade, bind the 1st, 4th, 7th and 10th struts.

To bind the top ring, place the end of the tape under the ring at the top of a strut (Fig.1). Bring the tape over the joint of the ring and strut and bind over the end of the tape. Continue binding as tightly as possible, keeping the tape at an acute angle and overlapping it slightly. At each strut, wrap the binding round the ring an extra time and then go on to the next section (Fig.1). To finish, stitch down the end of the tape on the outside of the ring. Turn the frame upside down and bind the bottom ring as above.

Below. *A pretty Tiffany lampshade looks its best in this kind of setting.*

BILL MACLAUGHLIN

For the struts, start at the top and loop the binding round the 'T' joint (Fig.2). Anchor the end of the tape and continue winding down the strut. Finish by winding the tape round the bottom ring on both sides of the strut and stitch the end of the tape firmly on the outside.

Unlined lampshade

Tailored cover

To calculate the amount of fabric, measure the circumference of the shade at its widest part and, if this is less than the width of the fabric, buy a piece equal to half the circumference. Otherwise buy a piece of the same measurement.

Cut the fabric across in two equal lengths and trim them to make two squares. With the 'right' sides together, place both pieces over one half of the frame with one corner of the fabric at the top. Pin it to the rings at points A and B. (Fig.3). Smooth out the fabric towards the bound struts and pin the fabric to them at the top and bottom. Easing away as much fullness as possible, pin the fabric down the struts, placing the pins at right angles. Pin along the rings, evening out any fullness (Fig.4).

Follow the line of the bound struts, mark the fitting line with pins or tacking, taking care not to catch the binding. Mark the lines of the rings in the same way. Unpin the fabric from the frame and, following the fitting lines of the struts,

machine stitch the pieces together along these lines only (Fig.5). Trim off the excess fabric to within $\frac{1}{4}$in. of the stitching and press the seam over to one side. Neaten the raw edges by overcasting them together. Remove the binding from the struts.

Place the cover, 'right' side out, over the frame and position it so that the seams are over the struts. Tuck the seams behind them. Pin the fabric to the ring at the top of the seams, smooth tightly down to the bottom and pin again (do not pin it down the length of the strut or you may leave pinholes).

Next, stretching and adjusting the fabric as you go, pin the fabric all round the rings, easing

in any fullness. Then oversew it to both rings, beginning at the base (Fig.6). Turn the surplus fabric back over the stitching, clipping where necessary, and stitch again (Fig.7). Cut off the excess fabric as close as possible to this second row of stitches.

Semi-fitted cover

Cut out a strip of fabric, on the straight grain, with the width equal to the height of the frame plus 2in., and with the length equal to the circumference of the frame plus $\frac{1}{2}$in. Make a tube by joining the short ends of the strip together with a plain seam. Trim the seam allowance to within $\frac{1}{4}$in. of the stitching, press the seam over to one side and neaten the raw edges by overcasting them together. Fit the tube over the

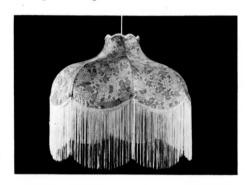

frame, positioning the seam over a strut. Pin it to both rings, gathering the fabric to fit it to the top ring. Stitch it firmly, as above.

Lined Tiffany

Lining a Tiffany lampshade is fairly 'fiddly', but well worth doing if the shade is to hang from the ceiling. Although the lining can be cut out and made up as for the tailored cover (see above), it is slightly easier if you cut it in four sections by fitting the fabric—on the bias grain—to the 1st and 4th bound struts. Mark the seam line as above and also mark the lines of the unbound struts. Cut out and mark the other sections in the same way and join them together.

With the 'wrong' side facing outwards, place the lining inside the frame, positioning it so

that the seams correspond with the bound struts. Pin the lining to the rings and along the bound struts, adjusting and easing the fabric as you go. Oversew the lining to the bound struts, and along the rings.

To prevent the lining from looking 'baggy' on the inside, you will also have to catch the lining to the unbound struts. Place one hand inside the frame and hold the lining to one strut. Starting at the top, secure the sewing thread to the binding on the ring. Working from the outside, take a tiny stitch in the lining on the tacked guide line about $\frac{1}{4}$in. from the top. Bring the needle out on the other side of the strut and pass it back over the strut and under the loop

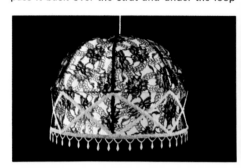

made by the thread (rather like blanket stitch, see Fig.8).

Continue down the strut, loosely catching the lining to the strut in this way at $\frac{1}{2}$in. intervals. Leave the end of thread free at the bottom of the strut and start again on the next strut.

When all the unbound struts have been attached to the lining in this way, it is possible to adjust the positioning by sliding the stitches along the strut. Tighten the stitches from the loose end and then secure the thread.

When you attach the cover, place its edge over the edge and stitching of the lining.

If the cover is a semi-fitted one, it is possible to attach it to the frame so that no stitching shows on the outside, making a trimming un-

necessary. With the wrong side of the cover facing out, and the bottom of the cover uppermost, fit this edge over the bottom ring of the frame. Taking a $\frac{1}{4}$in. turning, oversew the cover to the bottom ring (Fig.9). Then turn the cover up and over the frame and fit and stitch it to the top ring as above.

Trimming

Pin the trimming to the cover at top and bottom, covering the raw edges. Stitch it to the cover on both edges, working from side to side, and taking the thread underneath the trimming. Stitch a second piece of trimming inside the frame if you wish to cover the binding.

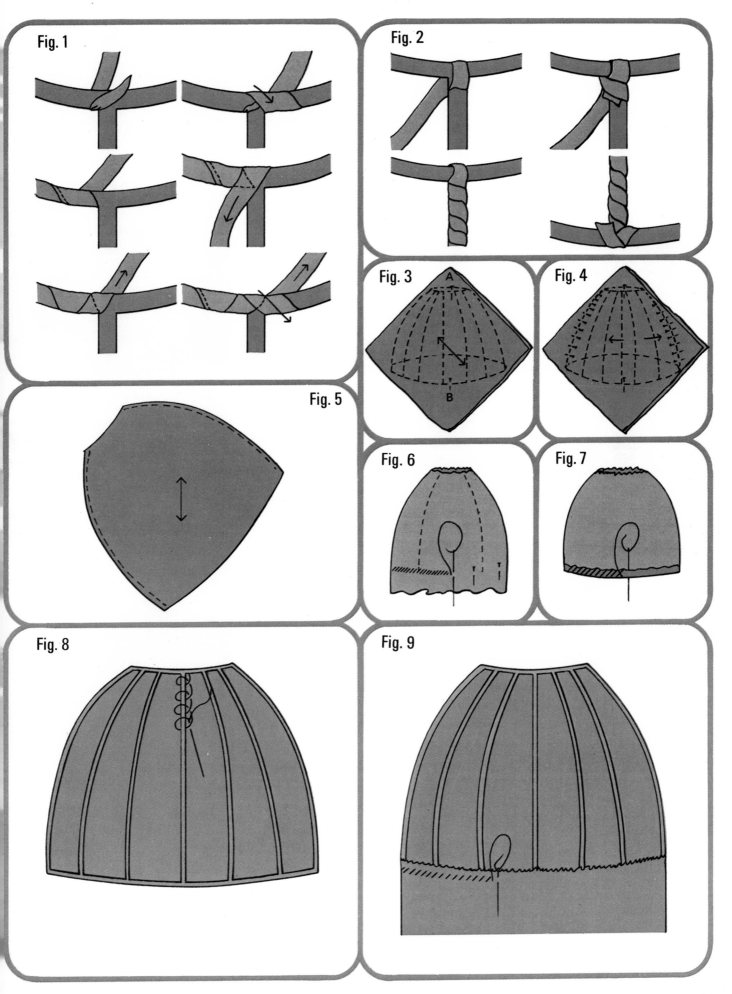

Fig. 1

Fig. 2

Fig. 3

Fig. 4

Fig. 5

Fig. 6

Fig. 7

Fig. 8

Fig. 9

Decorative swathed lampshades

Pleated fabric lampshades have long been popular because they are decorative and suit most rooms furnished in a traditional style. Yet they are the most expensive kind to buy, because they are hand-made and the pleating process takes time to do. The materials, however, are not expensive, so it is worth learning how to make your own.

There are three main styles of pleated lampshade. In the simplest kind, the pleats are straight and in line with the struts of the frame. Alternatively—and this is more tricky to do—they are slanted so that they swathe round the frame in a spiral motion. In the third type, which is the most complicated, they radiate from two central points on each side of the frame.

With all the styles, it is possible to work variations, such as alternating pleated panels with plain panels, perhaps of a fabric which matches something else in the room.

The frame

Most shapes of frame can be used, but they must have at least four struts between the top and bottom rings. Curved empire-shape frames are best kept for swathed shades only.

Prepare the frame by painting it and then binding the rings and struts as described on pages 249-251.

The fabric

For the outer cover, the fabric should be a soft and sheer one which will pleat easily and not look heavy. Chiffon, ninon, georgette and voile are all ideal, and are easier to use if made of silk or rayon, rather than nylon.

For *straight pleating*, allow a piece equal to the height of the frame, plus 2in. for turnings, × three times the circumference of the lower ring.

For *swathed pleating*, the width is the same as for straight pleating, but the depth of the fabric should be measured in a slanting line from the top ring to the bottom ring across a quarter of the frame (Fig.4). Add 2in. for turnings.

For *sunray pleating*, the depth is measured from the centre point of one strut in a straight line over one quarter of the frame to the junction of the side strut and bottom ring. Add 2in. for turnings. For the width of the fabric needed for each half of the frame, add together half the circumference of the top and bottom rings, plus twice the height of the frame, and allow 1½ times this measurement.

The pleats are always more successful if they lie along the warp threads (those that are parallel to the selvedges of the fabric), than along the weft threads. This means that because the total width required for making the shade will be considerably more than the width of the fabric, you will have to join it in one or two places. For straight and swathed pleated shades, the joins are not sewn, however, but simply concealed under the pleats. The turnings are hidden by the lining.

To calculate how much fabric to buy, divide the total width by the width of the fabric, and take it to the nearest whole figure above. Then multiply by the total depth needed. Usually you will have to buy a piece to the nearest quarter of a yard above this, but any spare fabric can usually be made into an attractive trimming.

For example, with a frame which is 9in. high and has a diameter of 10in. with a circumference of about 32in., for straight pleating you would need a piece of fabric 11in. long x 96in. wide. If the fabric you are using is 36in. wide, you should buy a yard, from which you can cut three 11in. strips.

If, on the other hand, the frame has a 12in. diameter and a circumference of about 38in., meaning that the fabric should be 114in. wide, you could then either buy enough to cut four widths, and have plenty left over, or else buy three widths and space out the pleats slightly to compensate. In this case any trimming would have to be a bought one.

The lining

This is not pleated, and is made in two sections, following the method given on pages 246-248. Use a fabric which will stretch easily and look attractive both as a backing for the outer fabric and inside the frame. Crepe back satin is particularly good for this, and looks attractive with either side facing out. Lingerie crepe, taiho and shantung can also be used.

The colour is obviously up to you, but generally you will find that even if you are using a dark colour for the main cover, it is best to use a pale one for the lining, as this will give the best light. If possible, hold both the outer cover and lining fabric together over a turned-on bulb so that you can see the effect.

For a sunray pleated shade, you will also need an interlining. This is made up in a similar way to the lining, but is attached like the main cover of a tailored shade as described on pages 246-248. It acts as the foundation for the pleating, so it should match the outer cover fabric as nearly as possible.

Right. *Pleated lampshades are ideal for bedrooms and living rooms furnished in a more traditional style. The swathed and sunray styles look best on Empire shades.*

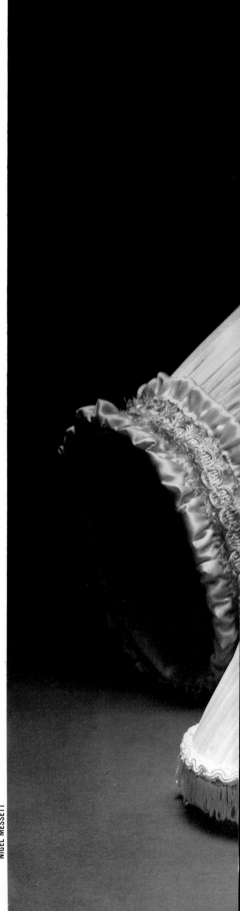

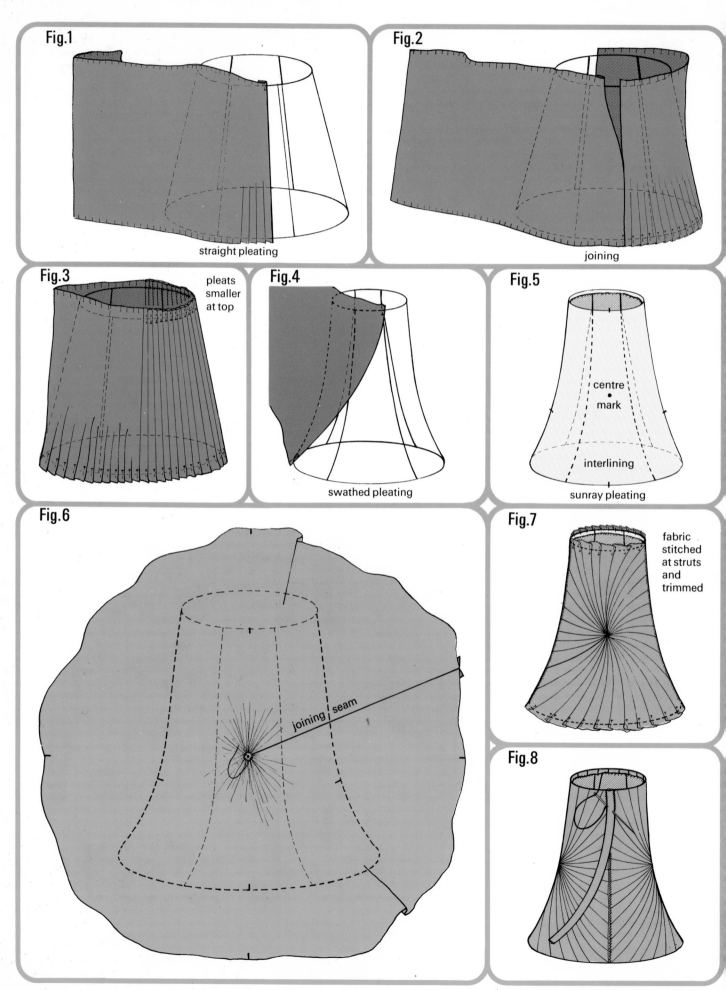

Fig.1

straight pleating

Fig.2

joining

Fig.3

pleats
smaller
at top

Fig.4

swathed pleating

Fig.5

centre
• mark

interlining

sunray pleating

Fig.6

joining seam

Fig.7

fabric
stitched
at struts
and
trimmed

Fig.8

Straight pleated shade

Prepare the lining, but do not attach it to the frame yet. Cut the outer cover fabric into pieces of the right depth, and trim off the selvedges.

The safest method of making the pleats an even size is to mark a pencil guide of dots along each long side of the fabric, about 1 in. from the edge. The dots should be $\frac{3}{4}$ in. apart (or $\frac{1}{2}$ in. apart for very fine pleats), and start $\frac{1}{4}$ in. from the short edge of the fabric on each piece. The corresponding dots on both edges must lie on the straight grain of the fabric, or the pleats will not form smoothly.

If the shade is a tapered one, the distance between the pleats will be less on the top ring than on the bottom ring, so as a guide for this, find the centre point between each strut on the rings, and mark it with pencil.

Place the shade on your work surface (or lap) with the bottom ring to the left (or to the right, if you are left-handed). Lay the fabric over the shade with one short edge towards you. Turn under $\frac{1}{4}$ in. along this edge, level with the first pair of dots, and pin it to the tape on the outer edge of both rings so that the fold lies along a strut (Fig.1).

Move to the next pair of dots and, using your thumbs and forefingers, hold the edges of the fabric taut between both hands. Make a fold along the straight grain between the dots by pinching the fabric on each side of them together. Roll this fold over to the first one, thus forming a pleat, and pin to the bottom ring. Do not pin it to the top ring yet. The distance between the folds should be $\frac{1}{4}$ in.

Go on to the next dots and make another pleat in the same way. Continue round the ring, forming pleats in the same way. If possible, place a pleat in line with the centre point between the struts, and a pleat directly over each strut. Pin the fold to the ring at the top of each strut too. Check that all the pleats are evenly spaced, and that there is an equal number in each section.

When you come to within 1 in. of the end of a piece of fabric, finish the pleat and trim off any excess to within $\frac{1}{2}$ in. of the fold. Turn under $\frac{1}{4}$ in. of the new piece, and place the fold over the raw edge of the previous piece so that it is $\frac{1}{4}$ in. from the fold of the last pleat formed (Fig.2).

When you have worked all round the bottom ring, trim the fabric to within $\frac{1}{2}$ in. of the last pleat, unpin the first fold, tuck under the raw edge and repin.

To complete the pleating round the top ring, turn the shade so that the top ring is now on your left and the first fold is uppermost. Unpin the first fold at the top, smooth it along the strut, stretching it slightly so that it is taut but not distorted, and re-pin it in position.

Next, find the dot which corresponds with the centre pleat in the section of fabric between the first fold and the next strut, and pin it temporarily, without making a pleat, to the corresponding centre point on the top ring.

Go back to the first fold and start making pleats following the method above, but decreasing the space between the folds if the circumference of the top ring is less than that of the bottom ring. You may have to adjust the pleats several times until you find the right spacing. On each section, however, the centre pleat must come level with the centre point between the struts, and the pleats on each side must be evenly spaced and lie on the straight grain of the fabric. On a very tapered frame, this may mean that the pleats have to overlap slightly at the top (Fig.3).

When you are completely satisfied with the spacing of the pleats, the fabric can be oversewn to the rings. Use doubled sewing thread, in a colour to match the fabric. Keep the stitches very small, and catch the tape on the outside of the rings only.

Cut away the surplus fabric at the top and bottom to within $\frac{1}{8}$ in. of the stitching. The shade is now ready for the lining to be fitted.

Swathed pleated shade

The general method for making this type is very similar to the straight pleated shade, the essential difference being that the folds are pinned diagonally across the frame. For this reason, you may find it easier to pin each fold to the bottom and top ring as it is formed, though you may have to unpin the folds to adjust them later.

Turn under the short edge of the fabric level with the first dots as before, and pin it to a strut at the bottom ring. Drape the fold across the shade, missing the first strut, and pin it to the top ring at the second strut (Fig.4.) Form the following pleats in the same way, adjusting the distance between folds evenly so that when you reach the next strut on the bottom ring, the fold will lie on the next-but-one strut on the top ring.

Sunray pleated lampshade

Make up the lining and interlining, and attach the interlining to the frame as for the main cover of a tailored shade (see pages 246-248).

The outer cover for this shade is made in two halves, each of which radiates from the centre point of the main panel on each side of the shade. Start by finding the centre point of each panel, and marking it in pencil on the interlining.

Next, measure the perimeter of half the shade —round half the circumference of the top ring, down one side strut, round half the circumfer-

Below. Chiffon and light-weight silks should be used for pleated lampshades because they drape well and are translucent.

ZEFA

ence of the bottom ring and up the opposite side strut. Divide this into quarters by marking the centre of the section on the top and bottom rings, and then the centre point between the marks on the struts (Fig.5).

Cut the cover fabric into pieces of the right depth, and join them along their short edges with running stitches, taking $\frac{1}{4}$ in. turnings, to make a circular strip of the right length.

Divide the length of the strip into quarters, and mark the divisions along both long edges. Along one long edge only, make two rows of fine gathering stitches and pull up the gathers tightly so that the fabric forms a small circle. Place the gathered edge with the right side facing out, to the centre point of the panel. Oversew neatly in position.

Smooth the ungathered edge of the strip out to the struts and rings, and match the division marks on the fabric to the marks on the interlining. Pin temporarily in position (Fig.6).

Starting at the bottom ring, and working from right to left, start forming little pleats, readjusting them as necessary until they are all evenly spaced, and any joins in the fabric are hidden on the inside of a fold.

The pleats must all lie in the same direction to complete the sunray effect, which means that on one side of the panel they will face upwards and on the other side they will face downwards. When one panel of the shade is pleated, stitch the fabric down to the rings and along the struts.

Work the other side of the shade in a similar way, but reversing the direction of the pleating so that it will correspond with the pleats on the other side where they meet at the struts. There should be the same number of pleats on each side. Stitch this panel down, placing the stitching at the struts over the previous stitching. Cut away the excess fabric carefully and as close to the stitching as possible (Fig.7).

The join can then be covered with trimming in the same way as for the top and bottom rings —a rouleau trimming, made from bias strips of the same fabric, usually looks best.

Rouleau trimming

A rouleau trimming to cover the turnings round the top and bottom rings can be made following the directions on pages 246-248.

To make a rouleau trimming for the side struts of a sunray pleated lampshade, cut a 1 in. wide bias strip of fabric long enough to cover the strut.

Fold it in three down its length, so that the side edges meet in the middle. Place this centrally over the strut so that the raw edges are underneath, and tack in position.

Stitch it down, making tiny catch stitches and working diagonally from side to side taking the needle under the strip each time (Fig.8).

To cover the raw edges at the centre of each section of the sunray shade, cut a strip of matching fabric approximately 1 in. wide x 6 in. long. Join it along the short edges to make a circular strip and fold it in half lengthwise with the seam inside. Run a gathering thread through the doubled fabric along the raw edges and draw up to a tight circle to make a 'rose'. Cover a small button mould with matching doubled fabric and stitch it to the centre of the 'rose'.

Place the 'rose' centrally over the raw edges of the shade and stitch down invisibly.